## ～ A Scapegoat in the New Wilderness

# A Scapegoat in the New Wilderness

## The Origins and Rise of Anti-Semitism in America

~

Frederic Cople Jaher

HARVARD UNIVERSITY PRESS
Cambridge, Massachusetts
London, England

First Harvard University Press paperback edition, 1996

Library of Congress Cataloging-in-Publication Data

Jaher, Frederic Cople.
  A scapegoat in the new wilderness / Frederic Cople Jaher.
    p.  cm.
  Includes bibliographical references and index.
  ISBN 0-674-79006-5 (cloth)
  ISBN 0-674-79007-3 (pbk.)
  1. Antisemitism—United States—History.  2. United States —Ethnic relations.  I. Title.
DS146.U6J34    1994
305.892'4073—dc20       93-34822
                CIP

To Hannah
with love for her, her family, and our people

# ∼ Preface

The Holocaust and the immense rage and sadness it stirs in me have deepened my Jewish identity and inspired me to try to understand how such a catastrophe could occur. This book is my attempt to comprehend that cataclysm intellectually and emotionally, and also an expression of my pride in being a Jew.

My thoughts about the Holocaust often linger on the Levin and Moshatzky families of Volkovisk, Poland. These are my wife's and stepson's relatives, and almost all of them were lost to Nazi brutality. I am particularly haunted by my wife's parents, Sarah and Aaron Levin, and her brother, Yair, who escaped the ovens but were also victims. Finally, and to some extent redemptively, I take pride in Lior Cohen, my stepson, a combat officer in the Israeli air force, who represents the hope and future of Israel and diaspora Jewry.

My feelings about the massacre of my fellow Jews have not blinded me to the realization that not all Gentiles hate Jews, and that even those who dislike Jews would not necessarily torment or liquidate them. In this book I trace the rise and fall, the continuity and discontinuity, of anti-Jewish attitudes and actions through the ages, with a particular focus on American anti-Semitism and its European roots. In the United States, anti-Semitism has steadily diminished since World War II. Although history indicates otherwise, I hope that the cycles will cease and the recent downward trend will continue until animosity against Jews, along with all other forms of bigotry, finally disappears.

∼

I thank the social history group of the University of Illinois for reading an early version of Chapter 2, Leonard Dinnerstein for useful bibliographical information and for reading most of the manuscript, the library staff of the University of Illinois for cordial and efficient assistance, Elizabeth Suttell and Donna Bouvier for effective and sympathetic handling of many publication details, and Aida Donald for her faith in my book. My manuscript editor, Camille Smith, significantly improved the book's clarity, organization, and style. My wife, Dr. Hannah Lavi-Levin Jaher, provided a brilliant critique of portions of the manuscript as well as the inspiration and emotional sustenance that enabled me to write this book. Above all, this book is for her and her family, as exemplifying wounded Jewry but also as epitomizing the virtue and will of the Jewish people to overcome catastrophe.

# ～ Contents

1    The Anatomy of Anti-Semitism    1

2    Historical Outsider    17

3    Ambivalence at America's Dawn    82

4    Progress and Problems in the Young Republic    114

5    Mid-Century Crisis    170

Epilogue    242

Notes    251

Index    325

~ A Scapegoat in
the New Wilderness

# ~ 1

# The Anatomy of Anti-Semitism

For more than a century, multitudes of Jews have immigrated to the United States, and this country is currently the home of nearly half of world Jewry. A major reason for the streams of immigration has been the mildness of American anti-Semitism relative to that encountered by Jews in other parts of the world. Nevertheless, anti-Semitic attitudes have been widespread here since the earliest colonial days, and it is important to investigate the course of this bigotry in the United States.

Comprehensive study of American anti-Semitism must address its scope, intensity, change, and causes. The ways in which it differs from anti-Semitism elsewhere are also important: What impact have republican beginnings and the absence of such factors as a medieval past, a legal nobility, and a national church had on America's reaction to Jews? Effective exploration of these matters requires comparisons with other forms of ethnic and religious bigotry and with reactions to Jews in other eras and countries, as well as investigation of domestic variations by region, social group, and historical period.

The historical and international continuities of anti-Semitism can be illustrated by the hallucination, long cherished by bigots, of a Jewish plot to destroy Christian civilization and rule the world. Over the centuries Jews outlasted more powerful enemies from the pharaohs to the Nazis, and dire consequences befell their oppressors. Anti-Semites interpreted their survival as evidence of a mysterious and powerful malevolence. In this fantasy Jews were allied with demonic forces in a global and cosmic conspiracy. From the Gospels onward, Jews were linked with Satan and

1

the Antichrist contending with Jesus at Armageddon. From the age of republican revolution they were suspected of belonging to a secret Masonic-Jewish insurgency against the established order. In nineteenth-century Europe and America emerged the chimerical cabal of parasitic Jewish bankers strangling productive peasants and artisans and the upright nation-state. In the twentieth-century the terrifying vision was of global Godless Jewish communism arrayed against Christian capitalism. These slanderous delusions, cumulative and mutually reinforcing, fed the fear and hate that culminated in the liquidation of European Jewry and intensified concurrent anti-Semitism across the Atlantic.

The persistence of anti-Semitism across time and around the globe raises doubts that its fundamental causes lie in specific historical forces or events. Permanent hostility indicates an origin in primal concerns about defeat, enfeeblement, and death, or in equally visceral responses of inter-group and interpersonal envy and rivalry.

If anti-Semitism springs from basic human impulses rather than from historical forces, then why have the Jews been so consistently singled out over so much of the earth? The historian Gavin Langmuir has identified three different types of hostility toward Jews: realistic, reactive, and illusionary. Realistic hostility arises for objective reasons. It may occur in war, for example. When combat ends, mutual antagonism often disappears, as happened between America and Germany after each World War and between the Romans and the Hebrews after the Jewish Wars between 66 and 135 C.E.

While reactive hostility, too, can be a realistic response, this disposition sometimes owes more to the beholder than to the threat. A group may be feared or disparaged because it has been conditioned by circumstances into antisocial, or least unpleasant, behavior. Oppressed and unoppressed peoples alike may evince traits attributed to Jews—obsequiousness, envy, competitiveness, cupidity, underhandedness, and aloofness. Reactive hostility was dramatically exemplified in the Middle Ages, when Jews were forced into trade and usury and into becoming agents for ruling elites, and were resented as commercial competitors or as surrogates for the real exploiters of the community. In modern times, many Jews have entered business or professional life, undertakings which have made them rivals of native majorities in their host societies, by whom they have consequently been derided and sometimes victimized.

Despite these distortions, reactive anti-Semitism is neither as dangerous nor as fallacious as illusionary anti-Semitism, which I shall call infernalization, demonization, or diabolization. As suggested by Langmuir, this third type of hostility is devoid of objective or reactive plausibility. The longest-lasting and deadliest attacks on Jews, from the First Crusade to the Holocaust, issued from delirious obsession. Fanatical fantasy conjured up the ritual murderer, the spreader of plague, desecrator of the Host, hater of Christians, kin of the devil and the Antichrist, and surreptitious schemer for world and cosmic domination. These deadly slanders did not have realistic or reactive causes, and they would not disappear with the cessation of conditions that created realistic and reactive animosity.[1]

Regardless of the balance among realistic, reactive, and hallucinatory elements in the phobic reaction, alleged Jewish misbehavior is assigned to heritage rather than to context, individual actions are taken to signify collective propensities, and traits admired in socially accepted groups are condemned in the outcast enclave. Furthermore, many of the accusations hurled at Jews are mutually contradictory. Full depiction of the supposedly evil Jew reproduces the symmetrical inversions or contrapuntal signifiers that Claude Lévi-Strauss perceived as part of the logical structure of all myths.[2]

All students of anti-Semitism, and anti-Semites themselves, agree that Jews have been alienated from the host societies in which they lived. Since the advent of Christianity, with its Manichean division of cosmic good and evil, Jews have been stigmatized as the antipodal antagonists of virtue and order. In contrast to the community of grace, they were the unredeemed disciples of the devil. To the disciples of Christ, they were the tribal enemies. To militant Christianity, they were enfeebled relics and yet also terrifying intruders. In the triumph of spiritual purity, they were the corrupt materialists, the dirty lechers. When Christian universalism gave way to the national state, the Jews, formerly denigrated as a particularistic remnant, came to symbolize the evil of universality. To the patriotism of blood ties, primal instincts, territorial roots, and an inherited culture, they were the cosmopolitan betrayers of all save their deracinated coreligionists. The Jews were either, and often simultaneously, too powerful or too weak, too arrogant or too servile, too superstitious and archaic or too modern and rational, too rigid or too insidious, too aloof or too eagerly assimilationist. Disloyal descendants of Judas, the Jews betrayed country and Christianity in conspiracies of Masonry, rapacious capitalism, atheistic, rootless radicalism, and arid rationalism—all in pursuit of world rule.

The outcast Jew is compounded of the interplay among these portrayals and their causes: Were defamation and alienation produced by real clashes with other groups or by pyschogenic fantasy or historical legend? Or was marginalization due to a mixture of objective and hallucinatory factors whose balance shifted with time, place, and social class? Historians generally feel more comfortable with explanations directly drawn from evidence of blood libels, from bigoted accusations against medieval Jewish creditors, from denunciation of Jews as subversive radicals, and from the labeling of Jewish bankers as rapacious international capitalists. Accessibility of direct evidence, however, does not necessarily determine relevance. Hence conventional social science research must be combined with analysis of metaphor and myth.

When examining economic aspects of anti-Semitism, social scientists conclude that risky, marginal, and degrading economic roles imposed on the Jews drew upon them the anger of the host society or coerced them into behavior that agitated the feeling against them. Economically induced or focused bigotry, in turn, rationalized and facilitated opportunistic and exploitative anti-Jewish actions, such as expropriating Jewish property, avoiding debts, or curtailing competition from Jewish merchants or artisans. At a more sophisticated mode of explanation, these episodes of hostility are categorized as symbolic or misconstrued contention for scarce goods of wealth and power; as ruses to deflect real grievances over poverty and oppression that might otherwise imperil established elites and socioeconomic arrangements; or as fears of anomic modernism projected onto the Jew.

Jews were forced into urban capitalism by church and state policies that barred them from manual and landed labor. They became influential and highly visible in international finance through connections with kin and other Jews throughout Europe and the Orient. These relationships evoked nightmares of a plot to undermine traditional Christian and national ways of conducting business. Jews were seen as draining the resources of country and Christendom, seizing for themselves inherited property, the products of manual and entrepreneurial endeavor, and the hard-won fruits of upright, rural life. Jewish property, charged the anti-Semites, is liquid not palpable, manipulative not productive. It is composed of shadowy, internationally negotiable abstractions—loans, stocks, bonds, paper money, and so on—rooted nowhere in time or place and unearned by sweat and hard work. The theme of Jewish commercial cupidity devouring the community's birthright ran through all these criticisms and was condemned by Christianity, reactionary nationalism, and radical socialism alike.

Christians could not, by belief and doctrine, easily accept a highly competitive economy and society in which existence was a series of contests in which one person's gain meant another's loss. Unable to square reality with religion, they projected the contradiction between church dogma and marketplace values onto the Jews. Criticism of them as the instigators of corruption in the community of grace reflected the strain generated by widespread fear of failure and envy of success.

To a lesser extent, Jewish business achievement could affirm as well as tarnish the Jews' image. In America especially, capitalist values of entrepreneurial and personal achievement, a bourgeois lifestyle, and an innovative outlook are less challenged by traditional, Christian, and communal allegiances that arise from a medieval past. The urban, rational, commercial image of the Jew, therefore, is more compatible with the American ethos than with a European culture still attached to feudal and church antecedents. While Jews have been derided for excessive display of capitalist traits, this stereotype has sometimes served to reassure America that they are worthy citizens.[3]

Political alienation worked in tandem with economic isolation to separate the Jew from western society. Opponents of Jews in the marketplace were unlikely to welcome them in the commonwealth. Consistent, irreversible disintegration in the civic standing of western Jewry began in the high middle ages. Jews had been Roman citizens, a status that helped sustain their rights until they became royal serfs. Until the twelfth century they were subject to occasional oppression and largely unimplemented legal and canonical prohibitions against intimacy with or the exercise of authority over Christians. Intermittent and ineffective restraints did not prevent them from maintaining good and equal relations, and a high degree of integration, with the larger community. Between the end of the eleventh and the end of the fifteenth century, however, these circumstances were disastrously reversed. Devastating victimization eventually culminated in banishment from England and nearly all of western Europe.

Reentry into the West began in the seventeenth century, and with the coming of the Reformation, the Age of Reason, republican and romantic nationalism, and left-wing militancy, several aspects of modernism emerged to oppose the harsh treatment of the earlier era. But these counterforces were ambivalent about Jews and offered freedom, equality, and citizenship only on condition that Jews lose their creedal and ethnic identity and be absorbed into the religion of man, the nation-state, or a socialist utopia. Nevertheless, Jews gradually acquired civic rights and privileges until they received full citizenship in England and western Europe during the last half of the nineteenth century. In eastern Europe attainment of equality was delayed until after World War I.

The United States, formed after medieval and early modern persecutions, did not impose federal legal restraints on Jews, and within fifty years of independence most residual state restrictions disappeared. Even in the American colonies, after a brief attempt at repression in New Amsterdam, discrimination was weaker than in the mother countries.

In America, however, voluntary associations and arrangements took the place of the more intense European legal exclusion of Jews from professions, neighborhoods, organizations, and schools. Here, as in Europe, the Jew was associated with other pariah groups—in this case other immigrants from southern and eastern Europe. Labeled nigger lovers, radical atheists, atomized intellectuals, and communists, anarchists, or union leaders, the Jews and their leftist allies were seen as seeking to overturn traditional, rural, Christian-capitalist America. Called international Shylocks and cutthroat domestic merchants, they would eviscerate American business enterprise and productivity. Defamed as lascivious and vulgar scoundrels, the Jews corroded moral and social order. Foreign agents of commercial, civic, cultural, and biological contagion, Jews polluted the Anglo-Saxon body politic. If America did not resort to legal segregation, coerced apostasy, government-decreed exile, and mass annihilation, in the 1920s it effectively barred entry to Jews, as well as to other allegedly infectious immigrants.

Modern nationalism did not inevitably engender anti-Semitism. In Spain, Portugal, and Germany patriotism did intensify historical Christian hatred of Jews. The effect was less strong in France, where the modern state emerged from an Age of Reason uprising against an aristocratic-Catholic heritage, and in the United States, whose founding fathers, also children of the Enlightenment, constitutionally forbade a religious establishment. But in France the revolutionary emancipation of the Jews was associated by defenders of the *ancien régime* with Deism, regicidal republicanism, and the rise of Napoleon. From 1789 through Vichy the clergy, the nobility, and their allies attacked every successive republic for being pro-Jewish, thus making Jews a major issue in the continuing conflict between republican and Bourbon France. In Holland, Britain, and America, where Jewish emancipation was not launched by revolutionary upheaval or by wartime defeats and other disruptions, Jews encountered fewer and milder difficulties than elsewhere. Even among the Axis powers, nationalist zealotry was not universally linked with hatred of Jews. Italian fascism belatedly, reluctantly, and incompletely acquiesced in its senior partner's genocidal policies. Japan, also authoritarian and xenophobic, rejected Nazi policy in this area. But Japan was not a Christian land, and Italy had been a comparative refuge in the pogroms of the late middle ages and the early modern period. In countries with a strong tradition of hostility toward Jews, extreme patriotism did encourage anti-Semitism. From the perspective of the nation divided into a band of virtuous insiders besieged by dangerous outsiders, the Jew became the extreme negative correlative. Fervent nationalists charged that Jews kept themselves aloof from sentiments and sacrifices that fostered national loyalty. Dispersed by God as punishment for the crucifixion, they were landless migrants, normless urbanites, without allegiance to the nation.

Both modern allegations of cosmopolitanism and, contradictorily, traditional Christian charges of tribalism disqualified Jews from good citizenship. As cosmopolitans they had far-reaching international interests and ties that took precedence over allegiance to their country of residence. As tribalists they put loyalty to their own group above commitment to the nation. Moreover, Judaism allegedly taught its believers that their primary loyalty was to lost Israel. For Jews, the Passover exhortation "next year in Jerusalem" was a rallying cry for communal solidarity; for anti-Semites it was proof of the Jews' betrayal of any other nation.

Suspicion of treachery was further aroused by the Jews' claim to be God's Chosen People. This aspect of Judaism was believed to account for the Jews' alleged feeling of superiority over others. Their imputed aloofness and arrogance, in turn, challenged the claim of other nations and creeds to be God's special favorites. How could Christianity have displaced Judaism, how could America be "God's country" and the "promised land," if the Jews were still closest to God and dreamed of returning to Israel?

The advent of racialism in Europe in the mid-nineteenth century and in the United States several decades later added an explosive ingredient to religious and xenophobic indictment of the Jews. Fraudulently concocted of evolutionary and genetic theory, racialism reinforced the notion that biology determined survival of cultures and groups. Healthy countries, which would prevail in confrontation with other nations and ethnic groups, had a pure racial stock. Jewish traits, considered innately foreign and defective, threatened genetic homogeneity. Whether racially identified as "Mediterranean," "Oriental," "Eastern European," "Judaic," "Negroid," or "mongrelized," the Jew was deemed biologically incapable of assimilating to—and yet inherently a defiler of—the Anglo-Saxon, Nordic, or

Aryan biocultural ideal types in Germany, Britain, and America. Xeno-phobic and racial anti-Semitism merged when the national ideal type was defined as the biological opposite of the Jewish stereotype. The most extreme traditional anti-Semitism, as in fifteenth-century Spain, gave Jews the choice of baptism, death, or flight. The most extreme racial anti-Semitism, however, led to genocide, the only cure for Jewish infection of the community.

Xenophobic and racialist hatred, like other aspects of anti-Semitism, were less virulent in the United States than in Europe. American xeno-phobes before the 1920s and 1930s rarely designated Jews the exclusive or chief genetic culprits. Indeed, they regularly preferred Jews to blacks and Orientals and intermittently to Irish, Indians, and other groups of immigrants from southern and eastern Europe. The diffusion of racial hos-tility was possible because, unlike most European countries, this "nation of immigrants" was made up of a multiplicity of ethnic and cultural groups. In fact, and also unlike the European experience, the ideal national ethnic type in the United States became a demographic minority and fell behind groups of European and Oriental newcomers in key status indicators of wealth, education, and occupational prestige.

By culture, creed, and race, then, the Jew was cast in the role of sub-versive alien. Anxiety and anger generated by this delusion targeted the Jews for a series of nefarious projections. The vast range of repugnant ste-reotypes meant that all social strata could find something despicable in Jews. Most societies crave homogeneity—even American allegiance to pluralism is grounded in the solidarities of ethnic assimilation and con-sensus on fundamental social values and structures. Ingroup unity was strengthened by the projection onto the Jews of personal and communal anxieties, resentments, and frustrations.

Modern-era liberation opened for Jews careers that multiplied contacts with Gentiles in competitive situations. Jews attained prominence in highly rationalized and/or individualized vocations that often were not integrated with or supportive of conventional social patterns. Thus the political equivalent of the Jewish capitalist *nouveau riche* was the aggressive Jewish subversive depicted as spy, lawyer, scientist, journalist, artist, theatrical performer and impresario, member of the intelligentsia, socialist, anarchist, strike leader, or financier-owner of political parties and public officials.

Both ancient and modern detractors were further enraged by the Jews' refusal to act the inferior and deferent role assigned to them. For anti-Semites, Jewish professional, business, political, cultural, and intellectual accomplishments were signs of social disorder, decline, and, if unresisted, disintegration. The irony was that in spite of their highly visible success, which gave rise to paranoia in the majority, the Jews were actually a weak minority. Jews were assailed not only because they were misperceived as an alien malignancy but also because they were a vulnerable scapegoat, easily isolated, humiliated, and slaughtered.

The worst episodes of anti-Semitism occurred during or soon after times of crisis—crusades, religious schisms, plagues, economic break-downs, wars, and revolutions—when the community felt most threatened. Jews have conventionally been identified with turbulence and frequently accused of profiting from it. Napoleon freed them in the countries he conquered, for example, and they received political equality and power in eastern Europe in the wake of the Russian Revolution and in the turmoil after World War I. In America, they achieved unprecedented political presence in the New Deal administration during the Depression.

American Jews, unlike those in Russia and France, were not liberated through gentricidal, regicidal, and dechristianizing upheavals. In this nation of diverse newcomers, devoid of legalized hereditary strata, medieval memories, homogeneous volk legends, and an established church, anti-Semitism was never officially sanctioned or politically institutionalized. Since Jews were citizens at the creation of the state, their freedom was neither subsequently imposed on the society nor granted by the government. In fact, their equality was widely considered to ratify the national ethos expressed in the inscription (written by a Jew) on the Statue of Liberty, that national icon of ethnic pluralism, and in Fourth of July, National Anthem, Flag Pledge, Declaration of Independence, and federal and state constitutional tributes to ethnic pluralism, equal rights, and liberty of conscience. The vital spirit of inclusive nationalism was exemplified in the most liberal immigration policy of any western country and epitomized in the American motto *e pluribus unum*. With singular good fortune, the country was also spared most of the traumas—bloody sectarian schism, recurrent revolution, and, except for the South and the Civil War, major military defeat, invasion, and conquest—that elsewhere aggravated anti-Semitism.[4]

~

Religious and secular factors intertwine as causes of hostility toward Jews. It is my contention that animosity embedded in Christian doctrine, while by no means the only source of anti-Semitism, has exerted a primary influence since the early days of Christianity. Research has uncovered abundant evidence of anti-Jewish sentiment in Catholic and Protestant theology, canon law, church councils, papal and clerical edicts, and abusive action. These persecutions are long-standing and range from ideological pronouncements to suppression of Jewish worship, segregation of Jews, and support for secular anti-Semitic rulers, parties, and policies. Readily available data consistent with secular prejudice, however, may disguise key aspects of the Christian response to Judaism. The relationship between these two intertwined monotheisms may be illumined by exploration of myth, metaphor, emotional drives, and personality disorders. Social scientists display considerable resistance to such inquiries, categorizing them as conceptually inapposite, analytically elusive, and unverifiable. Reluctance to pursue such topics, however, may handicap the investigation of why Jews are recurrent targets of hostility and why their victimization often takes such devastating forms. While Christianity's dispute with Judaism may account for the persistence of anti-Semitism, the cataclysmic consequences of revulsion may originate not in theology but in the depths of the human psyche.

Those who argue that anti-Semitism is created by worldly confrontations over precedence and power tend to rule out christological causes. They either claim that hostility derived from historical circumstances or attribute the infernalization of the Jews to universal human emotions unleashed by insecurities and frustrations unconnected to Christian doctrine. Those on the other side of the argument contend that anti-Semitism results directly and fundamentally from the relationship between Christianity and the faith that is both its progenitor and its monotheistic rival. Some trace diabolization of the Jews to the New Testament, others to the high middle ages, and the two groups differ in balancing circumstantial and christological, objective and obsessional influences in the Christian reaction to Judaism. Whether in exculpation or detraction, these scholars do agree that Christian feeling about Jews is as much familial and psychogenic as theological, economic, or political. Some point out that doctrines of crucifixion, martyrdom, sin, forgiveness, and redemption, and sacraments of baptism and communion, involve oedipal conflict, castration anxiety, and other psychoanalytic pathologies. These students of Christian-Jewish relations assert that human psychosis merged with Christian doctrine to make the Jew the despised outsider and villain in western culture.[5]

~

In the 1940s and 1950s students of anti-Semitism widely regarded that phenomenon—even in its relatively mild American version— as a ramification of severe emotional or social disorder. They realized that Christian prejudice, alone or in conjunction with economic and political factors, could not explain the firestorm that had nearly obliterated twentieth-century European Jewry. Those sources of anti-Jewish feeling and action coexisted with restraining countercurrents. Christianity revered as well as reviled Judaism. Jesus had been born a Jew, and according to Christian doctrine the Jews were to survive as witnesses to the truth and triumph of Christianity. Secular attitudes were also not wholly negative. Rulers found the Jews financially and administratively useful, and host societies admired their intelligence, professional and business achievements, charity, peaceful living, and other contributions to the community.

In the agonized post-Holocaust reassessment of western attitudes toward Jews, the most compelling question for American students of anti-Semitism was, could it happen here? Hannah Arendt and others touched on this issue as they speculated on how the delusive frenzy of Hitler and other charismatic anti-Semitic leaders became routinized into bureaucratized genocide, and why most European Christians reacted to the atrocities with passive opportunism or acceptance. As these attempts to explain a searing tragedy evolved into explanations for all aspects of anti-Semitism, their analytic applicability became a matter of extended controversy.

Some theorists, most originally and notably Sigmund Freud in *Moses and Monotheism* (1939), traced anti-Semitism to psychopathology in relations between Christianity and Judaism. Interactions between the monotheisms were interpreted from the perspectives of cosmic myth, macrocosmic models of family, and psychoanalytic theories about death, guilt, oedipal conflict, and castration anxiety.[6]

The greater the Christian animus against Jews, the greater the tendency of psychological inquiry to perceive religious anti-Semitism as an epiphenomenal mask for primal emotions. Psychohistorians, psychiatrists, and psychoanalysts tended to focus on flaws in the argument that anti-Semitism sprang from christological sources. They emphasized the alleged displacement of religious forms of hostility by the more recent phenomenon of racial anti-Semitism. Furthermore, some argued that racialist hatred of Jews was itself part of an anti-Christian movement. Xenophobes often directed against Christian belief the volk myth of blood, stock, soil, and fatherland, thereby erecting secular, particularistic, and biological barriers to the promise of universal redemption.[7]

The titles of many American works of the postwar period reveal the common theme of bigotry as primarily derived from psycho- and socio-pathologies. The most influential scholarly treatise on the subject was The *Authoritarian Personality* (1950), and other important works included *Anti-Semitism: A Social Disease* (1946) and *Anti-Semitism and Emotional Disorder* (1950). A recent psychoanalytical exploration is similarly called *Anti-Semitism: A Disease of the Mind* (1990).[8]

These types of studies describe anti-Semitism as an emotional disorder produced by intrapsychic tensions and sexual and social anxieties and frustrations. Aggression arising from these frustrations is diverted from the self or the real culprits onto the Jews by ego defense mechanisms of displacement, introjection, and projection. Jew haters accordingly exhibit grave personality disorders. They are asocial or antisocial, alienated, isolated, inhibited, anxious, repressed, rigid, regressive, infantile, narcissistic, hostile, punitive, conformist, dependent, delusive, guilt-ridden, paranoid, irrational, aggressive, and prone to violence. These troubled personalities crave authority figures and movements. They embrace fundamentalist and ritualized religious sects and totalitarian policies, parties, and leaders (usually, but not invariably, right-wing). These figures and organizations demand obedience and offer the spurious promise of security through preemptive violence against and suppression of a group erroneously supposed to be dangerous and evil conspirators. The psychiatrist Theodore Isaac Rubin has presented the most elaborate paradigm of disease in classifying anti-Semitism as chronic, pandemic (worldwide), endemic (an old sickness), ravaging both host and victim, metastatic (attacking everywhere), waxing and waning, and ranging in intensity from mild episodes (restricted to moderate dislike and the realm of thought) to mortal plagues (exterminating millions).[9]

Psychogenic interpretations of anti-Semitism derive from general classifications of neuroses and psychoses too inclusive to predict the incidence of xenophobia or ethnocentrism, let alone a specific case of scapegoating. Based primarily on data accumulated from opinion surveys, psychological tests, interviews, and patients in analysis, the methodology and findings, though suggestive, are not always applicable to historical research. Postulations that prejudice is caused by deformed personalities may also be culture and time bound. What is neurotic or psychotic in one time and place may be normal in different ages and locations. A medieval French peasant who claimed that Jews committed ritual murders, were agents of the devil, and had tails was expressing conventional opinion. A present-day descendant holding these beliefs would be called insane. When prejudice is a norm, people who conform to it do not always have the same emotional make up as when it is a deviant belief. In America after World War II, for example, anti-black and anti-Jewish attitudes had a much higher correlation in the North than in the South.[10] In some cases, as in the Third Reich, pathological traits may even become cultural and social norms and ideals.

Attribution of bigotry to emotional disorders may also ignore the importance of social factors. Hence it may inadequately account for why certain minorities are scapegoated with greater frequency and intensity; why anti-Semitism or other biases may vary with social stratum, level of education and wealth, region, and ethnic identification; and why different stereotypes are applied to different outgroups. Psychological theories are also prone to ignore the possibility that disturbed people living in happier times may display less anti-Semitism or xenophobia than mentally healthier individuals in times of social crisis.

It is well known that psychopathological explanations of prejudice may be substantiated by empirical evidence obtained and processed in contexts dissimilar to those in which bigotry is expressed in real-life situations. Conceptual difficulties also challenge theories of psychodynamic causation: Does frustration lead to repression and depression or to aggression? Are these moods necessarily mutually exclusive? Is the aggression passive or aggressive? Does it turn outward or inward? Is it explosive or implosive? Can conclusive correlations be made between the existence of frustration and attempts to rationalize or otherwise divert it through introjection, projection, and displacement? Does psychoanalytic interpretation, which comes from diagnoses of patients in long and deep analysis, hold for data obtained from brief and impersonal sources like questionnaires, one-time interviews, and psychological tests?

Psychological and sociological theories of bigotry are additionally open to criticism for inadequately distinguishing among reactive, conformist, and pathological hostility, between opinion and behavior, or among the finer gradations of disliking a group, acquiescing in its persecution, and taking an actively oppressive role. Related to these weaknesses is an inability to predict the intensity of the discrimination: Would the bigot stop at excluding the group from his country club or demand that they be liquidated? Attribution of prejudice to serious personality disorders in any case accounts for a fraction of the population. They may be a critical segment of inspirational agitators, compellingly depicted by Leo Lowenthal and Norbert Guterman in *Prophets of Deceit* (1970). But mobilizers of anti-Semitism get nowhere without a much larger number of followers, who may adopt the program for reasons of cultural conditioning or conformity or of occupational and economic opportunism.[11]

Several American examples demonstrate that the personality characteristics that create an affinity for authoritarianism or right-wing political causes are not necessarily correlated with anti-Semitism. Mormons, despite an authoritarian belief system and leadership structure, have always been friendly to Jews. A Louis Harris poll found that only 10 percent of those who voted for George Wallace in the 1968 presidential campaign blamed Jews for the nation's troubles, while 21 percent blamed the Ku Klux Klan. Supporters of Joseph McCarthy, according to a 1954 International Research Associates Survey, were 26 percent less likely than anti-McCarthyites to vote against a Jewish congressional candidate. This reactionary, anticommunist movement had Jews among its leaders instead of defining them as villains. Similarly, Robert Welch, founder of the anticommunist John Birch Society, explicitly attacked anti-Semites and dropped them from his organization.[12]

These attitudes of authoritarian and right-wing groups in America, not predictable by psychodynamic models of bigotry, indicate that outbreaks of prejudice, choice of scapegoat, and degree of victimization are highly selective. John Higham criticized *The Authoritarian Personality* and, by extension, intrapsychic theories of prejudice and anti-Semitism, from this perspective. The construct of an authoritarian or fascist personality, he asserted, is not a scientific truth, but an interpretation—by Adorno, Bettelheim, and other scholars whose religious heritage forced them to flee Germany—of the Jewish experience in Europe during the 1930s and 1940s. The Holocaust was the extreme case of anti-Semitism, hence its generalizability is uncertain. Right-wing conspiracy-defense and anticommunist movements bred anti-Semitism in Europe, but not as inevitably in the United States.[13]

Higham's critique suggests that a comprehensive analysis of anti-Semitism must consider the convergence of inner and outer environments, of psychological and social forces. America and Germany share the common culture of western civilization and Christendom and are the nations where Jews attained the highest assimilation and success, and there is no evidence that personality traits that encourage authoritarian and ethnocentric behavior are more common in Germany than in the United States. Yet one land slaughtered Jews and the other became a beacon of equality for them. American anti-Semitism was not an indigenous development but an inheritance from Europe. The "Jewish Question" was endemic in German volk nationalism and erupted into hatred in times of revolution, military defeat, and economic disaster. Consequently, German political and religious leaders, political parties, and prominent intellectuals made anti-Semitism part of their program. American nationalism, in contrast, was more inclusive than exclusive, and instead of taking over the country, as Hitler did in Germany, rabid anti-Semites hovered on the political fringe.

Analysis of the causes and nature of anti-Semitism is fundamentally an examination of how negative reference groups form and why Jews are singled out. Understanding these problems involves exploring the relationship between ethnocentrism and xenophobia. People locate and define themselves in significant ways by establishing boundaries between their group and others and seeing the other groups as potential or actual rivals. This psychosocial dynamic is ethnocentrism, that is, preference for one's own group. Ethnocentric preference may become ethnocentric confrontation if the ingroup defines what is socially normative and legitimate, and if in doing so it degrades the real or imagined traits of the outgroup. Ethnocentrism turns into xenophobia when the ingroup defines its essence, well-being, and cohesiveness as in opposition to an outgroup. In this case the ingroup will perceive the outgroup as a threat and adopt a policy of exclusion to resist a supposed enemy.

Unfavorable stereotypes may sometimes be realistic reflections of intergroup conflicts or unpleasant behavior provoked by repressive conditions. Incessant and long-term ill-treatment of Jews may have caused a collective secretiveness, distrust of Gentiles, clannishness, etc. Xenophobia, however, is composed of fantasies of the malevolent foreigner that symbolize inner anxieties and frustrations or personify and rationalize (irrationalize might be a better term) social crises or unresolved systemic conflicts. These delusions, destructive of self and community, come from a specious belief that maintaining distance from the despised group will bring clarity, coherence, and social control.

Nowhere is the pathology of prejudice better highlighted than in ingroup-outgroup stereotyping that makes qualities esteemed in insiders despised in outsiders. Even if the outgroup mirrors ingroup traits, through negative imaging those traits are delegitimized. All, and only, members of the outgroup possess the constellation of deprecated attributes. The ingroup is correspondingly solidified by supposedly having the contrary (praiseworthy) qualities. In fact, a hierarchy of xenophobia is registered in the degree to which the outgroup is negatively differentiated from the host society.

~

Any comprehensive analysis of anti-Semitism in America or elsewhere, as I have said, must consider the interplay of religious, social, and psychological factors. Of these factors, I believe that religious prejudice—specifically, Christian hostility toward Jews—is paramount. Other minorities have been heretical, commercially successful, intellectually accomplished, and prevalently liberal in politics, yet have not repeatedly been the focus of xenophobic and religious paranoia. None of the others, however, gave birth to Christianity, killed its God, and was assigned by Christian doctrine a pivotal role in the cosmic struggle between the saved and the damned. Uniquely cursed as unrepentant deicides, Jews became the most consistently demonized outcasts in Christendom. In fact a few Israelite leaders did assist in killing Christ, in Roman and medieval times some Jews did aggressively combat Christianity, many today still fear and dislike Christians, and all disbelieve in Jesus as the Messiah. As evidenced by vigorous Jewish advocacy of Jewish causes and historically low levels of intermarriage and other forms of structural assimilation, Jews have a high degree of group solidarity. But these facts are twisted into the essential anti-Semitic claim that all Jews are treacherous and murderous conspirators.[14]

Aversion for Jews is the oldest persisting ethnic and religious phobia. The anti-Semitism that the American colonists and later immigrants brought with them from Europe, which has persisted, in its less virulent American form, through the history of the United States, had its origins long before the European settlement of the New World. Hebrews were a significant people—and already a despised and beleaguered outgroup—in classical antiquity. Understanding the sources of American anti-Semitism requires investigation of its beginnings in the early days of Christianity, its gestation in the Greco-Roman empire, and its development in medieval and early modern Europe.

# ~ 2

# Historical Outsider

## Pagan Anti-Semitism

America is a Christian country, and the history of its anti-Semitism must include the influence that Christian beliefs have had on feelings about Jews for nearly two millennia. The importance of the christological component of anti-Jewish attitudes is a matter of debate; a careful look at that component from the early days of Christianity provides support for a major proposition of this book, that Christian hostility has long been basic to anti-Semitism. In America, I believe, this christological foundation continued to exert a primary influence even in an era when religious anti-Semitism was supposedly declining.

Anti-Semitism did exist when pagan cults were still the predominant sects. Experts concur that anti-Semitism, or at least anti-Judaism, emerged after a long period of cordial relations between Jews and pagans. Serious conflict arose in the mid-second century B.C.E., chiefly in Greco-Egyptian sectors of the Roman Empire: in large Hellenistic cities with numerous Jews, and in rural Egypt. Jews were disliked for being relatively prosperous, acting as middlemen between rulers and local subjects, and enjoying special privileges under the resented Roman imperium. Egyptians, further angered by the portrayal of their people in the Book of Exodus, spread rumors that Jews had syphilis and other diseases when they fled from the pharaoh. The Jews' claims to be God's Chosen and their dietary, Sabbath, circumcision, and other rituals were ridiculed, and they were reviled as corrupt, cowardly, vulgar, superstitious, fanatically reli-

17

gious, and intellectually primitive. They were also accused of grasping excessive political and economic privileges, being aloof and clannish, and scorning the civic religion and thus subverting the state and public order. These defects were associated with charges of snubbing, suppressing, and hating Gentiles. Other allegations included ritual murder (human sacrifice at the Temple) and related acts of cruelty and cannibalism. A widespread objection was that Hebrews dissented from the universal civilization that elevated and integrated the diverse peoples of the Hellenistic and Roman empires. Specific and general repetitions of this indictment would reverberate through the ages.

Official repression varied from the mild (several short-term banishments of Jews from Rome) to the severe (Selucid King Antiochus IV's attempts to stifle Israelite culture and creed). Unofficial persecution erupted in several pogroms in Alexandria and Antioch. In these assaults synagogues were defiled, Jewish property destroyed, and Jews murdered, residentially segregated, and deprived of civic rights.

Bigotry was initially less blatant in Rome. Until the Jewish Wars, which started in 66 C.E., Hebrews were usually respectfully treated as an imperial ally. Jewish insurgency, however, resulted in the burning of the Temple, the killing and enslavement of many Jews, and their exile from the Holy Land. In addition, special taxes were imposed on Jews—a mode of extortion that would intermittently victimize Jews down to the Nazi era.

Animosity cut across social strata, encompassing political leaders, upper-class circles, the intelligentsia, and the masses. Substantial differences existed, however, between classical and subsequent anti-Semitism. Jews in classical times were not defined as avaricious usurers, unscrupulous traders, possessors of uniquely ugly and unhealthy physical traits, impenitent deicides, or refusers of redemption. Although many of the stereotypes that plagued Jews in later eras did exist in antiquity, they generally conveyed disapproval rather than demonization. Violence against Jews was infrequent and brief. Government persecution, even rarer and rapidly reversed, faded after the suppression of the Bar Kochba revolt (132–135 C.E.), as Jews ceased to threaten Rome.

Classical ridicule and repression were spasmodic and pragmatic rather than ideological, passionate, or systemic. Official suppression usually resulted from Jewish uprisings, Roman alliances with Egyptian or Hellenistic groups to preserve local order or inspire imperial loyalty, and Hebraic subversion of pagan or imperial cults by proselytizing and attacks on polytheistic shrines. Roman persecution was specific to the time and place of violations or conflicts, and often occurred in reaction to judaizing motivated by the waning appeal of polytheism and the civic religion. Israelites were punished no worse than other transgressor peoples in the empire, continued to enjoy full rights as Roman citizens, and lived under their own ancestral customs and codes, undisturbed by laws incompatible with their autonomy. In fact, both before and after the rebellions they were frequently lauded for staunch religious faith and a philosophical temperament.[1]

Jews might be considered strange, stubborn, impious, and rebellious, but they were not yet assigned the role of archetypal aliens in law, theology, or popular belief. Their nonconformity, chiefly consisting of a distinctive faith, was not yet an irreconcilable evil, for polytheism was an inclusive belief. Jehovah and Jesus, not Jupiter, were jealous Gods, and by the time the Roman-Jewish troubles started, the imperial cult was a formal allegiance rather than a devotional passion.

## Early Christianity

The founding of Christianity drastically altered the equation between Jew and Gentile. Now appeared another monotheistic faith, with theological, historical, and psychological imperatives to combat Judaism. Little else, however, is agreed upon regarding the confrontation between Christianity and its progenitor. Disputes rage over the sources, motives, and dimensions of the new creed's side of the mutual hostility.

Disentangling a complex and sometimes interlocked chain of causation in Christian anti-Judaism necessitates a classification of causes moving from those contextual and incidental to church doctrine, to fundamental human feelings external to dogma, and finally to those factors embedded in the spirit of Christianity. The greater the convergence between animosity toward Jews and christological factors, the larger the role of the essence of Christianity, that is, its particular messianic form of salvation, in fomenting hostility. The more responsibility that Christian principles bear for such bigotry, the stronger the argument that since the United States has always been a predominantly Christian country, the antecedents of American anti-Semitism are historical, not modern; Christian, not secular; and endemic to western civilization, not exceptional. If anti-Semitism primarily derives from Christian doctrine, then the exploration of differences between American and European attitudes toward Jews may be most effectively directed to matters of degree rather than substance or genesis. Logically elegant models, however, may obscure real events. Massacres of Jews were exclusively Old World catastrophes; differences in intensity can overshadow a common essence or etiology.

If Christianity is the center of the proposed model, the outermost rim of causation concerns historical developments that, by definition, are temporal and changeable and thus separable from the message of eternal spiritual redemption through the martyrdom of Jesus. If contextual (nondoctrinal) factors mainly account for anti-Semitism, its cause cannot be christological. These external elements include absorption of pagan prejudice into Christian attitudes toward Jews; competition for converts between proselytizing monotheisms; defensiveness against judaizing elements within and Jewish attacks upon the younger creed; and attempts to reduce opposition from Rome by shifting suspicion of disloyalty from Christians to Jews.

Modern defenders of Christianity against allegations of intrinsic anti-Semitism emphasize historical causes, particularly continuity with Hellenistic and Roman anti-Semitism. Many negative feelings about and images of Jews, they point out, originated in the classical age. Christianity assimilated Greco-Roman culture, and anti-Semitism was part of this legacy.[2] However, not all aspects of Christian antipathy proceed from, or cohere with, Greco-Roman prejudice. Consider the case of accusations of ritual murder. By the thirteenth century blood guilt was a popular myth about Jews, yet it was mentioned only twice in antiquity. What had been occasional now became endemic. Other Christian condemnations could not even claim so tenuous a tie with the pagan past.

The conclusion that Christian anti-Semitism only partly derived from pagan anti-Semitism leaves unanswered the question of whether the latter was indeed the primary source of the former. The balance between inherited and original elements in Christian attitudes toward Jews cannot be reckoned by making an inventory of pagan and Christian fears and suspicions. Hence the inquiry must now turn to the ways the two belief systems related to Judaism. Even a differentiation of religious mentalities, however, may not locate the basic source of Christian animus, if that source lies in historical developments not concerning paganism or in universal human traits.

Analysis of pagan and Christian attitudes begins by distinguishing between polytheistic and monotheistic worship. The former tends to inclusive belief systems and willingness to incorporate additional gods into their pantheons. The latter leans toward an exclusive relationship with its god, which defines the deity as an absolute being, demands obsessive loyalty, and is therefore less likely to tolerate other gods. If these distinctions do not invariably hold, they do apply to differences between Greco-Roman polytheistic cults and Judaism and Christianity.[3]

They do not, however, entirely explain the fact that conflict between Christians and Jews has usually been far more intense than the relatively external confrontation of each with paganism. Christianity was an outgrowth of Judaism and both believed in one God, the sacredness of the Old Testament, and the coming of a Messiah. Despite these major agreements, monotheistic exclusiveness, inflamed by inhabiting a common territory and vying for the same souls, often made their relationship resemble the fratricidal rivalry of Cain and Abel rather than the brotherhood of Moses and Aaron.[4] Interfaith struggle was further destined by the fact that Jews and Christians, unlike most Romans and Hellenistic Greeks, derived their self, communal, and cosmic identities mainly from their religion and, further, that Christian identity was significantly formed by contrast with Judaism.[5]

Distinctions between paganism and monotheism do not indicate whether anti-Semitism was integral to Christianity or whether Christian hostility arose from historical factors. Consider the crucifixion. Biblical indictment of the Jews for slaying Jesus has been explained in contextual terms. According to this explanation, Christians and Jews refused to participate in the imperial cult, advocated apostasy from other faiths, and claimed a monopoly on religious truth, therefore incurring accusations of disloyalty to the state and the emperor. Christians, unlike Jews, neither enjoyed official tolerance and privileges nor could counter these charges by citing civil and military service to Rome.[6] Shifting responsibility for the death of Jesus from the Roman proconsul to the Hebrews, or at least to their leaders, was a way to evade suspicion of disloyalty. Transferring guilt from Pilate to the Jews absolved Christ of having aspired to the secular kingship of Israel and thus of having conspired against the *imperium*, and substantiated the claim, in an era of Hebraic uprisings, that Jews fanatically opposed their true God and defied the official agent of the emperor.

The contextual argument also attributes polemics against Judaism to Christianity's impulse to distinguish itself from its predecessor. This impulse, however, issued from human psychology as well as history: from Christians' need to seek self-definition and cohesion through ritual and emotional separateness from Judaism. For Christians, and probably for some Romans, the unsuccessful Jewish uprisings and their dire consequences to the Jews proved the accuracy of the Christian portrayal of sinful, stubborn, and subversive Israel ruined by God's displeasure with his once chosen, and now outcast, people. A vanquished and dispossessed Israel also confirmed for Christians that their new covenant had displaced a feeble, misguided, and obsolete religion.[7]

Assembling these arguments neither determines which is the most important causative factor nor measures the magnitude of antipathy. Is doctrine, history, human emotion, or some combination of these the basic cause of Christian anti-Semitism? And whatever the cause, was the church's acrimony a limited attack or total war—were the Jews wrong or evil, rivals or demons? If the ultimate explanation is all the above, with emphases varying with specific times, places, people, and issues, did New Testament and patristic doctrine lay the foundation for the hatred of Jews that led to their slaughter beginning in eleventh- and climaxing in twentieth-century Christendom?

A noted clerical opponent of the christological view of anti-Semitism suggests that Christian hostility toward Jews arose from psychological causes: the need to affirm one's own creed by belittling another, the tension generated by life's struggles and disappointments, the dialectical relationship between love and hate (in this case Christian love and hate for Judaism).[8] This postulation of universal human emotion as the prime motive for Christian anti-Semitism is, like the historical thesis, inadequate. Most pagans did not need to buttress their faith by undermining Judaism, nor did they generally seek an outlet from life's tensions by attacking Hebrews. The dialectic of ambivalence certainly existed in the Christian reaction to Judaism, but it may plausibly have stemmed from love-hate feelings about Christianity itself rather than about the older creed.

The historical argument has comparable weaknesses. Classical anti-Semitism subsided when a defeated Israel no longer alarmed Rome, but Christian animosity intensified after Catholicism irrevocably defeated its monotheistic rival.[9] Similarly, in high and late medieval Christendom and under the Nazi regime, merciless onslaughts, with considerable religious inspiration and clerical collaboration, continued long after Judaism buckled.

The analysis thus far invariably returns to the initial inquiry: Was the more prolonged and cataclysmic Christian anti-Semitism a heritage from antiquity or a legacy of early Christianity? Did it primarily erupt from historical and psychological factors or from Christology? These queries may also be applied to a related issue, the demonization of the Jews, which

Gavin I. Langmuir calls "chimerical antisemitism" and differentiates from earlier Christian "anti-Judaism." According to Langmuir, demonization emerged in the West during the First Crusade, subsided in the sixteenth century, resurged with unprecedented force in the late nineteenth century, and culminated in the near elimination of European Jewry.[10]

Resolution of the interlinked issues—putative medieval infernalization of anti-Judaism into anti-Semitism and the contribution of Christology to both modes of that prejudice—lies in evidence from New Testament and patristic writings, in mythic, metaphoric, and other visceral meanings the treatment of Jews in these writings aroused in believers, and in Christian behavior toward Jews in the ages of the Apostles and the church fathers. These texts inculcated ideas and sentiments that defined attitudes and prompted actions toward the Jews. This investigation of the allegedly christological provenance and nature of anti-Semitism, therefore, examines early church texts for evidence of christological and infernal features in anti-Jewish attitudes. The existence of such evidence does not prove that Christian anti-Semitism is solely christological in origin, that the church had no appreciation of Judaism, or that hostility always leads to demonization. But the discovery of a consistent and conjoined trend toward christological rebuke and diabolization of Jews substantiates the claim that Christianity is inherently and intensely anti-Semitic (even if it also harbors neutral and philo-Semitic impulses). If it is so, Christian doctrine bears some responsibility for the tragic development of western anti-Semitism.

Modern apologetics has assembled a complex resistance to charges of christological anti-Semitism. Tracing the causes of hostility toward Jews to historical and psychological instead of doctrinal factors is the primary rebuttal. Apologists, however, are also prepared to argue from scripture that the New Testament contains no doctrinal distaste for Jews. They cite favorable biblical commentary on Judaism while claiming that critical passages focus on interfaith competition and mutual hostility or are aimed at judaizers within the Christian community and, in any case, distinguish between Israelite leaders and masses. They dismiss even indisputably negative passages by suggesting that they may be spurious and subsequent interpolations, biased mistranslations and misreadings that distort the true message, or by claiming that the Jews are rebuked, not as a people or for their creed, but as "a theological cipher or symbol for a world that denies itself a Jesus." When all other disclaimers fail, the apologists interpret New Testament attacks on Jews as emotional outbursts rather than doctrinal declarations. Proponents of these arguments may be called the ABD (any-thing but doctrinal) school of Christian anti-Semitism. Midway between them and their adversaries stands Langmuir, who recognizes a theological dimension in early church anti-Judaism but judges it to have been an empirical (nondemonizing), though excessive, reaction to denigration by Jews of Christ and his followers.[11]

Plausible evidence against a christological basis for anti-Semitism can be found in scripture: Jesus and his disciples announced that the Jews killed him out of ignorance and would be forgiven, distinguished between the elite and the people, identified themselves as Jews, promised that Israel would be saved, and asserted that the Lord's covenant with his Chosen People was unrevoked. Indeed, the New Testament critique of Judaism derives extensively from Israel's prophetic tradition.[12]

~

Many passages in the Bible in which Jesus and his followers abominate the Jews, however, cannot be dismissed as anachronistic interpolations, biased renderings, or imitations of Old Testament Jeremiads. Echoes of the proph-ets were significantly modified to insist that Israel's reconciliation with God would be restricted to the remnant who accepted Jesus as Savior. Some pas-sages cited to refute doctrinal anti-Semitism leave the apologists open to accusations of tendentious and dubious interpretation. Consider first the Epistles of Paul, the oldest parts of the New Testament (ca. 40–63 C.E.), whose author transformed a Judaic cult worshipping Jesus as the Messiah into an autonomous religion that forsook Jewish law and ritual to focus its beacon upon Gentiles.

The fraudulent provenance argument is used only once, and partially, by the apologists, who assert that the one instance in which Paul blames the Jews for the crucifixion may be a later misrepresentation of his gen-erally high regard for Judaism and his Jewish origins.[13] In the contested passage Paul speaks of "the Jews: Who both killed the Lord Jesus, and their own prophets, and have persecuted us; and they please not God, and are contrary to all men" (1 Thess. 2:15; all quotations are from the King James Version). Unconditional divine damnation of Jews for deicide and other sins, asserted by the apostle who made Christianity independent of Judaism, if verifiable, would devastate the case against doctrinal anti-Semitism. But not according to the doyen of the apologists, Fr. John M. Oesterreicher. If this quotation were authentic, he "would continue to view it as an impassioned, uncontrolled outburst, something of a quite different order than doctrinal utterance."[14] Those suggesting that it is of dubious provenance, however, do not quote the continuation of Paul's remark, in which he is still referring to the Jews: "Forbidding us to speak to the Gentiles that they might be saved, to fill up their sins alway; for the wrath is come upon them to the uttermost" (1 Thess. 2:16). Oesterreicher asserts that Rosemary Ruether, his great antagonist, self-servingly mistranslates this verse as "God's wrath has come upon them at last."[15] Oesterreicher may be the more accurate linguist, but Ruether is the truer interpreter of Paul. Although this verse does not prove the veracity of its predecessor, it certainly can be read as a supporting sequence to that bitter denunciation, and it seems motivated by doctrinal as well as emotional estrangement.

Those who make Paul a veritable friend of the Jews note that he blamed "the princes of this world" for "crucif[ying] the Lord of glory," conceded that the Hebrew mob acted out of ignorance (1 Cor. 2:8), and declaimed that "I also am an Israelite, of the seed of Abraham, of the tribe of Benjamin" and that God has not "cast away his People" (Rom. 11:1-2).

Notwithstanding these sentiments, many of Paul's reprimands of the Jews and reports of God's disapproval, omitted by Oesterreicher and others, were harsher than those just quoted. These other reproofs, of undisputed authenticity, leave little doubt that Paul, both doctrinally and emotionally, is enraged against his people of origin. "For I could wish that myself were accursed from Christ for my brethren, my kinsmen according to the flesh," he laments (Rom. 9:3). Note the hint of demonization in the phrase "accursed from Christ." The Epistle to the Romans also prescribes divine justice according to Christian dogma: "because of unbelief they [the "branches" of Israel] were broken off" (Rom. 11:20). A remnant might be saved in eternity; meanwhile the Jews would be consigned to an earthly hell: "Behold therefore the goodness and severity of God: on them [the Jews] which fell, severity; but toward thee [Gentile believers] goodness, if thou continue in *his* goodness: otherwise thou also shalt be cut off" (Rom. 11:22).

Thomas Idinopulos and Roy Bowen Ward, prominent ABD analysts, move from evasion to casuistry in arguing that Paul "never says that Judaism was a false worship of God," and that "his acceptance of the gospel [does not] lead him to deny the holiness of the [Mosaic] law nor the election of the Jews." Transformation from Saul to Paul is not a repudiation of his earlier faith; "rather he claims that a new righteousness has been revealed which causes him to move into a new phase in the history of salvation."[16] The operative concept here is the emergence of a new, redemptive morality. Paul states, with blunt anti-Judaic invective, that for its believers the new revelation meant that the Gospel "delivered [us] from the [Mosaic] law, that being dead wherein we were held" (Rom. 7:6), and that "the letter killeth, but the spirit giveth life" (2 Cor. 3:6), and that "Christ hath redeemed us from the curse of the law" (Gal. 3:13).[17]

Striving to detach Christianity from Judaism, Paul elaborated on the penalty for stubbornly obeying a sterile code. "[I]gnorant of God's righteousness," Hebrews "have not submitted themselves unto the righteousness of God. For Christ is the end of the law for righteousness to every one that believeth" (Rom. 10:3–4). Israelites have therefore fallen (without being "cast away" as God's people), and "through their fall salvation is come unto the Gentiles, for to provoke them [the Jews] to jealousy" (Rom. 11:2, 11).

Paul does not merely trumpet the revelation of "a new righteousness" and "phase in the history of salvation." Judaism, unredeemed by faith in the Savior, is "false worship of God." Belief in Jehovah without Jesus, therefore, desacralizes Mosaic law. Idinopulos and Ward may define Paul's position as "theological imperialism" or a mere readjustment of Judaic belief, but the call for unconditional surrender of Judaic to Christian truth is doctrinal anti-Judaism.

Among Paul's christological polemics against Judaism, one argument blatantly contradicts Idinopulos and Ward's contention that "acceptance of the gospel" does not "lead him to deny . . . the election of Jews." Regarding Judaic law as imperfect and inferior to Christianity and as sanctified by Jesus, Paul concludes that "salvation" depends upon belief in "the gospel of Christ" (Rom. 1:16). Jews cannot be saved unless they become Christians, a core tenet of Christianity.

In focusing on Paul's plea that Jews accept the Savior and be redeemed, apologists ignore his christological scourging of the Jews. Although Paul does not explicitly address Jews in Romans 1, his recriminations are mainly directed at them. Paul was the architect and foremost advocate of Christianity's independence of Judaic law and ritual; strategy and conviction motivated him to discredit Judaism and its believers. He regarded the unredeemed Hebrews as his chief persecutors (Acts 13–28; 2 Cor. 11:24–25; 2 Tim. 3:11) and Christianity's primary adversaries (Acts 13:45–50; Rom. 11:25). He warned that "the wrath of God is revealed from heaven against all ungodliness and unrighteousness of men, who hold the truth in unrighteousness" (Rom. 1:18). The deity's anger is justified, for "when they knew God, they glorified him not as God, neither were thankful; but became vain in their imaginations, and their foolish heart was darkened" (Rom. 1:21; cf. 1:19).

The real object of Paul's denunciation becomes clear when these passages are read against the words of Paul and Barnabas to the Jews of Antioch: "It was necessary that the word of God should first have been spoken to you: but seeing you put it from you, and judge yourselves unworthy of everlasting life, lo, we turn to the Gentiles." The Gentiles rejoice at this, but "the Jews . . . raised up persecution against Paul and Barnabas, and expelled them out of their coasts" (Acts 13: 46–48, 50). In Romans Paul conveys the same message to the Jews: "that blindness in part is happened to Israel, until the fulness of the Gentiles has come in" (Rom. 11:25; cf. 11:11). If, as Paul asserts in Romans 1, God is enraged at those to whom he revealed himself and who yet rejected him, no people are more culpable than the Jews, to whom he originally appeared and who first and most totally spurned him.

Fulminations against those who dismiss the Christian message cross over from principled, ideological objections ("their heart was darkened") to the scurrilous attacks that pervade the letter to the Romans: When Jews no longer "worshipped and served" him (1:25), "God also gave them up to uncleanness," to "dishonour their own bodies between themselves" (1:24) and "to vile affections," in which they "did change the natural use into that which is against nature" (1:26). Men "burned in their lust toward one another; men with men working that which is unseemly, and receiving in themselves that recompense of their error which was meet" (1:27). For renouncing him, "God gave them over" to "all unrighteousness, fornication, wickedness, covetousness, maliciousness; full of envy, murder, debate, deceit, malignity." Disbelievers are "Backbiters, haters of God, despiteful, proud, boasters, inventors of evil things, disobedient to parents." They are "Without understanding, covenant breakers, without natural affection, implacable, unmerciful; who knowing the judgment of God, that they which commit such things are worthy of death, not only do the same, but have pleasure in them that do them" (Rom. 1:28–32). Whatever other feelings Paul held for his kinsmen, whatever other meanings apologists assign to his comments, Paul's diabolization of the Jews proceeded from intractable, creedal hatred.

Paul's invective is not exceptional in the New Testament, where Hebrews are frequently portrayed as a blind, bigoted, and backsliding people whose historic misdeeds culminated in the crucifixion. As well as

reiterating Paul's critique of Jewish law and ritual, accounts of the crucifixion in Matthew (ca. 60–65 C.E.), Mark, (?), Luke (ca. 80–85 C.E.) and
John (ca. 90–100 C.E.) introduce another aspect of Christian anti-
Semitism. The Gospels agree that Pilate exonerated Christ of accusations
by Jewish leaders. While Matthew and Mark assert that the chief priests,
scribes, and others in the elite incited the crowd (Matt. 27:21–24; Mark
15:13–15), Luke and John, the later writers, indiscriminately blame all
the Jews (Luke 23:4–5, 13–14, 16–17, 21–23; John 18:39–40; 19:1–
15). Luke reports that when the proconsul would have freed Christ, the
Jews "cried, saying, Crucify him, crucify him" (Luke 23:21). John accuses
the Jews of answering Pilate, "We have a law, and by our law he ought to
die because he made himself the Son of God." When the governor tells the
Jews that Jesus is their king, "they cried out, Away with him, away with
him, crucify him" (John 19:7, 15). Although Luke and John blame all the
Jews, it is Matthew, relatively moderate in this respect, who assigns them
perpetual guilt for the crime. To Pilate's craven plea, "I am innocent of the
blood of this just person: see ye to it," the mob retorts, "His blood be on
us, and on our children" (Matt. 27:24–25).

The biblical writers demonized the Jews by associating them with the
devil and the Antichrist: "I know the blasphemy of them which say they
are Jews, and are not, but are the synagogue of Satan," says Jesus of those
who disbelieve in him (Rev. 2:9; cf. 3:9). "Who is a liar but he that denieth
that Jesus is the Christ?" demands John. "He is antichrist, that denieth the
Father and the Son" (1 John 2:22).

The Prince of Peace can equal Jupiter and Jehovah in hurling vindictive thunderbolts: How much "sorer punishment" than the death
penalty prescribed for violating Mosaic law, is "worthy" for he "who hath
trodden under foot the Son of God, and hath counted the blood of the
covenant, wherewith he was sanctified, an unholy thing, and hath done
despite unto the Spirit of grace?" This question is answered in two
famous New Testament statements: "Vengeance belongeth unto me, I
will recompense, saith the Lord . . . The Lord shall judge his people."
For "It is a fearful thing to fall into the hands of the living God" (Heb.
10:29–31).[18]

Jesus the censorious patriarch, not Jesus the merciful martyr, harangued
the Jews at the Temple: "[I]f ye believe not that I am He, ye shall die in
your sins." "Ye are of your father the devil, and the lusts of your father ye
will do. He was a murderer from the beginning, and . . . there is no truth
in him" (John 8:24, 44). He pronounced stern judgment on those who,

unlike Gentiles, rebuffed him not from ignorance but out of stubborn spite: "If I had not done among them the works which none other man did, they had not had sin: but now have they both seen and hated both me and my Father" (John 15:24; cf. 15:22).

The disciple Stephen, if possible, surpassed his Lord's ire: "Ye stiff-necked and uncircumcised in heart and ears, ye do always resist the Holy Ghost: as your fathers did, so do ye. Which of the prophets have not your fathers persecuted? and they have slain them which shewed before of the coming of the Just One; of whom ye have been now the betrayers and murderers" (Acts 7:51–52). In Acts, the Jews respond to this denunciation by stoning Stephen to death.

～

Controversy over whether *adversos Judaeos* was doctrinal or incidental and over whether it had demonic elements persists in interpretations of the patristic age (the late first century through the seventh century in the Latin Church). Oesterreicher continues to minimize endemic bigotry by claiming that the anti-Jewish polemics of the church fathers made up a tiny share of their writings. This assessment, as well as Langmuir's insistence that chimerical anti-Semitism appeared much later, underestimates the magnitude of the church's quarrel with the Jews. Leading patristic thinkers viewed the crucifixion as the culmination of Judaic infamy. From the Jews' killing of Jesus and subsequent denial of guilt stemmed patristic vilification of Judaism for misinterpreting its own scriptures and for the defectiveness of its laws and rites.[19]

As Oesterreicher admits, Church Father John Chrysostom, exemplar of inherited New Testament diabolization of the Hebrews, hated Jews. In a series of "Homilies against Jews" preached between 386 and 388 in Antioch churches, Saint Chrysostom assails the "wretches" who "were called to the sonship, but they degenerated to the level of dogs" and acquired "blood guiltiness" in rejecting Christ. A putrid brew of inebriation, gluttony, lust, and thievery, "Their licentiousness has overshadowed the lechery of animals." Not "only the synagogue, but the souls of Jews are also the dwelling place of demons." Judaism is "the devil's snare." When "you go into a synagogue . . . make the sign of the cross on your brow" so that "the evil power which dwells in the synagogue flees." Otherwise, "the devil will afflict you with countless evils." In a later sermon (390–398), this Bishop of Antioch cautioned that "Jews . . . having deprived themselves of Him that is will fall into the hands of antichrist."[20]

Chrysostom's contemporary Saint Jerome, the abbot of a monastery in Bethlehem, anticipated modern anti-Semitic propaganda by predicting the emergence of an infernal Jewish conspiracy for global dominion. He asserted in 407 that the "Antichrist . . . is to be born of the Jewish people" and "by means of intrigue and deception" will "persecute the people of Christ" and "rule . . . the world." The "Jews mistakenly imagine" Lucifer's lieutenant their Messiah and eagerly receive him. He defeats Rome and restores Israel to the Jews, but he and most of his followers are destroyed in the apocalyptic fulfillment of Christianity.[21]

The demonization of Jews by association with the Antichrist originated in the New Testament (1 John 2:18, 22; 4:3; 2 John 1:7; Rev. 11:7; 13:1–10, 12; Matt. 24:4–5, 11, 23–24; Mark 13:6-7, 21-22). The "son of perdition" will sit "as God . . . in the Temple of God [that is, the Temple in Jerusalem]" (2 Thess. 2:3–4) and Jews worship the seducer of souls because they forsook their Savior (John 5:43).

Jerome railed against "the iniquity . . . of the Jews," who were "supplanted" and "cursed" for slaying the Redeemer. The "story of Judas; in general it is that of the Jews . . . The Jews take their name from the betrayer . . . from the traitor come the carnal Jews."[22] This identification with Judas not only implied that Jews were betrayers but also drew upon the diabolization of Judas in the Gospel of John: "After the sop Satan entered into him" and "supper being ended, the devil having now put into the heart of Judas Iscariot, Simon's son, to betray [Jesus]" (John 13:27, 2).

Saint Ambrose, Bishop of Milan and a powerful fourth-century force in ensuring that Catholicism prevailed among the ruling elite in the western Roman Empire, expressed what had become standard church dogma *contra Judaeos:* Christianity is the substance and Judaism a shadowy and displaced creed whose believers, a recalcitrant, blind, and "wicked" remnant, betrayed Jesus for money and killed him. Their descendants inherited this sin by continuing to reject the Savior and sacrilegiously torment Christians. As punishment for these transgressions, God abandoned his Chosen People and subjected them to an oppressive ordeal until their redemption at the end of days.[23]

Ambrose converted the most famous Church Father, Aurelius Augustine, Bishop of Hippo, in his time the preeminent prelate in Latin Christendom, chief architect of medieval church theology, and one of the two leading western Catholic philosophers (the other being Thomas Aquinas). In *The City of God* (ca. 415), Saint Augustine fortified a dictum that would reign until the High Middle Ages—that the misery of the Jews persisted because they had slain Christ and still repudiated his message. They were to live out a tormented existence as "testimony" and "witnesses" to Christ's "prophecies" of Christian truth and triumph. Augustine's relatively moderate theodicy of crime and punishment portrayed Jesus's persecutors and their progeny as deluded zealots. Unknowingly anti-God, they would ultimately be enlightened, remorseful, and forgiven. At the end of the eleventh century a harsher condemnation would emerge to challenge the Augustinian conception and inspire unprecedented persecution for the Jews.[24]

~

Ideological anti-Semitism fomented institutional anti-Semitism. Christianity underwent rapid elevation from repression to toleration to preferment after Constantine the Great became a believer in 313. The royal conversion had the opposite effect upon the legal status of Jews. From the fourth through the sixth centuries, edict and law attempted to constrain the political and religious liberty of the Jewish citizens in the empire. Roman laws called Jews impious, sacrilegious, deformed, pestilential, diseased, and execrable; accused them of being defilers; mentioned Jewish "perversity," "deadly superstition," and "abominable and vile name"; and referred to Judaism as an "abominable sect," a "nefarious sect," and "a fellowship in turpitude" and to its converts as "those who despised the dignity of the Christian religion and name and polluted themselves with the Jewish contagion."[25] Formal repression, however, rarely impeded real life, where Jews engaged in unlawful religious and civic activities without penalty.

Official discrimination worked in tandem with church policy. Contemporary synods and ecumenical councils sought to immunize the faithful from impiety, judaizing, and apostasy by forbidding Jews and Christians to take meals together or to intermarry. These religious rules formally, if not actually, defined Jewish-Christian interactions until well into the modern period.[26]

Government edict reflected Christian theology more than popular sentiment, and the church fathers themselves varied in their reaction to Jews; Origen's remonstrances, for example, are mild in comparison with Chrysostom's tirades.[27] For these reasons, actual relations between Jews and Christians and between Jews and the Roman government seldom reflected legal restrictions. Nevertheless, institutional anti-Semitism and its legal instrument, created after the Roman emperor became a Christian, would remain in force to a lesser or greater degree for more than fifteen centuries.

Although de facto conditions for Jews often did not match de jure restrictions, Christian attacks on Jews were not rare. The first recorded violation of a synagogue by Christians occurred in the fourth century. Multiplication of such incidents, sometimes led by local bishops, during the fourth and fifth centuries evoked a Roman law against vandalism. Ambrose, however, remonstrated that damaging Jewish holy places was not a crime and persuaded the emperor to rescind the protective law. In Alexandria in 414, after Jewish inhabitants were mobbed and their property confiscated, the first recorded Christian expulsion of Jews took place, under the leadership of Saint Cyril, patriarch of that city and a renowned church father. A year later, in Innestar, Syria, another mob attacked Jews because of an accusation of ritual murder.[28]

As the Roman Empire disintegrated and the patristic era came to an end, Jews retained imperial citizenship and religious autonomy, held public offices, owned land, bore arms, and lived among and exerted authority over Christians in reasonably harmonious and egalitarian circumstances. Legal oppression, canonical discrimination, and Christian-inspired assaults, even after Christianity became the dominant religion, were still partly external products of a struggle for worshippers and precedence between two vigorous monotheisms, of fears over judaizing tendencies among the faithful, and of Jewish attacks on Christians.

Nevertheless, this period foreshadowed the later persecution of Jews. Christianity now reigned in the Latin spiritual world, ideological and demonic anti-Semitism rooted themselves in church dogma if not yet in the popular consciousness, and institutional anti-Semitism created models for future public proscriptions. In theology and law, although not yet prevalently in practice, Jews retained autonomy over their own rituals but could exert no authority over Christians, were hindered in proselytizing, and were treated as outcasts. Toleration in exchange for subservience was not yet their lot, but the groundwork for later waves of repression had been laid.

~

The connection between ideological anti-Semitism and hostile behavior lies in the mythic and metaphoric, rather than in the cognitive, meaning of adversos Judaeos suggested in the New Testament and solidified in the thought of the church fathers. Doctrinal anti-Semitism and demonization denoted that antagonism toward Jews was essential to the Christian conception of salvation and to Christian spiritual identity. The emotional resonance of this theology would reverberate through the ages and give anti-Semitism its religious basis and much of its intensity.

Christian doctrine portrayed Judaism as a flawed and obsolete precursor and sometimes as a diabolic enemy. Designation of Judaism as a fossil faith ignored the spiritual, intellectual, and proselytizing vitality of rabbinical Judaism. According to Christian thought, the elder creed died with the accomplishment of its divine purpose, as stated in the Old Testament, in the birth of Christ. Repudiation of the Christian message and Bible was evidence of Jewish irrelevance and wickedness. Conversely, Christian reverence for the Hebrew scriptures gave the new religion historical legitimacy in a civilization that venerated the past. But Christianity's sanctification of the Old Testament, accompanied by its declaration of autonomy from its predecessor, necessitated general disparagement of post-Calvary Judaism and the specific cavil that the Jews malevolently misinterpreted their own holy book. Their refusal to recognize Jesus as Lord, and their clinging to a legalistic distortion of their own scriptures, fulfilled the Old Testament prophecy that Jews would deny and crucify the Messiah, epitomized stubbornly immoral Israel, and reassured Christians of the rectitude of their belief.[29]

Although Christianity largely failed to overcome Jewish resistance, it succeeded brilliantly in inspiring its followers and converting the heathen. The Old Testament, according to the christological interpretation, heralded the arrival of the Savior and proved that Judaism existed as a precursor of Christianity. Having issued in its successor, the older creed should now disappear. Christianity was a replacement, not an outgrowth, of Judaism. A prescription for theological genocide, supercessionism contrasted a ritualistic, legalistic, tribalistic, and corrupt relic, now fallen from grace, with a spiritual, vigorous, authentic, righteous promise of redemption. The Jews looked upon Jehovah as the only God and themselves as his Chosen People. Christianity asserted that Jesus replaced the Mosaic Covenant with a divine dispensation. Unable or unwilling (Christian thought embraced both possibilities) to accept this revelation, the Jews brought about their own downfall by rejecting the Messiah and thus abandoning their own prophetic tradition. In so doing, they chose evil over good, disobeyed the Lord, and compounded the wickedness amply displayed and reprimanded in their own scriptures.

Christian dogma contrasted Judaic particularism with Christian universalism. Moses, the paramount Jewish hero, who freed his people from bondage in Egypt, was eclipsed by the Son of God, who emancipated all people for all time.[30] The Jews' claims to be God's Chosen and expectation that the Messiah would restore their dominion over the Holy Land were contrasted with Christ's sacrifice of himself to redeem all who believed in him. Jehovah and his Messiah advanced only the worldly ambitions of the Jews; the Lord and his Son appealed to the spiritual aspirations of all humanity. Christian universalism, however, was premised upon a definition of sanctity no less exclusive than the Jewish claim of a special relationship with God. Deliverance was offered to all, but required acknowledging Jesus as the Savior. Damnation awaited those who denied his divinity. Both Jews and Gentiles could achieve salvation only by relinquishing their own faiths. Of all unbelievers, however, the Jews were most culpable, because Jesus had come to them first; unlike the Gentiles, they could not claim ignorance as an excuse. Christian prerogatives of exclusive universalism, divine election, and spiritual and moral primacy were asserted over all religions but particularly over the rival monotheism.

Israel plays both positive and negative roles in the Christian covenant, which simultaneously fulfills and cancels the promise of God to Abraham. The divinity of Christ involves immaculate conception, bloody crucifixion, and sublime resurrection. Jews are crucial at his birth and death. Mary, a Jewess, gives birth to Jesus, a symbolic enactment of Judaism creating Christianity. But in recognizing her child as the Savior she renounces her old faith, a symbol of the ejection of Judaism by Christianity. A more serious sign of dispossession is that those to whom Jesus initially belonged are accused of murdering him. Only after the end of his earthly life, in his resurrection, are Jews inessential.

Christianity is more preoccupied with turmoil than with transcendence, with death, betrayal, and guilt than with the virtuous paradise to come in the Millennium and in heaven. Crucifixion, not resurrection, is the palpable climax of the First Coming. In the doctrinal drama of salvation, Christians and Jews are bipolar signifiers of the conflict between good and evil. Christ incarnates absolute holiness and righteousness; those who impenitently destroy him are the enemies of perfect virtue. According to the Gospels and subsequent Christian depictions of the crucifixion, belatedly and incompletely revised in recent times, Jews commit unrepentant deicide. Slaying the Savior is a vile transgression; feeling no remorse makes it an inexcusable malevolence. Disregarding historical reality—Roman soldiers executed Christ, Pilate was a brutal proconsul unlikely to have been moved by sympathy for the innocent, most Jews were unaware of the alleged Messiah and did not dwell in Israel, much less in Jerusalem—Christian thought assigned collective blame to the Jews. Their descendants inherited the original guilt. Unwilling to repudiate their own creed by admitting the accursedness of the crime or the divinity of its victim, they perpetuated the ancestral atrocity. God's retribution was swift, severe, and deserved: the destruction of their Temple, dispersion from Judea, horrible carnage, and a defiled and anguished existence to last until a remnant would atone at the Second Coming. Until the end of history, however, Jews would be agents of the devil. Satan, epitome of evil in the Manichean struggle against the divine incarnation of goodness, was closest to God before he fell furthest from heaven. Similarly, the crucifixion made the Jews, once the Chosen People, the most distant outsiders. As Rosemary Ruether observes in *Faith and Fratricide,* the early church erected a double standard for persecution: the torment of Jesus, the apostles, and other followers is divine martyrdom, the suffering of the Jews is divine retribution.[31]

Armageddon finally resolves the conflict of good against evil, Lucifer against the Lord, and Jew against Christian. Christian eschatology identified the Jews with the Antichrist, an acolyte of the devil, often in the guise of a flying dragon. Jewish by birth and a champion of his people, this figment of Christian fear of Judaism stems from the union of a harlot with the spirit of Mephistopheles. Beloved by the Jews, he rebuilds the Temple in preparation for the end of the diaspora. He then seeks to conquer the world but is defeated by Jesus at the head of the Army of the Saints. The dreadful antagonist and most of his Jewish supporters perish at Armageddon and the rest convert, thus fulfilling the ultimate Judaic role in Christendom by witnessing the triumph of Christianity and ushering in the earthly reign of the Savior. Disappearance of the dissenters, by the sword or voluntary apostasy, realizes the claim of Christian universalism declared at the First Coming.

Although a minority survive by converting, apocalyptic liquidation of the Jews is a doctrinal anticipation of the Holocaust. Thus Judaism disappears through both armed rebellion and spiritual reconciliation, another of its dual roles in Christian eschatology. The sinister Jews, the Antichrist and his minions, must die because, as the devil's servants, they can never enter the Christian community. The good Jews, millennial apostates, are absorbed into this community after renouncing their erroneous creed.[32]

The eschatology linking crucifixion with redemption, the First Coming with the Last Judgment, formulated the view of the perfidious Jew. Unrepentant deicides are capable of all other (and lesser) outrages. From the Middle Ages almost to the present day, the Jews were often accused of murdering Christians as part of their ritual and of plotting to rule the world and destroy Christianity. Such libels already appeared in early Christianity. The same eschatology, however, put restraints on retaliation against the sinners. The Jews could not be eliminated: they had to survive to endure lengthy chastisement and finally to affirm the dominion of Christianity at the Second Coming. This doctrine on Jews as propounded in the New Testament and by church fathers would dominate Christian opinion until after World War II.

The Christian indictment of the Jews abounded in Manichean dualisms, not surprising in a creed based on cosmic moral divisions into body and soul, heaven and hell, salvation and damnation, a corrupt past and present and a glorious future, God and the devil, and according to some principles and some worshippers, Christians and Jews. These oppositions issued from the theodicean essence of Christianity: the arraignment of divine goodness and omnipotence against the powers of evil, a prolonged conflict whose resolution in favor of God awaits the outcome of a mighty millennial struggle.[33]

A highly suggestive rendering of good and evil came from the tale of Cain and Abel (Genesis 4:1–15). The older brother, envious and enraged about forfeiting his birthright to his nobler, younger sibling, becomes an outcast for killing him. From the Christian perspective, Cain and Abel respectively represent Judaism and Christianity. The tainted creed, jealous and vengeful about being superseded by its younger and better brother, crucifies the founder of the new faith. As a result, Jews plummet from a special state of grace to a depth even lower than that of the pagans. Inseparable in eschatological crisis, Judaism and Christianity are connected in the Christian version of the primal myth of death and rebirth, for out of the fall of the former comes the elevation of its successor. In this clash of dualisms, Judaism means debasement and history and Christianity perfection and eternity. While Christian thought also encompasses neutral and pro-Jewish impulses, doctrinal anti-Semitism makes Judaism the antipathetic antithesis of the anointed faith.

Long after rivalry ended in victory for the younger brother, unresolved historical, emotional, and theological problems continue to hinder interfaith harmony. Though these persisting tensions have historical and psychological components, to an important degree the friction is christological in source, deriving from unreconciled contradictions in

Christianity that reflect and produce ambivalence toward Jews. Primary and pervasive in these conflicts is an ontological dialectic that penetrates to the heart of Christianity: in this religion love and forgiveness and the attainment of eternal life define the central revelation and purpose of the Supreme Being, and yet striving for salvation involves a contrary preoccupation with sin, strife, judgment, and death.

When preoccupied with corruption, conflict, and retribution, Jesus and his Father replicate the vengeful moods of Jehovah and Greco-Roman gods. In sacralizing the murder of Christ, associating death with life and destruction with creation, Christianity is closer to classical paganism than to Judaism. Gospel accounts of the coming of the Savior and the formation of Christianity complement and are meant to complete pentateuchal exposition of the creation of the world and the emergence of Judaism. Both geneses involve vengeance and forgiveness, violence and adoration, betrayal and atonement, defilement and grace. In Judaism, however, martyrdom is not an aspect of the deity, much less a condition of redemption. Nor does the Jewish Messiah require a bloodbath at Armageddon to usher in a millennial dawn.

~

Judaism figures prominently and ambivalently in Christian contemplation of the violent transition from its own founding to its expected fulfillment. Oedipal rebellions abound in ancient myths, dramas, and cults, and pagan antiquity envisioned secular and godly order issuing from wars between fathers and sons. Christianity conceived of its relationship to Judaism as a struggle between creator and supplanter, a notion that, like many Christian ideas, is partly borrowed from Hellenistic and Roman polytheism. According to the primal tale that originated in pre-Hellenic times and passed down to imperial Rome, Cronos castrates his father (Uranus) and, fearing that his own children will overthrow him, swallows his offspring— all but Zeus, whose mother deceives him into thinking he has also eaten this child. Zeus grows up and defeats Cronos, displaces his father as the chief deity, and forces him to disgorge his brothers and sisters. One conclusion to this legend leaves Cronos languishing in prison; another has him becoming the king of the golden age, where humanity lives in innocent bliss.

Zeus, the sky god, assuming the paternal function of dominant deity, was looked upon by the Greeks as their functional, though not biological, father. Jupiter, his Roman counterpart, had a corresponding role. Their names were etymologically related and their cults sometimes associated with each other. One striking difference, making Jupiter in this respect resemble Jesus instead of Zeus, was that Jupiter became the moral exemplar of the Roman civic religion. Parallels between Christianity and Greco-Roman paganism are obvious. Both Jesus and Jupiter-Zeus conquer and supplant the paternal faith and in the process morally elevate their believers.

As Sigmund Freud noted in *Moses and Monotheism,* an oedipal conflict arose between Judaism and Christianity. Expropriating the virtues of Judaism while emancipating itself from it, Christianity rendered the parental religion irrelevant at best. The offspring sect, in effect, slew the father faith.[34] It is no coincidence that the doctrine of immaculate conception (Matt. 1:18–24; Luke 1:27–35) virtually eliminates Joseph, the historical father of Jesus, from the Holy Family. Nevertheless, fatherhood is an important feature of monotheism. Such religions usually posit an omniscient and omnipotent male deity, often making the earthly vehicle a mortal, but still formidable, founding father. Judaic patriarchalism is epitomized by Jehovah and Abraham. Paternal masculinity is also represented in Christianity, as in all messianic cults. The gender and power of the Almighty and his Son proclaim this virility. But the patriarchal presence is softened by the filial, forgiving dimension of the Son and, in later times, by the rising influence of his mother. Patriarchy, filiation, and exclusive demand for loyalty, however, remain fundamental in the oedipal struggle between Judaism and Christianity.

Judaism as the father faith, according to psychoanalytic thought, means that in Christendom Jews stand for the parental-punitive superego. Jehovah is a judgmental God and the Hebrew prophetic tradition contains elements of this stern, patriarchal authoritarianism. Thus Christianity's insurgency against Judaism is a displacement of the revolt of the id against the superego.[35] Desiring to kill the father is a basic taboo in western culture. Combining murder with incest, the oedipal desire generates enormous guilt and must be suppressed. Christianity, guilty over dethroning its paternal creed, projects its guilt onto the father, charging Judaism with deicide. Projecting blame onto the Jews gives Christianity a socially legitimate target for the aggression caused by the anxiety that results from repressing forbidden desires.[36]

Cast as the villain in this oedipal struggle, the Jew must be given traits making him a credible deicide. The crucifier cannot embody the superego. Hence the Jew assumes one of a series of dual and contradictory images in

Christian consciousness, a dichotomy reflecting irreconcilable divisions within Christianity. In addition to the stern, distant parent, the Jew becomes an id figure—the primitive, degenerate savage who killed Christ. These opposing roles are perpetuated in secular as well as religious form. Inaugurated in the letters of Paul and inscribed in the treatises and sermons of the church fathers, the ascription to Jews of lasciviousness and other types of physical and moral uncleanness was stereotypical by medieval times and has remained so. Since the nineteenth century, in the United States as well as Europe, the Jew has also become an exemplar of reason, restraint, and success and, in the mass martyrdom of the Holocaust, a reminder of Christian guilt.

Christianity underwent a corresponding transformation, taking on superego characteristics. God the Father demands penitence from backsliding believers as well as from dissenters. Even the saved must be pardoned by a censorious Messiah-Father, and to be absolved they must repent their sins. The association of repentance with redemption exacerbates Christian guilt and anxiety and spurs the quest to displace this burden onto a permissible and plausible scapegoat.

The oedipal relationship between Christianity and Judaism is, therefore, not a bilateral father-and-son conflict—both religions contain paternal and filial elements. Jews are children of God, the Chosen People, as well as the parents of Christianity. Similarly, the Trinity merges God the Father with God the Son. Consequently, Christkillers not only slew the Son of God but violated the fatherhood of God. The crucifixion was an oedipal uprising against the Father of all. In Christian ideology, however, the filial rebellion of Christians brings salvation while that of Jews ends in damnation. The difference is explained by the Freudian principle that sons perceive fathers as both nurturing and threatening, good and bad parents. Jehovah, alternatively jealous, punitive, and tyrannical and sympathetic, supportive, and loving, combines these opposites. Christianity, by supplanting Judaism, eliminated the bad father; Judaism, by defying God and spurning his monumental benefaction, the sacrifice of his Son, assaulted the good father.

A sanguinary father-son battle involving castration, crucifixion, and cannibalism takes place between the religions. According to Freud, Christian rejection of the Jewish rite of circumcision stems from fear of castration. In any case, circumcision has been identified with alleged Jewish sexual, mental, and physical deviance and disease and has set Jews apart from other peoples.[37] Castration anxiety is embedded in the oedipal myth, as in Cronos's castration of Uranus. Apart from oedipal terror, the urge for independence from the paternal creed induced Christian repudiation of this central Jewish ritual.

The climactic act of violence in the oedipal conflict is crucifixion, not castration.[38] This horrible deed unites the ancient myth of oedipal murder, Old Testament lore, official Roman methods of execution, and Christian dogma. From pre-Hellenic and Greco-Roman religious sources came the murderous impulses of father and son toward each other. The Hebraic element is that Abraham, when promised by Jehovah that his progeny will become the Chosen People, proves worthy of this promise by obeying Jehovah's order to sacrifice his son, Isaac (Gen. 22:1–18). Thus both covenants, the original one between Jehovah and the Jews and the superseding one between Jesus and the Christians, involve filial sacrifice.

A theological ancestor of the crucifixion and of Abraham's willingness to offer Isaac in obedience to God is the legend of Molech. Jehovah commands Moses on Mt. Sinai that his people must not worship this archaic monster of fire, blood, and human sacrifice (Lev. 18:21). Molech figures in the Christian version of deicide as an antecedent of Judaic animal sacrifice, and by extension, of the crucifixion. He also indirectly surfaces in the death of Jesus because his name is a cognate of *moloch,* the Hebrew word for king. The Messiah is often called the King of Kings, and Christ's Jewish accusers try to convince Pilate of his guilt by charging that in defiance of Roman sovereignty he declared himself King of the Jews (Matt. 27:11, 37; Mark 15:4, 9, 12; Luke 23:2–3; John 19:12, 14–15, 19, 21). Echoes of the pre-Judaic cult of Molech also appear in the role in the crucifixion assigned to Jews. Refusing the life of Isaac, the God of Israel signified disapproval of human sacrifice, which Judaism replaced with animal offerings. Nevertheless, Christians blamed Jews for the crucifixion, both human sacrifice and deicide.[39]

The purely Christian component in the theology of Calvary is that the crucifixion plunges Jews into despair and disrepute and raises Christianity to their former preeminence. With Moses at Sinai the Jews' mission was to glorify God and prepare the way for his Son, hence they were God's Chosen. At Calvary the Jews' mission was to destroy God, a horrible sin that justifies their dispossession as the Chosen People.[40]

But this reversal of statuses and roles also changes Jesus. The Good Shepherd reveals that, like Jehovah, he can be jealous, censorious, and stern. Assimilating the traits of Jehovah is part of Christian displacement of Judaism. The vehicle for displacement is Christ on the cross, for salvation depends upon crucifixion. The crucifixion, in turn, derives from the Jews' denial of the Messiah. In his sacrifice is their iniquity. In their punishment, the victorious faith gives its God attributes of the vanquished Mosaic God.

The messianic drama of eternal life through death, salvation through the sin of deicide, exculpates the Romans (the actual executioners) and blames the Jews (in Hyam Maccoby's splendid term, "the sacred executioners"). The sequence of rejection, resurrection, and ultimate redemption pits the paternal creed, literally the "elders" of Israel (Matt. 26:3; Mark 15:1; Luke 22:52), against the Son of God, body and spirit of the religion that grew out of Judaism. As interpreted by Maccoby, the crucifixion is a kinship between victim and murderer. Pilate's washing his hands and proclaiming the innocence of Jesus means that the community of Gentiles is not responsible for Christ's death. This leaves Jews and Christians as respective antagonist and protagonist. But this antithesis is too simple, for the Son of God is betrayed by his own apostle Judas, a treachery he announces at the final communion feast with his closest disciples (Matt. 26:21–25; Mark 14:18–21; Luke 22:19–23; John 6:70, 13:10, 18–30). This suggests that Christ could be renounced by Christians as well as Jews (Judas is both a Christian apostle and a former Jew, and his name is a close cognate of Judaism), especially since he died not only as a result of Jewish transgressions but for everyone's sins.[41]

If Christian triumph involved absorbing the attributes of the defeated Jehovah, Christianity also consecrated a more direct ingestion of the qualities of its own Messiah, possibly a derivation from the myth of Cronos's eating his offspring. Cannibalism, manifest in the sacrament of Holy Communion, completes the violence associated with the oedipal rebellion. In the Gospels and the Epistles of Paul, the Eucharist is a Passover meal eaten by Jesus and his apostles the night Israel's high priest and elders seize him. The Eucharist also relates to the Jewish kiddush ceremony, the blessing of the wine and bread at the start of a festival or Sabbath meal. Performed by Christ at the Last Supper, this ritual was sacramentalized into Holy Communion, the consumption of the blood and body of Christ necessary for salvation.[42]

Jesus asks the apostles to "eat" the bread, "this is my body," and "drink" the wine, "this is my blood of the new testament, which is shed for many for the remission of sins" (Matt. 26:26–28; see also Mark 14:22–24; Luke 22:19–20; 1 Cor. 11:23–25). The Lord's Supper, a fundamental part of the church service since the dawn of Christianity, celebrates the union of worshippers, symbolically with one another and literally with the Savior, in the *corpus christi*. Freud argued that through Jesus's martyrdom the son displaced the father because Christianity emphasizes the Son in the Holy Trinity. The faithful consume the blood and body of Christ, not of God, in order, as in other cannibalistic rites, to absorb his spirit. Thus Christians expiate their sins by accepting the gift of their Savior's sacrifice.[43]

The oedipal confrontation is cataclysmally resolved in the Second Coming, in a bloody engagement between good and bad fathers, respectively the Savior and the false Jewish messiah known as the Antichrist.[44] Acceptance of salvation through Jesus is the true renewal of the Jews and resolves the conflict with the father-founder, who must die in order to be replaced, but who must be loved in order to be incorporated into Christianity. Restoration of the Chosen People to divine grace heals an equivalent cleavage in the Trinity: the merciful filial forgiver of sin is now in harmony with the punitive paternal God of righteousness who sentenced the Jews to generations of misery.

The conversion of the Jews that ends the strife represents yet another contradictory interaction between the religions. Jews, who await their own Messiah, and whose belief was established before Christ, do not need Christianity for completion of their religion. Yet, although Christian doctrine claims that Judaism is incomplete, its fulfillment being displacement by (and adoption of) Christianity, it is eschatologically essential for the millennial consummation of the Christian religion. The sinful Jews are preserved because their misery and abasement verify Christian triumph and truth. A remnant of Judea, surviving to acknowledge the Savior upon his return, is necessary to, and ultimate witness of, universal redemption. Seeking validity from an outside source that questioned the essence of Christianity doubly wounded the Christian psyche. The requirement of external authentication produces a crisis of faith and involves the Jews in that crisis by designating them ultimate arbiters of millennial truth. Such primacy in the outcome of Christianity makes Jews resented, as well as valued, by Christians.

In the end, as at the beginning, of Christianity the Jews play an ambivalent role. They are good and bad fathers, creators and would-be destroyers of Christianity, they kill the Savior and impenitently compound that crime, but he forgives them at Calvary because "they knew not what they did" and at the Millennium because, in admitting their guilt and surrendering to his will, they finally and fully do know what they did. Conversely, crucifixion is a grievous sin, in which parricide (murder of the paternal spirit) merges with regicide (killing the King of Kings) and culminates in deicide (an attack on the Heavenly Father). Christ may forgive his tormentors but Christianity demonizes them by making the Jews agents of the devil at the crucifixion and in the final battle.

The oedipal explanation of Christian rage against Judaism, which distinguishes this rage from hostility toward other peoples and among Christian sects and groups, is most illuminative when placed in the contexts of pagan precursors of Christian myths regarding filicide, parricide, and deicide and of the embattled progenitive relationship between Judaism and Christianity. The weaknesses of this explanation reduce but do not negate its interpretive relevance. Christian attacks on Jews often can be traced to causes that are not primarily psychological, much less psychoanalytic and oedipal. Furthermore, as a psychoanalytic principle of displaced aggression, oedipal conflict applies to a variety of familial and intergroup problems remote from Christian-Jewish friction. Myths of violence, Christian or otherwise, are usually allegorically expressed fears of mortality and loss of identity that cannot be faced on the conscious level. According to Carl Jung, they are archetypal symbolic manifestations of a universally shared historical unconscious and, especially in religious legends, often contain contradictory images and themes of good and evil, sin and salvation.[45]

While the war between fathers and sons, transposed from family and biology to myth and theology, may clarify Christian prejudice against Jews, displacement of aggression, a basic premise of oedipal theory, is less apparent in early Christian thought. This premise would attribute anti-Semitism to a diversion of resentment from the Messiah to the Jews. From the Gospels onward, Christian theology testifies to the filicidal, parricidal, regicidal, and deicidal elements in the crucifixion but reveals no direct evidence that blaming Jews for the death of Jesus is a deflection of Christians' anger against their own Savior. Given the lack of this important aspect of Freudian theory, the oedipal hypothesis is a tantalizingly plausible explanation of Christian bigotry but one that is too speculative to be accepted uncritically or totally.

~

Ambivalence toward Judaism, as I have said, is systemic in Christianity. Sin, guilt, and, mortality haunt both religions, but in different ways, and their impact on Christianity shapes its reaction to Judaism. Christianity is more preoccupied with death, as in the crucifixion, and with repression of instinct, as in its concern with gluttony and sex. Unlike Judaism, Christianity has a Savior who died and became a historical phenomenon. Believers thus must resolve the paradox, defined by Ruether, between history and eschatology. Jesus sacrificed himself to redeem humanity, yet humanity has not visibly become more virtuous. This apparent contradiction is uneasily bridged by doctrinal declaration that awareness of sin and admission of guilt are conditions of absolution and salvation. History, in fact, seems to support the Jewish insistence that the Messiah has yet to come because sin still pollutes the world. Christian dogma, from its earliest days, turned this argument against its proponents, blaming the Jews particularly and other dissenters generally for the continuing presence of vice in the world. The morbid features of Christianity—negation of physical needs, unreachable standards of morality accompanied by fear, shame, and guilt at failure to meet them, obsession with penitence and death—aroused tremendous anxiety, frustration, and aggression among the faithful. But these feelings were deflected by dogma and belief from their natural target, God the Father and Son, to Judaism, the real father and, by sacred writ, the perverse foe of Christianity in a manichean dynamic of good against evil. History, psychology, and theology conjoined to make Christianity a force for unprecedentedly rigorous religious animosity toward Jews.[46]

## The Middle Ages

Transition from Roman to medieval civilization little disturbed the lives of European Jews. An equilibrium was established with the triumph of Christianity in the late empire, and the standing of Jews in western Christendom remained stable for six centuries. Gone was the summit of monotheistic prominence that Jews proudly inhabited before the victory of Christianity, yet to come were the torments inflicted upon them in the long turbulence from the crusades to the waning of the Counter-Reformation. In this period Christian theology consigned Jews to the position of sinful outcast, but secular action seldom reflected doctrinal bigotry. Persecution that would later become conventional was still remarkable, and whatever the masses prayed about Jews had not yet extensively disrupted harmonious interaction. This relatively comfortable situation persisted until the tenth century, when hostility began to increase gradually but immensely, leading to the catastrophic outbreak of anti-Semitism during the First Crusade (1096).

From the fifth through the ninth centuries the vast majority of rulers over most areas of western Europe retained, and sometimes expanded, rights and privileges that Roman citizenship and law had given Jews. Some rulers even repealed repressive Roman edicts, which in any case usually went unenforced. Informal imperial precedents also guided the cordial secular relations between Jews and Christians. For Jews this meant communal self-government and religious autonomy, disregard of legal and canonical restrictions, unhindered entry to all occupations, and ability to own land, bear arms, serve in high government posts, and hold positions of authority over Christians. Jews and Christians mutually proselytized and lived comfortably and closely together. At a time when pagan tribes and Muslim invaders were harshly treated, Jews were unique among non-Christians in being governed by their own laws, rituals, and leaders and integrated into Christian society on singularly intimate, equal, and amiable terms.[47]

Several portents of future trouble nonetheless can be discerned in this halcyon period. Although prosecutions for heresy ended in the West around 590 and were not revived until the end of the tenth century, structural anti-Semitism did not abate. Roman Catholic theology, dogma, canon law, and policy disparaged and discriminated against Jews. In the later Middle Ages, when suppression turned into savagery, the church was the most protective, though still a punitive, institution in western Christendom. But in the early medieval era official doctrine and action usually promoted repression. Secular rulers also sometimes brutalized Jewish subjects. While onslaughts could result from Jewish communities being involved in dynastic and local political conflicts, or even from occasional Jewish attacks on Christians, they also stemmed from endemic Christian animosity that anticipated the catastrophes that would be inaugurated at the end of the eleventh century.

Repression, though reversible and intermittent, did occur. Visigoth kings generally accorded Jews substantial parity with Christians, but King Sisebut (612–621) ordered Jews to convert or depart, the first such decree affecting an entire Christian country. His successor, however, permitted Jews to return. Resistance by local lords and clergy inhibited royal and ecclesiastical oppression. Consequently, anti-Jewish decrees generally failed to undermine the political, economic, and cultural standing of the Jewish community.[48]

Secular anti-Jewish policies were short-lived, primarily politically and economically motivated, never fully implemented, and usually unsuccessful. Church policies were more consistent, widespread, ideological, and specifically christological. Catholic theology persisted in demanding punishment of the Jews for their sins. The church, as in the Roman era, fearing competition for the souls of pagans and Christians, sought to separate Jews from the community and place them in an inferior position. Dogma and canon law, repeatedly promulgated in church synods and councils, ecclesiastical conferences, and pronouncements from popes and bishops, prohibited conversion to Judaism, Jews' and Christians' taking meals together, maintaining friendships, or intermarrying, and Jews' owning Christian slaves. Clerical parties, also fearing competition from Judaism, advocated dismissal of Jews from public posts and supported factions and government authorities aiming to curtail Jews' freedom.[49]

A particularly determined clerical confrontation with Carolingian tolerance was mounted by Bishop Agobard of Lyons against Louis the Pious. Along with several other Frankish prelates, Agobard used canon law to prevent Jewish proselytizing and close Jewish-Christian relations. In a tract written to Louis and the palace bishops (ca. 822–828), he called Jews "Antichrists" who "daily satisfy the biddings of their father [Satan], despising the law, spurning the prophets, persecuting the church, and blaspheming the very son of God." Why "should the servants of sin be preferred (by the emperor, etc.) to the servants of God," he asked; "the disinherited to the heirs, the sons of the Devil to the sons of God?"[50]

Western Catholicism consistently attempted to constrict Jewish existence and to segregate Jews in order to better missionize them, prevent reverse conversion, and impose a just ordeal on those who denied Christ. During the early Middle Ages this policy usually failed because of secular governmental and community opposition. Secular contravention of ecclesiastical bigotry was exemplified when Louis replaced Agobard with a pro-Jewish bishop in 833. The few monarchs and lesser authorities who did launch repressive programs met with resistance in their own lands, including dissent from local bishops and priests.[51]

Thus divisions within the church over treatment of Jews, as well as ecclesiastical political weakness and secular opposition, hindered official Catholic oppression. The Spanish church hierarchy and numerous local priests, doctrinally bound to abjure forced conversion of Jews, fought Sisebut's suppression. Pope Gregory I (590–604) affirmed Augustinian temperance and opposed forcible conversion and interference with Jewish rituals. He defended Jewish rights guaranteed by Theodosian law, in preference to the harsher Justinian Code, and allowed Jews to have Christian slaves.[52] While Gregory's restraint better predicted subsequent papal policy, Agobard's diabolization regrettably proved a truer harbinger of the sinister mystification of the Jews in the popular mind.

~

Long before the First Crusade, adversity eroded Judaic freedom and good relations and near equality with Christians. The expansion of urban centers and a money economy produced conflict. The worsening of conditions for Jews, however, significantly derived from the growth and consolidation of the power of Latin Catholicism and from fears sparked by a simultaneous revival of heretical movements. In addition, the fervor of the masses was aroused by the expected Millennium of the year 1000 and by the crusades. Paralleling the rising institutional power of the church, and sometimes opposing it, was centralization of secular political power and the emergence of prototypes of nationalism.

Latin Christendom was traumatized by internal rifts, epitomized by struggles between popes and anti-popes for control of the Holy See, and by conflicts with other denominations, religions, and sovereignties. Institutional and spiritual friction within the church spawned anticlerical and dualist dissent. Dualism resurrected an early Christian Manichean movement, which contended that benevolent Providence ruled the spiritual realm but that the material world was created and governed by Satan, hence good and evil had separate creators. The return of heresy in the West, particularly in conjunction with anticipation of the apocalyptic prelude to the Millennium, excited fear of a resurgent Antichrist and Lucifer.[53]

By the late tenth century interrelated secular and spiritual developments had had a discernibly negative impact on Jewish life. The changes degraded and endangered western Jewry and exploded in the annihilations of 1096. For the next five hundred years conditions for Jews drastically worsened, as manifested in pogroms, demonization myths, enforced segregation from the Christian community, coerced conversions, interference in religious practices, and, finally, ejection from most of western Europe.

Hatred and persecution of Jews, intrinsic in Christianity but long latent, first flared up in the late tenth and early eleventh centuries. In 992 Jews in Le Mans were accused of making a figurine of the local count, putting it in their synagogue, and piercing it to destroy the count. Here began medieval infernalization of the Jew, which drew upon New Testament and patristic sources and associated Jews with murder and black magic and obviously presaged charges of desecration of the Host. In subsequent decades, for diverse reasons, anti-Jewish incidents proliferated in French and Spanish cities. Economic anxiety and disorder directed hostility as much to Jews as businessmen and newcomers as to their religion. Another mundane factor, suspicion of Jews' betraying towns to the Muslims, drew upon the great betrayal of the crucifixion. Rumors of purely religious offenses, such as mocking of crucifixes, also increased hatred. Punishment often took the form of forced apostasy—sometimes in reaction to outbreaks of Christian heresy. Sometimes, however, Jewish communities were not offered the alternatives of exile or conversion but were summarily slaughtered.[54]

Religious turbulence increased after 1050. Challenges to ecclesiastical authority appeared in papal and monastic reform movements; in the lay investiture controversy, the initial major medieval conflict between church and state; and in the breach that opened between Rome and Constantinople. Both threats to the church and victories over Muslims in Spain and Italy—both the anxieties of an agitated church and the arrogance of a conquering one—stimulated Catholic militancy, triumphalism, and claims of the primacy of Rome over temporal power.[55]

Internal and external strife spilled over into enmity toward Judaism. In 1062 Jews in Artemo, Italy, were charged with blaspheming a holy image. A year later Jewish communities in southern France and Catalonia were attacked by bands of knights on their way to fight the infidels in Spain. In the next decade a church council reiterated traditional commands against Jews' owning Christian slaves and reasserted the doctrine of Judaic social and theological inferiority. The deterioration in relations between Christians and Jews was not limited to the West; the eleventh-century Orthodox church in Russia also experienced a wave of antagonism against Jews. An initially favorable but eventually ominous development occurred at the end of the eleventh century, when Jews were declared royal serfs in England and the Holy Roman Empire and formally assumed the same status under French kings and nobles.[56]

The spiritual and secular tumult of the eleventh century climaxed in the First Crusade, which magnified tensions between Christians and Jews and marked the beginning of a long period of persecution of Jews. Holy war, accompanied by widespread crop failure, starvation, and religious frenzy, ignited unprecedented and shocking anti-Jewish violence. The first large-scale pogrom in western Europe occurred between May and July 1096. Peasants, burghers, and crusaders killed approximately ten thousand people, about one-fourth to one-third of the Jewish population, in the German Rhineland and in northern France.[57]

The carnage had several features that indicate Christian ambivalence and a residue of goodwill toward Jews. Violence was spontaneous and short-lived, and Jews were given the choice of conversion or death. Many Christians tried to save the victims, and many Jews sought protection from the Christians among whom they lived.

Most earlier anti-Jewish campaigns had arisen in Spain, southern France, or Italy, but the troubles of 1096 centered in northwest Europe, until then a relatively moderate region. Racked by famine, agricultural disaster, and a battle for supremacy between church and state, this area became the locus of anti-Semitism. Fear of Jewish economic rivalry and lust for Jewish wealth, especially among townspeople and a few urban clergymen, led not only to murder but to extortion of Jewish property in exchange for protection. Crusader troops and mobs, avid for loot and provisions, also took both Jewish wealth and Jewish lives. But the primary motive for the rampage was Christian anti-Semitism. Jews who converted under threat of death gave their persecutors a sense of triumph over Judaism and reassurance against theological dissent.[58]

Christological factors inspired crusading hysteria. Pope Urban II's call for the crusade declared Christian possession of Jerusalem a precondition for the appearance of the Antichrist and, therefore, of Judgment Day. His plea addressed preoccupations that had gathered strength throughout the eleventh century—with Jerusalem, with holy war against unbelievers in Spain and elsewhere. Crusader attacks on Jewish communities were largely provoked by charges that the Jews had killed Christ. Those who took up arms for the Savior and against infidels did not always distinguish between deicides and Mohammedans. In the religious mania inspired by holy war, many crusaders began battling for the Lord long before they reached Jerusalem. The Saracens, after all, were not the ones who had crucified Christ—and it was thought that Jews would ally themselves with any opponent of Christianity. Crusaders desecrated synagogues, Torah scrolls, and Jewish cemeteries, compelled Jews to worship Jesus, took Jewish property, and murdered Jews. Popular crusader preachers like Peter the Hermit may have engaged in more coercive proselytizing than did regular soldiers, for few Jews were forced to convert outside of western Europe and none in Palestine. Converting Jews, crushing infidels, and conquering the Holy City were aspects of imperial Christianity. The church militant would follow driving the Muslims out of Spain with an offensive against them in the Holy Land.[59]

The ravages of 1096 were the first step toward disaster for western Jewry. It did not, however, mark an abrupt end to harmony and parity between Jew and Christian. Assault and compelled apostasy lasted only a few months and focused in one sector of Europe, and a minority of the populace participated. Most authorities, from the church and the Holy Roman Emperor down to local bishops and lords, denounced coercion and violence. In future attacks, monarchs and the clerical hierarchy would protect Jews. Acts of neighborly compassion indicated that Jews were still accepted in Christian communities, and sites of major depredations were quickly rejuvenated. Jewish population growth and immigration and advancement of Jewish culture and economy in northwest Europe continued for another century. Later crusades, furthermore, brought less violence against Jews.[60]

During this period, nevertheless, danger signs abounded. Christological hostility intensified, and Jews were more often made scapegoats for political instability, economic catastrophes, heresy, and conflicts between church and state. Crusades continued to stir up zeal against infidels and to focus attention on the crucifixion and the rescue of Jerusalem, thus underscoring militant and vengeful dimensions of Catholicism and stimulating further hatred of Judaism. Moreover, however brief and seemingly anomalous the attacks of 1096 had been, they had introduced large-scale massacres of Jews into European reality. Visions of Jewish enmity, cruelty, and malevolence began to penetrate popular perceptions and provoke terrible actions. The stark choice of apostasy or death had undermined the Christian doctrine dictating toleration of Jews until the Second Coming.[61]

Although crusader attacks on Jews diminished after the First Crusade, many Jewish communities were massacred during the Second Crusade, especially in Germany in 1146. England, where formerly Jews had been decently treated and mob violence unknown, belatedly succumbed to anti-Jewish passion at the time of the Third Crusade. Riots, massacres, and forced conversions began in 1189 and continued through the rest of the century, as did a special tithe imposed on Jews for the campaign to rescue Palestine.[62]

Holy war was not the only factor inciting Christian anti-Semitism. The church was racked in the twelfth century by pontifical disputes, battles for supremacy between civil and ecclesiastical forces in Britain and the Holy

Roman Empire, and heresies in France and northern Italy. Dissent now went beyond rebuke of clerical corruption and bureaucracy to question the sanctity of the sacraments and the divinity of Christ. Fears that the church would be overwhelmed by heterodoxy led to a counteroffensive culminating in the calling of the Third Lateran Council (1179) to unify the church.[63]

These pressures on the church provoked harsher anti-Jewish polemics. After 1150 hostility encompassed postbiblical Judaism, categorizing rabbinic, midrash, and Talmudic elements as blasphemous and irrational barriers to acceptance of Christ's divinity. According to the new Catholic critique, the Talmud, by contradicting Old Testament prefigurement of Christianity, promoted refusal of redemption. The argument was hazardous for Jews, for it encouraged christological intolerance. If postbiblical and contemporary Judaism was perfidious, the Jews could not be saved without intervention by the church in their holy rites and governance. In the twelfth century, this challenge to Augustinian laissez-faire regarding Jews was a minority opinion. Regrettably, the theology of repressive judgmentalism would subsequently prevail.[64]

Crusades, church-state conflicts, heresy, and factional squabbles within Catholicism cannot entirely account for the crescendo of anti-Semitism in the twelfth century. Two other factors were the new and ominous identification of Jews with usury and sharp business practices and the demonization of Jews in charges of ritual murder and other sinister activities.

Since the eighth century the church had forbidden Catholics to lend money at interest, a ramification of Christian glorification of the poor and corresponding disapproval of material acquisition. New Testament sources of this belief appeared in the Sermon on the Mount and elsewhere in the Gospels: "Ye cannot serve God and mammon" (Matt. 6:24; Luke 16:13). The poor are particularly "blessed" for they enter "the kingdom of Heaven" (Matt. 5:3), but it is impossible "for a rich man to enter into the Kingdom of God" (Matt. 19:24). In an episode foreshadowing condemnation of usury, Matthew and Mark reported that "Jesus went into the temple of God, and cast out all them that sold and bought in the temple, and overthrew the tables of the moneychangers" (Matt. 21:12; Mark 11:15). By 1100 money was deemed an instrument of worldly corruption, and at the Second Lateran Council (1139) Christian usurers were denied communion and Christian burial. Jews were not subject to the ban on usury, and since Christianity did not prohibit borrowing at interest, they found a niche in the Christian economy in practicing this despised but indispensable profession.[65]

Theological constraints on credit came at a particularly awkward juncture when crusades and economic expansion rapidly increased demand for capital. The conflict between church doctrine and rising material needs created opportunities that compensated some Jews for exclusion from other vocations. Driven off the land by increasing observation of injunctions against having Christian servants and other legal obstacles, required to pay special taxes, and refused admission to guilds and many professions, Jews found in financial endeavor an alternative to the poverty to which officially sanctioned anti-Semitism might otherwise have reduced them. This calling was also appealing to Jews because money was an asset easily hidden or portable in emergencies, one that displayed affluence less visibly than land or other forms of property and was therefore less likely to inspire Gentile envy or extortion.

Lending money for profit temporarily curbed the economic and vocational decline of the Jews but also further stigmatized them. Both in Britain and on the continent, the grasping creditor became an anti-Semitic stereotype. Resentment of Jewish business practices was not new: as early as the tenth century Jewish entrepreneurs had aroused the anger of the bourgeoisie. Many eleventh- and twelfth-century burgher governments impeded Jewish commercial activity, and merchant guilds excluded Jews. Moneylending also drew Jews into the unpopular role of fiscal agents for rulers and bureaucracies. Medieval states and cities often had difficulty taxing powerful enclaves of nobles, clergy, or merchants. To gain indirect access to the affluence of these elites, rulers exacted revenue from Jewish creditors, either regularly through large levies or by sudden expropriation of personal fortunes.

At times fiduciary usefulness made Jews indispensable to public authority, but government support was fragile because as creditors they naturally were resented by their debtors, who came from all levels of society. Ruling groups often sacrificed Jews to popular demand for financial relief, made them scapegoats for economic adversity, and failed to discourage the poorer classes from venting their resentment upon the minority. Nor were public or clerical authorities above mounting attacks on Jews in order to default with impunity.[66]

The image of the Jews as protocapitalists, creditors, traders, estate agents, economic intermediaries, and so on stigmatized them as parasitical victimizers. Since property is an extension of person, the threat to property in the form of debt collection or foreclosure became a threat to self. Jews could readily be identified as exploiters and blamed for economic frustrations by both masses and elites. This negative association was reinforced by the historic role of the merchant and moneylender as outsider and stranger, whose wealth is liquid and easily moveable and who often comes from afar and tarries briefly. Traders since ancient times, the Jews maintained religious and social as well as economic distance from their host communities. Acting as merchant, primitive banker, and economic intermediary between rulers and subjects inevitably kept the Jews somewhat aloof from other groups. These functions also fed the stereotype of the Jews as urban rationalists who often obtained advantages through calculation. In a traditional and impulsive society distrustful of rationality, innovation, intangible property, and nonmanual labor, the roles imposed upon Jews fated them to be unwelcome aliens. By the eleventh century money itself became suspect, associated with contamination and social change. Nascent urban capitalism in general, and specifically the Jewish businessman, represented as a greedy, crafty creditor, was seen as sabotaging old values and ties of blood, rank, and community. Although most Jews did not lend money and Christian businessmen far outnumbered their Jewish competitors and at least rivaled them in ruthlessness, the image of the Jewish creditor helped to make the Jews a despised out-group.[67]

For such reasons King Philip Augustus of France, in 1179, seized for ransom the goods and persons of the Jews, his fiscal agents and royal serfs. Two years later, supported by monastic orders, and deeming persecution a just response to usury, he expelled Jews from his domain and ordered bishops to consecrate synagogues as churches. Needing the Jews' services, however, he readmitted them in 1198. These policies signaled the new status of Jews as royal fiscal agents and serfs—protected, exploited, or terrorized at the king's pleasure. As royal and noble fiduciaries, subject to special taxes and laws, Jews were further distanced from the community. The withdrawal imposed upon them was cited by their oppressors as proof of Jewish aloofness.[68]

Christian resentment of Jewish usury and commerce was based in religion as well as economics. Dogma defined lending money at high interest as a major sin, and many religious houses and foundations owed money to Jews. Crusading fervor, combined with the exigencies of financing the crusades, added to the church's resentment of Jews. In 1198 when Pope Innocent III called for Holy War to recover Jerusalem, he ordered that Jewish creditors remit to crusader debtors any profits from interest on such loans. Repeated in 1199, this decree commanded all

Christians to cease commerce with Jewish moneylenders who disobeyed the pope.[69]

Jews, money, and evil became firmly linked in the public mind. Satan was depicted in writing and art as avaricious, counting cash and defecating coins. The Jewish creditor was seen as not only a ruthless businessman but a demonic transgressor of Christianity. The vicious moneylender, agent of the devil, was also linked to the horrible sin of ritual murder. Financial extortion amounted to an anti-Christian act in which the Jew seeks to kill the Christian by taking his money—the equivalent of draining his blood in ritual murder. The myth of the vengeful creditor who demands a pound of flesh circulated for centuries before Shakespeare created Shylock. Usury joined deicide and blood guilt in the trinity of Jewish abominations, an interrelationship scripturally sanctified by the charge against Judas. Behind the association between money and blood, extortion and crucifixion, loomed the specter of the paternal faith, Judaism, controlling its offspring, as fathers frequently do, by granting or withholding cash.[70]

Like other infernalizations, the nefarious usurer is rooted in the Gospels. Judas, the apostle possessed by Satan, who betrays Christ for "thirty pieces of silver" (Matt. 26:14–16; John 12:4–6), also handles the funds of Jesus and the apostles (John 12:6; 13:29). Judas, the archetypal disloyal sinner, whose name in Hebrew is Judah (Judea), also the name of the southern kingdom of Israel and one of the twelve tribes, symbolizes his people. Twelfth-century Christian thinkers identified Judas with money, cupidity, Jewry, and betrayal of Jesus. In legends he was also portrayed, sometimes grotesquely, as fratricidal, patricidal, and incestuous with his mother.[71]

The Jew as evil usurer was associated with another imagined Jewish ogre, the ritual murderer. The one devoured the resources of Christian communities, the other the blood of Christian children. Here, too, diabolization may be traced to the New Testament. "I have sinned in that I have betrayed the innocent blood," says Judas in bringing "the thirty pieces of silver to the chief priests and elders" (Matt. 27:3–4). The priests respond: "It is not lawful for to put them into the treasury, because it is the price of blood." Instead, they use the misbegotten gain to buy "the potter's field, to bury strangers in. Wherefore that field was called, The field of blood" (Matt. 27:6–8). Judas dies in this field (Acts 1:18–19): an outcast from redeemed society lies eternally with other aliens. The biblical connection of betrayal, blood, greed, and money was resurrected in medieval blood libels instigated by borrowers to avoid paying debts to Jews. The related stereotype of the blood-sucking creditor, later epitomized by Shylock, also linked usury and ritual murder.[72]

Blood libel, the definitive twelfth-century diabolization, was crucial in transforming anti-Semitism from a theological and legal prescription with limited impact on community life to a widely held view of the Jew as sinister outcast. An epidemic of accusations of ritual murder evoked repression, expropriation, violence, and finally banishment. Doctrinal and legal sources of anti-Semitism now were joined with popular anger and anxiety directed at a supposedly fiendish foe.[73]

The legend behind accusations of ritual murder was that to make unleavened bread for the Passover rite Jews needed Christian blood, preferably from children. Jews were also believed to need this blood to cure ailments peculiar to them and to use in malevolent magic. It was also said that Jews crucified Christian boys to insult Christ at Easter and Passover and to return Palestine to their people. The victims were reported to be chosen by prominent Jews in a remote place; for example, it was said that chief rabbis and leading Jews in Spain selected a victim from a different European country each year. The fantasy of ritual sacrifice reappeared in England in 1144, after a seven-century hiatus. Allegations of ceremonial killing of children, formerly extremely rare, swiftly spread throughout western Christendom. Local members of the clergy frequently brought the charges, supposed victims were deemed martyrs and sometimes canonized, and pilgrimages were made to where their bodies had been discovered. Accusations and reprisals were also prompted by the desire to escape debt and plunder Jewish property. Jewish communities were sometimes exterminated in fury over the "crime," especially if suspected killers were tortured into confessing.[74]

No such homicide was ever proven, Jewish dietary laws require that all blood be removed from meat before cooking, and unleavened bread is made with water. But blood libel is based on myth and emotion, not logic or reality. The Jewish Passover occurs around the time of Easter. The older holiday celebrates the central events of Exodus, flight from Egypt and the journey to the Holy Land. Jehovah forced the pharaoh to free the Jews by slaying the Egyptians' first-born children. Jewish children survived because Jews were warned to smear lambs' blood on their doors. Commemorating these events, Jews sacrificed the paschal lamb at the Temple before eating it at the holiday meal. The lamb is also a symbol for Jesus and for Easter, which comes three days after his death and commemorates his resurrection. The relationship between the celebrations, ceremonies, and symbols of Passover and Easter suggests that blood libel is a projection onto the Jew of Christian guilt over the crucifixion and cannibalistic urges. (Maccoby suggests that cannibalistic urges in the Eucharist are an oral-aggressive compulsion to eat the sacred God—a pregenital fixation also reflected in Christian fear of sex and suppression of women.) Christians at Holy Communion sacramentally drink the blood and eat the body of Christ. Yet the Jews, whose creed abjures blood in their food and in their services, are accused of consuming Jesus by eating the Passover lamb, and of using the blood of young Christians to make the bread they eat on that holiday. Passover is also linked to the crucifixion through the Last Supper. Other evidence supports the assertion that ritual murder stands for the crucifixion: the children symbolize the innocence of the Savior, and some accusations of ritual murder included the contention that they were crucified.[75]

The images of ritual murderer and rapacious creditor contradicted the medieval portrayal of Judaism as decrepit, obsolete, and overborne by Christian virtue and vigor. Stereotypes of the Jew as evil power reflected fear that Judaism still formidably challenged the church militant. Blood libel revived the Jew as cruel patriarch and "sacred executioner"—Abraham's descendants doing what God saved him from doing to Isaac, actually killing the children of God, and through them the Son of God. Diabolization of the Jew as cruel father was additionally prompted by the eleventh-century advent of the cult of Mary, who figures in the ritual murder legend because the child-victim is frequently her devotee.[76]

Blood libel had other implications that made it the extreme infernalization of the Jew. In the Middle Ages blood was considered to have medicinal and magical properties. The Jew was seen as a villainous sorcerer with uniquely demonic physical traits. Among such traits were diseases related to the blood, such as menstruation in males. The remedy was to drink Christian blood to replenish the blood lost through menstruation and circumcision. Another link between the devil and the Jews appeared in allegations that the victims were sexually seduced or violated. Legends based on the death of Hugh of Lincoln (1255) suggested seduction and incest. A blood libel associated the slaying of boys in Fulda, Germany (1235), with seduction and sexual orgies. An accusation of 1475 noted that young William of Trent had been stabbed in the penis, conjoining ritual murder with circumcision and castration. Such canards made blood guilt a product of lechery, a vice shared by Jews and Satan. Since Christian folklore abounded with blood-sucking monsters and witches, blood libels merged with vampire fantasies. Tales of both Dracula and ritual murder feature killing, black magic, lust, purity, and Christian faith. Dracula also drains the blood of his innocent victims, but they can fend him off by displaying the cross. Like the Jew as usurer and as murderer, the vampire must kill in order to survive and feeds on the vitality of his victims. Fears about sex, death, demons, and damnation coalesced in the widespread delusion that Jews committed ritual murder.[77]

In the Middle Ages the crucifixion was an event remote in time and a sacrifice as much symbolic as real; charges of ritual murder, derived from that event, gave it relevance and immediacy. Blaming Jews for killing Christians, especially children, was a vivid contemporary reminder of the primal deed and the inherited guilt of the descendants of its perpetrators. The subliminal message of the legend was the fragility of Christianity. In an age of religious strife, blood libel reflected anxiety that the church could not protect its flock. By the twelfth century the legend had entered mass consciousness and was perpetuated in folklore, ballads, sermons, incantations, passion plays, and vernacular literature. Centuries later it would become a staple of Nazism and other anti-Jewish movements.[78]

Akin to blood libel was the charge of desecrating the Host (the body of Christ consumed by the faithful in Holy Communion), which appeared in France during the First Crusade and proliferated in the Holy Roman Empire. Jews supposedly pierced the wafer to make it bleed, stoned or gestured lewdly at the image of Christ, stabbed crucifixes, and polluted the sacred wine and wafers with blood, offal, or poison. Their imputed motive was to subvert transubstantiation, thus desanctifying the sacrament of Communion. Jesus was depicted at Holy Communion as an infant, hence the Christ Child was believed to be present in the Eucharist wafers. Cutting the wafer and causing it to bleed was therefore equivalent to taking the blood of a young Christian at Passover. The two accusations, which were sometimes combined, both arose out of fear of Catholic weakness and derived from conceptions of Jews as defiant murderers of Christ dedicated to evil, black magic, satanic rites, and depraved hatred of Christians. Related as reenactments of the crucifixion, they both emphasized a Jewish conspiracy to exterminate Christianity.[79]

In the fantasy of desecration of the Host, the role assigned to Jews verified the Christian vision of salvation. In molesting the consecrated Host in order to torture Christ, the Jews testified to their belief in the supernatural presence of Christ's body in the Eucharist. Thus even these sinister dissenters demonstrated their faith in the Redeemer.[80]

Jews were also accused of poisoning wells. Early rumors of this foul deed emanated from central and eastern Europe, initially from Bohemia in 1161.[81] Like charges of ritual murder and desecration of the Host, the charge of contaminating water expressed fears of a Jewish scheme to destroy Christianity.

In the twelfth century Jews began to be associated with filth and lechery—attributes assigned to the devil and to other outcast groups. Putrefaction, dirt, stench, and sensuality now alike designated Jews, lepers, heretics, the devil, his allies (such as witches), and other spurned categories. These detested figures had interchangeable images and were commonly targeted as threats to Christian order. A reason given for the expulsion of Jews from France was that they used sacred objects and images as privies. Similar claims were later made in Britain, Austria, and Flanders. Allegations of ritual murder and desecration of the Host also contained scatological references.[82]

The devil and the Jews, both considered greedy, salacious, and smelly and identified with bodily functions and filth, began to be portrayed in unholy alliance: in painting and sculpture Lucifer rode on the back of a Jew or on top of a synagogue, and his evil qualities were assigned to the church of Satan, the Jews, who, like witches and Lucifer, celebrated the sabbath on Saturday. The "beast" was a synonym for the devil, who was portrayed as an animal with horns, talons, a tail, a goat's beard, and an acrid odor. The goat, the animal symbol of lechery and the devil's creation and favorite beast, was thought to be the Jew's pet. Jews were depicted with horns, bulging eyes, goatees, tails, cloven feet, and diseases of the blood. They had the oversized genitalia of Satan, and their malodorous sores and unique diseases gave them his smell. Physically, as well as in avarice, lust, defiance, necromancy, and demonic hatred of Christianity, the devil and the Jews were in manichean opposition to Christ and Christians.[83]

In contrast to his lascivious and dirty enemies, Jesus was immaculately conceived, his mother was a virgin, and the ideal of his church was an ethereal spirituality devoid of sex and other bodily functions. Myths of ritual murder and profanation of the Host emerged at a time when celibacy, doctrinally imposed upon Christian priests in the fourth century but widely disregarded in the early Middle Ages, was once again being enforced as a requirement for the priesthood as a result of late-eleventh- and twelfth-century reforms. Meanwhile, nuns were designated virginal "brides of Christ." These developments coincided with the rise to prominence of the cult of the Virgin Mary. The atrocities ascribed to Jews, in contrast, featured seduction and violation of innocence, blood lust, and cannibalism.[84]

As elegantly evaluated by Langmuir, diabolization dehumanized Jews into semblances of Christian doubts and anxieties. No longer seen as real people, Jews became figments of the needs, neuroses, and disturbed imaginations of later medieval and early modern society. In the twelfth century arose the first of the recurrent hallucinations of secret Jewish plots to rule the world. Supposedly a Jewish government, then said to be located in Spain and run by a rabbinical council, was preparing for war against Christendom. Previous anti-Semitism had had some basis in reality, being partly derived from historical confrontations and rivalries between Jews and Gentiles. The image of the Jew as malevolence incarnate, however, was a fantasy not linked to any reality, and its development marked an acceleration of the long descent into rabid hatred.[85]

The deterioration in conditions for western Jewry was most dramatic in England, previously a relative haven for Jews. Persecution of Jews in Britain was particularly portentous because in the twelfth and thirteenth centuries Britain was the most united, well-governed, and orthodox western European country and heresy was rare. In addition to the ravages at the time of the Third Crusade, in 1181 Jews were enjoined from having or bearing arms, a legal prohibition that further divided them from other Englishmen, weakened their defenses against attack, and hence increased the likelihood of onslaughts and made them dependent upon other groups for protection.[86]

Withdrawal of goodwill from Jews in Britain narrowed the area of tolerance to places relatively untouched by crusader zeal and nascent capitalist pressures and places where Jews were better integrated into society. In Hungary, Romania, and Poland Jews generally enjoyed the same rights of Gentiles, and there were comparatively few restrictions on Jewish businessmen, forced conversions, or massacres. Jews were also better treated in Italy and in Moslem and Catholic Spain. The papacy, which was opposed to anti-Jewish violence, had its greatest influence in Italy, especially in Rome. Consequently, the Holy City was the only major western metropolis that never excluded Jews.[87] The primary locus of anti-Semitism had shifted: England, France, and Germany had become inhospitable, while Spain and the papacy, once leading harassers, were now less threatening.

~

In thirteenth-century northern and Mediterranean Europe the long ordeal of oppression finally reversed Jewish cultural, commercial, and demographic growth. Conditions were not yet wholly negative, however. Consistent with the principle that Jews must endure to witness the triumph of Christianity, most thirteenth- and fourteenth-century popes and some theologians repudiated pogroms, forced conversions, and charges of ritual murder, well poisoning, or having caused the Black Death. Outside papal territories such remonstrances regrettably had little effect. Intermittent royal defense of Jews as useful sources of capital and business management sometimes curtailed secular persecution and church restraints upon Jewish moneylending. Both elites and masses sometimes afforded refuge to, or at least did not inevitably loathe, Jews. They did not always support blood libel persecutions launched by local lords and bishops. Nor did the populace rally around Edward I of England or Philip IV of France for banishing Jews, respectively in 1290 and 1306, from their domains.[88]

Conditions worsened in the thirteenth and fourteenth centuries as old grievances against Jews continued to fester and new ones came into being. Jewish entrepreneurship, particularly moneylending, continued to enrage Gentile competitors and debtors. Theologians and ecclesiastics reaffirmed traditional opinion about perfidious Jewry, and accusations of occult and lethal Jewish malice toward Christians penetrated deeper into the mass consciousness. Heresy, schism, and internal strife still threatened the church, and crusades generated religious frenzy. The agitation and aggressiveness triggered by spiritual and social crises often found a target in Jews.

Pope Innocent III (1198–1216) renewed the offensive against long-simmering heresy by proclaiming the Albigensian Crusade (1208) and convening the Fourth Lateran Council (1215). Similarly pursuing spiritual conformity, rulers of France, Germany, and Aragon in the 1220s and 1230s banned heretics and confiscated their land. Two newly founded mendicant orders were given a mission to fight heterodoxy. Franciscans and Dominicans, drawn largely from the urban middle class and, unlike other monks, seeking engagement in the world, wielded the church's most powerful weapon against dissent and the devil—the Inquisition (begun in 1233). Early battles were chiefly waged against renegades, such as the Cathari, who blasphemed that the church and its sacraments were works of black magic and of Satan. Not coincidentally, witchcraft trials began amid these troubles.[89]

As pope, Innocent III confronted Saracen rulers of Palestine and large parts of Spain, emperors disputing papal authority in Italy, a rising commercial class whose way of life and work often conflicted with Catholic values and dogma, and a formidable challenge from heresy, especially in Languedoc and Lombardy. In addition, he believed the apocalypse to be imminent—an expectation that infused his defense of the church with eschatological immediacy. His comprehensive solution was to convene the Fourth Lateran Council in 1215. The many topics dealt with by this gathering included clerical reform, efforts to root out heresy and to drive Muslims out of the Holy Land and their remaining strongholds in Europe, and the fortifying of papal dominion within the church and over secular rule.[90]

The grand resolution of 1215 also regulated Jews. Many injunctions against Jews recapitulated the 1205 Papal Bull *Etsi Judaeos,* Innocent's summation of Rome's official combination of toleration and oppression. Jews could maintain their houses of worship, could not be forced to convert, and were free to obey their rituals and laws unless these contradicted canon or civil law. *Etsi Judaeos* also barred them from taking meals with Christians or having Christian servants, holding government posts or exercising jurisdiction over Christians, testifying against or converting Christians, and required them to wear distinguishing marks on their clothing (the Jew badge). It also mandated confinement to ghettos, prohibited Jews from appearing in public at Easter, and forbade Jewish converts to Christianity to continue to observe Jewish rituals. The last interdiction was intended to prevent false conversion and curb judaizing tendencies which the church suspected in Jewish-born Christians and heretics. Following a papal decree of 1208, the council also declared a moratorium on collection of the principal, as well as the interest, on usurious debts contracted by crusaders. Thus within the framework of orthodox theology and policy, Innocent significantly increased restrictions upon Jewish liberty.[91]

Later in the century Thomas Aquinas, whose *Summa Theologica* (1266–1273) ranks as one of the monuments of medieval Christian unity, also contended that though Jews should not be harmed or forcibly converted, they were forbidden to marry, or exert authority over, Christians, and must wear distinguishing marks on their garments. Inherited betrayal of Christ destined them for "perpetual slavery," a penalty legally entitling "sovereigns of states" to "treat their goods as their own property." Aquinas felt that custom and Christian decency ruled out such harsh measures, but, along with his illustrious mentor and fellow Dominican scholastic Albertus Magnus, he believed that the Antichrist had Jewish parents and would become the Jewish messiah and lead his people at Armageddon.

Despite papal disclaimers of Jewish guilt for ritual murder and well-poisoning, affirmation by the church's preeminent philosophers of the association between Jews and the Antichrist weakened Rome's opposition to infernalization.[92]

Traditional theology endangered Jews, but they were at greater risk from departures from the Augustinian synthesis. Jews, as tolerated nonbelievers, were formally outside the jurisdiction of the Inquisition, but they were also considered proponents of heresy. Popes accordingly commanded Franciscans and Dominicans to investigate allegations that Jews incited heterodoxy. This mission gave inquisitors an opportunity to interfere in Jewish life and ritual. The old notions that Jews had killed Christ out of ignorance and should not be impeded in the practice of their rites gave way to charges that as intentional and remorseless deicides they must be firmly restrained, persecuted as heretics, forcibly converted, and possibly expelled from Christendom. This theology of the Jews as a nefarious outgroup accompanied late medieval accrual of Christian unity and papal power. Corresponding nationalist aggrandizement also cast Jews in this role. The new theology not only promoted Catholic and nationalist anti-Semitism but also reflected resentment of Jewish competition and stimulated popular fantasies of Jews as demonic aliens.[93]

Condemnation brought repression. Growing suspicion of postbiblical Judaism led to the first major church interference in Jewish religious life when Pope Gregory IX in 1239 accused the Talmud of blasphemy and demanded that Jewish books be confiscated and examined by Paris-based Dominicans and Franciscans. These judges found the Talmud guilty of doctrinal error and sentenced it to be burned at the stake. Inquisition tribunals thereafter regularly censored, suppressed, and destroyed Jewish texts. Pontiffs and kings or clerical courts summoned by them passed similar sentences against Hebrew sacred literature. After 1240, tracts against the Talmud appeared. Less exalted watchdogs of doctrinal purity took up arms against Jewish books: in Bourges in 1251 a mob threw them into a fire. Censorship, impounding, and mass burning of Jewish writings lasted to the end of the Middle Ages and would be revived in Hitlerian Germany.[94]

Suppression of post–Old Testament Hebrew texts proceeded from the assumption that rabbinic Jewry corrupted the Jewish Holy Book and that, without later perversions of their own Bible, Jews would be likelier to embrace redemption. These texts were considered blasphemies of Christianity as well as of biblical Judaism. The Talmud, Christian theologians argued, instructed Jews to deceive and kill Christians and defame Christ, his church, the pope, and Mary. Contradiction, as always, defined the Christian perspective: Was Judaism a doddering remnant of ancient Israel, embodied in the legend of the Wandering Jew and in the contrast between the synagogue as a bent old lady and the church as a vibrant young woman? Or was it, through rabbinic-Talmudic malediction, still a threatening opponent?[95]

Beginning in the 1230s Jews were compelled to attend conversion sermons preached in synagogues, a graver intervention in Judaic religious practice than the suppression of texts. Pope Innocent IV regarded the right to impose such harangues as part of the papacy's sacred mandate to control the internal religious affairs of the Jewish community. A generation later Pope Nicholas III made missionizing, including preaching, to Jews part of the apostolate of the mendicant friars. Canon law ratified these policies, and the Inquisition and European monarchs implemented them. The homilies emphasized Judaic perfidy and its sole remedy—embrace of Christianity. A variation of this technique, disputation between Catholic and Jewish theologians, first appeared in 1242. The latter were required to take part in these debates and the former were given the advantage, being encouraged to disparage Judaism while their adversaries could not criticize Christianity.[96]

Jewish houses of worship were violated in other ways as well. In thirteenth-century England, where Rome's anti-Semitic enactments were implemented with uncommon vigor, the Archbishop of Canterbury forbade Jews to build synagogues, the main London temple was assigned to an order of friars, and private houses of prayer were confiscated. Under Inquisition writ, between the thirteenth and fifteenth centuries, synagogues in southern Italy and Spain were converted to churches.[97]

Grudging Catholic tolerance, inherent in the belief that Jews were to survive and to suffer, gave way during the thirteenth and fourteenth centuries to severe persecution that included forced apostasy, banishment, and violence. Local clergy and secular authorities in Italy, France, Spain, Portugal, and Britain, including the pious French king and passionate anti-Semite Louis IX, often ignored papal abjuration of forced conversion. Popes Innocent III and Nicholas III themselves compromised this position by allowing Jews to be forced to choose between conversion and exile and loss of property; for them only the choice of conversion or death was an unacceptable inducement to apostasy. Moreover, church law prevented converts from returning to their former faith. Inquisitors also scrutinized recent Jewish converts. *Relapsi* were punished, as were judaizers and Jews promoting backsliding.[98]

Implementation of Christianity's self-ordained task to rebuke and rescue Jews ranged from polemic to pogrom, from sermon to suppression, from segregation to banishment. Ecclesiastic imposts, injunctions against exerting authority over Christians, and regulations that Jews swear special legal oaths were joined in this period by enforced isolation, extorted conversion, massacre, and expulsion. Church councils, papal decrees, canon law, and secular ordinances segregated Jews from Christians and required them to wear special insignia. Thirteenth-century French provincial councils banned Jews from the countryside. Jews were also expelled, partly by Inquisition suggestion, from Britain and part of Naples. Fourteenth-century pogroms forced thousands of Spanish Jews to choose baptism or death.[99]

~

Repression permeated worldly as well as spiritual dimensions of Jewish-Christian interaction. Longstanding Catholic condemnation of usury and command that Jews be subordinate and deprived drew the church hierarchy into regulating Jewish economic behavior. Aquinas claimed that the church could dispose of Jewish property because the owners were its subjects and Mosaic law did not intend "to sanction the acceptance of usury from strangers; but only to tolerate it because of the proneness of Jews to avarice." Popes, prelates, and church councils reiterated that Jewish prosperity rewarded infidelity. Innocent III complained about Jewish moneylenders' seizing Christian goods, and the Fourth Lateran Council prohibited Jews from charging excessive interest on debts as well as from collecting loans made to crusaders. Canon law and subsequent church pronouncements forbade Christians to charge interest and Jews or Muslims to impose high rates. Taking interest on loans was defined as a sin in itself and hence an offense against Christianity. Jews, identified as usurers, were therefore anti-Christian. In fact, conversion of Jews was promoted as means of stopping usury. Accordingly, thirteenth-century Jews in England paid tithes to parish priests on profits from loans and could not take church books, vestments, and ornaments as collateral. Pope Alexander III's Bull of 1257, calling usury a heresy, officially linked Jews, usury, and heterodoxy—a connection all the stronger because moneylending was now a major calling of western Jewry.[100]

As in earlier medieval times, Gentile businessmen exploited the imputation of usury to weaken and eliminate Jewish rivals. The masses continued to blame Jewish moneylending for their burden of debt. Elites were ever ready to sacrifice their Jewish financial agents and creditors to the popular outcry against poverty and economic oppression. Moreover, attacks on Jewish commercial and financial activity afforded opportunities for virtually all groups in society to avoid debt payments and gain wealth.

The thirteenth-century British crown levied draconian taxes upon Jews and forced them to become the king's revenue gatherers. They thus became more visible and immediate causes of financial difficulties among tenants and minor nobility. In addition, their economic activities were curtailed by limitations placed on loans and exclusion from landholding, trading in towns, and merchant and craft guilds.[101]

Identical pressures plagued Jews on the continent. Property was regularly confiscated during major thirteenth-century crusades (1234, 1246–47, 1268). In Austria and Germany Jews were subject to special taxes and became increasingly unpopular because they were financial middlemen for princes and burghers. There and in Switzerland and northern Italy, artisan and merchant guilds impeded Jewish entrepreneurs and craftsmen by curbing their residential and trading privileges and barring them from guilds. Jewish businessmen and communities were also widely and violently (and often falsely) accused of debasing and counterfeiting coins.

Envy, fear, suspicion, and opportunism besieged Jewish enterprise. As the French monarchy consolidated power it tried to uproot usury, suppressed Jewish business endeavors, imposed heavier taxes on Jews, and imprisoned them for ransom. In fourteenth- and fifteenth-century Spain and Portugal, Jews were employed as tax collectors and blamed for usury and other social problems, and laws were enacted curtailing Jewish trade and money-lending. From the twelfth to the fifteenth century, Jews had to give "gifts" to nobles, kings, and municipalities, the church hierarchy frequently repudiated debts to Jews, and governments in Britain, France, Spain, and the Holy Roman Empire curbed interest rates and the rights of Jews to collect debts. Jewish moneylenders made many petty loans to artisans, small traders, and peasants, liabilities that turned the masses against all Jews.[102]

By the thirteenth century, Dives, a symbol of greed, affluence, lechery, dirt, and offal, was often represented as a Jew. Dives was the traditional name for the rich man in Jesus's parable of the beggar Lazarus (Luke 16:19–25). He wears opulent clothes and eats sumptuously while Lazarus lies at his gate ill and starving. In the afterlife, however, Lazarus finds a comfortable haven in Abraham's bosom while Dives languishes in hell. Scriptural allegory again was the source of venomous contrast between Judaism and Christianity.[103]

Demonic exaggeration of Jewish economic exploitation joined resentment, jealousy, and avarice in provoking mob violence against Jews in thirteenth-century England and in fourteenth-century France, Switzerland, and the Holy Roman Empire. Usury was also a major justification given for the eviction of Jews from England and France.[104]

Crusading fervor also continued to be a source of danger to Jews, although later carnage never matched that of the First Crusade. The spiritual militancy aroused by holy war, combined with recurrent rumors that Jews collaborated with Arabs and lepers against Christianity, led to coerced conversions, massacres of several thousand Jews, and destruction of hundreds of Jewish communities in Catholic Spain and France.[105]

High and late medieval western Christendom was riven by sectarian disputes, holy, civil, and foreign wars, conflicts between church and state, peasant rebellions, social and economic upheavals associated with emergent capitalism and nationalism, and catastrophic plague. Political and economic disorders involved concrete issues that the populace might comprehend, but theological turmoil, famine, and epidemics were calamities that conjured up occult forces.[106] In an age of faith and mystery, ruled by the Lord but tempted and tormented by Lucifer, spiritual dissent and natural disasters were interpreted as fiendish plots. An atmosphere of turbulence, ignorance, and fear fomented demonization of the Jews. Blood libel and rumors of desecration of the Host, poisoning of wells, and necromancy became more vivid and menacing in these troubled centuries.

The accusation of ritual murder, the earliest medieval diabolization to capture the popular mind, underwent one substantial change in the thirteenth century. Previously it had focused on reenactment of the crucifixion as a continued Jewish insult to the Savior. In Germany in 1235, and soon after in France and England, the charge was increasingly linked to the Jewish religion and to Jewish black magic and fear of Jewish doctors. Blood libels now stressed that the sacrifice of Christian children was to get blood for Jewish medical and religious rites, especially for Passover services. Despite papal denial of these canards, Dominicans and Franciscans took the lead in ritual murder charges. During the twelfth and thirteenth centuries approximately 150 trials were convened; in one episode more than 80 Jews were executed. Such malicious gossip helped instigate the exile of Jews from Britain, caused attacks on thirteenth- and fourteenth-century Jewish communities from Naples to Poland, and provided a fourteenth-century French monarch with an excuse to seize Jewish property.[107]

Desecration of the Host and well poisoning, the other widespread dia-bolical fantasies about Jews, underwent more substantial modification in the late Middle Ages. In Berlin (1242) and in Paris (1290) Jews were burned and their property seized for allegedly polluting the Host for malevolent sorcery or to wreak vengeance on Jesus. This imaginary outrage exceeded blood libel in jeopardizing Jews in the Holy Roman Empire. Germany was engulfed by civic turmoil in the thirteenth and fourteenth centuries, beginning in the 1230s with the outbreak of war between the Holy Roman Emperor and the King of Germany and Sicily and a campaign in Germany to suppress heresy. The latter involved a crusade against those purportedly maltreating the Eucharist and crucifying clerics. Rumors of profanation of the Host led to the first major massacre of Jews in Germany since 1096, accounting for thousands of Jewish deaths and widespread pillage of Jewish property. One hundred known trials of Jews for this transgression took place in the Middle Ages; they resulted in flight, expulsion, and extermination of Jews in fourteenth- and fifteenth-century Holland, Belgium, Luxembourg, and Switzerland.[108]

Two thirteenth-century theological developments also contributed to the upsurge in accusations of desecrating the Host. In the wake of the Fourth Lateran Council, transubstantiation of the Host at Communion became official church doctrine (1264). It nevertheless remained a matter of dispute. Doubts and efforts to still them combined to intensify attacks on Jews for violating the Body of Christ.[109]

Accusations of well poisoning were linked to profanation of the Host and blood libel because Jews supposedly polluted the water supply with hearts and blood obtained from Passover victims and powder from the violated Host. Rumors circulated in France in 1320–21, a period of social unrest and crusading fervor, that Jews and lepers allied to kill Christians by contaminating their drinking water. Merged with an accusation of ritual murder, this lie resulted in the destruction of 120 Jewish communities. An incident in Germany in 1336 resulted in extensive bloodshed and intro-duced the charge, later augmented by the Plague, that Jews participated in a conspiracy to kill all Christians. Jews were now malign carriers and com-municators of plague. Once again formerly favorable images of Jews were turned into harsh condemnations: Jewish physicians, previously famed for their healing powers, were now feared as sorcerers and, with other Jews, as spreaders of disease. From the late twelfth century, the church forbade Christians, on pain of excommunication, to be treated by Jewish physi-cians.[110]

Well-poisoning fantasies became more deadly than ever before in response to the Black Plague (1347–1349). This scourge wiped out approximately one-third of Europe's population, aroused apocalyptic visions, and heightened obsession with the devil and the Jews. Epidemic-induced hysteria intensified the conviction that Jews served Satan and the Antichrist. Already deemed lethal foes of Christianity, Jews were blamed for causing the Plague by poisoning wells with spiders, frogs, lizards, and other symbols of dirt, corruption, and the devil. As the Lord had brought a plague upon Egyptians to emancipate the Hebrews, Lucifer and the Jews brought a plague upon Christians to take revenge upon God the Father and Son. Placing the blame on Jews explained the mystery of the epidemic and absolved God and Christians of any suspicion of guilt, impotence, or immorality. Instead, mortal fear and moral outrage brought retribution against the foes of Christianity. Jews were slaughtered across Europe as far east as Poland.[111]

Another delusion about Jews that intensified at the time of the Black Death was the charge of a world Jewish conspiracy against Christianity. The terror that bred this nightmare also vented itself in murderous attacks on Jews.

The rampage during the Plague, like other outbreaks of violence against Jews, was stimulated by social conflict and religious frenzy. During the fourteenth century, particularly in Germany, struggles intensified between mercantile elites and craft guilds. The landed gentry allied with the urban merchants. Since Jews were associated with commerce, often acted as agents of the nobility, and lent money to artisans at high rates, the workers took a prominent role in the pogroms. In addition, Jews were frequently killed after the appearance of Flagellants, itinerant religious enthusiasts who whipped themselves to ward off the epidemic. Neither official church denials that Jews caused the Plague nor the quick declaration of Flagellants as heretics saved the Jews. The gap between ecclesiastical authority and local religious feeling could not be bridged by official pronouncements.

The greatest medieval massacres of Jews, those associated with the First Crusade and the Black Death, centered in Germany. During the latter, German Jews, unlike those elsewhere, were given no choice between baptism and death. Even Jewish-born Christians were slain, foreshadowing Nazi elimination of Jewish blood and Jewish belief.[112]

In the late medieval period as in the twelfth century, Jews were identified with blood, the devil, sexuality, and dirt, and thus as offensive opposites of the spiritual, ascetic, and immaculate values of Christianity.[113] They were also believed to be allied with other groups considered unclean, such as lepers, in the imagined conspiracy to infect Christians with mysterious and deadly diseases. The stereotype of Jews as disgusting and diseased prefigured the racial anti-Semitism that many experts believe originated after 1850. This modern bigotry, too, argued that Jews had uniquely degenerate inborn physical and temperamental traits. These traits were infectious as well, and could irreparably damage the Christian or national community in body and soul. The key difference between historical (Christian) and modern (racial) variants of this prejudice was that the former included the belief that baptism could purify Jews of defilement. Traditional Christian anti-Semitism preserved the Jews so they could repent and be rehabilitated; the modern version sought to annihilate the Jews as innately and irrevocably debased and destructive.

Rotten in spirit and flesh, deicide and deadly foe of Christianity, archconspirator, Lucifer's collaborator, financial and sexual despoiler—the Jew became an obsession in the manichean apocalypticism of the high and late Middle Ages. Anti-Jewish images traveled via every possible avenue of communication: in religious propaganda by sermons, treatises, canons, dogma, and liturgy; in folklore by ballads, tales, legends, incantations, charms, jokes, passion and miracle plays, and carnival sketches; for the more intellectual audience in chronicles and pamphlets; through such literary devices as satire, scatology, and ridicule; and in sacred and secular art and sculpture. The birth of vernacular literature in the fourteenth century quickened its transmission. In Geoffrey Chaucer's "The Prioress' Tale" (ca. 1390), the Jew is a ritual murderer, an agent of Satan, and an extortionate moneylender, who cuts the throat of a Christian widow's seven-year-old son. Chaucer alludes to the death of eight-year-old Saint Hugh of Lincoln as the same type of crime. One hundred years after being driven from England the Jews were still viewed as a menace.[114]

In an era when most people were illiterate, the printed word had a less persuasive impact than church sculpture, iconography, painting, stained glass windows, illuminated manuscripts, prayer books, hymnals, Bibles, woodcuts, and monuments on bridges, city halls, and public squares. By this time, as noted above, nefarious representation of the Jew was a verbal and pictorial convention. Artistic works present the church as a stalwart, self-confident woman and the synagogue as an old, downcast, and blinded woman, symbolizing her obsolete faith and its obstinate refusal to recognize Christ as the Messiah. Judaism was also portrayed as a faltering widow, sometimes with the head of a goat or a sow. The goat evoked lechery and Lucifer; the pig evoked dirt and bodily functions repulsive to Christian ideology. Despite their taboo against eating pork, Jews were shown in intercourse with sows or as part swine and wallowing in excrement. Jews were also portrayed as scorpions or other animals. Even when human elements predominated, Jews were delineated with hooves, claws, and horns, and sometimes as actual devils. When cast as human, they were pictured riding goats or with goatees, with pigs' ears and teeth, with misshapen bodies and distorted features such as long and hooked noses, with bloody hands and feet (like the wounds of the Savior), and with worms in their mouths (symbolizing death). They were shown as disheveled and wearing the Jew badge and conical hats to conceal their horns. Motif, as well as physical description, emphasized depravity. Illustrations abounded showing Jews and Satan together as allies, thirsting for blood and poisoning the Savior's wounds. These caricatures would persist through the ages and appear in twentieth-century anti-Semitic propaganda.[115]

Government-decreed dress codes made Jewish isolation and degradation official and conspicuous. Costume signified rank and status much more closely at that time than it does today. The Fourth Lateran Council provision about distinctive attire was implemented in 1218, when Britain required Jews to wear a badge. Conical caps, badges, and other items singling out Jews subsequently appeared in southern France (1294), Portugal (1325), Spain (1391), and fourteenth- and fifteenth-century Italy. Saracens, sorcerers, heretics, and disgraced priests, prostitutes, lepers, and criminals also had to wear badges, and Jews were connected in the popular mind with these outcast groups. The Jew badge, usually circular and yellow, probably denoted money. Yellow was also the color for prostitutes, who, like Jews, personified lewdness and thus were at odds with spiritual purity and the Christian community. The Jew badge was also a "mark of Cain," signifying Judaism as the murderous older brother of Christianity. Jews were sometimes forced to wear a horned hat, illustrating the popular conviction that they, like the devil, had horns.[116]

Distinctive apparel set Jews apart, emphasizing their spiritual separation from Christendom. Church edict and canon and secular ordinance, though not always consistently observed, enjoined additional forms of isolation. As with all segregated and stigmatized groups, sexual relations were rigorously regulated, though not necessarily effectively controlled. Seduction of Jewish women by Christian men was sympathetically treated in law and literature, but sexual relations between Jewish men and Christian women could be punished by death. Gentiles who married or cohabited with Jews were arraigned for the crime of bestiality, a charge that addressed popular assumptions about Jews having animalistic traits and insatiable sexual appetites and preying on innocent Christians.[117]

Christian reverence for chastity and the immaculate conception and repugnance toward fleshly urges and functions made carnality a sin. Since Judaism did not denigrate sexual activity and Jews in any case were regarded as immoral, they were inevitably judged guilty of malicious lust. The medieval exaltation of the Virgin Mary compounded theological condemnation of carnality in general and Jewish lechery in particular. Extolling the Mother of God also evoked the oedipal element in Christianity with its implied rivalry with the paternal religion, thus further complicating Christian attitudes toward sex, women, and Jews.

Jews were also distanced from the Christian community by enforced residential segregation in ghettos. This separation derived from the contradictory views of the Jews as feeble relic and potent malevolence. The ghettos were a geographic parallel of the Jews' religious isolation and their displacement by Christianity. Segregation also protected Christians from the malignant influence of the Jews. Enforced segregation of Jews into ghettos began in the thirteenth century, even in relatively tolerant east central and eastern Europe. During the next century legally mandated ghettos were established in France, Germany, and Spain.[118]

Christians felt it necessary to be distanced from Jews not only in life but also in death. Hence Jewish tombs, like Jewish homes, were removed from proximity to their Christian counterparts. Attacks on Jews also continued after death: Jewish cemeteries were vandalized or otherwise desecrated. These violations were sometimes mandated by local law, when governments used Jewish gravestones for town walls or executed criminals in Jewish burial grounds. The latter practice constituted an additional identification of Jews with a stigmatized outgroup.[119]

Separation ended in mass removal, which made the West virtually without Jews by 1500. Until the thirteenth century, expulsions were intermittent and uncommon and usually confined to towns and other relatively small communities. During the late Middle Ages, Jews were more regularly and permanently banished from large districts or entire countries. Exclusion on a national scale was facilitated by yet another type of segregation. "Chamber serfdom" in the Holy Roman Empire and France, beginning in the twelfth century and fully implemented in the thirteenth, made Jews a separate class of king's subjects governed by special royal law. Similar arrangements were made in Britain and Spain. With this development, Jews were completely segregated: visually by insignia on their clothes, economically by unique taxes and business restrictions, legally by their legal status as royal serfs, and residentially by confinement to ghettos. In the public mind they were also set apart religiously as infidels, physically as bearers of peculiar traits and illnesses, morally as evildoers, and spiritually as demons.[120]

Banishment on a large and irreversible scale came from a variety of causes. Kings were gradually consolidating their power; this made them better able to defend their royal serfs but also gave them less incentive to do so and encouraged persecution. Infernalization made Jews a more alien and widely hated minority. Their economic usefulness was diminishing as extortionate levies depleted their resources. At the same time, the growth of a Christian middle class reduced the need for governments to rely on Jews for economic services, while increasing the risk of antagonizing an anti-Jewish bourgeoisie. As moneylenders, estate agents, business competitors, and fiscal servants of lords and kings, Jews were targets of all sectors of society.[121]

Britain, the least hospitable land for Jews, expelled Jews in 1290, the final stage in a century-long erosion of Jewish rights. The drastic move had a variety of opportunistic and tragically false causes already discussed: Jews were scapegoats for civil and religious strife and economic frustration and indigence; victims of crusading ardor; blamed for ritual murder, black magic, and abhorrence of Christianity; hated as usurers and tax gatherers; and no longer economically useful. The mendicant orders were leaders in the drive for eviction, in which Edward I was primarily motivated by the desire to expropriate Jewish property. Clergy, barons, and businessmen called for their departure. The masses, mostly peasants, did not demand eviction but had sufficient resentment and fear not to resist it. Jews would not return for almost four centuries.[122]

Similar causes, along with an eruption of crusading fervor in 1320, well-poisoning rumors, and imputed guilt for the Black Death, drove Jews out of most of France. Unlike England, however, France did not exclude Jews either abruptly or completely. Exploited for profit by the monarch and nobility, the royal serfs were expelled when they did not pay various fees and required to agree to even higher fees upon readmittance. Financially exhausted after 1394, Jews officially vanished from France; outside Avignon and other papal districts, no Jews officially lived in France for three hundred years.[123]

Jews fared no better in the Holy Roman Empire. In 1346 they lost citizenship rights and became the emperor's serfs. Immediately after the Plague the emperor gave princes and cities the right to determine Jewish residence; expulsion from many German towns ensued, rationalized by charges of usury or anti-Christian activity. Italian disunity created local variations in policy toward Jews, but they were tolerated in Rome and the Papal States. Black Death hysteria and accusations of extortion and commercial chicanery resulted in exile, starting in the late fourteenth century, from Swiss and Low Country cities.[124]

Approximately one hundred years after the expulsion from England, once a relative haven for Jews, a similar turnabout occurred in Catholic Spain, another former refuge. Thirteenth-century Iberian literature facilitated this reversal by portraying good Jews as apostates and bad Jews clinging to their obsolete faith and as usurers and ritual killers. Beginning in the fourteenth century Jews were confined to ghettos, inhibited in business activity, prohibited from holding public office, forbidden sexual relations with Christians, and required to wear badges. They were accused of conspiring to cause the Black Plague, of plotting with lepers, and with increasing frequency of committing ritual murder and poisoning wells, and they were subjected to a rising number of conversion sermons, forced conversions, and pogroms. Violence peaked in 1391 in a bloodbath, incited by the clergy, in which possibly fifty thousand Jews lost their lives.[125]

At the close of the Middle Ages, with Spain now hostile, Rome and the other papal territories alone afforded modest protection and privileges for Jews in western Europe. Aside from ideological considerations that prompted papal protection against anti-Semitic violence, most of the Holy See lands were in Italy, a region that was spared the worst depredations of the Black Death and crusading mania and where Jews were less prominent in moneylending. Hence Jews were better integrated into Italian life and cities than elsewhere in Europe, a circumstance that mitigated medieval, Renaissance, and subsequent Fascist anti-Semitism.[126]

As the Middle Ages ended, conditions for Jews in the Christian world were at a nadir. Until the 1930s, only in Iberia would their position deteriorate further in western Europe. Embodying primal fears buried in dark recesses of western consciousness, the Jews inspired savage disapprobation. Attitudes do not always dictate action, but in the Middle Ages prejudice easily erupted into pogroms.

Weakening of the Jews' defenses as hostility grew worsened their predicament. Their chief refuges, the church and the monarchy, were dubious protectors. Eschatological imperatives made the papacy a guarantor for survival, but Christian belief demanded punishment of the remnant of Israel. Moreover, papal bulls and canon law did not necessarily determine conduct in local parishes. Secular rulers provided even less security. Sovereigns tolerated Jews to enrich the royal treasury but readily sacrificed them to deflect popular unrest, to confiscate their wealth, or when they were no longer economically useful.

Jews were at best marginal figures in a host society of the baptized. They were stigmatized as dissenters and dangerous outcasts. Like lepers, whores, and heretics, they were shut out of respectable society. They gradually were excluded from membership in guilds, town corporations, and government posts, and they could not own land or bear arms. Retaining a shaky status as the king's serfs, they were increasingly isolated by law, as well as by custom.

Progenitors yet betrayers of the Savior, validators yet deniers of salvation, and victims yet potential vanquishers of Christian civilization, the Jews incarnated unresolved conflicts in medieval society. They were feared and hated as demonic fantasies, as symbols and projections of Christian fear and self-doubt. For Christians falsely accused Jews of doing to them what they now did on a large scale to Jews. It was Christians who stole and despoiled Jewish property, desecrated Jewish objects and places of worship, compelled conversions, seduced and raped Jewish women, and slaughtered Jews, including children.[127]

## The Renaissance and the Early Modern Period

Consolidation of national states in Renaissance and Early Modern times amplified the importance of Christianity's national, as well as universal, appeals for validity and loyalty. Contemplated as a whole or nation by nation, however, momentous economic, political, religious, and cultural changes did not radically modify behavior toward Jews until the seventeenth century. As with an earlier transformation, the collapse of the Roman Empire, monumental changes in Europe had little impact upon treatment of Jews.

In fifteenth-century Iberia Jews continued to face suppression, segregation, forced apostasy, expropriation of property, pogroms, and, in Spain in 1492 and Portugal in 1497, the alternative of baptism or expulsion. Exile from Iberia, the last in the series of national banishments that had begun in 1290 in England, brought to an end the second stage of Jewish history in Latin Christendom: the first great transitional stage, the emergence and triumph of Christianity in the Roman Empire, lasted four hundred years from the birth of Christ; the second, from subordinacy to suppression, occurred between the eleventh and fifteenth centuries.[128]

Although no Jews were allowed in Spain until 1869, Jews remained objects of hatred. Spanish literature continued to ridicule and reprimand Jews. In fifteenth-century Spain syphilis was called the "Peste of the Marranos," an epithet that helped to inaugurate the stereotype of Jews as carriers of venereal disease and, hence, infectors of the body politic. The Inquisition, introduced to Spain in 1480, was conducted there with unsurpassed savagery. Jesuit investigators ruthlessly probed the souls of Marranos and converted Jews for evidence of clandestine judaizing. Many priests claimed that adoption of Christianity could not purge innate Jewish vices, and Jews were widely thought to be inherently tainted. Many apostates and their descendants died by *auto-da-fé* or mob violence. Survivors were barred from guilds and government posts and some dioceses and religious orders. "Blood purity" statutes, inaugurated in the sixteenth century, as requisites for entry into the nobility and public office and not officially repealed until 1860, launched Portuguese and Spaniards on elaborate genealogical expeditions to disprove Jewish ancestry. These and other persecutions distinguished between old and New Christians on the basis of Jewish lineage. New Christians were considered inassimilable because of "polluted blood" through descent from the crucifiers of Christ, which made them secret infidels. In a related attribution of inborn stigma, seventeenth-century Spanish physicians still claimed that Jewish males had tails and menstruated. The situation in Spain contravenes the assertion that racial anti-Semitism replaced religious anti-Semitism because of waning Christian influence and belief. From the reign of Ferdinand and Isabella through the seventeenth century, patriotism and Christian messianism fused in a vision of Spain as the paladin of Catholicism. This nationalist ethos underlay expulsion of Jews, refusal to accept converts, and the ferocious idealism of the Spanish Inquisition.[129]

The persecution of Iberian New Christians, which lasted from the fifteenth to the eighteenth century, anticipated the search for Jewish forebears by the Nazis and the Gestapo's refusal to distinguish between converts and those remaining Jewish. The most virulent varieties of racist anti-Semitism emerged in Spain and Germany, where Jews were more integrated and influential in national life than in other western countries and thus incurred greater fear and resentment.

Anti-Jewish hostility, unsubdued by Renaissance Humanism, radically reduced Jewish settlement in western Europe. Old images of and policies against vile Jewry continued in force. Sixteenth-century popes banned study and publication of the Talmud, ordered it burned, and renewed the mission of the Inquisition friars. Charges of ritual murder and desecration of the Host continued to circulate, and Jews continued to be expelled and forced to pay special taxes.

Religious turmoil persisted as well. Heretical movements, such as the fourteenth-century Wycliffites in Britain and the fifteenth-century Hussites in Bohemia, and the Reformation and Counter-Reformation fueled theological controversy, for example over the sanctity of transubstantiation. Catholic-Protestant confrontations increased public preoccupation with the Antichrist and with Gog and Magog. These associates of Satan in the infernal axis eschatologically confronting Jesus (Rev. 20:8–9) now stood for the reemergent lost ten tribes of Israel. Yet another supernatural stereotype solidified itself in public opinion. The Wandering Jew, that symbol of the diaspora, became well known in fourteenth-century England and mid-sixteenth-century Iberia and Germany immediately after expulsions of Jews in these places. During this age of denominational conflict Ahasuerus and his people were strongly identified with the Antichrist and his apocalyptic campaign against Christianity.[130]

Some fifteenth- and sixteenth-century Humanists, most notably Germany's Johannes Reuchlin, criticized blood libels and destruction of the Talmud, but even such relatively enlightened figures retained aspects of medieval bigotry. Reuchlin asserted the collective guilt of the Jews and applauded their sixteenth-century expulsion from many sectors of the Holy Roman Empire. Erasmus blamed the Peasants' War (1524–1526) on a Jewish conspiracy and rejoiced that France was free of Jews.[131]

Jews were also maligned in England, the country of their longest absence. Christopher Marlowe's The Jew of Malta (ca. 1589) and William Shakespeare's The Merchant of Venice (1596–1598) brought memorable Jewish villains to the Elizabethan stage. Jewish poisoners, traitors, schemers, Christkillers, murderers, foreigners, evil enchanters, rapacious businessmen, and Shylock and Barabbas types became standard Tudor theater characters. Similar types appeared in plays, narratives, and songs on the continent.[132]

The Reformation and Catholic retaliation had substantial but mixed impact on conditions for European Jews. While Catholic vigilantism was intensified by the Reformation, it focused on Protestant enemies and paid less attention to its older antagonist. Protestant sects were divided in their response to Judaism, but sixteenth-century anticlericalism bred hostility when opponents of ecclesiastical authority associated Jews with the church.[133]

German and Scandinavian Lutheranism fomented Jew hatred, partly prompted by the dislike for Jews that their founder evinced late in life. Like many Catholic anti-Semites, Martin Luther believed in the Antichrist and Gog and Magog and lumped together Jews, Turks, and false Christians. Luther's notorious pamphlet of 1543, *On the Jews and Their Lies,* and his last sermons pilloried "those miserable and wicked people" for idolatry, blasphemy, deicide, well poisoning, enslavement, child murder, collaborating with the devil, usury, and greed. He called Jews "blood-thirsty enemies of our Christian and human name" who brought "plague, pestilence and all misfortune." Luther advocated segregation of Jews, avoidance of synagogues and Jewish schools, confiscation of the Talmud and other sacred books, outlawing of usury and rabbinical teaching, and curtailment of Jewish travel, and he suggested banishment as the best solution to Jewish criminality and sinfulness.[134] And Luther was not the only anti-Semitic father of the Reformation. Huldreich Swingli, a founder of Swiss Protestantism, also felt that Jews threatened Christianity and the world's well being.[135]

British Puritans, Scottish Presbyterians, and the Dutch Reformed Church, in contrast, revered the Old Testament and its Chosen People, and that sentiment diluted animosity toward descendants of the Hebrews. Lutheran hostility also somewhat abated in the seventeenth century, but in the 1500s, along with charges of Christkilling and financial predation and traditional Catholic anti-Semitism, it perpetuated the persecution that eventually overwhelmed Jewish enclaves in Germany and Austria. When not evicted from towns and states in central Europe, they endured pogroms, suppression of holy texts, confinement to ghettos, outlawing of sexual and other relations with Christians, economic restrictions, accusations of desecration of the Host, and enforced display of the Jew badge. In some respects the predicament of Jews actually worsened in that region after the medieval period. Between 1388 and 1519 ninety expulsions of Jews, often for usury, took place in the German empire. While such banishments became rare after 1520, hatred of Jews did not diminish. The Peasants' War inflamed suspicions of Jews as ruthless creditors and currency devaluators and linked protection of Jews with defense of elite authority, high taxes, and extortionate interest rates. Required wearing of the Jew badge and other distinguishing marks spread to Germany in 1434 and Austria in 1551. Cumulative oppression in the Holy Roman Empire and adjacent lands impelled the exodus to eastern Europe.[136]

Expulsions were rarer in France only because fewer Jews remained there. The big difference from central Europe was that in France regular slaughters of Jews stopped in the 1490s instead of in the next century. Massacres ended largely because Protestants assumed the Counter-Reformation role of foe of the church and because Jewish inhabitants were scarce. Resentment, however, did not dissipate. In the years 1481–1486, when Provence was incorporated into France, its Jews were expelled.[137]

Outside Italy, by 1520 the Jewish presence in the west was sparse and scattered. Jews had been banished from Iberia and England, and, after the usual persecution, from Switzerland and the Low Countries as well. Some communities remained in Germany and Austria and in the papal territories within France.[138]

Salo Wittmayer Baron, the preeminent historian of world Jewry, argued that the humanistic study of Hebrew language and history and the advance of individualism mitigated hatred of Jews during the Renaissance.[139] But his research in northern and western Europe indicates that the drastic decline in Jewish populations, rather than decreased hostility, accounts for the reduction of abuse. Baron's evidence from Italy even more convincingly contradicts his claim of Renaissance tolerance. A seemingly irresistible onrush of hatred now threatened to overwhelm western Jewry's last shelter. In southern Italy Jews were occasionally massacred, and in Sicily and Naples they were forced to choose between baptism and exile.[140]

Jews fared better in the center and north of Italy, the citadel of the Renaissance, but even here their situation actually deteriorated during the Renaissance and Baroque periods. Artisans and merchants reviled Jewish competitors. Legal ghettos appeared in 1430 and subsequently multiplied. Jew badges and other mandated insignia originated in the fourteenth century. In the fifteenth century Jews were forbidden to own land and in the 1400s and 1500s Italian municipalities restricted social relations and activities between Christians and Jews. In the sixteenth and seventeenth centuries Hebrew works were confiscated and burned in Florence and elsewhere. Jews were expelled from sixteenth-century towns, including Milan and Genoa.

The increase in repression was mainly due to Counter-Reformation resistance against religious dissent. In Italy, unlike the situation in other parts of western Europe, Jews were acutely victimized by aggressive defense of the faith. Rome and the Papal States, until this time the securest shelters for Jews, reversed their policies. Here and elsewhere in Italy Jews were pressured to convert and, in defiance of canon law, their children were sometimes baptized despite parental opposition. During the sixteenth and seventeenth centuries Rome censored and destroyed Jewish sacred texts and forbade Jews to possess them. Both in papal areas and elsewhere in the sixteenth century, synagogues were destroyed or turned into churches, Jewish cemeteries vandalized, and converts who returned to Judaism arrested and executed. Mobs frequently molested Jews in Rome, Florence, and other areas. At the height of the Inquisition, Pope Paul IV (1555–1559) confined Jews in Rome to a ghetto, prohibited their owning land, required them to wear yellow badges and listen to conversion sermons, and destroyed all but one synagogue. While Jews were not driven from the Holy See, Pius V evicted them from other pontifical territories in 1569, partly to prevent interfaith sexual activity.[141]

By the fifteenth century most Jews had fled to the east, where oppression was milder. Migration began in the thirteenth and fourteenth centuries, when Jews went to Poland to escape rampages prompted by the Crusades and the Black Death, and culminated between the fourteenth and sixteenth centuries, when that nation became the world center of Jewry. Displaced by increasingly sophisticated Gentile capitalists in the west, Jews flourished in the backward eastern European economy as bankers, moneylenders, and financial agents of nobles and kings.[142]

Poland proved to be an imperfect and impermanent haven. From the beginning, the church was antagonistic. The national hierarchy and clergy feared that a large influx of Jews might uproot newly planted Christianity (Catholicism had come to Poland in the tenth century) and consequently campaigned for segregation and compulsory wearing of the Jew badge. Church-organized outbreaks against the new arrivals began in the thirteenth century. The earliest pogrom (1347) resulted from an accusation of ritual murder and came at the time of the advent of ghettos and rumors of blood libel, plots to cause plague, well poisoning, and desecration of the Host. Such suspicions and hysteria caused by the Black Death led to additional fourteenth-century rampages. Traders and artisans, growing envious of Jewish rivals, supported harassment. After 1450 native merchants became powerful enough to compete with Jewish businessmen, and in the 1500s large towns limited Jewish entrepreneurship and moneylending and

Jews were barred from guilds. In the sixteenth and seventeenth centuries Jews were driven out of a number of cities and victimized by urban riots. These attacks were usually organized by businessmen, with artisans preponderant in the mobs that devastated personal property and synagogues and brutally assaulted Jews. Secular persecution coalesced with Counter-Reformation militancy. The sixteenth-century Polish church circulated accusations of Host desecration and blood libels, suppressed the Talmud, and outlawed synagogue building. In the following century rivalry turned Polish physicians against their Jewish counterparts. Meanwhile, the rural masses grew to hate Jews as tax collectors, middlemen between landowners and peasants, and administrators of aristocrats' estates. Jews also were innkeepers and ran the liquor industry, another source of peasant indebtedness and anger. Festering peasant grievances ignited the bloodiest annihilation of Jews until the Holocaust. A rebellion of Eastern Orthodox Christian serfs, conflated with a Ukrainian cossack uprising against the Polish King, incited Russian intervention on behalf of the peasants in 1648-49. At least 100,000 Jews died in the ensuing war, and the survivors, deposed as urban bankers and businessmen, sank into rural poverty. Pogroms persisted in later times, provoked by Catholic fanaticism, clerical complicity, and general perception of Jews as Christkillers and ritual murderers.[143]

Rabid anti-Semitism on the part of the Russian Orthodox Church and the ruling classes kept all but a few Jews out of Russia until the late-eighteenth-century partitions of Poland. Sixteenth-century monarchs tried to obliterate vestiges of Jewish life in Russia, and Czarist invasions and conquests of Poland and Lithuania in the 1500s and 1600s invariably resulted in Jewish eviction and extermination or the choice of death or apostasy. Newly arrived masses of Jews from formerly Polish territories lived in the Pale, a restricted area of settlement in western Russia. Changing nations did not alter status or circumstances. Jews continued to be blamed for the same crimes, excoriated for the same reasons, and forced to suffer the same tribulations.[144]

Similar ordeals befell Jews elsewhere in eastern Europe. Alleged collaboration with Turks in 1594 provoked a pogrom in Romania. Hatred of Jews was also endemic in contemporary Hungary, where debts owed to Jews were canceled, their taxes were increased, their cemeteries were damaged, and they had to swear the Jew oath. Merchants agitated against Jewish competition, and Jews were driven out of several cities. Seventeenth-century Hungary also penalized judaizers with death or deprivation of property.[145]

As the bulk of Jewry moved eastward, momentum toward tolerance swung in the opposite direction. Conditions began to improve in western Europe in the seventeenth century, inaugurating the third stage of the Jewish experience in Latin Christendom. Gradual recovery culminated in nineteenth-century emancipation. England and Holland now treated Jews better than Poland or Italy. The sinister Jew was still embedded in Christian ideology and public opinion, and often aroused horrendous behavior toward real Jews. But the modern age, which eventually wreaked destruction upon the Jews, opened with, and for a long time held, considerable promise. From the 1650s to the 1880s only one incident of violence, a Ukrainian pogrom in 1768, massively endangered Jewish life. The last expulsions of Jews from Germany and Austria occurred in Frankfurt in 1616 and Vienna in 1671 and the last expulsion from western and central Europe, a temporary exile from Prague, in 1744. Serious accusations of well poisoning and desecration of the Host ended in the seventeenth century.[146]

~

The waning of hostility toward Jews in western Europe reflected an expanding confidence created by such developments as the defeat of long-standing Muslim enemies, consolidation of nation states, economic growth, cessation of religious wars, and advances in science providing solutions to hitherto fearful mysteries. Another manifestation of increasing optimism and control was the colonization of distant lands. Many of the new provinces were in North America; this chapter has been a prelude to an examination of anti-Semitism in the United States from colonial days through the Civil War. The European developments combined with conditions peculiar to the New World to diminish anti-Jewish feeling, but the legacy of animosity examined in this chapter would ensure the perseverance of that prejudice.

# ~ 3

# Ambivalence at America's Dawn

Ambivalence is the word that best describes the colonial attitude toward Jews. While amply negative, New World opinion of Jews was higher than was customary in Europe. Factors in provincial life hindered transmission of Old World hostility and blunted its autonomous renewal in the infant communities across the ocean. British North America's beginnings during the Counter Reformation and transatlantic reverberations of England's wars with France and Spain made Catholicism the main threat to Protestantism. The founding of permanent colonies also coincided with relaxation of anti-Semitism in Britain, Holland, France, and Germany—primary mother countries of the settlers. Spain and Portugal, where hatred did not abate, lost hegemony in the Old and New Worlds to nations where Jews were comparatively advantaged.

## Europe

In 1590 Holland, a leading capitalist country, set the example for western nations by admitting, after long exclusion, a small enclave of affluent Jewish traders. Dutch Calvinists revered the ancient Israelites and accepted their descendants for the same eschatological reasons as did British Puritans. Rulers and entrepreneurs in both countries also saw secular advantages in allowing reentry. Improvement in the prospects for Jews in Britain coincided with the Puritan Revolution and the emergence of Britain as the foremost maritime and imperial power in the West. A 350-year hiatus officially ended in 1656 when a few rich Jewish merchants were permitted residence. Puritans esteemed the Old and New Testaments as the divine foundation of their faith and the biblical Hebrews as the Chosen People whose descendants could save themselves and usher in the Millennium by adopting Christianity. The economic usefulness of wealthy Jewish businessmen combined with spiritual imperatives to inaugurate the slow, partial, and regrettably reversible dilution of western anti-Semitism. When Puritan zeal was displaced by Restoration indulgence, material considerations provided the main impetus for gradual enhancement of the tiny Jewish community. Medieval exploitation of Jews as a source of revenue, however, was replaced in England and Holland by a new economic incentive for tolerance. The momentum toward modernization inherent in commercial capitalism motivated their governments to invite rich Jews in order to promote trade and finance. By 1700 the historical situation had diametrically altered and Jews were less constrained in England than on the continent. The Enlightenment, glorifying individual rights and the primacy of reason, further eroded traditional Jew hatred, despite jaundiced tirades by various *philosophes*.[1]

A few years after Jews returned to Britain they were again tolerated in France. Contemporary Jewish businessmen in Germany also benefited from the conditional reception characteristic of the West and marking the emergence of the "court Jew."[2] Spain was the exception to this amelioration of conditions for western Jewry, a difference associated with its failure to modernize economically, its fall from commercial preeminence, and its messianic Catholic nationalism.[3]

Seventeenth-century beachheads of tolerance did not develop into a rapidly conclusive campaign against historical hostility. Reentry was at first rigorously selective, confined to urban centers of capitalism, and due to informal and reluctant consent rather than radical change in popular sentiment or public policy. Dutch Reformed church synods, particularly in the first half of the century, condemned "Jewish blasphemies." Jews in Holland were also victimized by special taxes and occasional violence and were required to swear the discriminatory Jewish oath. Opposition in Britain came from royalists and in both nations from merchants fearing Jewish competition. English and Dutch rulers severely limited the number and activities of the newcomers. Jews received legal authorization to dwell in Britain in 1664, almost a decade after their official reappearance. France was even more reluctant. Pamphlets, theological treatises, histories, travel tales, and belles lettres uniformly portrayed Judaism as superstitious and legalistic and Jews as dark and dirty with an unpleasant odor; as deceitful, mercenary, selfish, and sexually degenerate; and as hating Christians. Not until the mid-eighteenth century, save for peripheral places like Alsace and Lorraine, did organized Jewish life exist in France.[4]

Curbing of traditional anti-Jewish abuses followed rearrival, particularly in Holland and England. After 1650, and especially after 1676, the Dutch Reformed church, guided by millennial expectations, tried to convert Jews and became less intolerant. While subject to restrictions, even the earliest immigrants, instead of being governed as a corporate body in the medieval manner, were treated as individuals, like other Dutch residents. By 1657 the government of the United Netherlands required that Dutch Jews living abroad be recognized as citizens, an act of emancipation never repealed. Across the North Sea in England, in 1673 Crown and Parliament officially recognized the religious status of Jews.[5]

In spite of tentative sufferance, progress for western European Jewry proceeded at a fitful and sometimes glacial pace. Even in relatively liberal seventeenth-century England and Holland, Jews were prohibited from engaging in retail trade. Driven by fear of entrepreneurial rivalry, London merchants during the reigns of Oliver Cromwell and Charles II protested against Jewish immigration and agitated for legal restraint of the commercial activity of the newly settled community. Time did not tame hostility. Widespread opposition caused the withdrawal of a parliamentary bill of 1753 to naturalize rich Jewish merchants and allow them to own land. Conferral of other economic and civic rights was no less reluctant. Eligibility for membership in guilds and the City of London, initiated in the eighteenth century, awaited full implementation for another hundred years.[6]

Prospects elsewhere were even grimmer. Jews in France were excluded from trade in Marseilles in 1652, and the municipality of Paris opposed Jewish settlement in 1767. Until the 1780s French Jews paid special taxes and could not own land, belong to guilds, or pursue certain professions. Those in German states encountered severer adversity: during the seventeenth century, appearance of Jews in streets and Christian neighborhoods was regulated, their dress was dictated by sumptuary laws, their marriages were restricted in order to stifle demographic increase, and they were occasionally expelled from a few cities. Frederick the Great later limited the number of Jews in Prussia by cultivating a few wealthy capitalists and casting out the rest. He mandated special taxes upon those privileged to remain and barred them from certain occupations.[7]

Restrictions and humiliations derived from obdurate convictions about the perfidiousness of Jewry. Trials for ritual murder ended in the West, but belief in blood libel persisted. Similarly mythic charges of desecration of the Host, poisoning of wells, and religious infidelity also resisted, while adversely influencing, the Age of Reason and subsequent evolution of the rational temperament.[8]

Despite the tenacity of such repugnant stereotypes, an emancipation movement emerged just as the American colonies won independence. After 1750 French culture was less censorious of Jewry. In 1782 the last medieval anti-Jewish laws were abolished in France and Emperor Joseph II of Austria issued the Edict of Tolerance, a limited decree of Jewish emancipation. But the emperor's decree would be withdrawn in the reactionary revival of the 1790s and citizenship for French Jews would be a gift of the Revolution. Here, as everywhere, complete emancipation came after the United States constitutionally guaranteed civic equality for all creeds.[9]

## Colonial America outside the Future United States

New World attitudes toward Jews reflected those of the mother countries. Reactions ranged from exclusion and Inquisitorial persecution of Judaizers and Marranos in Iberian outposts to relative freedom in Dutch and British territories.

French colonies were governed by policies midway between repression and tolerance. Jews were initially barred from the French West Indies, admitted by a 1671 royal decree, banished in 1684, and soon allowed to return. Although Jews had economic freedom in the eighteenth century, they were still threatened with official expulsion, had few civil rights, and suffered frequent personal and public rebuke. Not until the 1760s were they released from paying special imposts, and not until 1777 were they formally allowed private worship. Jews probably encountered heavier oppression in the Islands than in France.[10]

Circumstances in the British West Indies had much greater impact upon Jewish life in the mainland northern settlements. Although the status of Jews varied from island to island, immigration in the seventeenth century was encouraged for economic reasons and to offset an overwhelming numerical imbalance between black and white residents. Accordingly, Jews were early allowed extensive political rights and public worship. By the eighteenth century they served on juries in some islands and in the militia everywhere, and many were naturalized citizens. Nevertheless, they were barred from public office and endured other indignities. In Jamaica, with by far the largest number of Jews in the New World, until 1787 they could not become lawyers and until 1820 they could neither become jurors nor vote. The main proponents of discrimination and insult, as in England, were businessmen who feared competition. In Barbados, Gentile traders petitioned to make Jews swear the medieval Jewish oath in order to expose their alleged commercial chicanery. They were partially successful, for until the end of the eighteenth century Jews had to swear Christian oaths in business dealings. In Britain, in contrast, as early as 1667 Jews were permitted to swear on the Old Testament in all cases. London was also more liberal on other issues of economic equality. In Jamaica and Barbados, respectively until 1739 and the 1760s, despite royal opposition, Jews had to pay special taxes. Notwithstanding imperial encouragement of political and economic rights, Jews were not enfranchised in Barbados until the nineteenth century. They did not win full citizenship in Jamaica until 1831, a few years after blacks received de jure equality.[11]

Many Jews also came to Dutch New World territories. The imperial government in the Netherlands, as in England, for mercantile motives encouraged this migration and gave Jews broad economic privileges and the right of public worship. If Jews in Dutch and British possessions had similar advantages, they also had identical problems. Dutch West Indian Jews did not acquire full citizenship until the nineteenth century and encountered economic and social hostility from Gentile traders.[12]

## The Future United States

Intermittent, hesitant, and partial advances sometimes diluted and obscured, but never eradicated, western hostility. At best Jews were candidates for economic exploitation or spiritual apostasy. In more ominous phases and times, they could be regarded as implacable foes of nationality and Christianity. Hence, in Europe de jure granting of equality did not reflect or engender deep and widespread de facto awareness of national solidarity and common humanity between Jew and Gentile. Conversely, in America, more extensive and confident de facto assumption of civic rights anticipated de jure recognition of interfaith parity and approximated a more profound, though flawed, empathy between Jews and Christians.

Absence of a medieval past and convergence of settlement with Protestant and Age of Reason countervailence against traditional Jew hatred contributed to the relatively positive response to Jews in America. In contrast to their historic legal status in Europe, Jews in this nation were born free from the time of colonization. In contrast to their role as ultimate outcasts from the High Middle Ages to the Reformation, Jews seemed the less despised enemy to combatants in the Catholic-Protestant wars still raging as early settlements took root. Indigenous factors made an even greater contribution to the comparatively favorable reaction in America. Extermination of Indians and enslavement of blacks were vigorously under way well before the seventeenth century ended. Never in this country would Jews be so marginalized. Long before nationhood, characteristically pluralistic trends were visible in American society. By the 1680s, for example, sectarian diversity and free association created a polycentric spiritual life concurrent with economic and political voluntarism. Pluralism helped neutralize the Christian propensity to absolutize the world into a battleground between unadulterated good and evil. Tolerance was further fostered by the opportunistic and optimistic orientation of the young society. Need for settlers and competition for congregants gave practical appeals precedence over traditional sectarian and ideological exclusiveness. Isolation from Europe's historical lamentations and disasters, blessed abundance, and the unbowed innocence of youth diluted transmission of the European sense of sin, damnation, and worldly hazard and the tendency to incessant conflict. Relatively peripheral in America, these forces underlay the pessimistic ideology of Christianity in Europe, the belligerence of the nobility, the anxiety of the precarious middle class, and the despair of the peasantry. Views of Jews as unrepentant and unredeemed crucifiers, invulnerable and pitiless rivals, and insidious underlings, therefore, had less immediacy in the new land. Together these developments promoted resistance to legal sanctions singularly applied to Jews, precluded the rise of a hegemonic church, accelerated progress toward civil equality and liberty, and thus hindered conveyance of Old World anti-Semitism.

## The Seventeenth Century

Lord Baltimore and Lord Shaftesbury, in the 1630s and the 1660s, attempted to restore earlier social forms by providing respectively in their Maryland and Carolina proprietarial charters for seigneurial privileges, patents of nobility, and manorial courts. Analytic elegance would be served if animus toward Jews had been another medieval relic that made the overseas journey. Anti-Semitism did surface in these colonies, but any relationship between feudal fantasy and provincial bigotry seems coincidental. The Fundamental Constitutions of Carolina (1669), in which

Shaftesbury and his aide John Locke elaborated their scheme for a hereditary landed aristocracy, also explicitly guaranteed freedom of conscience.
Lockean liberalism merged with the desire to lure settlers to bring about
this rare colonial declaration of comprehensive tolerance. Jews could vote
and hold office and in 1697 became naturalized residents. By the early
1700s, however, South Carolina had stabilized and needed fewer newcomers and, at least according to law, naturalization and the other political
privileges were withdrawn. This deteriorating legal status did not result
from vestigial feudalism; feudal titles meant little in a country of plentiful
land and scarce settlers, conditions contrary to those prevailing in Europe.
Nor were Jews singled out for discrimination. Catholics received harsher
treatment: Jews worshipped openly, Catholics were denied this privilege.
Early in American history began the tendency to view Catholics as more
dangerous foes who needed severer constraint.[13]

A more plausible connection between the vision of a medieval social
order and animosity toward Jews existed in Maryland, where in the late
1630s immigration was limited to Christians. In fact, the ugliest legal case
of purely religious anti-Semitism in American history transpired there in
1658—but by then Lord Baltimore's baronial aspirations had dissolved
just as feudal echoes had ceased in South Carolina. The Act Concerning
Religion (1649), better known as the Toleration Act, gave religious
freedom only to Trinitarians and forbade denial of the divinity of Christ.
Nine years after its passage Jacob Lumbrozo, the sole Jew in Maryland,
was indicted for blasphemy, a capital crime under the statute. He was
charged with declaring that Jesus was neither divine nor resurrected and
that his miracles were acts of a "necromancer." He was not tried, however,
and went on to become a prominent citizen of Maryland. He may have
avoided trial and execution by adopting Christianity, or more probably,
because of an amnesty grant celebrating Richard Cromwell's accession as
Lord Protector of England. Although Judaic belief was presumptive evidence of the crime of blasphemy, Lumbrozo was the only colonial North
American Jew ever arrested or in any way mistreated on exclusively religious grounds.

When Maryland became a crown colony in 1691 and the Church of
England was established in 1702, Catholics fared worse than Jews. Congregants of the faith embraced by the original proprietor were now denied
freedom of worship, subjected to special taxes and oaths, suspected of
treason, scrutinized, and threatened. Jews were spared these persecutions.
As in other colonies, anti-Catholicism intensified because of the Revo-

lution of 1688 against the Catholic James II, and because of chronic warfare between Britain and France.[14]

The most serious secular mistreatment of Jews occurred in New Netherland, a commercial venture of the Dutch West India Company that harbored no medieval nostalgia and originated in the nation most tolerant of Jews. In 1654 twenty-three Jews arrived in New Netherland from Brazil, a Dutch colony retaken that year by Portugal, fleeing the certain imposition of Inquisitorial oppression. Soon after they disembarked, Governor Peter Stuyvesant wrote the Company directors in Amsterdam that the colonists "deemed it useful to require them [the Jews] in a friendly way to depart." Mixing modern and medieval stereotypes, he asserted that many of the Jews were poor and would be a public expense, "that they (with their customary usury and deceitful trading with the Christians) were very repugnant," and proposed "that the deceitful race,—such hateful enemies and blasphemers of the name of Christ,—be not allowed further to infect and trouble this new colony." The governor also feared that admission of Jews would attract Quakers and Lutherans, other groups he detested.[15]

Stuyvesant's recommendation and evaluation were not unusual for him; as the nominal administrator of contemporary Curaçao he also resisted Jewish entry and rights there. The directors' response was as consistent: in New Amsterdam, as in other colonies, the Company encouraged Jewish settlement. It rejected removal because the Company was nearly bankrupt and desperately needed trade and settlers, and Dutch Jews had commercial connections and capital invested in it. New Amsterdam suggested a policy concordant with conventional conduct; old Amsterdam refused because the Jewish community, sixty years after its return, now had critical financial leverage in the Company and the country. Effective intervention by a Jewish business elite on behalf of less fortunate brethren was novel in mid-seventeenth-century Holland and unprecedented in the New World. The different perspectives of the "planters" in the wilderness and the "adventurers" back home led to a duel of several years' duration between the local colonial government and the "Amsterdam Chamber." In 1655, after the latter's reply, Stuyvesant and the New Netherland Council resolved, on the grounds that militiamen abhorred serving with Jews, that Jews pay a tax in lieu of military service. At the end of that year the provincial administration denied a petition of three Jewish merchants to travel and trade on the Delaware River and at Fort Orange, a request already granted by the parent company. In addition to these restrictions, Jews were prohibited from owning land and houses, engaging in retail operations or trading with Indians, working as craftsmen, and, along with other non-Calvinists, from publicly observing their religion. By 1657, however, the Dutch West India Company, fortified by pressure from Jewish merchants in Holland, had prevailed. Jews successfully petitioned for burgher rights in New Amsterdam, which ended discrimination in trade, public worship, service in the militia, and taxation. Disenfranchisement and ineligibility for government office persisted because these rights were reserved for Dutch Reformed congregants.[16]

Stuyvesant was the son and son-in-law of Dutch Reformed ministers, and the head of that denomination in New Amsterdam lent spiritual support to the battle against the Jews. "These people have no other God than the unrighteous Mammon," said Dominie John Megapolensis, "and no other aim than to get possession of Christian property, and to win all the other merchants by drawing all trade toward themselves." Megapolensis echoed the castigations of clergymen and merchants in the mother country and in other Dutch territories. In 1640 his counterpart in Brazil, then a Dutch colony, likewise called for limitation of Jewish immigration because the newcomers were "attracting the trade" and acquiring the "shops" of Dutch businessmen.[17]

The most significant anti-Semitic episode in provincial North America unfolded in a profusion of paradoxes. It appeared in an outpost of the most liberal nation in Europe, a settlement that was a capitalist venture rather than a Christian commonwealth and did not attempt to revive a medieval way of life in the wilderness. Reversing the usual course of persecution, it originated in the New World and was resisted in the Old World. The etiology of seventeenth-century New Amsterdam bigotry is easier explained than its evolution. Traditional prejudice was still rife in Holland and its overseas empire. Improvement in the position of the Jews, however, partly shifted the focus of aversion from historical and theological factors to economic competition. The latter was an especially powerful motive for proscription or exclusion in a settlement founded for profit rather than principle. Parenthetically, and again paradoxically, if the reemergence of influential Jewish commercial communities stimulated the anti-Semitism of entrepreneurial rivalry in New Amsterdam, it was the presence of an influential Jewish mercantile elite in old Amsterdam that halted discrimination. The simplest explanation of this case of anti-Jewish agitation, however, may be that New Netherland was the only seventeenth-century North American colony where Jews as a group permanently settled and New Amsterdam was the site of their most populous settlement.

While no sensational anti-Semitic event surfaced in New England, Jews figured importantly in its creedal consciousness, and, because of the region's religious and intellectual prominence and the mobility of its population, its attitudes were influential in other places and future ages. The Protestant attitude toward Judaism received fullest expression in the New Canaan along the Charles River and in Connecticut and Rhode Island, colonies that arose after theological disputes resulted in voluntary or forced exodus from Massachusetts Bay Colony.

Puritan New England's behavior did not substantially deviate from the contemporary norm. Although the first known Jew in Boston was "warned out" in the 1640s, this policy was short lived and also applied to adherents of Christian sects. During the next decade Jews entered New England intent on permanent residence and, as in other settlements, were undisturbed in their private worship and less oppressed than Catholics. In fact, Jews were tolerated while Catholics, Quakers, and Anglicans were not. Rhode Island, founded by the defender of freedom of conscience Roger Williams, not only admitted members of all denominations but, unlike Massachusetts and Connecticut, did not tax them to support the Congregational church. In this early citadel of religious liberty, however, Jews were not formally allowed to vote or hold office.[18]

Theological sophistication and dedication, rather than action, chiefly distinguish New England from other early colonies in its reactions to Jews. Puritan sentiments were complicated and paradoxical. Pragmatic, pluralistic, and optimistic religious practice and belief promoted America's comparatively cordial accommodation of Jews. New England Calvinism, at least in the generation of arrival, was principled, pessimistic, and, outside Rhode Island, monolithic. Its Reformational nonconformity entailed no renunciation of received dogma regarding perpetual Jewish guilt for the crucifixion, Judaism as a supplanted and flawed belief, or salvation dependent upon acceptance of Christ as Savior. Where the theology of corruption and punishment was embraced (inflicted alike on Jew and Gentile), however, its anti-Jewish potential might be mitigated, as in New England Congregationalism, by ideology and circumstance. Puritans in America, as well as in England, associated their Protestantism with ancient Israel. They feared Catholics more than Jews, praised the Hebrews as heroic progenitors of Christianity and the Old Testament as the book of divine revelation, and believed that Jewish entry into the state of grace would bring about the Millennium. New World Puritans further identified with the Chosen People because they were establishing a new Israel in the wilderness. Such reverence inspired John Cotton and Nathaniel Ward in 1636 to propose a body of laws for Massachusetts based on the Mosaic Code, the Connecticut Colony Enactment (1685) to prescribe that Code as fundamental law, and the Plymouth Colony Legislature in 1658 to recommend that Israel's law be a model for all, and especially Christian, governments.[19]

Pilgrim and Puritan leaders so repeatedly drew parallels between their people and Israel that the Book of Exodus became a veritable metaphor for the experiences of its self-defined successors. Likenesses between Hebrews and New Englanders sometimes stressed reappearing faults, but also focused upon common ordeals and glories. William Bradford constantly associated Plymouth Colony inhabitants with God's Chosen in Egypt and Palestine. Recommendations of Old Testament morality and wisdom and similes between the Pentateuchal and prospective wanderers in the wilderness also proliferate in *A Model of Christian Charity*, written by John Winthrop aboard the *Arbella* as it sailed to the new holy land. "This Israel in the wilderness," Increase Mather called New England. His son Cotton compared the voyage to Massachusetts with the flight from Egypt.[20]

Qualified deference to ancient Judea did not engender empathy for contemporary Judaism, but New Englanders did express esteem for what John Cotton called "the mother church of the Jews." "God tells us of a special love he yet bears the Jews from Abraham's sake," wrote Roger Williams. "The holy scripture, saith . . . that they are a people above all the peoples and nations in the world, under most gracious and express promises."[21]

Cotton and Williams, preeminent early New England divines, Cotton's son-in-law Increase Mather, a premier religious figure of the second generation, and his son, Cotton Mather, a luminary of the third generation, believed that grace would be restored when Jews embraced Jesus. Upon their "accept[ing] the Messiah, as the only help of their souls against all the Guilt of their Sins," promised Cotton Mather, "God will remember his Covenant [with them]."[22]

Apostasy was as critical for Christian redemption. For Mather senior, "news of the Jews conversion will put life into all the churches upon earth," and "be unto the Gentiles as life from the dead. For Gentiles shall be enlightened, and therefore enlightened from Jewish churches." Mather junior and John Davenport, another religious leader, "perceived the mystery of the salvation of Israel" as a "glorious coming of the Lord Jesus Christ." According to the former, Jewish redemption would "confirm us Christians in our faith exceedingly to see every article of it asserted in the express words of the Old Testament."[23]

Israel's cherished contributions to Christianity, combined with the greater fear and threat of Catholics, made Jews the less hated minority in Protestant America. Williams, Cotton, and the Mathers assailed the Catholic church and the pope as agents of Satan, "the great whore," "the bloody whore," "the Harlot of Rome," "the beast," and "a bastard Christianity."[24] Slurs against Judaism were rarely as vitriolic.

Reverence for biblical Hebrews did not prevent New England magistrates and ministers from viewing Judaism as rigid and legalistic and Jews as stubborn and sinful scorners and slayers. It "would make us odious to all Christian commonwealth," thought Winthrop, "to allow and maintain full and free tolerance of religion to all men . . . Turk, Jew, Papist." The Massachusetts Bay governor also regarded with distaste " the Synagogue of Antichrist in her superstition."[25]

John Cotton luridly affirmed the conventional Christian critique. Although less often than in anti-Catholic remonstrance, "the Church of Israel" was a "Harlot" that "had gone whoring after false gods." Adherence to Judaism resembled "bondage under Antichrist" and renewal of the covenant between the Lord and his Chosen People awaited penitence for "the greatest sin that ever was committed upon the face of the earth." Cotton Mather similarly described the "Jewish church" at the time of Christ as "under an extreme degeneracy" and thereafter as the "leprous and outcast church of Israel." This reprobate people employed "magical tricks," the "black arts," and "witchcraft" to raise "the devils" among them and "blast the miracles of Jesus."[26]

Roger Williams, the early New England champion of religious tolerance, actually exceeded Cotton and Mather in vituperating Catholics and Jews, in addition to Quakers, Baptists, Moslems, and atheists. He also was more sparing in praise for the scriptural Hebrews. Mundane, corrupt, and coercive, old Israel was the prototype of "the national church" that prompted Williams to leave Massachusetts and that was the most formidable foe of Christianity. Williams's other calumniations were more conventional: Jews "blaspheme" the "true religion." They wallow in "pits of rotteness" and "stand . . . for Satan against Christ" as abjurers of guilt for the "horrible crime" of deicide. Alone of these famous divines, Williams mixed secular with spiritual castigation, a compound malice he shared with Dominie Megapolensis. With "horror," Williams thought "of the Jews killing the Lord Jesus, of their cursing themselves and their posterity; of the wrath of God upon them; of their denying the Fundamentals of our Christian worship." He then left the lofty realm of theological admonition to denounce Jews for "their known industry of enriching themselves in all places where they come."[27]

Increase Mather also rebuked premillennial, and therefore unreconstructed, Jewry. In *The Mystery of Israel's Salvation Explained and Applied* (1669), he asserted that Judaism is merely "antiquated ceremonies" and that "the unconverted Jews" are under the power of Satan. The "sin of Hell, and of the Devils" means that "that people is desperately moved with envy and malice against the true Religion," and therefore "lie[s] under the guilt of blasphemy . . . against the Son of God." Another grave transgression is "that [the] most prodigious Murder that ever the Sun beheld hath been committed by the Jews; and that the guilt thereof lyeth upon the Jewish Nation to this day, even the guilt of the blood of the Savior."[28]

Always the orthodox Calvinist, Mather believed that the Jews would recant and be forgiven by his stern but merciful deity. No "Nation [is] guilty of such prodigious wickedness as the Jewish Nation hath been guilty of, whereby they have infinitely provoked" the Lord to bring upon Israel "the greatest calamity that ever shall befall any people to the world's end." Eschatological contrition, however, ensured that "the Jews shall be saved from the blindness of their minds, saved from the unbelief of their souls, saved from that curse and wrath of God which lyeth upon them." "[The] Jews, who have been trampled upon by all Nations, shall shortly become the most glorious Nation in the whole world, and all other Nations shall have them in great esteem and honour." Belief in repentance and restoration restrained Christian hostility. But Mather also went beyond the prescriptions of orthodoxy and proclaimed that Jews neither poisoned wells nor ritually murdered Christian children.[29]

Attitudes in other colonies generally resembled those of New England. William Penn affirmed eventual Jewish salvation, but until the Millennium conjoined "Jews, Turks and Infidels." Although he permitted adherents of all creeds to live and worship in Pennsylvania, officials and electors had to proclaim Christ's divinity. Jews also could not vote or hold government positions in North Carolina and Virginia.[30]

Political constraints aside, by the end of the seventeenth century the approximately 250 Jews in America enjoyed de facto and, for the most part, de jure economic equality and religious liberty.[31] Only the test oath, which universally disqualified Jews from public office, impinged upon their freedom of business activity by preventing them from practicing law. A significant sign of the clement atmosphere for American Jewry was that when de facto assumption clashed with de jure denial, resolution favored reality above legality. Such was the outcome in 1685, when Rhode Island Jewish merchants were tried, and their goods impounded, for violating the British Navigation Act of 1660, which prohibited aliens from trading. Though guilty under the law, the defendants were acquitted by the jury.[32]

Also in 1685, more than ten years after the colony again became an English province, another de jure decree disrupted established commercial operations in New York. Governor Thomas Dongan, withdrawing privileges that Jews had wrested from Stuyvesant, enjoined them from pursuing retail trade and handicraft occupations. Before the decade ended, however, they resumed these endeavors. Dongan's edict was reversed, over the objections of Gentile merchants, through denization (semi-naturalization) grants from the governor or the assembly.[33]

While contravening a New Amsterdam practice that benefited Jews, Dongan reaffirmed another that impeded them. A second decree of 1685 reserved the right of public worship to Christians. Dongan compounded this regressive colonial anomaly by rejecting a petition by Jews to extend this right to them. Thus the coming of British rule initially left Jews still conducting devotions in private homes. Repeal of this order in the next decade enabled Jews at last to pray in a synagogue.[34]

Litigation was as important as legislation and determined whether enactments commanded actual obedience and were fairly applied. Although the Jews' scant numbers limited their total involvement in lawsuits, such actions were frequent enough to rule out the possibility that Jews were reluctant to participate in the judicial process because they felt justice was unobtainable. Evidence shows that Jews were as often plaintiffs as defendants and as likely to win as to lose trials. A decision that reflected public or, at least, governmental sympathy for Jews came in 1670 when the Court of Assistants at Hartford reduced Jacob Lucena's punishment for lascivious conduct because he was Jewish and then further lightened the sentence out of respect for another Connecticut Jew who intervened on Lucena's behalf.[35]

Refusal to convict in Rhode Island and justice mellowed by mercy in Connecticut indicated that Jewish defendants would not be victimized, but in New Amsterdam this could be a misleading expectation. Huge fines were levied on Jewish businessmen for minor offenses, and one was heavily fined, flogged, and banished for contempt of court. Miscarriage of justice induced by bigotry did not, however, discourage Asser Levy, a burgher of New Amsterdam and of New York after British conquest, from incessant litigation. Levy usually acted as plaintiff and successfully sued Nicholas Bayard, the colony clerk, and other high officials. During the 1670s he was a court trustee for property disputes between, and executed wills for, Christians.[36]

~

Elimination of religious and economic constraints and gradual attainment and vigorous exercise of civil rights disguised the popular image of the loathsome Jew. Along with salutary aspects of Jewish life in America, this poisonous weed from Europe took root in colonial times. "I believe she has vile thoughts of us," remarked Rev. Hugh Peter of Massachusetts Bay during the dispute between Anne Hutchinson and the Puritan oligarchy, "and thinks us nothing but a company of Jews." "Jew" was also a reproach in New Amsterdam, where one citizen sued another for calling him a Jew. "You are a Jew," said a burgher of that town involved in a suit against a Jew; "you are all cheats together." Balthazar D'Haert, another citizen of the Dutch colony, in 1668 sought exculpation from accusation of fraud in a commercial transaction by pleading that the damaged goods had been meant only "for a devilish Jew." Jacob Rader Marcus, the foremost historian of colonial American Jewry, reports that in the seventeenth and eighteenth centuries the word "Jew" conveyed disapproval or contempt. Conversely, he notes, the phrase "worthy Jew" or "honest Jew" exempted certain Jews or Jewish merchants from the habitual detraction of their people. Religious affiliation as a derogatory allusion also applied to Catholics and Protestant dissenters from the established church in each colony. Marcus asserts, however, that epithets directed at Gentiles were not equivalent instruments of opprobrium. According to him, colonists seldom referred to wily Quakers or greedy Papists.[37]

In general, whatever the variation in form, Jews were no more subject to aspersions based on their creed than Catholics or dissenters. A major exception, however, was the charge of deicide, which traveled more viscerally than through sermons, theological speculations, or Bible lessons. Carried over from the Old World were folktales, ballads, exorcisms, incantations, and charms blaming the Jews for killing Christ. American versions of this legacy resounded throughout the colonies, appeared in both black and white folklore, crossed the continent as the frontier receded to the Pacific, and are not yet entirely stilled. Crimes and medical advice were linked to this sin. "The Jews crucified Christ, they did the worst of deeds to him," began an Anglo-Saxon charm chanted to avenge the stealing of cattle, "they hid what they could not hide. So may this deed never be hidden, *per crucem Christi.*"[38]

From Ireland came this popular item of medical wisdom: "If ointment is to be rubbed on a sore place, do not use the forefinger, but the second one, the first finger having been poisoned ever since Judas Iscariot betrayed our Lord by pointing out him to the Jews with that finger."[39] Jews as crucifiers appear in an eighteenth-century German incantation to alleviate colic:

> O Jerusalem, thou Jewish town,
> Thou, who the Christ did crucify,
> Who spake that fresh water and fresh blood,
> Were for bowel and colic good.
> Strike the side Three Times with the hand.
> XXX.[40]

A cradle hymn sung by Puritan mothers bore the same message:

> Yet to read the shameful story
> How the Jews abused their king
> How they served the Lord of Glory,
> Makes me angry while I sing.[41]

Crucifixion fantasies spawned blood libels. Ballads and stories from England and Ireland, "Sir Hugh," "Sir Hugh or Little Harry Hughes," "Sir Hugh and the Jew's Daughter," "The Jew's Daughter," "It Rained a Mist," "The Little School Boy," "A Little Boy Threw His Ball So High," and "Little Harry Houston," were narrated by whites and blacks in every colony. In most versions a young boy (based on Hugh of Lincoln, a child whose murder in England in 1255 was falsely blamed on the Jews as a ritual killing) is enticed into a Jew's garden by a Jew's daughter, who stabs the child and collects his blood for the holy day service. The victim is a cognate of the martyred Jesus and the temptress represents Eve; the crime of Calvary is repeated in a personal, renewable, and sexualized variant. In Virginia alone sixteen texts and seven different melodies have depicted this tale,[42] which merges the dogma of the Jew as archetypal betrayer and murderer, slave of sterile Mosaic law, and pernicious foe of Christianity

with the later myth of the Jew as sensual desecrator of Christian innocence.

~

The colonies made indisputable progress, after early controversies, in
bestowing rights and privileges on Jewish inhabitants. Indications of routine transference of Old World prejudice were temporary and atypical.
Stuyvesant was the uniquely rabid anti-Semitic colonial leader, New
Amsterdam made the sole serious effort to deport Jews, and Lumbrozo
alone among colonial North American Jewry was arrested or in any way
mistreated on purely religious grounds. Baptists, Quakers, and other dissenting Protestants, in contrast, were regularly persecuted, and Catholics
were more resented than non-Christians. By the 1690s Jews freely worshipped and conducted business, lived where they chose, and sometimes
voted. Hence, Jewish life in what later became the United States was substantially more favorable than the experience of Jews elsewhere—possibly
excepting Holland and England.

Direct comparison between these nations and their American provinces
is called for. Jews received better treatment in the Netherlands and Britain
than elsewhere in Europe, the Dutch and the British were predominant
powers in this part of the New World, and the United States has been universally credited with unprecedented and unrivaled tolerance of Jews.
Both the mother countries and their possessions had minuscule numbers
of Jews, so no variations in treatment can have resulted from disparate size
of Jewish enclaves in the Old and New Worlds. Exploration of the
question of how the mother countries influenced the reception of Jews in
their New World territories yields no single answer. Although Holland lib-
eralized New Amsterdam's behavior toward Jews, the British Navigation
Act of 1660 reversed the direction of this momentum by prohibiting
aliens, which meant most Jews, from engaging in trade. The Act was
widely flouted, indictments were rare, and juries refused to convict. Thus
in this case the settlers fostered tolerance by resisting the will of imperial
officials and merchants.

Findings about the influence of the center upon the periphery do not
necessarily apply to a vital comparison, that of actual differences in the
scope of freedom in Europe and America. Mother countries might be more
tolerant abroad than at home, or the type of influence they exerted might
harmonize with their own practices. The separability of these facets of
comparative history deserves mention here but not extensive exploration,

particularly since no definitive statement can be made about whether the impact of Holland and England upon their empires was primarily progressive or regressive.

The Old and New Worlds can be compared with respect to various freedoms. Little difference exists in religious liberty. With brief exceptions in New Amsterdam and New York, which lagged behind their parent countries in this regard, European and colonial American Jews concurrently enjoyed public freedom of conscience. Although Britain and the Netherlands anticipated several of their outposts in this facet of denominational emancipation, New Jersey and early Rhode Island were the first to levy no tax for an established church.

In economic freedom America clearly took precedence. Well before most British and Dutch craft and mercantile guilds admitted Jews, all occupations save law, except for a few years in New Amsterdam, were open to colonial Jews. When Britain later attempted to restrict mercantile endeavor, her impositions were ignored by American Jews and their enforcement defied by American Gentiles. Linked to business and vocational opportunity was geographic mobility. Here, too, the colonies led their mother countries. Excluded from certain towns in Holland and even more confined in England, Jews had unobstructed access to the colonies. Their movement to, or in, America was also unregulated by property requirements, while only rich Jews could enter England and western Europe.

The gap narrowed in civil rights. Jews in Britain and the colonies encountered no proscription in the legal system, while those in Europe had to swear the Jewish oath. They nowhere held public office, but by the 1690s informally voted in some provinces and, to a lesser extent, in England. New World Jews had slightly more legal and political privileges and were more secure in person than in the parent lands. Mob and individual violence occasionally befell Jews in Holland and England. In America, Catholics and dissenting Protestants were subject to punitive action, usually by the government, but Jews never suffered from legally sanctioned or casual violence.[43] Aggregating different aspects of freedom shows America undoubtedly, but not dramatically (as usually claimed), ahead of enlightened European nations in accepting Jews.

## The Eighteenth Century

Circumstances for eighteenth-century American Jewry were only marginally altered by the erosion of Puritanism and other ideological commitments caused by an increasingly pragmatic and pluralistic atmosphere, transatlantic dissemination of the Enlightenment, and the decline of denominational passion after the Counter-Reformation and the Glorious Revolution. These profound changes, starting in the late seventeenth century and inaugurating the gradual and irreversible eclipse of Christianity by other forces as the arbiter of life, prepared the way for nineteenth-century emancipation of western European Jewry. In colonial America, where Jews already exercised all public rights save political equality, these developments had a modest impact. Severe examples of early hostility such as the incidents in New Netherland and Maryland were rare even in the relative intolerance of the earlier century, and found no successors in the benign climate of the later provincial era. The tangible effect of the growing subscription to principles of free expression, individual judgment, and the primacy of reason over faith was to hasten the assumption of full civic rights by Jews in the early national period, several generations before European Jews attained equivalent status.[44]

Eighteenth-century colonial society clearly moved toward acceptance of Jews. Older currents of affirmation flowed into new waves of positive feeling. Ancient Israel still stirred adoration in pastors and their congregations. At the final rite of passage from province to independence, Americans still envisioned biblical Hebrews as their model. During the Revolutionary era Ezra Stiles, Charles Chauncy, and other celebrated clergymen, in New England election day sermons delivered to high officials and legislators, noted parallels between present and Old Testament events. They compared their leaders and travails with scriptural figures and struggles and recommended that prospective state and national commonwealths emulate the law and government of ancient Israel. John J. Zubly, a highly respected Georgia Presbyterian, preached a similar message to the Provincial Congress of Georgia in 1775. A secular version of this theme appeared in 1765 in an editorial in the *Connecticut Courant*, which compared British rulers and the Stamp Act to Roman tax collectors oppressing the Chosen People.[45]

In 1776 when the Continental Congress was considering designs for the new nation's seal, Benjamin Franklin proposed that the seal represent Moses dividing the Red Sea while the Pharaoh's army drowned in its waters, and Thomas Jefferson suggested that it portray the children of Israel in the wilderness following a cloud by day and a pillar of fire by night.[46] Pentateuchal symbolism did not become a civic icon, but the infant republic, inventing its own past, sought roots in scriptural Israel.

Praise for contemporary believers was less forthcoming but reflected greater acceptance of Judaism. The Congregationalist pastor Ezra Stiles was fascinated by Hebrew language, history, theology, and ritual and sought Jews as friends. Upon attending, along with high officials of Rhode Island, the opening of the Newport Synagogue in 1763, he lauded the building, the services, and the congregation. Ten years later, Stiles told his Newport flock that the "Seed of Jacob are a chosen and favorite people of the most high and the subjects of the peculiar care of heaven." Approval in the press, though also rare, had greater import than the occasional encomium from an eminent minister. Newspaper notice may have better mirrored, and more strongly affected, popular opinion. The *Boston Daily Evening Traveller* and the *Newport Mercury,* respectively in 1754 and 1763, reporting the consecration of synagogues in their cities, were impressed with the attendance of "prominent citizens," the handsome edifices, and the exotic ceremonies. For the *Traveller,* the service recalled "the Majesty and Grandeur of the Ancient Jewish Worship."[47] Curiosity about the "oriental" customs of Judaism helped account for the Gentile presence, nonetheless the social and political elite thought it worthwhile to attend and the journals were commendatory.

Whether or not these fragments replicated prevalent opinion, it is uncontestable that after the 1680s Jews were free of encroachments upon religious liberty. The original charter of Georgia (1732) excluded only Catholics from the right of free worship. In New Hampshire, New York, and South Carolina non-Protestant services were forbidden, but such orders were imposed on Catholics and sometimes on dissenters, while Jews were ignored. In Pennsylvania after 1729, the Christian oath of abjuration was required of alien Catholics, but not of Jews. Parliament mandated in the Plantation Act of 1740 that Jews and Protestants, but not Catholics, were eligible for naturalization and the former could omit the otherwise required Christian oath. Blasphemy laws were passed in Massachusetts Bay, Pennsylvania, Delaware, New Hampshire, Virginia, Maryland, and other colonies, but, except in Lumbrozo's case, these laws were never used to persecute Jews. Presbyterians in New York, Moravians in Connecticut, Baptists in Connecticut, Massachusetts, and Virginia, and Catholics almost everywhere (by the Revolution only Pennsylvania provided for unmolested Catholic worship) were excluded, arrested, and beaten. Such mistreatment never befell Jews.[48]

Veneration for the parent of Christianity was reinforced in colonial colleges, whose acknowledged purpose was to inculcate morality and train ministers and whose presidents and faculty were usually clergymen. Hebrew was taught at the Congregationalist strongholds of Harvard and Yale. From the founding of Yale (1701), the college seal was inscribed in Hebrew, and an oration in that tongue was requisite for the Harvard A.B. examination and graduation ceremonies. Israel's history and language also entered colonial intellectual life through study at private academies and through books on these subjects printed at provincial presses. Obligatory courses in Hebrew led to the appointment of Judah Monis, an apostate Jew, as a Harvard instructor. Two years before his conversion, Monis received a Harvard A.M. (1720); he was the sole Jew enrolled prior to the nineteenth century. The waning of religious and social bigotry also allowed the presence of Jews at other colleges. One was awarded an A.B. from King's College (later Columbia University) in 1774. Benjamin Franklin's Academy (later the University of Pennsylvania) began admitting Jews in 1757, and ten or twelve matriculated before the Revolution. Although Jews at the time attended colleges in Germany and Italy, their appearance in American institutions of higher learning antedated by over a century their entry into Cambridge and Oxford.[49]

The most extraordinary example of equality for Jews in higher education occurred at Rhode Island College (later Brown University). In 1769, five years after the college was founded, several Jews from Charleston, South Carolina, made a donation to the school. In acknowledgment of their generosity, the trustees and fellows amended the charter to grant Jews admission, freedom of worship, exemption from chapel attendance, a Jewish tutor if justified by the number of Jewish students, and permission to establish their own chair in Hebrew and fill it with a member of their own religion.[50] Remarkable for their tolerance in 1770, these principles would still be noteworthy in 1900.

Acceptance of Jewish students reflected a respectability unusual for this long-despised minority. By the 1740s and 1750s Jews had helped found or joined such elite organizations as the Union Society of Savannah, Georgia, a patrician philanthropic endeavor; the Music Club of Philadelphia; the Philadelphia General Assembly, an association for exclusive society balls; the Redwood Library in Newport, Rhode Island; Franklin's Public Library in Philadelphia; and the Lancaster (Pennsylvania) Library Company.[51]

Jews ornamented the beau monde in other ways. Rhode Island Lopezes and the Levy-Franks clan in New York and Philadelphia belonged to the urban gentry. In Pennsylvania in 1781 a Jew became grand master of a Masonic lodge and deputy inspector general of Masonry. A Jewish merchant in Manhattan joined the city's prestigious Chamber of Commerce, signaling Jewish entrepreneurial success in New York, Rhode Island, and other colonies. Jews served as Revolutionary army or militia officers up to the rank of colonel in Pennsylvania, Virginia, Georgia, and South Carolina; in Europe Jews were generally excluded from the military. Daughters of distinguished Jewish families married scions of the upper class, as in the match between Phila Franks, child of an affluent Manhattan merchant, and the aristocratic New Yorker Oliver DeLancey.[52]

Progress was not confined to prominent spiritual, educational, and social circles. Goodwill spread throughout colonial society, a truer measure of its scope and depth. Newspapers respected Judaism and portrayed believers as pious, charitable to needy coreligionists, and having commercial acumen that would enrich the colonies. In the 1750s and 1760s, Gentile publishers in Pennsylvania reissued a German pamphlet calling for tolerance of Judaism. Public approbation indicated that Jews generally maintained good social and economic relations with Christians. Jews were designated beneficiaries of their Christian friends and vice versa, and members of the two groups witnessed each other's estates and were business partners. Many Jews married Christians, and occasionally the Gentile wife converted. Even Jews charged with grave offenses were not always vilified for their religion. When David Franks, a member of the leading Jewish colonial family, was tried for Loyalist sympathies, his creed was not reviled.[53]

Marcus observes that colonial Jews achieved social but not political equality, while through most of the subsequent history of the republic this situation was reversed.[54] Perhaps overly optimistic about early social approval, this interpretation nevertheless credibly describes the situation in provincial and national America. By 1700 Jews acquired respectability, had nearly total economic and religious freedom, and encountered no uncommon difficulty in law courts, but had yet to attain political parity with other citizens. Eighty years and a revolution later the same conditions prevailed: Jews worshipped unmolested, transacted business, and figured in lawsuits, but were substantially excluded from the polls and public office. Progress in government service, but not in enfranchisement, proceeded in the eighteenth century.

Jews were barred from public posts by the requirement of swearing to the divine inspiration of the New Testament. Edict, however, did not always determine practice. Not surprisingly, Jews held office first and foremost in South Carolina, where in Charleston in 1703 one became head of what would later be called the police. Public office was also available in Rhode Island, that other early colonial beacon of liberty, but no Jews lived there. Remarkably, shortly after the appointment of the Jew in Charleston, Jews also joined the police, though in the humble post of constable, in relatively intolerant New Amsterdam and Boston. While Jews in the colony of New York were never elected to public office or even chosen for jury duty, in 1731 Rodrigo Pacheco became a colonial agent to Parliament, the highest appointment in that province held by a Jew. By the 1760s and 1770s, mainly in Georgia and South Carolina, Jews served more regularly and in higher positions than in earlier colonial times. They were initially port officials, an outgrowth of their commercial prowess. While a Jewish constable patrolled the streets of Manhattan in the 1760s, Moses Lindo, the South's leading Jewish merchant, was inspector general of indigo for South Carolina. A decade later another Jewish trader became inspector for tanned leather at the port of Savannah and Jews were justices of the peace in Georgia. By the Revolution, Jews held offices of greater power and prestige and of political rather than economic jurisdiction. This development reflected an overwhelming Jewish preference for the patriotic cause, a preference due to lack of prejudice in America compared to England and to the fact that most Jews had few ties to the mother country or the imperial establishment. Appreciation for siding with the rebels, who soon controlled the majority of the colonial governments, particularly in the South, along with their own social and economic distinction, enabled a few Jews to attain political prominence. The Whig merchant Mordecai Sheftall in 1774–75 headed the most important Georgia county government as chairman of the parochial committee of Christ Church Parish (Savannah and its environs). During the war he was colonel of a Georgia brigade and commissary general for South Carolina and Georgia. A newly arrived Jew from London sat in the First and Second South Carolina Provincial Congress, and after independence, when the Provincial Congress became the General Assembly, he was the first Jew in an American state legislature.[55]

Gains were balanced by some losses, but the pattern was more consistently ascendant in officeholding than in Jewish suffrage. Uncertainty in both aspects of citizenship surfaced in South Carolina. After initial promise, by 1716 Jews could neither hold office nor vote. They regained these rights and were high officials in the 1760s and 1770s, but the 1778 state constitution excluded non-Protestants from the Assembly. Early-eighteenth-century Rhode Island also withdrew rights of public service and suffrage, but Lopezes and other affluent Jews probably voted for local office. Between the early 1700s and 1737 Jews went to the polls in New York. Formal disenfranchisement lasted until 1761 at the latest, when they were on an elector list for an Assembly contest. Legal permissions or prohibitions were somewhat irrelevant, for Jews participated throughout the century in New York elections, though in lesser proportion than their share of the population. Jews probably voted, but could not hold office, in New Jersey, and were ineligible for both in Connecticut, Pennsylvania, Delaware, Maryland, and Virginia. They went to the polls, at least intermittently, in Massachusetts, New Hampshire, and North Carolina and seem to have had uninterrupted suffrage in Georgia. Not until the New York State Constitution (1777) did Jews approximate the de jure political equality granted them in early Rhode Island and South Carolina. Even in an age of revolutionary republicanism, however, New York was singular.[56]

The Plantation Act illustrates advancement toward, and ambivalence about, making Jews citizens and attests to their relatively superior political status in the colonies. Parliament designed this bill to strengthen the settlements by naturalizing Protestants and Jews to increase immigration. Providing full economic, but not political, rights, naturalization was a middle ground between denization (already given Jews in several seventeenth-century colonies) and citizenship. Resistance in some provinces and previous exercise of these rights meant that few Jews (under sixty—mostly in New York and Pennsylvania) became naturalized. Nonetheless, London had significantly advanced civil legitimization of Jews.[57]

Naturalization applied only to Jews abroad, not those at home in England. When Parliament in 1753 legislated this procedure for the homeland, the bill aroused such ire that it was revoked within a year. Similar, if weaker, sentiment appeared in North America. Outside Massachusetts, New York, Pennsylvania, the Carolinas, New Jersey, Delaware, and possibly Maryland, objections obviated implementation. Recalcitrance was most flamboyant in Rhode Island, where Aaron Lopez, the preeminent Jew in that colony, was denied naturalization in defiance of the Act of 1740 on the grounds that a 1663 Rhode Island law restricted this status to Christians. Lopez and other Jews transferred their legal residence to Massachusetts or New York. Outraged by the Rhode Island Superior Court's rejection of his friend's petition for naturalization, Stiles pronounced it a "mortifying sentence and Judgement," that would "prevent their [Jews'] incorporating into any Nation, that they may continue a distinct people." The "opposition it [naturalization] has met with in Rh. Island, forebodes that the Jews will never become incorporated with the people of America."[58]

It is often mentioned in acclaim of American tolerance that Jews were not singled out for deprivation of civic rights. South Carolina Protestant dissenters in 1704 complained to Parliament that "Jews, Strangers, Sailors, Servants, Negroes, and almost every Frenchman in Craven and Berkeley Counties" voted in elections. Three-quarters of a century later a petition from Amherst County, Virginia, demanded that Catholics, "Jews, Turks and Infidels" be barred from government office. The proposition that inclusiveness dilutes bigotry has won considerable agreement though the contrary is equally plausible, namely that multiple prejudices may be mutually reinforcing. In any event, before independence only Rhode Island, Pennsylvania, and Delaware gave Protestant dissenters full political rights, and test oaths in these provinces disqualified atheists and Deists in addition to Jews. Catholics, blacks, and Indians nowhere enjoyed unfettered citizenship.[59]

Discrimination was sometimes precisely expressed in legislation and commentary. In 1723 James Logan of Pennsylvania disparaged a political rival as "an apostate Jew or fashionable Christian proselyte." After a bitterly contested election in 1737 the New York Assembly disenfranchised Jews. Addressing the legislature, Assemblyman William Smith, attorney for a defeated candidate, justified the action by arguing that Jews had crucified the Savior and that letting them vote compounded this abomination. Jews were also specifically targeted in Maryland in 1776, when Catholics but not Jews were made eligible for public office.[60]

During the Revolution, as in other crises, expressions of anti-Semitism multiplied. The Tory James Rivington satirized the Continental cause, in a 1774 issue of Rivington's N-Y Gazetteer, by announcing a bogus work entitled "Disappointment or the Sure Way to make a Patriot: Exemplified in the History of a Polish Jew." The Pennsylvania Evening Post, during the state constitutional debate of 1776, printed several letters advocating that Deists, Jews, Turks, Catholics, and other "enemies of Christ" be ineligible for public office, lest Pennsylvania become a bridgehead "for Antichrist" and "unsafe for Christians." Henry Melchior Muhlenberg, the foremost German Lutheran pastor of the colonial period, also feared that if the state constitution did not ordain Christianity as the civic religion "a Christian people" might be degraded under "rule by Jews" or some other depraved group. The drafters of the document heeded these imprecations by including a test oath disqualifying infidels from holding office. After the Massachusetts Constitution was ratified in 1780, the state Baptist leader

Isaac Backus, long a critic of Judaism, applauded the article that kept Jews from becoming Commonwealth officials. This particularly offensive provision uncommonly mandated a general allegiance to Christianity which ruled out Jews alone.[61]

Commercial, as well as constitutional, issues drew fire. "An American" (a Charleston merchant) wrote to the *Charlestown Gazette* in 1778 that the "Tribe of Israel" deserted Savannah, "after taking every advantage in trade," when "it was attacked by the enemy." They "fled here for an asylum with their ill-got wealth, dastardly turning their backs upon" Georgia. "Thus it will be in this State if it should ever be assailed by our enemies." Two days later in the *Gazette* appeared a rebuttal from "A real American."[62] Thus began the cycle of charge and denial that would become a crescendo in later wars. Stemming from wartime anxiety, slander of Jews for profiteering, cowardice, and treachery would recur in every major armed conflict.

Liberalization of ideology and behavior in the Age of Reason and the age of revolution and independence did not curb religious or political invective. A Calvinist theological text assigned at Yale described "the obstinate Jews" as "open foes of Christianity," who "deny the Trinity and the coming of the Messiah, and interpret carnally, what is spoken of Christ's Kingdom in the Prophets spiritually." In "the crucifying of Christ, it was Pilate's purpose to continue in the favour of Caesar, and of the Jews: the Jews drift was to satisfy their desire with hatred and revenge; but God's end was to redeem mankind."[63]

Calvinist intolerance persisted in the Great Awakening, a series of spiritual paroxysms from 1720 to 1750 led by Presbyterian, Congregationalist, and Dutch Reformed preachers. North America's original mass revival reiterated the Puritan millennial commitment that made Jews indispensable to the coming of the Heavenly Kingdom. Supplementing the dominant Calvinist voice in the Revival, prominent German Lutheran pastors reprimanded Jewry.[64]

America's most profound theologian, the revivalist preacher Jonathan Edwards, was a postmillennialist who awaited the temporal return of the Messiah. Recapitulating his Puritan heritage, the Massachusetts Congregationalist contemplated Old Testament Hebrews as "types" foreshadowing the agony and victory of the Messiah. Judaism, therefore, had no independent existence; its essence was christologically stipulative and its purpose was to be the imperfect instrument of Christian fulfillment.[65]

Preparatory to the reunion of errant Jewry and the Second Coming is Judaic wickedness and chastisement. The "Christian religion prevailing against the opposition of Jews and heathens," moved Edwards to "prophe[sy]" the "mutual slaughter of the Jews and heathen, the common enemies of the Christian faith, and persecutors of the Christian religion." Jewish "dispersion" was "dreadful and signal punishment of their unbelief." They have "continued a distinct nation, that they might continue a visible monument of his displeasure, for their rejecting and crucifying their Messiah." When the Jews "openly profess" Christ's "gospel," they reunite in their Holy Land as "a monument of God's wonderful grace and power in their calling and conversion."[66]

In *The Great Christian Doctrine of Original Sin Defended* (1758), Edwards again voiced traditional condemnation of Jews. He contrasted "particular [Mosaic] law" with "the law of nature" promulgated by the Redeemer and "written in the hearts . . . of all mankind." Israelites "boast[ed] of the[ir] law," but "it condemned them, and was an occasion of their being sinners in a higher degree, and more aggravated manner, and more effectually and dreadfully dead in and by sin agreeable to those words of Christ."[67]

The Messiah's martyrdom and the remorseless evil and retributive misery of his executioners, for Edwards, were the compelling themes in Original Sin. His "coming, and his doctrine and miracles . . . and the glorious things that attended," produced "an infinite increase in their wickedness. They crucified the Lord of Glory, with the utmost malice and cruelty, and persecuted his followers." This abomination, "contrary to all men," merely foreshadowed Jewish iniquity. They grew "worse, till they filled up the measure of their sin, and wrath came upon them to the uttermost." As "tokens of the divine abhorrence and indignation . . . The bigger part of the whole nation were slain, and the rest scattered abroad through the earth, in the most abject and forlorn circumstances." In "the same spirit of unbelief and malice against Christ and the gospel, and in their miserable dispersed circumstance, do they remain to this day."[68]

In the most famous sermon of the Great Awakening, "Sinners in the Hands of an Angry God" (1748), Edwards invoked for his flock "The vengeance of God on the wicked unbelieving Israelites" who refused "the means of grace." Muhlenberg, another Great Awakening evangelizer, from a Lutheran perspective scourged Jews for killing Jesus and his followers. Those who regretted their sin and wrongful creed would be saved; the rest were eternally doomed.[69]

Reproval was not a monopoly of revivalists. Identical sentiments resounded from election day pulpits, including a sermon preached by a Harvard College president, and from New England dissenters. Exemplifying the latter was the Baptist Backus, who decried Jewish law and ritual as a form of bondage, proclaimed Jewish rejection and murder of the Messiah as canceling the Lord's election of the Jews, and suggested that Judaism should disappear, having accomplished its divine task of paving the way for Christianity. Even Stiles, that admirer of Judaism and friend of Jews, mused in 1770 at a New York synagogue service, "How melancholy to behold an Assembly of Worshippers of Jehovah. Open and professed enemies to a crucified Christ."[70]

Clerical grumbling strayed from sacred concerns. "The Jews in general are said to be very strict and punctual in the observance of some of the traditionary ceremonies of their law," declared Rev. David McClure, an Anglican missionary educated at Yale and Dartmouth, "but hesitate not to defraud, when opportunity presents."[71]

Even Stiles expressed worldly rancor. Accusing Jewish merchants of violating the 1770 non-importation agreement against Britain and consequently causing Boston and Philadelphia to stop trading with Newport, he confided to his diary that "five or six Jews & three or four Tories may draw down Vengeance upon a country." Three months later he recorded more serious delinquencies, whose delusive, conspiratorial content smacked of later anti-Semitic accusations. He was convinced that a Jewish cabal had set up, with imperial government support, "a secret *Intelligence office* in London." With "Correspondents" in Boston and Newport, paid by the "Ministry" for the colonies, "this office boasted of having Intelligence of every Occurence of any consequence in America." After the outbreak of war Stiles again attacked Newport "Jews" for being "very officious in informing against the [patriotic] inhabitants."[72]

Ministerial reproach occasionally went beyond rhetorical rebuke. Boston's Protestant clergy in the 1720s forbade a marriage between a Jewish man and a Christian woman. The couple defied this attempt to revive an antique Christian ban against Jews. In 1782 in Philadelphia a congregation of the German Reformed sect, a Protestant denomination that had advocated the test oath in the state constitution of 1776, objecting to a temple being built on a lot next to their house of worship, also went back into history to rejuvenate a sixth-century papal decree against putting synagogues near churches.[73]

Anti-Semitism was conspicuous in eighteenth-century America. Historians have underestimated the influx of this virus because of its relatively low intensity—the infection seldom spread from denunciation to action—and its greater toxicity elsewhere. Yet Jews were subject to blatant worldly, as well as religious, abuse, usually verbal but sometimes more dangerous.

Commercial relations routinely evoked insult if a competitor was Jewish. Christian traders in Rhode Island and Connecticut employed the word "Jew" as an epithet against rivals of that faith. The New London businessman Andrew McKenzie, hearing in 1753 that a commercial correspondent had availed himself of the services of a Jew, criticized him for "being led by the nose by a faithless Jew whose nation sold their God for money, and crucified him afterwards." An entrepreneur, feeling duped in a transaction with the eminent Philadelphia merchant Michael Gratz in 1776, slandered Gratz's religion. James Kenny, a Quaker who traded with Indians in Pittsburgh during the 1760s, complained that a Jewish rival cheated Indians and sold them rum.[74]

More symptomatic of the instinctiveness of this response was defamation in the absence of a Jewish competitor. "I have almost turned Jew," wrote the patrician New York merchant Gerard G. Beekman about some vigorous bargaining he undertook in 1760. Fiction, as well as real life, stigmatized Jewish businessmen. The *Philadelphia Gazette* in 1753 carried a story about "A Jew pedlar" who tricks the wife of a customer into having sex with him. The seducer is, in turn, outwitted by the customer and his errant spouse, who destroy his goods. The villain in this tale exemplifies two medieval caricatures: the dishonest and lecherous Jew, and the trickster tricked, a sly Jew swindled by a Gentile.[75]

Random or spontaneous disparagement was the surest sign of obsessive prejudice. For Major Robert Rogers, a famed fighter in the French and Indian War and explorer of the Northwest Passage and also an embezzler, Rhode Island Jews were a "rascally set" who "infest[ed]" the province. In some Indians, Rogers discovered a "guilty Jewish cast." New York Jews were "selfish and knavish (and where they have an opportunity) an oppressive and cruel people."[76]

While Rogers spewed out contemporary venom, other bigots introduced slurs that would become future stereotypes. A 1749 letter in the *New-York Weekly Journal* anticipated the next century's censure of the Jewish nouveaux riches by ridiculing the extravagance of a Jewish family recently resident in the neighborhood and reporting the exclusion of these parvenus from the local social club. If the *Weekly Journal* article heralded future attitudes, the strategy at a 1768 trial in North Carolina reflected a historical grievance in attempting to impugn the testimony of a witness by calling him a Jew.[77]

An older recrimination, indicating greater hatred of and danger for the Jewish community, surfaced after a riot in 1768 in Frederick Town, Maryland. The spectacle of a mob of Nonconformist German settlers, reportedly led by a Jew, attacking the local Anglican parson provoked the comment that the alleged agitator was motivated by "the principles upon which his forefathers crucified our blessed Savior and stoned the apostles." This accusation also appeared in James Kenny's answer to an Indian's query about Christmas. Kenny explained that the holiday concerned the "Son of the God Spirit . . . who suffered the Jews to put him to death."[78] The anathema, transmitted from European to American folk belief, of the Christkilling and still homicidal Jew was indelibly imprinted in the Christian consciousness and reinforced by successive waves of immigrants from places of its inception.

Although fulmination did not, as in other times and places, rationalize and foment major repression, thought and action had some correspondence. From the seventeenth century until recently Sunday laws constituted a formidable economic nuisance for devout Jews. Although legally liable in many colonies, Jews were never prosecuted for not going to church on the Christian sabbath. Beginning in the 1650s, however, they were penalized for not observing the Lord's day of rest, worship, and contemplation.[79] Such legislation disadvantaged orthodox Jews, who could work neither on Saturday nor on Sunday, and were an intrusive reminder that even liberal communities demanded minimal obedience to Christian rituals.

Prejudice was more dramatically manifested in several edicts in Virginia and Georgia. In Virginia in 1705 an unusual departure from the equality generally accorded to Jews in colonial courts enjoined this minority, in addition to blacks, Catholics, and convicts, from testifying in trials. Provinces occasionally reverted to medieval ordinance to vent bigotry. When its legislature in 1705 and again in 1753 forbade Indians, blacks, and "any Jew, Moor, Mahometan, or other infidel" to own or hire Christian servants, the Old Dominion resurrected another anti-Semitic relic from the Dark Ages.[80]

Although possibly the most hospitable place for eighteenth-century Jewry, Georgia nearly adopted a policy of malicious intent unsurpassed in the later provincial period. The founding trustees of the settlement in 1733 urged deportation of Jews from Savannah, fearing their presence would inhibit immigration. Governor James Oglethorpe, over the trustees' objections, granted Jews plots of land. Reconsidering their earlier proposal, the trustees in 1737 gave a Jew a large loan to encourage the growing of grapes.[81] The clash between the London trustees and their executive in Georgia illustrates that reality in the provinces sometimes overruled bias in the imperial capital and that the colonies were better disposed toward Jews. The conflict between Georgia and London also reversed the sides of the same debate, conducted eighty years before, between old and New Amsterdam.

Death, the rite of passage over which religion was the supreme arbiter until its displacement by the medical profession, frequently provoked attacks on Jews. In 1743 a mob assaulted a Jewish funeral cortege in New York. Jewish graves were desecrated there and in Philadelphia. In 1762 and 1770 Savannah freeholders disputed the enlargement and government confirmation of a Jewish cemetery in the town commons. The petitioners "apprehend[ed] that no person would choose to buy or rent a house" near "a burial ground of any kind, particularly one belonging to a people who might be presumed from prejudice of education, to have imbibed principles entirely repugnant to those of our most holy religion." As the colonial age ended, hatred erupted in Rhode Island: the Newport synagogue was vandalized in 1773, and the Jewish cemetery two years later.[82]

Jews were especially vulnerable in territories ruled by Catholic powers, which would become part of the United States early in the next century. Here, like Protestants, Jews were legally excluded and subject to the Inquisition. None lived in Florida because their expulsion from Spain in 1492 covered the empire. In 1724 the French king, in an order to the governor of New Orleans to extend the West Indian Code Noir to Louisiana, made Catholicism the only tolerated religion and evicted Jews. In 1769, shortly after France ceded Louisiana to Spain, the new authorities expelled some Jews, and others were reluctant to enter because of the Inquisition. Nevertheless, these proscriptions, as in the North, were frequently breached toward the end of the colonial period, and Jews did dwell in the territory under French and Spanish sovereignty. Formal exclusion ended in 1789, when the Spanish governor was ordered not to disturb non-Catholic private worship and to expel the New Orleans–based inquisitor. Imposed to foster immigration from the United States, these measures still left Jews appreciably less free than their northern coreligionists.[83]

~

As Jews belatedly progressed toward sufferance in Louisiana, northward a new nation was emerging. The American Revolution differed markedly from the French and Russian upheavals in many ways, including its consequences for Jews. In France and Russia 1789 and 1917 transmuted Jews from despised and oppressed outsiders to legally recognized, if not popularly accepted, citizens. In the United States, Jews worshipped freely even before the Bill of Rights (1789) incorporated religious liberty and parity into the Constitution, and the freedom of conscience provision in the federal document did not prevent states from perpetuating provincial restrictions. Independence and nationhood thus brought little departure from the customary experience of American Jewry.

# ~ 4

# Progress and Problems in the Young Republic

Most historians find a quiescence of anti-Semitism between the early American republic and the Civil War. In contrast with slower progress in Europe and with later American circumstances, Jews fared well during this period in the United States. Even so, the era yields evidence of persistent prejudice and periodic outbreaks of discrimination.

## Europe

As the colonies achieved nationhood two seemingly irresistible forces emerged in western civilization and united to ameliorate conditions for the Jews. The Age of Reason and the rise of the nation-state did indeed bring improvement, especially concerning legal rights and during the revolutionary era. But the light of reason was a flickering beacon and the age of insurgency unleashed a strident nationalism whose apocalyptic particularism boded ill for Jews.

Affirmations of individual liberty, human equality and perfectibility, and the primacy of reason contradicted traditional, theological, mystical, and exceptionalist bases of Jew hatred. Enlightenment thought, however, also compounded bigotry. The natural rights principles of philosophers like the Encyclopedists Denis Diderot and Baron d'Holbach left undisturbed their disdain of Judaism. "If the blood of Jesus Christ cried for vengeance against the Jews," wrote Diderot in 1746, "'tis because in shedding it they turned a deaf ear to Moses and the Prophets who foretold the Messiah." Reflecting Enlightenment ambivalence in *Rameau's Nephew* (1774), Diderot featured

114

contrasting Jewish characters. An honest and trusting Jew, who is robbed and betrayed by a renegade Christian, is counterbalanced by a stereotypical lecherous, dishonest, showy, upstart Jew, always looking to cheat Christians and observing the letter—but not the spirit—of the law.[1]

Holbach's feelings were less ambivalent: "Jews" were "the most stupid, credulous, savage, unsociable people that ever existed on earth." Scorning all religions as fanatical and superstitious perversions of human imagination, the atheistic Baron, in an attitude typical of Enlightenment enthusiasts, charged that "Christianity is but a reformed Judaism," and asserted that "even now the remainder of this unfortunate nation is looked upon as the vilest and most contemptible of all the earth, having no country, no superiority." Voltaire, the most vicious critic among the Deists, shared these views and called Jews clannish, fraudulent, and avaricious.[2]

English and German rationalists agreed with these ideas. British Deists attributed Christian superstition to Judaic primitivism. In Germany as in France, some Enlightenment thinkers defended Jews and some disparaged them. The rationalist theologian and Bible critic Johann David Michaelis castigated Jews for atavistic worship, moral deficiency, and tribalism. Immanuel Kant condemned Jews for being exclusive, contentious, usurious, and greedy, and the "Judaic spirit" for rigid legalism that stifled reason, contradicted natural law, killed the genius of religion, and was morally inferior to Christianity. He recommended "euthanasia" for Judaism.[3]

Such sentiments demonstrate that values of reason, secularism, universality, and modernism harmonized with and could reinforce beliefs about Judaic obsoleteness, aloofness, particularism, superstition, and barbarity. Proponents of Reason persisted in denouncing Jews for clinging to their creed, but reprimanded them for renouncing secular, not theological, truth. As Emil L. Fackenheim has put it, modern thinkers invited Jews back into history and society on condition that as believing Jews they remain outside. Rationalists and redeemers, proclaiming different versions of universalism and ethical preemption, nevertheless agreed on making these principles into demands that Jews reject their creed and forfeit independent existence.[4]

Not all reactions of the illuminati were negative, however. Even Voltaire could express tolerance when opposing religious persecution. Jean Jacques Rousseau called ancient Hebrews "the vilest of all people," but deemed all creeds equal because all men were equal and hence opposed conversion and excoriated Christians for vilifying Jews. Diderot also argued against religious oppression and praised Jewish wisdom and morality. Kant held contradictory ideas about Jews, whose freedom of thought impressed this advocate of liberty of conscience. Enlightenment doctrines fostered the favorable portrayal of Jewish characters in the theater and literature of France, England, and Germany. Deistic and natural rights concepts also contributed to the decline of sinister mystifications of the Jews. The Wandering Jew, now journeying through the Age of Reason, acquired the benign persona of a sage.[5]

Behavior, as well as attitude, improved. Citizenship for French Jews resulted partly from revolutionary dedication to the rights of man. Allegiance to natural rights also helped inspire Austrian Emperor Joseph II to free Jews from restrictions and humiliations going back to the Middle Ages. But his edict was limited to officially tolerated Jews with rights of free residence, thus excluding most Jews in the empire; certain vocations were still closed even to the privileged elite; and Jews could not become citizens. Napoleon, another enlightened despot, simultaneous betrayer and acolyte of the Republic of Reason, emancipated Jews in countries he defeated. Through his victories and influence Jews obtained civil rights in the 1790s in Italy, Holland, and Switzerland, during the next decade in French vassal states in Germany, and in 1812 in Prussia. Prussia, however, limited freedom to "privileged Jews," who were now able to own land and enter professions but barred from public office. Napoleon did not act with unblemished liberalism: personally disliking Jews, in 1808 he accommodated popular demand by hampering Jewish movement, settlement, trade, and financial transactions.[6]

The most dangerous aspect of the French emperor's policy was his advocacy of assimilation. He shared the basic response toward Jews of believers in natural rights and the revolutionary cult of reason, insisting that Jews relinquish their separateness and beliefs to assume citizenship in a secular state. In the First National Assembly on September 28, 1789, a liberal aristocrat from Paris set the terms of the debate and anticipated those of emancipation in 1791 when he argued that "There cannot be a nation within a nation. One must refuse everything to the Jews as a nation but one must give them everything as individuals; they must become citizens." The debates reflected anger expressed in the Estates-General "Cahiers," which seethed with objections to Jews as greedy, underhanded business competitors. Hostility erupted in the Alsace pogroms of 1789, but First Republic repression of Judaism was part of a Jacobin crusade against all religion.[7]

Citizenship for Jews was part of the demolition of the *ancien régime*. Contractual obligations among different classes and corporations, each group having a separate legal status that stemmed from feudalism, gave way to citizenship, which made most French inhabitants equal under the laws of the state. Jews were included in a rationalized system of uniform national status. Emergent nationalism curbed Christian and other historical sources of anti-Semitism but engendered other perils. Secularization and nationalism, reversing the priorities of western theology, gave precedence to this world over the next. Christianity could accommodate earthly Judaism because the Jews would ultimately be converted in the more important eternal realm of the spirit. Proponents of nationalism, or socialism for that matter, could not indulge in such tolerance. For them, Jews had to be absorbed, evicted, or eliminated. Granting citizenship to Jews raised the expectation that they would be assimilated into the national culture. If the Jewish minority was perceived as unassimilable and exclusive, and when a weakened Christianity no longer provided millennial guarantees of survival, its civil rights could be withdrawn, or it could be expelled or otherwise eliminated from the state. In all countries save Holland, civil rights ordinances for Jews were repealed in the reaction against the Age of Reason, Revolution, and Napoleon: in Austria during the 1790s and elsewhere at the Congress of Vienna (1815).[8]

Anti-Semitism predominated in the church, drama, fiction, popular culture, and economic life despite some inclinations toward tolerance in the Enlightenment rear guard and early-to-mid-century liberalism and Romanticism. Vicious caricature reached a post-Elizabethan peak in early Victorian England, when Charles Dickens's *Oliver Twist* (1838) featured filthy, ugly, cringing, miserly Fagin, the most memorable Jewish monster since Shylock.[9]

Jews were also assailed from the left, an attack launched during the Revolution of 1789 and intensified in France during the 1820s and 1830s, when the utopian socialist and communitarian Charles Fourier reviled Jews as ruthless, unreconstructible capitalists.[10] A more ominous ideological portent was rehabilitation of the fictional Jewish plot to rule the world. Napoleon sparked the renewal of this rumor by convening an Assembly of (Jewish) French Notables in Paris in 1806 and again in 1807 to satisfy himself that Jews were loyal and assimilated Frenchmen and to stop money lending. Royalist émigrés interpreted these meetings as an anti-Christian cabal—especially since the emperor called the 1807 body "the Great Sanhedrin," after the high court of ancient Israel. Austrian anti-Semites accordingly claimed that Napoleon was a henchman of the Jews.

A variant of such paranoia was suspicion of a conspiracy of Jews, Masons, Deists, and regicidal republicans to rule the world by overthrowing Christianity and aristocracy.[11]

Napoleon's bestowing of political rights on Jews in the imperial and satellite territories was regarded, especially in Germany, as foreign subversion of national solidarity. When romanticism became the dominant cultural mode and then merged with nationalism, the romanticists, like their deistic predecessors, were divided over the "Jewish Question." They were usually more anti-Semitic, however, seeing Jews as incompatible with the organic unity that they exalted as the fulfillment of Gothic grandeur and volkish spirit. They also resorted to conventional charges of avarice, separateness, remorseless deicide, and overall sinfulness.[12]

In this spirit, the statist philosopher and Christian apologist Georg Wilhelm Friedrich Hegel berated Judaism as enslaved by sterile law and Jews as aloof and fanatically stubborn and thus inclined to form a state within a state. Jews were a "fossil nation," a "parasite race," yet Hegel believed these and other deficiencies might be overcome if Jews were given citizenship. Another nationalist thinker, Johann Gottlieb Fichte, advocated conceding elementary human rights to Jews but denying them citizenship because their creed was "founded on a hatred of mankind."[13]

Bigotry fomented discrimination. Prussian peasants and burghers opposed the 1812 emancipation law, and between 1815 and 1841 privileges of Jews in that kingdom were gradually curtailed. During the post-1814 conservative resurgence in Germany emancipation was revoked and assaults on Jews increased. In the infamous "Hep Hep" urban pogroms of 1819 Jews were beaten, their property and synagogues damaged, and their expulsion demanded. Anti-Jewish riots recurred in France and Germany, triggered by the successful uprising of 1830 against Bourbon restoration. In that turbulent year, Jews were also victimized in eastern Europe. In Poland, during and after the Polish revolution against Russia, Jewish insurgents were segregated into special military and police units because they were considered pro-Russian enemies of the revolution. Similar suspicion of treachery fell on German Jews in 1819, suspected of aiding France, and on Jews in France and central and eastern Europe in 1848, slandered as German agents. Nineteenth-century European crises evoked the notion that Jews were at best incapable of loyalty and at worst plotting against their nation of residence.[14]

Measured against struggles of their European coreligionists American Jews had dramatic advantages in emancipation and participation in quasi-public and honorific institutions. Even comparatively liberal England and intermittently enlightened France conceded such gains belatedly, conditionally, or inconstantly. Jews in other nations encountered greater obstacles. During the 1790s and early 1800s the numbers of Jews permitted to live in Vienna were limited, and not until 1838–1840 could Jews settle everywhere in Hungary. Commercial and vocational as well as residential rights were curbed. In Prussia and Austria, for example, Jews were excluded from certain trades and professions.[15]

Eastward, where the majority of world Jewry now dwelled, the situation was worse. In Romania Jews could not rent land except in towns or serve in public office; they would not acquire full citizenship until after World War II. Conditions for Jews in Poland reversed the upward course observed in America and western Europe. Between 1772 and 1795, when Poland was partitioned, long-term enmity from the peasantry, the nobility, the church, and commercial competitors left the Jews even more beleaguered than their Gentile countrymen. Blood libels, restrictions on residence and real estate purchases, exclusion from craft and merchant guilds, and imposition of special taxes continued to undermine Jews during the nineteenth century.[16]

By 1814 two-thirds of world Jewry lived in Russia, the vast majority confined to the "Pale of Settlement," former Polish territories where most Jews had dwelled before partition. A similar coalition of hostile forces—Russian Orthodox clergy, peasants, aristocrats, traders, and artisans—perpetuated old miseries under new sovereignty. Jews were restricted in settlement and occupation and drafted into the army, where many were forcibly converted. Display of skullcaps and side curls was outlawed or taxed. Jews were legally forbidden to have Christian servants or build synagogues near churches; their books were censored, and presumed anti-Christian texts were burned. These outrages were compounded by repeated accusations of ritual murder.[17]

## America

### From Tolerance toward Equality

Compared to England and Europe, the United States significantly advanced western Jewry's struggle for freedom. Special circumstances persisted after independence and combined with Enlightenment liberalism and the newly formed nation's zeal for reform to improve conditions for American Jews. A legacy from the colonial era was that Jews never lived in enclosed communities governed mostly by their own laws and leaders. American society permitted Jews to mingle with other groups, a situation facilitating assumption of full citizenship.

There were still very few Jews in America at this time. Given the rudimentary state of statistics and demographic records before the mid-nineteenth century, calculations of the Jewish segment are necessarily inexact, but its minuteness is indisputable. In the 1750s approximately 500 Jews lived in the colonies. Estimates for 1790 range from 1,300–1,500 to 2,000 (0.04–0.06 percent of the population), with the lower figures more likely. The numbers increased to about 2,700–3,000 in the next thirty years (under 0.03 percent of the population) and plausibly doubled between 1820 and 1830. In 1840, after an influx from Germany, the Jewish population possibly totaled 15,000.[18]

These small numbers probably contributed little to the relative benignity of American attitudes. Whatever may be the case for other outgroups, past and present experience on both sides of the Atlantic contradicts the argument that Jews are tolerated until their numbers reach a critical mass that gives them negative visibility. Long after leaving England Jews were detested there, and their return was only grudgingly accepted. Nor did the annihilation of central and eastern European Jewry still anti-Semitism in that area. In the young United States, frequent criticism was directed at the infinitesimal cluster of Jewish residents. Bigotry increased with the size of this enclave until World War I, but dramatically intensified from the 1920s until the end of World War II—despite cessation of mass Jewish immigration. Conversely, although the number of Jews in the United States remained stable, hostility drastically declined between 1947 and 1980.

The Age of Reason is a more likely explanation of the relative quiescence of this prejudice than demographic invisibility. In America as in Britain and Europe, related doctrines of Deism, natural rights, individual liberty, human perfectionism, and rationalism worked against anti-Semitism. Beginning in 1740, the writings of John Locke were used as college texts. Between the 1770s and the 1790s, Locke, Voltaire, Rousseau, and Thomas Paine were widely read both inside and outside colleges. A domestic variety of Deists, rationalists, and believers in natural rights, most notably Ethan Allen, Benjamin Rush, Benjamin Franklin, and Thomas Jefferson, also flowered in the new world. Although the French Revolution made Enlightenment principles anathema to Federalists, the rise of another revolutionary republic reinforced these ideas among many Democratic-Republicans.[19]

New York in 1777 was the first state in the western world to confer total citizenship upon the Jews. The second provision for full emancipation was Article 6 of the U.S. Constitution, which ruled out religious tests for federal office or trust. The First Amendment prohibited a national religious establishment and interference with liberty of conscience. Although the original state constitutions—formulated during the Revolution or carried over from colonial times—also proclaimed unfettered worship, all states but New York curbed rights for Jews. Around the time of ratification of the federal Constitution most states required taxes to support Christian denominations and/or religious oaths that excluded Jews from government posts. New Hampshire, Massachusetts, Connecticut, Maryland, and South Carolina had established churches. Only Protestants could hold office in New Jersey. Connecticut discriminated against non-Congregationalists, atheists, Catholics, and Jews. North Carolina required state officials to accept the divine inspiration of the New Testament and prohibited Jews, Quakers, atheists, and sometimes Catholics from holding office. Eleven of the thirteen original states limited officeholders to Christians or Protestants.

Between the 1780s and 1830s these restraints were eliminated except in New Jersey, North Carolina, Rhode Island, and New Hampshire, and were absent from the fundamental charters of newly admitted states. From 1789 to 1792, for example, Delaware, Pennsylvania, South Carolina, and Georgia, impelled by Enlightenment ideas and postrevolutionary fervor for reform, enfranchised Jews.[20]

As in colonial times, Jews were sometimes in government service despite constitutional proscription. Acquisition of civic rights, however, did not inevitably secure total equality. Jews occupied high public posts in Georgia, but only judges and Christian ministers could legally perform marriages there. After 1818 Connecticut disestablished the Congregational Church and Jews could hold office, but the new state constitution granted full citizenship rights only to members of Christian denominations. Political progress notwithstanding, early-nineteenth-century Jews were allowed to practice law only in Pennsylvania, Virginia, South Carolina, and New York. Enthusiasts of freedom of conscience advocated unqualified rights for religious minorities, and many people opposed federal interference in these matters. However, most Americans remained uncommitted to equality for Jews and Catholics, wanted to be governed by Protestants, and were willing in some states and on some issues to legalize this preference.[21]

American Jews immediately implemented total or qualified constitutional conferrals of rights and assumed government positions decades before such opportunities were available in other countries. During the 1780s Jews were elected to the Richmond, Virginia, city council and the Georgia assembly; in 1801 David Emanuel (generally thought to be a Jew) became governor of Georgia; Moses Levy was recorder of Philadelphia in 1802 and shortly thereafter became a judge. Samuel D. Franks sat on an early-nineteenth-century Pennsylvania state court. In 1809 a Jew was elected to the North Carolina House of Commons. He avoided the required pledge of the divinity of Christ and took his seat without betraying his creed. The next year a Jew became a New York State senator, in 1818 a Jew served as recorder and acting mayor of Richmond, and in 1825 a Jew presided over the Baltimore city council. In South Carolina, Jews served in the legislature beginning in 1796 and as state treasurer between 1817 and 1822. Jews were commissioners, aldermen, and mayors in Charleston, Georgetown, and elsewhere in South Carolina.[22]

American Jews set precedents in many public and quasi-public fields. Ineligible for military service, or at least discouraged from bearing arms and prevented from obtaining commissions, in Prussia and other nations, from the Revolution onward Jews in America were in elite militia companies and served as regular army and navy officers. The original class at West Point (1802) included Jews, as did those of 1823 and 1832. Well before Jews entered English and most European universities, they enrolled in Yale (1809) and Harvard (1837), and a distinguished Manhattan rabbi was a Columbia College regent and trustee between 1784 and 1815. Jews were masters of high-status Masonic lodges, founders of the New York City and Georgia medical societies, and members and officers of prestigious professional organizations, social clubs, and cultural societies such as Richmond's Commonwealth Club, the Philadelphia Club, the Philadelphia Dancing Assembly, the Philadelphia Academy of Fine Arts, the Philadelphia County Medical Society, the Richmond and Boston Atheneums, the Charleston Medical Society, the Literary and Historical Society of Charleston, St. Andrews Society in Charleston, the Charleston Antient Artillery Company, and the Virginia Historical Society. Offspring of rich Jewish mercantile families had little trouble gaining acceptance from the east coast urban and rural gentry. Marriage with prominent Gentile clans was extensive, although apostasy in these unions invariably meant that the Jewish spouse adopted the Protestant (usually Episcopal) faith.[23]

Renowned figures of the Age of Reason in America defended religious liberty and often supported Jews. Benjamin Franklin, along with a coterie of local patricians, in 1788 subscribed to a fund for a new synagogue in Philadelphia. "The Rabbi of the Jews locked in the arms of two ministers of the gospel," said Benjamin Rush, commenting on Philadelphia's Fourth of July parade in 1788, "could not have been a more happy emblem" of "that section of the new constitution which opens all its power and offices . . . to worthy men of every religious sect."[24]

Thomas Jefferson, America's preeminent Enlightenment thinker and fighter for freedom of conscience, bore a primary responsiblity for the "Act for Establishing Religious Freedom in Virginia." Proposed by him to the House of Burgesses in 1785, it forbade compulsory denominational atten-dance or support.[25] The sage of Monticello proclaimed while president, as well as in retirement, that choice of worship was not subject to govern-mental interference. He also assured his Jewish correspondents of his high regard for their creed, regret for persecution of their people by misguided Christians, and hope that religious equality would be inscribed in American hearts, as well as in national law.[26]

Enlightenment figures were not alone in advocating religious freedom or praising Judaism and American Jews. Unlike European political leaders of the time, U.S. statesmen repeatedly expressed such sentiments, thus enlisting their celebrity on behalf of Jews. In this respect the first four pres-idents, also heroes in the formation of the republic, became exemplars of tolerance. John Adams "insist[ed] that . . . fate ordained the Jews to be the most essential instrument for civilizing the nations" by "propagat[ing] to all mankind the doctrine of a supreme intelligent, wise, almighty sovereign of the universe, which I believe to be the great essential principle of all morality, and consequently of all civilization." Adams found among Jewish acquaintances "liberal minds, as much honor, probity, generosity and good breeding as any I have known in any sect of religion or philosophy." Jews collectively should "be admitted to all the privileges of citizens in every country of the world. This country has done much. I wish it may do more; and annul every narrow idea in religion, government, and commerce." With typical asperity, Adams assured a correspondent that he disliked Jews no more than any other nationality or people.[27]

James Madison, Jefferson's chief collaborator in legislating religious freedom in Virginia, memorialized the General Assembly in 1785 to pro-scribe state sponsorship or subsidy of any sect. Years later, as an ex-pres-ident, he acclaimed the "good citizenship of such as have been most distrusted and oppressed elsewhere, a happy illustration of the safety and success" of the "just and benignant policy, equal laws protecting equal rights." These principles, he wrote to a Jewish correspondent, were "the best guarantee" of "love of country" and "good will among citizens of every religious denomination." They were "necessary to social harmony" and "advancement of truth." "The account you give of the Jews of your Congregation," he continued, "brings them fully within the scope of these observations."[28]

Jefferson's and Madison's efforts on behalf of religious freedom influenced and reflected broader opinion in Virginia. In the legislative battle several county petitions advocated tolerance of Jews, and Amherst County repudiated its 1779 plea for exclusion of "Jews, Turks and Infidels" from public life.[29]

The substance and timing of his actions and his fame as founding father made George Washington the paramount model for religious tolerance and affirmation of American Jewry. Replying to encomiums from synagogues in Philadelphia, New York, Charleston, Richmond, Savannah, and Newport, Washington expressed commitment to freedom of belief and his respect for Jews and Judaism. These communications particularly reinforced the principles he avowed because they were publicly voiced while he was president and praised contemporary Jews instead of Old Testament Israelites.

"For happily the government of the United States, which gives to bigotry no sanction, to persecution no assistance, requires only that they who live under its protection should demean themselves as good citizens," responded Washington in 1790 to the head of the Newport congregation who had thanked him for visiting the temple. Like other champions of tolerance, Washington linked interfaith equality with respect for Jews. "May the children of the stock of Abraham who dwell in this land," he told the Newport congregation, "continue to merit and enjoy the good will of the other inhabitants."[30]

Washington's behavior, even more than his sentiments, enhanced respect for Judaism. The president's visit to a synagogue conferred civic recognition on American Jews. Another emblematic legitimization occurred at the Fourth of July parade in Philadelphia in 1788, when Christian and Jewish clergymen marched arm in arm. At the feast following the parade a kosher table was laid for Jewish citizens.[31] Thus began the gradual admission of Judaism into the civic religion of America, an interfaith parity now mandating every major national celebration or political convention to be blessed by a rabbi, a priest, and a minister.

The postrevolutionary generation, perhaps because of the passing of the Age of Reason, a decline in political innovation and idealism, or diminished zeal—especially in the elite—to differentiate itself from Europe and England, less frequently and forcefully proclaimed religious equality and praised the Jews. Further progress toward absorption into the civic religion was nonetheless evident in 1829, when a Richmond rabbi gave the invocation at the Virginia Constitutional Convention. Three years later Henry Clay disavowed anti-Semitic intent in alluding to someone in a U.S. Senate debate as "the Jew." Clay reassured Solomon Etting that no offense was meant against his people and that "I judge men not by their nation, religion etc., but by their individual conduct."[32]

Support also came from clergymen, local officials, and other Christians in New York, Philadelphia, Charleston, Newport, Richmond, and Cincinnati, who attended synagogue services, especially consecration ceremonies, and gave gifts to Jewish congregations. Christopher Gadsden, a leader during the Revolution and a prominent merchant, donated old Hebrew books to Congregation Beth Elohim of Charleston as a testament of "respect" and "regard" for that body. A few ministers, including the Episcopal Bishop of New York and the Charleston aristocrat Edward Rutledge, rector of Episcopalian parishes in South Carolina and New England and assistant professor of moral philosophy at the University of Pennsylvania, praised modern Jews. Sectarian tolerance in Manhattan went even further: Rabbi Gershom Mendes Seixas of Congregation Shearith Israel occasionally preached in St. Paul's (Episcopal) Chapel.[33]

New York and Charleston, the two largest centers of Jewish settlement in the United States between 1790 and 1830, were the sites of important steps toward parity for Jews—providing persuasive evidence against the contention that anti-Semitism rises as the number of Jews increases. New York's 242 Jews in 1790 and 550 in 1820 respectively composed 0.73 percent and 0.40 percent of the city's population.[34] Though small in number and share of the population this was the second largest American Jewish enclave. Its relative prominence did not preclude Seixas from being the first rabbi to preach in an American Christian pulpit and the first Jewish trustee of an American college. Over a century would pass before a second Jew would serve as a Columbia College trustee.

Greater evidence of interfaith equality appeared in 1811, when New York's mayor DeWitt Clinton drew up and sent to the state legislature a memorial for a charity school run by Congregation Shearith Israel. The legislature granted the Polonies Talmud Torah the same privileges it conferred upon Protestant and Catholic parochial institutions, and the city council made payments retroactive to the school's beginning.[35] Inclusion with other religious charities was a gesture that went beyond individual appreciation of, or patrician benevolence toward, Jews. Positive institutional interaction between Jewish and official, Gentile-dominated organizations endorsed Jews as citizens.

Jews were even more visible in Charleston, where 188 believers in 1790 constituted 2.5 percent of the population. During the 1790s the Jewish enclave expanded much faster than its New York counterpart and Charleston had the biggest contingent in the nation. By 1820, 674 Jews made up 5.0 percent of Charleston's inhabitants. If relatively high numbers and consequent negative visibility created animosity, they would have done so in antebellum Charleston. Yet Jews there never even lived in a religiously separate neighborhood. Residential integration, widespread officeholding, membership in elite organizations, and acceptance by leading citizens indicate that Charlestonians were exceptionally tolerant. When Beth Elohim Synagogue was dedicated in 1794, three years after the state constitution was amended to provide full religious liberty, the *South Carolina State-Gazette* applauded the decline of anti-Semitism and the fact that Jews "are here admitted to the full privileges of citizenship." In 1812 Governor Henry Middleton apologized to Congregation Beth Elohim for leaving Jews out of his Thanksgiving Day proclamation. The patrician planter assured "his fellow citizens" that calling exclusively upon Christian denominations to celebrate the holiday had been an unintended slight.[36]

Favorable notices also appeared in newspapers, which were closer to, better reflectors of, and possibly of greater influence upon the public than was the attitude of elites. The *New York Commercial Advertiser* in 1822 welcomed Jewish immigrants because their "wealth and enterprise" advanced the "interests of the United States." "[P]articipating in the blessings of liberty," the newcomers had "every inducement to become valuable members of society." A few years later the editor of the *Virginia (Constitutional) Whig* admired Jews for being proud and surviving two-thousand years of oppression, praised freedom of religion in America, and asserted that Jews had an equal right to be Americans. Accordingly, he denounced anti-Semitism and inherited guilt and punishment for the crucifixion.[37] When the bill to extend full political rights to Jews in Maryland suffered defeat in 1819, the legislature was censured by Democratic-Republican journals in Maryland, Philadelphia, Charleston, and elsewhere for fostering "bigotry," subverting America's mission as "the asylum for the oppressed," and "dishonor[ing] . . . Our National charter, our various state constitutions."[38]

Other publications directed at general audiences also praised American Jews. Hannah Adams, the nation's first female professional writer and author of *The History of the Jews from the Destruction of Jerusalem to the Nineteenth Century* (1812), the earliest American book on that subject, lauded Jews for unity and perseverance through their troubles and rebuked Christianity for persecuting its parental faith. A founder of the Female Society of Boston and Vicinity for Promoting Christianity among the Jews (1816–1843), Adams had an agenda and a perspective that sometimes clashed with total equality and empathy for non-Christian beliefs. Less compromising (and less compromised) in advocating equity was S. G. Goodrich's *The Fourth Reader* (1839), a primary school text. "Lesson LXIX" introduced a passage from *The Merchant of Venice,* frequently included in such anthologies, with the unusual disclaimer that it was not meant to reproach and that Jews could be good members of society and, like everyone, should be judged by acts not by preconceptions.[39]

Popular fiction and belles lettres in both the Old and New Worlds conventionally portrayed Jews unsympathetically, but the demonization customary in medieval and early modern writings, plays, and folktales was undermined by Enlightenment ideas. As America made the transition from province to federal republic, the literature of England, France, and Germany, whose cultures had the strongest influence upon and closest relationship to the young nation, began to portray Jews less negatively. Antagonism was now less habitually savage and more often, though still infrequently, interspersed with neutral or positive representations.[40]

Among the positive works, *Ivanhoe* (1817) had the strongest impact in America, particularly in the South. Sir Walter Scott's novel featured a hook-nosed, elderly, rich, obsequious, cowardly, suspicious, stubborn, shrewd, parsimonious, mercenary patriarch and his daughter, the exotic, beautiful, sensuous, generous, and proud Hebrew maiden. While not omitting negative literary conventions, Scott explained Isaac of York's vices as responses to interminable and severe oppression of his people and himself, especially promoted by fanatical medieval Catholicism. The author also emphasized Isaac's admirable traits: family loyalty and love for his daughter, Rebecca, outweigh an obsession with money and survival. Grateful to Ivanhoe for saving Isaac's life, father and daughter rescue the hero. Isaac is basically kind, in crisis he overcomes timidity, and he and Rebecca would give up their lives rather than convert. Moreover, Scott attributes praiseworthy qualities, such as intrepid tenacity in crisis and loyalty to Judaism, to all Jews.[41]

Jewish rogues were sometimes sympathetically portrayed in the New World. In the 1752 Williamsburg performance of *The Merchant of Venice,* Shylock was the first Jewish character portrayed on the American stage. In this initial professional production in America of a Shakespearean play, the moneylender was almost certainly depicted by the British touring company as a harsh, vindictive figure. The English actor George Frederick Cooke's Shylock, diabolic, enraged, and vengeful, was a box office and critical success in 1810–1812 in New York, Boston, and Philadelphia. But another renowned British thespian, Edmund Kean, played the usurer as a person of mixed and justifiable motives instead of a fiend. He acted this version before approving New York audiences in 1820–21. Junius Brutus Booth, the premier American tragedian of the period, made Shylock a guardian of Hebrew law and grandeur. This favorable depiction was possibly motivated by Booth's belief that he had Jewish ancestry.[42]

American writers also demonstrated positive feelings about Jews, or, at least, supported freedom of conscience. The New Yorker Philip Freneau, a Jeffersonian Republican editor and poet and advocate of the French Revolution and the light of reason, in "Robert Slender Argueth with the Parson" (1800), ridiculed intolerance and state interference in matters of conscience by satirizing a fictional Presbyterian pastor who argued that false worshippers, Catholics and Jews, had no right to dispute Protestant truth.[43]

The first American Jew in fiction appeared in Charles Brockden Brown's *Arthur Merwyn* (1799–1800). A journalist as well as a novelist, Brown was the nation's first professional author. His gothic romance features the conventional Jewess, graceful, noble, altruistic, dark, and beautiful, with lustrous and piercing eyes. "Her nation has suffered too much by the inhuman antipathies of religious and political faction," remarks the hero. Against these sentiments, however, must be weighed the heroine's concealment of her Jewishness and description of her father: "He had few of the moral or external qualities of Jews; for I suppose there is some justice in the obloquy that follows them so closely."[44]

In the next generation, William Ware, a Unitarian clergyman and son of the noted Unitarian minister and Harvard professor Henry Ware, wrote a trilogy (*Zenobia,* 1837; *Aurelian,* 1838; *Julian,* 1841) on the struggles of the early Christians. These popular novels exploited bourgeois fascination with the exotic East and reinforced the notion of Christianity as the supremely noble and true faith beset by vindictive Jews and heathens. Although the books charge that Jews persecute Christians because they consider any worshipper of the Messiah "a rival—a usurper—a rebel," the major Jewish character is lauded. Isaac the Jew, a peddler in Rome, is wise, loyal, good hearted, honest, and courageous. Hatred of Christianity and denial of Christ does not prevent him from loving and aiding Christians as human beings. He never recants Judaism, and he declares that his deeds belie the image of Jews as usurious extorters, nefarious wizards, and ritual murderers.[45]

If *Zenobia* and *Aurelian* contained a Jewish protagonist who denounced anti-Semitism, William Gilmore Simm's *Pelayo: A Story of the Goth* (1838) bordered on the philo-Semitic. The Charlestonian Simms, the foremost antebellum southern author, apparently imbibed the tolerance of his city. Unlike Ware, Simms suggested no invidious comparisons between Judaism and Christianity and no christocentric evaluation of tensions between the religions. A historical romance of eighth-century Spain, yet another setting underscoring the exotic appeal of Hebrews, *Pelayo* featured the standard aged patriarch, Melchior of the Desert, and his virginal, gentle, beautiful, dark-eyed, and raven-tressed daughter, Thryza. But Simms departed from literary stereotype by portraying Melchior as a brave commander leading Jews in battle against Gothic tyranny. In another break with tradition, he depicted the Jewish villain as betraying, rather than confirming, his heritage. *Pelayo* conforms with the predominant view of Judaism only when Thryza displays an affinity for Christian doctrine and dies with a cross in her hand. But Simms weakens the conversion theme, virtually a ritual in this genre, by noting that she seized the cross unconsciously.[46]

Fiction of the early republic reflected the comparatively favorable attitudes toward Jews. References to Jews were few and contemporary Jewish characters were even fewer, an indication that Americans were not obsessed with Jews. Sparser still were the types of diabolic representations abundant in Europe. When Jews appeared, even negatively, authors sometimes noted that interminable oppression produced flawed types and that Jews, at least in Europe, were downtrodden. In addition to mentioning foreign bigotry, the diplomat and newspaper editor Theodore Sedgwick Fay, in *Sidney Clifton; or, Vicissitudes in Both Hemispheres* (1839), which featured a stereotyped Jewish villain, uncommonly observed that Jews were socially discriminated against in the United States.[47]

## Anti-Semitism, 1790–1840

Progress toward full acceptance was far less uniform and certain than appears from a superficial marking of milestones along an alleged climb to equality. The Holocaust and dramatic advances made by American Jewry after World War II encouraged Americans to judge the domestic record by the current and possibly impermanent situation. From this understandable and seductive perspective derives a tendency to exaggerate positive and minimize negative aspects of the Jewish experience in pre–Civil War America.

Age of Reason republicanism and the successful struggle for political and religious parity in the federal and many state constitutions are important signs of America's unique accommodation of Jews. But exploration of the very forces earnestly disposed toward freedom and citizenship for Jews reveals the intense conflict over, and the elusive realization of, these aspirations.

The Enlightenment enthusiast Benjamin Rush, for example, a scientist, Continental Congressman, signer of the Declaration of Independence, and social reformer, revealed views of Judaism shaped by Christian apologetics. He "anticipated the time foretold by the prophets when this once-beloved race of men shall again be restored to the divine favor and when they shall unite with Christians" in "praises of a common and universal savior." Belief in redemption of the estranged Hebrews and in Pentateuchal prefigurations of the Prince of Peace led Rush to endorse another tenet of Christian triumphalism. Contrasting Christ's message with "Jewish infidelity," he "condemn[ed] the Jews for looking for a temporary deliverer" instead of "our savior" and warned against "act[ing] their folly" by seeking "a mere temporal instead of a spiritual kingdom in the Millennium."[48]

Jefferson denied the divinity of Jesus but, in a letter to Rush, strongly attacked Judaism. He found that Jews' "ideas of him [God] & of his attributes were degrading & injurious" and their "Ethics . . . often irreconcilable with the sound dictates of reason & morality" and "repulsive & anti-social, as respecting other nations." America's champion of natural rights and freedom of worship wrote to Joseph B. Priestly that Judaic beliefs and morality "degraded" Jews and "presented" the "necessity" for their "reformation."[49]

## Politics and Law

Apart from Age of Reason ambivalence, victories in expanding the rights of Jews disclose a detractive countercurrent. A few ordinary citizens and dissenting members of state conventions to ratify the U.S. Constitution disagreed with unrestrained liberty for Catholics and non-Christians. "[T]hose gentlemen who formed this constitution," said a North Carolina convention delegate, objecting to the clause prohibiting test oaths for national office, "have given this invitation to Jews and heathens" to "come among us." An influx of such peoples "might endanger the character of the United States" because "the Christian religion is best calculated of all religions to make good members of society, on account of its morality . . . those who have any religion are against the emigration of those people from the Eastern Hemisphere." A western Massachusetts resident similarly opposed the Constitution: "There is a door opened for the Jews, Turks, and Heathens to enter publick office, and be seated at the head of the government of the United States."[50]

Such sentiments were not common. Few members of the federal constitutional convention disapproved of outlawing test oaths for federal office, and the lack of controversy over this issue in the ratification conventions and debates was a monumental accomplishment in securing citizenship for Jews. Some delegates in Philadelphia, however, especially Federalists, supported the federal provision and yet voted for religious tests in their own state charters.[51] This seemingly contradictory strategy was not a mere trade-off by those poised between tolerance and bigotry. Since the states were then the primary instruments of government, particularly in domestic matters, those reluctant to extend federal liberties to state and local authority pursued an asymmetrical policy reflecting resistance to, rather than advocacy of, political equality for Jews.

The Massachusetts constitutional revision convention of 1820–21 removed the declaration of belief in Christianity requisite for state officials. Largely owing to a ten-to-one margin in Boston, this amendment narrowly (13,782 to 12,480) won. The outcome obscured formidable opposition, both among the members, who rejected by 242 to 176 an attempt to vitiate the resolution, and in the popular vote. In the convention debate Joseph Tuckerman, a Unitarian minister and founder of a city mission to the poor in Boston that became a model for similar agencies in France and England, ardently supported retention of the test oath to keep Massachusetts a Christian commonwealth. "If men should be elevated to high and responsible states, who are enemies of Christianity," he warned, "may we not look with some apprehension to the consequences." Leverett Saltonstall objected that "jews, mahometans, deists, and atheists" were "opposed to the common religion of the Commonwealth and believe it an imposition, a mere fable, and that its professors are under a wretched delusion." "Are such persons," he asked, "suitable members of a Christian state?"[52]

Brahmin Federalists like Saltonstall could take comfort in another constitutional provision stating that Massachusetts residents might voluntarily pay taxes to support Christian institutions and instruction and in the retention of a de facto (if limited) establishment of Congregationalism.

The greatest antebellum controversy over granting Jews full citizenship occurred in Maryland, where the original state constitution (1776) also required a pledge of Christian faith for state officeholding. Although in colonial times proscriptions had usually applied to Catholics and dissenting Protestant sects as well, exclusion from civic rights in the early national period focused on non-Christians. Debates in Massachusetts and Maryland focused on Jews, Mohammedans, Deists, atheists, and, less frequently, Unitarians. Although not the only victims of discrimination, Jews were in a smaller group of potential outcasts than in the provincial era. Maryland Jews unavailingly appealed to the legislature in 1797 and 1804 for repeal of the test oath. Not until 1818 was a "Jew bill" introduced, but it failed to pass. Similar legislation, defeated in 1822, finally became law in 1825.[53]

Democratic-Republicans in the legislature were more likely than their Federalist counterparts to support the statute, and in the state Catholics were more favorable than Protestants, especially rural Protestants. Jeffersonian newspapers in Maryland and neighboring states approved full citizenship for Jews, as did the Catholic Bishop of South Carolina. This impressive show of support, however, did not prevent a long and bitter battle between initial introduction and final passage. The power of the opposition dramatically manifested itself in the election a year after the 1822 defeat. Candidates running against broadening the franchise bested sixteen incumbent supporters. Among the losers was the Jeffersonian Thomas Kennedy, the main sponsor of the "Jew bill," who represented a normally Democratic-Republican stronghold in western Maryland. Benjamin Galloway, the victor, called himself the candidate of the "Christian ticket" and Kennedy the head of the "Jew ticket." A Galloway election handbill labeled Kennedy's proposed law "an attempt to . . . bring into popular contempt, the Christian religion." Since Galloway preferred "Christianity to Judaism, Deism, Unitarianism, or any other sort of new fangled ism," he "deprecate[d] any change in our State government, calculated to afford the least chance to the enemies of Christianity, of undermining it in belief of the people of Maryland."[54]

Kennedy was reelected in 1824. By 1826 Jews could run for office, and in that year two were elected to the Baltimore city council and one served as its president. According to one scholar, however, in the repeal of the oath Maryland's need for more rich settlers outweighed other factors such as belief in religious liberty.[55] Perhaps this order of precedence explained continuing difficulties for Jews. In 1829 the Baltimore Jewish community wished to charter the building of a synagogue and incorporate themselves for that purpose, a matter requiring permission from the state legislature. In 1830 the Assembly voted down the enabling statute because the congregation was Jewish. It passed only through special request.[56]

Unlike Massachusetts and Maryland, North Carolina modified the test oath in a way that still excluded Jews from officeholding. An 1835 state constitutional convention broadened the original declaration by substituting a pledge of Christian for Protestant belief. Subsequent attempts to make the oath nondenominational were voted down by about two to one. The amendment included Catholics as full citizens, thus leaving Jews even more isolated in deprivation of political rights.[57]

Federalist resistance to equality for Jews partly derived from xenophobia exacerbated by anxiety over the French Revolution and Democratic-Republican electoral success. Confounding the latter with the former by perceiving Vice President Thomas Jefferson as a domestic Robespierre, the Federalist-dominated congress passed the Alien and Sedition Acts during the administration of John Adams. These laws reflected Federalist distaste for Deism, atheism, revolutionary republicanism, and transatlantic incubation of the Terror. Designed to curb the anti-Federalist press and hinder aliens, especially French immigrants, from becoming citizens, they evoked many protests, most notably in the Virginia and Kentucky Resolutions, written respectively by Madison and Jefferson.

Several years after the French Assembly granted citizenship to Jews, James Rivington, an ex-Tory who had become a Federalist publisher and newspaper editor in New York, attacked the Democratic Society in that city for alleged Jacobin propensities and harboring of French agents. "This itinerant gang [Democratic Societies] will be easily known by their physiognomy," he wrote in 1795. Anti-Federalists seditiously sympathized with the French Revolution and were property levelers who "seem to be like their *Vice-President,* of the tribe of Shylock: they have that leering underlook and malicious grin, that seem to say to the honest man *approach me not.*"[58]

Rivington's diatribe was not an isolated example of Federalists' grouping of Jews, Jeffersonians, and Jacobins in an imagined plot against America. The *New York Journal* in 1795 criticized Jewish Republicans for belonging to Democratic Societies. The Presbyterian minister and Dickinson College president Charles Nisbet wrote to a fellow Pennsylvania Federalist in 1797 (referring to a state senator who was not in fact Jewish), "A Jewish Tavern Keeper, with a very Jewish name (viz Israel Israel) is chosen one of the Senators of this commonwealth for the city of Philadelphia solely on account of his violent attachment to the French Interests." When the *Tree of Liberty* appeared in Pittsburgh in 1800, a Federalist broadside accused its editor, John Israel, of being Jewish and "a mother of sedition" and the Jeffersonian journal of belonging to "the Jew Press" and spreading "Jacobinism."[59]

The *Gazette of the United States,* edited by the famed Federalist publisher John Fenno, whose patron was Alexander Hamilton, was the party organ in Philadelphia. This journal also identified Jews with Jacobins and Republicans as a treacherous trinity. "An observer" derisively reported in 1800 that "Citizen N——the Jew" had responded to a request for small contributions to pay for the room at a meeting of the local Democratic Society: "I hopsh you will consider dat de monish is very scarch, and besides you know I'sh just com out by de Insholvent Law."[60] In this stereotype of the corrupt Jew, the accent identifies him as an alien, the scene labels him a Republican, and the title "Citizen" associates him with French radicalism. The combination of these negative references reinforces their separate and cumulative derision.

Anti-Semitism in the *Gazette* reflected the outlook of its staff member Joseph Dennie. Poet, satirist, essayist, editor, and critic, Dennie had a versatile literary career of which political journalism was only one facet. After Charles Brockden Brown he was the nation's earliest professional litterateur. The son of a prosperous Boston merchant, Dennie attended Harvard, regretted independence, wished to live in England, and was an Episcopal lay reader, a devotee of hierarchy and order who despised democracy, and a passionate Federalist who hated Deism and the French Revolution and dreaded the Jeffersonian triumph of 1800. His letters evinced casual contempt for Jews. This "Republic, this region [Pennsylvania]," he ranted in 1800, is "covered with the Jewish and canting and cheating descendants of those who felled the Stuarts." He also felt antipathy for Boston because "I have not a friend in that Jewish, peddling, and commercial quarter."[61]

Along with Dennie, John Quincy Adams belonged to the generation of Federalists who matured after ratification of the national constitution. Their attitude toward Jews indicated no abatement of hostility. Indeed, compared to his father, Adams displayed considerably greater prejudice.

His animosity surfaced early and lasted throughout his life. In 1794, when minister to Holland, he confided to his diary that a Jew offered him a low exchange rate for British guineas. This reference, ambiguous in itself, becomes a credible sign of anti-Semitism in the context of another Adams remark about Jews. Subsequently, and publicly, he said in describing Frankfurt, a city with numerous Jewish inhabitants, that the "word *filth* conveys an ideal of spotless purity in comparison with Jewish nastiness."[62]

Bigotry so permeated the party that according to David Hackett Fischer, a prominent historian of Federalism, "During the 1790s there had been a wide and fetid stream of antisemitism in Federalist thought."[63] Fischer and other students of that era note that the Republicans were appreciably less anti-Semitic and that Jews accordingly supported the party of Jefferson. One indication of the comparatively favorable Republican attitude was the publication in a New York Democratic journal of denunciations of Rivington's ravings about Jews.[64]

Less fearful of aliens and the French Revolution and more imbued with the spirit of the Age of Reason, Republicans were likelier defenders of religious freedom. Nonetheless, adherents of that party sometimes revealed anti-Semitism, especially in attacks on Hamilton's financial plan. One New York Republican accused speculators of "Israeltish avarice." Another charged that Hamilton's policies enriched "British riders, Amsterdam Jews, American Tories, and speculating lawyers and doctors." A third claimed that nine-tenths of the original state debt was held by "brokers, speculators, Jews, members of congress and foreigners." A Republican poem of 1790 noted that "Each day a fresh report he [Hamilton] broaches, / That spies and Jews may ride in coaches."[65]

If some Federalists identified Judaism with treasonous attachment to a cataclysmic Republicanism of natural rights and political disorder, at least one Jeffersonian blamed Judaism for a Federalist deluge of state-sponsored worship and religious and political oppression. In an address honoring Jefferson's second election to the presidency, Nehemiah Dodge, a Baptist elder and a Connecticut Republican, called Congregationalism, which was still officially privileged in Connecticut, an unholy branch of Federalism. He agreed with his fellow Baptist Isaac Backus that the "corrupt fruit . . . springing from a connection between church and state," was a "Jewish plan." The "Jewish covenant" was a "yoke of bondage," repudiated in 1776. Imposed by Britons, royalists, aristocrats, "high-toned federalists," "Federalist Clergymen," Catholics, and "Jewish rabbies," the "Abrahamic" agreement was "the devil's purpose." All these plotters were "Judaizers" and "leaders for a long time in the Jewish Church." He protested against "continu[ing] your standing in Jewish churches and constantly pay[ing] your money to support these Judaizing teachers who are constantly trying to gull you out of your inalienable rights."[66]

The turmoil inherent in the founding of a new nation undoubtedly aggravated anti-Semitism. Invective cast in the early days after independence, however, derived more from colonial and older attitudes than from anxiety over new beginnings. A Georgia pamphleteer, probably an ex-loyalist, charged in 1784 that Jews in that state were enemy aliens with no judicial rights. He mentioned medieval ritual murderers—a reference relatively rare in political, if not religious, discourse—and accused their descendants of entering "politicks . . . to favour that system which is most promotive of their pecuniary interests, the principle of lucre being the life and soul of all their actions." According to this anti-Semite, "Jews always insinuate themselves most into favour among those nations who remain in darkness and in the shadows of death." With "these people eternally obtruding themselves" in Georgia's public life, he asked, "what are we to expect but to have Christianity enacted into a capital heresy, the synagogue become the established church and the mildness of the New Testament compelled to give place to the rigor and severity of the Old?"[67] Also in 1784 the Quaker lawyer and ex-Tory Miers Fisher argued for a charter for the Bank of Pennsylvania to lower interest rates and to protect people from money and stock speculation, evils he blamed on Jewish brokers.[68]

The significant changes that occurred when the early national period gave way to the age of Jackson brought little alteration in attitudes toward Jews. Nationally prominent Jews were constant targets of disdain. Mordecai Manuel Noah (1785–1851), lawyer, politician, journalist, and playwright, was the best-known American Jew until supplanted in celebrity in the 1850s by Judah P. Benjamin. Incessant derision of Noah's faith reflected the continuing antipathy toward Jews. When he served as consul to Tunis (1813–1815), the editor of the *Charleston Investigator* employed standard slurs, such as "Hooked Nose," to describe the Jewish diplomat. In 1820, the Clintonian faction of the New York Democratic Party unavailingly fought the appointment of Noah (a supporter of Martin Van Buren) as sheriff of New York City. The opposition's organ, the *Columbian,* wondered whether the prospective sheriff would be a "Shylock" in office. Two years later, running for election to this post, Noah was pilloried by the local press. "Should it be the unfortunate lot of any Christian to be brought to the gallows during this man's administration," charged the Clintonian and former Federalist editor of the *New-York Evening Post*, "with what a venomous satisfaction would he give the last pull at his legs." The *New York Commercial Advertiser* regarded Noah's incumbency as evidence that "the Jews prevailed against the Gentiles." The election occurred during a yellow fever epidemic, prompting Rev. Pascal Strong, recording secretary of the American Society for Meliorating the Condition of the Jews, to sermonize that the plague was God's "judgement" because eminent citizens were "publically abetting the election of an infidel in pref-erence to a Christian." Noah lost the contest, in which his opponent notified voters that a Jew could not give absolute allegiance to America.[69]

Similar bilge gushed forth from the *New York Herald*, the *New York American*, the *National Advocate*, and the *Washington Globe*. The *Herald* editor, a journalistic adversary of Noah's *Evening Star*, claimed in 1837 that his rival belonged to a "secret conspiracy entered into by a portion of the Jews and infidels to uproot" Christianity. A *Globe* editorial of 1833, "Mor-decai Mammon Noah," the captious modification of his middle name insin-uating personal and creedal love of lucre, portrayed him as a journalist vending "cast off falsehoods and stale jokes, instead of pursuing the hon-ester calling of his tribe—the traffic of selling old clothes. But lying to sell a newspaper, is akin to lying and selling rags." Outrage over this libel caused the *Globe*'s editor Francis P. Blair, an intimate of Jackson's, to apologize in the next issue for ill-chosen language, decry distaste for Jews, and praise them as good citizens.[70]

Other Jewish public figures were also censured. Uriah Phillips Levy, the only Jewish officer in the U.S. Navy, in 1816 faced the first of many court-martials and courts of inquiry, provoked by his violent response to insults to his creed, that would haunt his career.[71]

This period also saw the emergence of Jewish cartoon figures, har-bingers of the anti-Semitic caricatures that would be habitual after the Civil War. A lampoon of Jacksonian banking practices in 1834 pictured "Levi Stock an Exchange Broker" speaking in Yiddish dialect. In 1838 a lithograph on New York election fraud ridiculed Dr. Moses Jacques, a Tammany leader. In the German-Jewish dialect fashioned by bigots here and abroad, he says: "Shtop my friendsh I vill shave you shome troublesh. It is moneysh vat maksh de Mayor go!!" Jacques was portrayed as the ste-reotypical bald, long-nosed Jew.[72]

The oncoming generation of political reformers proved no more immune to bigotry than were Jacksonians and Whigs, and bitterness festered during the era of sectional turmoil. Letters written in 1836 and 1837 by the abolitionist crusader and *Liberator* editor William Lloyd Garrison bristled with anti-Semitism. "Judaism and Romanism," he said, were responsible for the moral blight of Protestantism. A *New England Spectator* fusillade against Garrison, the *Liberator*, and Boston blacks indicted him for refusing to attend Sunday church services. "There is no such holy locality," retorted Garrison; "if you were not groping in Jewish darkness you would perceive this truth." Habitual denigration was characterized by the editors of his correspondence as exemplifying "Garrison's Anti-Jewish Protestant Fundamentalism."[73]

Through test oaths, provisions for state support of Protestant sects, and the career difficulties faced by Levy and Noah, anti-Semitism expressed itself in action as well as rhetoric. Several minor incidents of discrimination posed further obstacles to Jews in public life. Jacob Henry was reelected to the North Carolina legislature in 1809, but a colleague demanded his removal because Henry, as a Jew, was constitutionally prohibited from serving in the state government. In the end Henry was not forced to take the prescribed test oath, and the election was upheld. When James Monroe removed Noah in 1815 as consul to Tunis, the president wrote him that his religion "produce[d] a very unfavorable effect" on Noah's performance in office.[74] Monroe's decision was not due to personal prejudice against Judaism, but it is doubtful that the administration would have attributed withdrawal of a Protestant diplomat to denominational ties. In a more flagrantly anti-Semitic episode, the first governor of the Louisiana Territory canceled the appointment of a Catholic civil commandant in a district whose inhabitants, also Catholics, protested against the official because his family had been Jewish. In a turnabout typical of American ambivalence about Jews, several years later the discharged candidate became justice of the peace in another district.[75]

The heaviest burden imposed by public policy upon the majority of American Jewry was a relatively mild display of anti-Semitism. Civil enforcement of Sunday as a day of rest obligated no hatred of Jews but demanded considerable material sacrifice from devout believers in the Mosaic Code. From the 1790s until well into the twentieth century local and state governments often prohibited business activity on the Christian sabbath. These laws hurt orthodox Jews, ritually prohibited from working on Saturday. Judicial affirmation of the constitutionality of such legislation was often based upon the secular principle of the need for a day of rest. These decisions were also sustained by the assertion of sabbatarians and their evangelical allies that America was a Christian nation and that Sunday observance accorded with the status of the municipality, state, or nation as a Christian community. Similar reasoning validated governmental compulsion of Jews to participate in court proceedings on their holy days.[76]

Evangelical sabbatarians were not the only, or necessarily the most powerful, proponents of legal privileges for Christianity. Joseph Story, a justice of the U.S. Supreme Court, ardently advocated Christian nationalism. The Massachusetts-born and Harvard-educated Story was a Unitarian, a Jeffersonian, a former congressman, a stellar American jurist and legal scholar, and a founder of Harvard Law School. At his investiture in the chair of jurisprudence at the Law School in 1829, Story maintained "that Christianity is part of the Common Law, from which it seeks the sanction of its rights, and by which it endeavors to regulate its doctrines." No "act" or "contract" under "Common Law" can therefore be "offensive" to Christian "duties" or "morals." In *Commentaries on the Constitution of the United States* (1833), Story asserted that "it is impossible for those, who believe in the truth of Christianity, as a divine revelation, to doubt, that it is the especial duty of government to foster, and encourage it among all its citizens and subjects." Believing in federal interdiction of the test oath and in the Bill of Rights guarantee of freedom of worship, Story claimed that the purpose of the latter "was not to countenance, much less to advance Mahometanism, or Judaism, or infidelity, by prostrating Christianity," but to prevent "rivalry among Christian sects" and a "national ecclesiastic establishment."[77]

Another legal giant of the early republic, James Kent, a conservative Federalist who was the first professor of law at Columbia University and then became chief justice of the New York supreme court and chancellor of the New York court of chancery, similarly appreciated the political priority of Christianity. "No government," Kent argued in 1811 in a state supreme court opinion upholding a lower court's decision to fine a freethinker for calling Jesus a bastard and Mary a whore, "ever hazarded such a bold experiment upon the solidity of the public morals as to permit, with impunity and under the sanction of their tribunals the general religion of the country to be openly insulted and defamed." As evidence that Christianity was the creed of the people and sanctioned as such by the legislature, he noted that the government enforced laws forbidding gainful employment on the Christian Sabbath. He further affirmed that defamation of Christianity was a public offense under New York law. "Nor are we bound . . . to punish indiscriminately like attacks" upon any other creed, "for this plain reason, that the case assumes we are a christian people."[78]

## Religion

A review of the civic commentary of this period discloses that Christian anti-Semitism was a primary cause of political discrimination against Jews.[79] Age-old accusations against Judaism mingled with a belief in Christian triumphalism and the association of proper governance with a Christian commonwealth.

These attitudes were articulated by clergymen as well as laymen. I have already mentioned the Unitarian Joseph Tuckerman's rationale for retaining the test oath in the Massachusetts constitution, the Baptist Nehemiah Dodge's indignation over the "Abrahamic Covenant," and the tireless proselytizer of Jews Pascal Strong's invocation of divine punishment for those aiding an "infidel" electoral candidate against a "Christian" opponent.

Ezra Stiles Ely, a Philadelphia Presbyterian pastor, brewed another concoction of clerical and political animus in "The Duty of Christian Freemen to Elect Christian Rulers," an Independence Day speech of 1827. He called for a party of the worshippers of Jesus to choose only Christian governors so that the nation would be ruled according to Christian principles. He expressed the hope that "all Christians may agree that it is more desirable to have a Christian than a Jew, Mohammedan or Pagan, in any civil office."[80]

Ministers had reprimanded Jews since the initial American settlements hovered between the wilderness and the sea. The birth of the republic in a time teeming with ideas of liberty did not curtail attacks from the pulpit. Survivors from the pre-Revolutionary period like Isaac Backus did not discard their jaundiced views. Backus, a member of the Massachusetts convention to ratify the federal constitution and an outspoken champion of the Commonwealth's exclusion of Jews from public office, continued to scold "the envious Jews" for their killing of the Messiah, which revealed the "difference between true believers and reprobates." For "unto the defiled and unbelieving is nothing pure but even their mind and conscience is defiled."[81]

John Carroll, the scion of an aristocratic Baltimore family and the country's first Catholic bishop and archbishop, also bore a grudge that bridged independence and nationhood. In the early 1770s Carroll complained that church patrimonial funds "in Alsace were loaned to Jews, who swarm throughout the province" and that "a company of Jews" in Lorraine "bought and carried off" paintings of the Catholic hero King Stanislaus of Poland. Later, addressing American Catholics in 1784, he mentioned that "the Jews thought they crucified" Christ. At the first Diocesan Synod in the United States (1791), he declared that "Christians . . . do not, like the Jews, possess the shadow of Goodness, but possess Truth itself and the fulfillment of all [Old Testament] prefigurements."[82]

Ambivalence toward Jews pervaded the theology of the generation of Christian clergymen and thinkers who matured after the nation was born. The balance between aspersion and admiration shifted against Judaism in the thought of the Congregationalist John D. Marsh. In transit from a Connecticut pulpit to high office in the American Temperance Union, Marsh wrote *An Epitome of General Ecclesiastical History* (1827). In the next forty years sixteen editions were issued of this standard and influential christological glorification of the disciples of Jesus and denunciation of biblical Israel. According to Marsh, Hebrew history, the Old Testament, and Moses and the prophets had meaning solely as supplanted foretokens of the Messiah. Well before the First Coming Jews debased themselves by sectarian squabbling and belief that "obedience to Mosaic law . . . could atone for the vilest transgressions." Capitulating "to the grossest wickedness," Israelites "looked for the Messiah . . . as a temporal prince, who would deliver them from Roman bondage, by a zealous performance of external rites." To halt moral decay, the Savior "prescrib[ed] in place of the ceremonial worship of the Jews, a new, simple, and spiritual worship which should be offered by the people of God, not only in Jerusalem, but in all parts of the world."[83]

Executing "his prophetic office," Marsh continued, "Christ abolished the Jewish, and established the Christian Church," a step that aroused the enmity of the priestly elite. Marsh rendered the passion of Jesus provocatively: "Pilate could find not fault in him," but "the Jews demanded his crucifixion, and wished that his blood might be upon them and their children. Afraid of the mob, the Roman governor shamefully yielded to their entreaties." An "unbridled populace" then "dragged him amid the grossest insults and abuse to Golgotha." They "stripped off his raiment, and nailed him through the hands and feet, to the accursed instrument of death." By "rulers and people, he was ridiculed, as he hung suspended in the air." The stereotypical depiction of the crucifixion concluded by noting: "Infidelity has seldom had the effrontery to deny the existence of this illustrious founder of the Christian religion."[84]

Deicide reflected perpetual Judaic evil. In "betraying and murdering Christ, they had but imitated the conduct of their fathers, who treated Moses and the Prophets with contempt." Repeating ancestral transgressions, this "degenerate race, . . . the blood of Christ come upon them and their children, . . . persecuted the followers of Christ with relentless rage." Ingrained "ingratitude, perverseness and rebellion . . . called aloud for the vengeance of God."[85]

The "judgements of heaven [cast] upon the first oppressors of the gospel of Christ" made "the Jews . . . incredibly wretched." No "longer a nation," they "were scattered through the earth and have continued to this day, a wonder, a reproach, and a by-word among all the nations." Outside America, Jews "had an iron yoke of bondage put upon their necks."[86]

Marsh merged traditional with modern chastisement. Conventional condemnation of "inflexible obstinacy" in adherence to perverted and obsolete law and ritual was conjoined to the fashionable imputation that "Infidels, among the Jews . . . reject all belief in revelation, and moral accountability, and any Saviour." To the nineteenth-century cavil of Jewish moral nihilism he added the contemporary complaint of cultural barrenness: "The Jews have never been a literary people. Rabbinical knowledge is all that has been esteemed by them of any value."[87]

The suffering of this defiantly iniquitous people, however, was not an eternal destiny. "The extension of civil liberty and rational Christianity and the efforts making for their illumination and conversion, are fast placing them on the same footing with other nations, and are bringing them into the kingdom of God." *An Epitome of General Ecclesiastical History* brought forth the timeworn theology of Judaic sterility, sinfulness, and displacement overborne by Christian virtue, vitality, and spirituality. The conclusion is routine: "The preservation of the Jews through 1800 years of awful suffering and disgrace" is "a 'reproach and a by-word' among all nations." A "wonderful fulfillment of prophecy," it "affords incontestable evidence of the truth of the Bible. He who can contemplate it and be an infidel, must renounce all claim to a candid and considerate mind."[88]

Among Christian clergymen, the reservations of Carroll are more representative of attitudes toward Jews than are the hectoring of Backus and Marsh. Particularly in the New World, tolerance partially sheltered western Jewry from the late eighteenth to the late nineteenth century. Total elimination of resentment, however, was blocked by revered canons of Christian apologetics, which stipulated Judaism as the correlative outcast of the true faith.

Such sentiments characterized the American Society for Meliorating the Condition of the Jews (ASMCJ; 1820) and the American Sunday-School Union (1824). These organizations were evangelical products of the Second Great Awakening—a series of revivals from the 1790s to the 1830s. The resurgence of Protestant piety revitalized millennial urges and hence heightened eagerness to convert Jews.

Charles Grandison Finney, a famed antebellum revivalist preacher, ordained as a Presbyterian and later a Congregationalist, was, like Jonathan Edwards in the First Great Awakening, a postmillennialist, convinced that the next thousand years would pave the way for the earthly kingdom of God. Edwards and Finney agreed that Israel and its history and theology, as revealed in the Old Testament, constituted a typology, that is, a prefigurement of the Messiah and his life and doctrines, as revealed in the Gospels. "When Christ came, the ceremonial or typical [Jewish] dispensation was abrogated, because the design of those forms was fulfilled, and therefore themselves of no further use," wrote Finney in *Lectures on Revivals of Religions* (1835), a handbook on conducting revivals that sold twelve thousand copies in its first three months after publication. "He being the anti-type, the types were of course done away at his coming," Finney contended. "The Jews accused him of disregarding their forms. His object was to preach and teach mankind the true religion."[89]

If *An Epitome of General Ecclesiastical History* expressed the punitive impulse in orthodox Christian thought about Judaism, the ideas and strategies of the ASMCJ and similar missionary societies marked the opposite margin of sympathetic condescension. Aspiring to redeem dissenters through gentle persuasion instead of harsh remonstrance, and using ex-Jews as spokesmen, these proselytizers professed great friendliness for the unrepentant. They revered the ancestral faith and the Hebrews as progenitors of Jesus and regarded the descendants of old Israel as victimized by persecution and still in special relationship with the Lord.[90]

The ASMCJ, modeled on its English sister organization, was founded by an apostate Jew, several college and seminary presidents, and professors, clergymen, and Federalist patricians, mostly from New York and New Jersey and of Presbyterian and Dutch Reformed affiliation. Its membership included presidents of Queens College (now Rutgers University), Yale, Harvard, and Princeton, and a Federalist congressman and ex-president of the Continental Congress, as well as Stephen Van Rensselaer and De Witt Clinton. John Quincy Adams was an ASMCJ vice president. In spite of this impressive list of supporters, the ASMCJ did not implement its plan to transplant a colony of former Jews from Germany to a wilderness tract in New York and convinced few Jews to embrace Jesus. By 1840 the society was moribund; partially revived in subsequent years, it staggered on until 1870.[91]

Notwithstanding earnest enticements by proselytizers, the movement was ambivalent about the objects of its pursuit. Desire to convert Jews arose from genuine concern for their spiritual and mundane misery. It was no coincidence that the decline of the ASMCJ and the Boston Society for Promoting Christianity among the Jews coincided with a rise of anti-Semitism that began in the late 1830s and climaxed during the Civil War. But missionary zeal also sprang from the dual premise that denying Christ as the Messiah brought divine retribution and that redemption required recanting disbelief in him. Following Jesus meant forsaking Judaic ritual and belief.

Clashes between benevolence and severity, respect and reproach, agitated would-be rescuers of Jews. Hannah Adams, of the Boston Society, in an exceptionally appreciative history of the Jews, assured her readers that "he was ignominiously rejected and put to death by the Jewish nation." The "tremendous calamities which befell them after perpetrating this horrid crime; the fulfillment of our Saviour's predictions, respecting the destruction of their city and temple, and their consequent dispersion and sufferings will be related in the following pages."[92]

Adams went on to tell her readers that after "dispersion" Jews "adhered with inflexibility to those customs and religious rites" which earlier had led them to forsake the "divine Redeemer." Although she recognized some persecution of Jews in the Roman Empire, she repeatedly accused them of massacring and torturing Christians. Conceding that Jews were forced into usury, she nevertheless argued that "infamous on account of their religion," they "had no honour to lose" and "were therefore apt to exercise a profession, odious in itself, by every kind of rigour, and even sometimes by rapine and extortion." Jewish "industry and frugality," giving "that nation" all "the ready money" of England and Europe, "enabled them to lend at an exorbitant and unequal interest." Parading the avaricious Jew, she caricatured the reaction of the victims to their persecutors. They "oppose[d] oppression by fraud. These acquired habits were continued from age to age, all the energy of their minds directed to the pursuit of gain."[93]

With an ambivalence characteristic of the movement, Adams concludes by admiring Jews for surviving their tribulations, upbraids Christians for tormenting their lost brethren, and predicts restoration of the prodigal wanderers to saving grace. Contrition and redemption, however, are a projected ending to long and deserved misery. "The history of the Jews exhibits a melancholy picture of human wretchedness and depravity," as Adams and her readers "contemplate the lineal descendants of the chosen people of God forfeiting their inestimable privileges by rejecting the glory of Israel, and involving themselves in the most terrible calamities."[94]

Philip Milledoler, professor of theology and president of Queens College and minister of the largest Presbyterian church in the country, in the 1816 presidential address to the newly formed American Society for Evangelizing the Jews (ASEJ), voiced the usual attitudes of the proselytizers. He imputed to Jews "laxness of morals," called them "Infidels," and claimed that "their religious exercises are scarcely conducted with the form, much less the spirit, of devotion." Such ethical and spiritual impairment moved Milledoler to ask, "What contempt do they not experience? What opposition do they not encourage from their associates?" No matter "how dreadful is the veil that is upon their hearts," however, they should not "be suffered to perish before our eyes." Their "situation [is] calculated to excite our sympathy and call forth our exertions." Since Jews were the first worshippers of the Lord, guarded the gift of Providence, brought forth the Redeemer, and were oppressed by Christians, their lapses did not license persecution. True to evangelical optimism that the doubters would eventually welcome the Savior, he "still hope[d] better things of some of them, and especially that part of the nation which is resident in this country." Positive reception of Jews here and in "the general opinion of the Christian world," indicates that "Israel's restoration is at hand." Milledoler was not unmindful of the ultimate item in the agenda of apostasy: redemption of the Jews would be "a signal for the conversion of the great body of Gentiles" and the advent of the Millennium.[95]

The ASEJ was a forerunner of the ASMCJ, which absorbed attitudes as well as members from its predecessor. A "Director's Report" of 1823 heralded "one of the grandest events in the vista of prophecy, connected with the subsequent universal triumphs of the Gospel, The Conversion of the Jews." Belief that "that repudiated race is still 'beloved [by God] for their fathers' sakes,'" confidence in the glorious outcome, and sympathy for Jewish suffering went hand in hand with reproval: "The blood of the Messiah, 'the Prince of Life', was shed by their faith and judicially visited, according to their own imprecation, 'upon them and their children.'"[96]

A year later, John H. Livingston, a founder and vice president of the ASMCJ, expressed similar dualism. The knickerbocker aristocrat, president of Queens College and professor at the Theological Seminary of the Reformed Dutch Church in America, praised the "industrious people," secure and free in America, while calling them "infidel Jews."[97]

Harvesters of souls for Christ could be less hopeful and less compassionate when confronted by real issues and candidates for conversion than in abstract aspiration to uplift the unredeemed. John Quincy Adams, after listening to a Presbyterian missionary back from the Turkish empire, reported that the sermon conveyed "a melancholy picture" of the empire's inhabitants. The speaker called "Jews" "the worst" of these peoples and asserted that "their hatred of all Christians is rancorous beyond conception."[98]

The American Sunday-School Union, although it had a broader evangelical scope than the missions to the Jews, was even more important than the proselytizing organizations as an indicator of and an influence upon Christian attitudes to Jews. Sabbath education was a larger and more prominent development in what Martin Marty has called the righteous empire of nineteenth-century Protestantism, and as a vehicle of mass learning it more extensively shaped popular culture. This movement spanned the sacred and secular spheres, socialized Protestant children, influenced the presentation of religion in the public schools, and, since Protestants rarely attended parochial schools, became a fundamental means of sectarian inculcation and propagation.

The Sunday-School Union capped a crusade that began in the 1790s and quickened with the founding of associations in New York, Philadelphia, and Boston several years before the emergence of the national institution. In 1830 the Union resolved to establish a school in every town where none already existed. Apart from that task, the Union and similar bodies in the various sects published a journal, monthly magazines, and didactic juvenile pamphlets and books. While operations for converting Jews floundered, Sunday school organizations flourished. Supreme court justices, governors, congressmen, state legislators and jurists, businessmen, lawyers, physicians, and others in local and national elites became superintendents and teachers and officers of the national and denominational societies.[99]

*Union Questions* set forth the Union's position on scriptural matters and therefore on the biblical and, for this evangelical institution, basic relationship between Christianity and Judaism. Designed as a guide for Sabbath school Bible class teachers, it was originally issued in 1827 by the Union's publication committee, which included Baptists, Congregationalists, Episcopalians, Methodists, Presbyterians, and adherents of the

Dutch Reformed church. According to the 1834 edition, 1.6 million copies of *Union Questions* were sold in seven years.[100]

The book was divided into lessons, each with several subheads consisting of questions. Through this format the sections dealing with Jews and Christians imparted an orthodoxy of total guilt, betrayal, savagery, and dispossession on one side, and pure innocence, perfection, and predominance on the other: Question 9, Lesson 8 asked: "Who are said to be the true children of Abraham?" Question 17, Lesson 11 asked: "What is the difference in this respect ['grace and truth'] between the [Mosaic] law and the gospel?" Some queries stressed the superiority of the newer religion; others were blunter indictments of the Hebrews: "How was Christ rejected by the Jews?" went Question 25 of Lesson 25. And Question 26: "Will you now try now to think who it was that bore all this treatment—bound, struck, spit on, mocked, scourged, and delivered to a mob to be killed . . .?" Further interrogation emphasized the guilt of Israel, as evinced in the two-part Question 39 in Lesson 37: "Did those who saw Jesus pity him? What is the meaning of reviled?" The catechism in Lesson 38 hammered home the indictment of deicide: "Who condemned Christ to death? Who crucified him? Who caused him to be condemned and crucified? Had they any reason for this?"[101]

The Union published works for children and adolescents on the same themes of Christian superiority and the terrible fate awaiting the unrepentant and unconverted.[102] *Elisama* (1835), written by Rev. Jarvis Gregg for the Union, was a juvenile novel about Hebrew history from the Babylonian Captivity to the building of the Second Temple. A cautionary tale recounted in the format of a Sunday school class, it took as its theme "Judah's glory and disgrace," with emphasis on the disgrace. Jehovah's punishment for Israel's impiety and defiance, the initial diaspora, humbled the pride and curtailed the corruption, if not of all Israel, at least of those with the fortitude and faith to restore themselves and the Holy Land. Even the devout, however, are not fully rejuvenated. Responding to a question from a pupil as to whether these Jews were "pious," the teacher insists that "most" had "no conception of the spiritual nature of the law, nor of the real meaning of its rites." A "'veil' covered their hearts. And so even it is today."[103]

The teacher recites a "beautiful hymn," expressing a clergyman's self-righteous sacrilege of Judaism. While attending a synagogue service, the minister "fervently" prays that "light" from the "mighty [Torah] scroll" will "break on every soul" in the congregation so that "on their hardened hearts the veil might be no longer dark." The "film shall fall," he entreats God, when "Judah . . . see[s]" the "Messiah's signs in Christ" and "by Jehovah's nameless name, invoke[s] the Nazarene."[104]

The first dispersion foreshadows the second exile. Reverting to habitual sins and disobedience to divine will, the Jews are again banished from a devastated Jerusalem and a wrecked Temple. Once more they suffer the just wrath of God. Another surrender to the Lord is required before Israel is fully and finally rehabilitated. "Daughter of Zion, from the dust / Exalt thy fallen head," fittingly ends the lesson of *Elisama*. "Again in thy Redeemer trust, / He calls thee from the dead."[105]

Using the same format, Gregg wrote *Selumiel; or, A Visit to Jerusalem* (1833), which was also published and endorsed by the Union as a Sunday school text. *Selumiel* focuses on Jerusalem in the age of Jesus and his apostles. As in *Elisama,* the narrative is a Christian apologetic designed to fortify young souls. To attain these ends, Gregg again makes Judaism the antithesis of the true faith.

*Selumiel,* taking as its topic the torment of Christ and the conflict between Judaism and Christianity, is harsher than *Elisama* in its treatment of Jews and Judaism. Compare, for example, the passage quoted above from *Elisama* on the shortcomings of Jewish law and ritual with severer rebuke in *Selumiel,* which says Jews "trusted in external forms and . . . honoured him [God] with their lips, but their heart was far from him." In their "outward reverence and seeming holy joy, God was only mocked."[106]

Selumiel, the hero of the novel, is an apostate with a residual Jewish identity manifested in nostalgic pride over the glories of Israel in the age of the patriarchs, poignant grief for the tribulations about to befall the Jews, and expectant joy that in the fullness of time they will return to grace. Nevertheless, when "he remembered that this offended lord had sent even his only son," and they "conspired against him and put him to a cruel death, then he felt that the decision of God, that one stone of the proud towers of Jerusalem should not be left one upon another, was just." "Ill-fated Jerusalem," begins the protagonist's most impassioned malediction. "Poor, infatuated people! Sad was the curse which they imprecated on themselves when in the madness of their bitter zeal against Christ, they exclaimed, 'His blood be on us and our children!' Fearfully will that curse be executed."[107]

Conventional complaints about Judaism issued not only from evangelical denominations but from the liberal Unitarians as well. A biographer of William Ellery Channing, a founder of Unitarianism, perceived anti-Semitism in Channing's disapproval of the Jews' claim of "chosenness." For Channing, the self-designated and now displaced Chosen People claimed an entitlement that clashed with Christian universality and ecumenicism —core tenets of Unitarianism. "The Dispensation of Moses [Old Testament]," he preached in the 1819 sermon that soon became the shibboleth of rational Christianity, "compared with that of Jesus [New Testament], we consider as adapted to the childhood of the human race, a preparation for a noble system, and chiefly useful now as serving to confirm and illustrate the Christian Scriptures."[108]

James Walker, a Unitarian leader who taught religion, morality, and politics at Harvard and became president of the college (1853–1860), agreed. In "The Day of Judgement" (1817) he insisted that "the Old Testament . . . was never understood to come up to the Christian standard" and "Judaism is marred throughout . . . by the narrowness and arrogance of a people educated in the belief that God was their God in a sense in which he was not the God of all mankind."[109]

The most direct, exhaustive, and influential Unitarian indictment of Judaism was formulated in "The Worcester Catechism," a text published in 1815 by recent graduates of the Harvard Divinity School, including the future first president of the American Unitarian Association (1825). This work, which was used by youngsters in Unitarian Sunday schools and churches, differed little from *Union Questions* in its evaluation of Jews. On the subject of Jews, liberal Christianity and evangelical conservativism shared the same doctrine.

"Elements of Religion and Morality in the Form of a Catechism" (1813), the early part of the Unitarian catechism, was written and published by Channing and Samuel C. Thatcher. Question 31 asked: "What did Jesus Christ suffer for us?" According to one prescribed answer: "He was constantly opposed and persecuted by the Jews, who did not hearken to him." Later questions and answers underscored traditional opinion:

Q. 34. How did the Jews manifest their displeasure at the conduct of Jesus?

A. By watching for opportunities to take his life.

Q. 48. What did Pilate do with Jesus?

A. When he found that the Jews insisted on his death, he delivered him up to them to be crucified, although he himself was satisfied of his innocence.

Q. 93. How did God punish the Jews for rejecting the Messiah and for their other crimes?

A. Forty years after the death of Jesus Christ, Jerusalem was taken and destroyed by the Romans; their beautiful temple was consumed by fire; a vast number of the Jews perished; and those who escaped death, were reduced to slavery, and dispersed throughout the world; and their descendants remain to this day in a state of dispersion, yet a distinct people.

Answers for queries regarding Jewish persecution of the apostles also reproduced orthodox dogma. "The Jews excited a tumult against" Paul, and the Romans had "to protect him from the malice of the Jews, who sought his life."[110]

## Secular Education

Through mutual teachings and influence Sunday schools and secular schools were a channel between Sabbath learning and the American ethos. Public and sectarian education shared the same clientele and inculcated similar values. One common element was a shared attitude toward Jews. Readers of *American Popular Lessons* (1820), designed for lower primary school classes and in its tenth edition by 1848, learned, as in Sunday school, that "Jesus Christ was killed by the Jews at Jerusalem."[111]

When textbook authors were clergymen, Sabbath and public school lessons on this topic were indistinguishable. One such author was John Pierpont, a Harvard Divinity School graduate who preached from a Unitarian pulpit in Boston. Besides his pastoral calling, Pierpont was a well-known Federalist poet, an abolitionist, and an activist for temperance and pacifism. He also wrote enormously successful readers and recitation books used in Boston public schools and elsewhere. Equally solicitous of the well-being of the nation's children as of other causes, Pierpont introduced *The American First Class Book*, originally published in 1823 and in at least twenty-five editions by 1835, by noting that "the book will fulfill my hopes" by helping the pupils "attain the end of their Christian faith,—the salvation of their souls."[112]

Pierpont's didactic anthologies express mild reservations about Jews, in the fashion of the missionizers. An essay in the *National Reader* (1827), which was adopted in 1829 for upper grades by Boston schools and went through at least seventeen editions by 1854, praised Judaism for giving to the world the Savior and heralding Christianity and requested Christian "sadness" for the trials of a once glorious people. But Pierpont nevertheless portrayed the Jews as debased by their own acts: "[S]hall the moral ruin, the spiritual decay, the symptoms of eternal perdition, excite no feeling in our bosoms?" What "ruin," he asked, "is so mournful, and so complete, as that which the moral aspect of Judah now presents to our view?"[113]

John L. Blake was another New England clergyman and author of textbooks whose works sometimes read like Protestant tracts. A graduate of Brown and ordained first as a Congregationalist and later as an Episcopalian, he published didactic readers, histories, geographies, and science books as well as volumes on agriculture and popular encyclopedias. In addition to writing, Blake was a church pastor, proprietor of a girls' school, and editor of the official periodical of the American Episcopal church.

In *A Geography for Children* (1831), Blake interspersed items more appropriate in sermons and Sunday schools with worldly information (and misinformation). Lesson 28, "History of Asia," claimed that when the Jews "became disobedient and wicked, He abandoned them, and they have been subject to reproach and derision for nearly eighteen hundred years . . . wicked people soon become unhappy, while the virtuous and good usually live in peace and happiness." Defining Jews as dissenters from the divinely inspired New Testament, Lesson 45, "Different Religions," noted that in "Christian countries, the persons, who disbelieve the Bible, are called infidels." We "consider them exceedingly wicked to reject a religion given to them in so much mercy." Some "infidels" are "so inveterate in their opposition to the gospel, as to use the utmost exertions to overthrow it."[114]

An equally uncompromising critique of Judaism was advanced in *The Columbian Orator* (1797), Caleb Bingham's common school anthology on oratory, which by 1860 was in at least its fortieth edition. Like Pierpont, Bingham was a Connecticut-born college graduate with reform inclinations, as manifested by his advocating of free public schools. A bookseller and a textbook writer, Bingham was not a clergyman, but Christian exhortation resounded in his works, which were frequently used in conjunction with the Bible in New England schools. "Christ's Crucifixion," a poem in *The Columbian Orator*, epitomized Bingham's indoctrinational zeal and his quarrel with Judaism. The "partition-wall [between Jews and Gentiles] by Moses built, / By Christ was levell'd." The "birthright of the elder born, / Heirs of the promise," was similarly "forfeited" when those who had been God's chosen slew God's son. After Jesus died "dire denunciations" of "lamentation, mourning and of woe," fell "fast on Israel's wretched race."[115]

By including "Infernal Conference" in *The Columbian Orator*, Bingham descended from conventional criticism to demonization, then seldom encountered in America. In this poem the Jews are manipulated by Satan, who says that "Jews may be urg'd to envy, to revenge, to murder: a rebellious race of old!"[116]

Other textbooks of this era belittled Judaism, though more moderately than *The Columbian Reader*. A catechism in *Geographical Compilation for the Use of Schools* (1806) represented routine textbook opinion:

Q. What is the Jewish religion, or Judaism?
A. It is the religion which God gave on Mt. Sinai, which was nothing but the figure of the religion that Christ was to establish after ages.[117]

Various contributions to *The Art of Reading* (1800), which was reissued at least eleven times by 1817, also cast shadows upon Jews and their creed. The Hebrews, "blinded by prejudice," were important only as forerunners of Christianity, a faith infinitely better than their narrow, exclusive outlook.[118]

Similar sentiments were expressed by the Dartmouth College professor John Hubbard in a personalized, and hence more provocative, context in *The American Reader* (1804), a primary school text that went through at least five editions in seven years. "A conceited doctor of the Jewish law, with a design to insnare our blessed Saviour," debates with Christ over attainment of eternal life. The Israelite, whose "sect had limited the sense of neighbor to those of their own nature and religion," argues from particularistic principles commonly imputed to Judaism by Christian apologetics. But the Savior "leave[s] the doctor speechless" by telling the story of the good Samaritan, that allegory of universal benevolence. Hubbard later quotes from the New Testament "St. Paul's Defence Before Agrippa and Festus" to show Paul as a Jew persecuting Christians and later as an apostle being threatened by his former coreligionists.[119]

Although textbook authors more often accused Jews of religious offenses than of secular vices, mundane stereotypes were not rare in their works. *The Art of Reading* contained an account of "a Jew peddlar . . . who paid" poor servants "in specie scarce a fifth part of our nominal and intrinsic value." Another cautionary tale for young readers, in *The Book of Commerce* (1837), reprinted at least six times by 1862, recounted the experience of an impoverished lady from whom a Jew wanted to buy a precious stone. "The woman was shrewd enough to know that a Jew would not give five shillings for any thing unless it were worth a great deal more." Refusing his offer, she later discovers the stone to be a large diamond for which she gets a thousand guineas.[120]

Abraham T. Lowe, in *Second Class Book* (1825), a history and geography text for the lower grades that was in its third edition by 1831, employed the customary artifice of making Jewishness synonymous with deplorable behavior. A contributor to this volume described modern Greeks as "more barefaced in their impositions than even the Jews."[121]

Joseph E. Worcester, a celebrated lexicographer and opponent of Noah Webster's attempt to create a national language, attacked Jews on intellectual grounds. As restrictions on Jews loosened in the eighteenth and nineteenth century, their increasing participation in western culture created a new confrontation with an old foe. Worcester, an anglophilic New Englander who came from a family of Congregational ministers, attended Yale, and was a schoolteacher, historian, and geographer as well as a lexicographer, did battle for western culture against invasion from the ghetto. In *An Epitome of History* (1827), in its third edition by 1836, he told grammar school pupils that "Hebrews . . . were in some degree enlightened; yet they were never, in any age, distinguished for science or philosophy."[122]

An older kind of attack appeared in Lowe's *Second Class Book*. From the patristic age onward, Israel was identified with the enemies of Christendom as an underling of Satan and an ally of the Moors. In modern times these unholy alliances have been updated to link Jews to the Russian Revolution and other Communist movements or to attribute Jewish "blood" to Hitler, Lenin, or other current anathemas of the West. Lowe employed this strategy by including in his anthology "Mahohmet," an essay describing the founder of Islam as venal, despotic, impious, and megalomaniacal and the Muslim creed as repressive and dictatorial. The author claimed that the prophet had a Jewish mother and hired Jews to help write the Koran and "to accomplish his purpose" of tyrannical self-aggrandizement.[123]

In 1836, at the end of the Jacksonian era, appeared the first of the legendary *Eclectic Readers,* unsurpassed among American textbooks in readership, influence, and commercial success. Seven million *Readers* were sold by 1850. Written by William H. McGuffey, a professor and college president and Presbyterian minister, these selections of poetry and prose aimed to teach reading and a conservative outlook. McGuffey sought to instill in young readers a traditional Protestant piety; a middle-class ethic of education, industriousness, honesty, and individual achievement; and a Federalist-Whig reverence for social order and private property and repugnance against Jeffersonian-Jacksonian demagoguery and mob rule.[124]

Christianity is "the religion of our country," McGuffey told an audience of professional pedagogues in 1835. He warned against threatening "our country's quiet, by teaching . . . revolutionary principles of modern infidelity." Two years later, Lesson 19 of *The Eclectic Third Reader,* "More About the Bible," addressed an older infidelity: "consider the Jews as the keepers of the Old Testament." Their "sacred volume . . . contained the most extraordinary predictions concerning the infidelity of their nation, and the rise, progress, and extensive prevalence of christianity [sic]."[125]

## Popular Culture

Sabbath and secular school references to Jews ensured that aversion would be imparted to the next generation. Disparagement from the pulpit and by Christian organizations and politicians further inculcated anti-Semitism. The deeply embedded dislike of Jews also revealed itself in other products and shapers of popular culture, including journalism, literature and folklore.

~

Newspaper attacks on Mordecai Manuel Noah and his religion went beyond the usual invective of party squabbles and electoral contests. A *New York Herald* editorial of 1837 reached new depths of scurrility in its vilification of Noah and his creed. The *Herald's* publisher was James Gordon Bennett, a Scottish immigrant and former Catholic seminarian who had virtually inaugurated sensational journalism by founding the penny daily. His grievance against Judaism naturally projected itself onto Noah, its most visible American proponent, and was compounded by the *Herald's* rivalry with Noah's *Evening Star* and by Bennett's feud with Martin Van Buren, of whom Noah was a supporter.

The editorial was entitled, "Roy's Hebrew Lexicon—Secret Conspiracy against Religion Developed." The Redeemer and apostles, it claimed, fought "superstitious infidelity and ferocity of the Jews." Present "opposition" to Christianity is "stimulated by the same people who, in Jerusalem, cried out 'crucify him'," by "a certain portion of the blaspheming, infidel Jews of modern times." Recent "leading atheists and deists—the prime infidels were all Jews." Without "a country—without a home—without a nation, this singular people still continue to make war in disguise on that great system of revelation . . . which subverted the people and name of the Jews." The Talmud "show[s] the real sentiments of this race of secret conspirators against religion." Jews "beguile and deceive those among whom they live, in order to better crush all religion under the secret poison of infidelity and atheism, but their Talmuds and Targums are evidences against them." Noah and his paper are "evidence of this modern Jewish conspiracy against the principles, mysteries, or morals of the Christian dispensation." Bennett accused the Jews of sexual, as well as spiritual, degeneracy. "On the great question of morals," he claimed to have realized "from their own sacred writings" that "Jews of the present day retain still their own notions of polygamy . . . love, founded on purity and intellect between man and woman—is not a tenet in their book of morals."[126]

Another major daily, the *New-York Evening Post,* in an editorial of 1822 concerning a pamphlet on the Jews, recognized their rights of "hospitality and citizenship." But the *Evening Post* was outraged that the Jewish author questioned the divinity, and even the existence, of Christ and called the ASMCJ a moribund falsifier of Judaic beliefs. The pamphlet, the writer asserted, mounted "the most daring, impious and indecent attack on the Christian religion that has ever yet appeared." Although entitled to "quiet and undisturbed worship," Jews must "not abuse these privileges" and "turn upon the hand thus extended toward them." Let "them refrain from open and outrageous attacks upon this community," a "wanton species of cruelty . . . no society, who duly regards the welfare of its members, can ever tolerate."[127]

In this editorial the *Evening Post's* editor William Coleman, once Alexander Hamilton's chief journalistic spokesman and still head of the newspaper founded by the Federalist leader, prescribed the limits of tolerance for the Jews. America was a Christian land. So long as Jews acknowledged subordination by tacitly accepting a dual standard, as in medieval debates between priests and rabbis in which their creed could be challenged but they could not challenge the dominant faith, they would be permitted to worship as they pleased, to hold formal rights of citizenship, and to participate in the national community. Given the circumstances of their coreligionists elsewhere, the United States was generous, but its Jews had not yet achieved equality. Most Americans would have disavowed the *Herald's* fulminations. But they would have endorsed the *Evening Post's* warnings against overstepping the boundaries of benevolence by demanding equality. The national motto might be "in many one," but for Jews it meant "in tolerance deference."

Even journals noteworthy for defending Jews could also resort, though less often and less viciously than did the *Herald* and *Evening Post,* to anti-Semitic commentary. Hezekiah Niles, founder and editor of *Niles' Weekly Register,* usually championed the rights and virtues of Jews. The *Register,* eventually located in Washington, was the nation's earliest national news-paper and most influential weekly; its editorials were widely reprinted in the press and its subscribers included presidents, cabinet secretaries, con-gressmen, and prominent state and local officials. Niles lampooned con-version societies, objected to foreign and domestic persecutions, welcomed Jewish immigration, lauded Maryland's "Jew bill," and commended Jewish charity, zeal for education, and progenitorship of Christianity.

The Quaker editor, however, lapsed into conventional objurgation. Edi-torials in 1816 and 1822 accused Jews of shunning honest labor. An edi-torial advocating equal rights for and free admission of Jews also contained Niles's most extensive critique. Maryland constitutional constraints and "deprivation of Jews from human rights almost everywhere had a moral cause." Their "interests do not appear identified with those of the commu-nities in which they live." Jews "create nothing and are mere consumers. They will not cultivate the earth, nor work at mechanical trades, preferring to live by their wit in dealing, and acting as if they had a home no where."[128] Thus contrary sympathies and principles notwithstanding, Niles slandered Jews as rootless parasites and clever traders who avoided productive work and had tenuous ties to the larger community. Even admirers lambasted Jews.

~

The theater, fiction, and folklore were less explicitly didactic and christo-logical than Sunday schools, theological tracts, missionary organizations, and sermons, less worldly than politics, and less purposefully instructional than public schools or newspapers. Drama, novels, poetry, and folktales, however, as society's designated and self-conscious purveyors of myths, symbols, and passions, expressed popular and primal facets of American culture. Bigotry was an elemental force in this culture. A primordial nega-tive correlative, the Jew therefore appeared in various literary and folk characterizations as sinister alien and ludicrous intruder—an object of fear and ridicule.

As a rule in American culture, the greater the pretension to lofty thought and refined sentiment, the closer the emulation of European, especially British, gentility. The stage was no different in this respect from architecture, painting, prose, or verse; consequently, villains, heroes, and heroines in American plays resembled their foreign cousins. But the simi-larity of Jewish caricature also stemmed from the derivative yet inde-pendent existence of New World anti-Semitism.

The late eighteenth and early nineteenth centuries brought a reduction in the number of diabolic Jewish characters portrayed in English, French, and German drama. Grotesquely criminal or comic rather than cosmically malevolent, Jewish characters were now usurious skinflints, unctuous clothing salesmen, scheming peddlers, deceitful spies and forgers, or other embodiments of venality. In these guises the Jews in contemporary European plays bore greater mutual resemblance to their American counterparts than would have been the case if the Hebraic fiend had still dominated old world depictions. Increasingly in the nineteenth century, on both sides of the Atlantic, modern figures spoke in simulated Yiddish and German that induced malapropisms and thus burlesqued their ethnicity and reminded the audience of the alien and humiliating status of Jews.[129]

Few Jewish characters appeared, but their depiction was preponderantly derisive, whether in works from abroad performed here, American adaptations and imitations of such plays, or indigenous theatrical productions. According to the historian of anti-Semitism on the American stage, "Disparaging references, stereotypical personae, and caricatured behavior mark the first century of theater in American as routinely anti-Semitic."[130]

Of the foreign imports, Shylock, despite occasional sympathetic versions, was the most widely seen despicable Jewish character. Another familiar type transplanted from abroad appeared in *Trial without Jury; or, The Magpie and the Maid* (1815), a play adapted from a French melodrama by John Howard Payne, an actor, playwright, critic, and theatrical journalist, publisher, and press agent. Among the characters is Solomon Isaac, a peddler speaking in Yiddish dialect. A cunning bargainer, Isaac buys a silver spoon for a pittance from the heroine, an innocent maiden who needs the money to save her father. "I'll wager now he's got it for nothing," observes another character. "For they are so Jewish, these Jews." The sly peddler is a coward, another trait frequently assigned Jews.[131] Late in life, in 1842, as a reward for his literary fame, Payne, this lampooner of Jews, was made consul at Tunis, a post formerly held by another versatile American playwright, Mordecai Manuel Noah.

Jewish sharpers also appeared in plays by American authors. The earliest was the villain Ben Hassan in *Slaves in Algiers* (1794), not coincidentally the first American play with Jewish characters. *Slaves in Algiers* was a patriotic rescue drama by English-born Susanna Haswell Rowson, who lived most of her life in Massachusetts and was a well-known actress, playwright, novelist, literary magazine editor, children's textbook author, and educator. She appeared in the first run of the play, performed in Philadelphia and Baltimore. Hassan is a former "old cloathes man," a reviled occupation ascribed to Jews almost as often as usury, forgery, and pawn-broking. In fact Hassan also engaged in these other pursuits, forging bank checks and lending money at fifty percent interest. "So, having cheated the Gentiles, as Moses commanded," and fearing the gibbet as a result, he flees from London to Algiers. There he gets rich by collecting ransom money for Americans captured by the Barbary privateers. He acquires greater wealth by betraying his clients so that they may be recaptured, or by falsely claiming not to receive the money their families send and asking for additional payments. To accentuate Hassan's deviousness, Rowson has him profess to Christians his good intentions but speak to himself in asides that reveal his true purpose. "I feel very much for poor Christians," he tells one potential victim. "I should be very glad (aside) to have a hundred or two of them my prisoners."[132] She further associates Judaism with duplicity by writing Hassan's dialogue in the bogus German-Yiddish dialect that was the lingua franca of anti-Semitic hyperbole. The archetypal Jewish villain, treacherous, avaricious, and cowardly, Hassan was the first of many similar characters on the American stage.

Roswell introduced another hackneyed European image to American drama—the evil Jew's angelic daughter. As virtuous as Hassan is vicious, his daughter Fetnah saves the Christian hero and, drawn to his faith, leaves her father for him. The typology of Jewish fictional characters distinguishes between father-daughter, male-female, old-young, ugly-beautiful, evil-good, corrupt-innocent, damned-saved, and, ultimately, Jewish-Christian. Some of these distinctions arise from the Judaeo-Christian view of Judaism as a patriarchal religion. Christian theology posits Judaism as a father or an elder brother, but never as the mother of Christ and his creed, and, as discussed in Chapter 2, Christianity is in oedipal rebellion against the older faith. Christians attribute putatively feminine qualities of nurturance such as empathy, pacifism, spirituality, love, mercy, sacrifice, unconditional forbearance, and universal forgiveness to Jesus and his earthly mother. To the Hebrews they ascribe masculine faults of belligerence allegedly displayed in being obdurate and warlike, craving conquest and vengeance. It is chiefly male Israel that dreamed of a messiah who would slay its enemies and restore its territory, and Hebrew men bear the primary responsibility for the crucifixion. Jewish women, according to this dichotomy, are more open to Christian grace. Moreover, despite the seductive and despoiling Jewess in ritual murder myths and other folklore and in literature, the Jewish man is the basic incarnation of Judaic lechery and therefore the likelier violator of Christian innocence. He assaults this purity in its divine form of Christ and in its highest state of earthly chastity—Christian maidenhood.

The shady Jew also appeared, though less blatantly than in *Slaves in Algiers* or *Trial without Jury,* in a work by Nathaniel Parker Willis, a literary figure of greater renown than Payne or Rowson. Willis was well known as an aesthete and as the editor of the short-lived but influential belletristic *American Monthly Magazine,* a playwright, a poet, an author of short stories and sketches, and a foreign correspondent whose specialty was high society. In Willis's romantic tragedy *Tortesa the Usurer* the hero, against type, is a Jewish moneylender. In an otherwise sympathetic portrayal, however, Willis has Tortesa aphoristically refer to the mercenary Jew: "Has, like a penny in a Jew's close pocket, / Stolen the color of a worthier coin." The drama opened in 1839 with the famed American actor James W. Wallack in the title role. After a successful run in New York, it was produced elsewhere in the United States and in London.[133]

Jewish characters in American plays invariably resided in exotic lands, a strategy that heightened the image of the Jew as a mysterious outsider. Willis placed his Jewish protagonist in Renaissance Florence. For Rowson, the scene was Algiers, then on American minds as a Barbary State to which the nation paid tribute for passage of her ships in the Mediterranean. In 1801–05 and 1815 the United States ended Barbary piracy through successive victories over Tripoli and Algiers. Two leading Barbary Jewish families financed the Turkish proconsul in Algiers, supervised buccaneers, and lent money to ransom prisoners of the brigands, often at extortionary rates.[134]

Another playwright who wrote about Algiers and the Jews was Royall Tyler, whose *The Contrast* (ca. 1787) was the second play and first comedy written by an American. To that play and to a novel, *The Algerine Captive,* Tyler owes his stature as the foremost man of letters in the early republic. A Federalist and a friend and literary collaborator of Joseph Dennie's, Tyler also distinguished himself as a lawyer, jurist, and professor of jurisprudence. Fortunately, the reputation of this literary and legal luminary did not depend on his biblical dramas.

Tyler wrote four unproduced and unpublished plays, three of them, *The Origin and Feast of Purim, Joseph and His Brethren,* and *The Judgement of Solomon,* in blank verse. The exotic surroundings in which Tyler placed Jews were their scriptural settings of Babylon, Egypt, and Israel. Each play is subtitled "A Sacred Drama," but they are more sententious than inspirational. Old Testament narratives are turgidly transformed into harbingers of Christian triumphalism. In these homiletic dramas Jehovah's Chosen ungratefully and unremittingly complain to him, defy their creed and their Lord, and regress to heathenism. A Jewish prophet in *The Origin of the Feast of Purim* foretells the coming of the "glorious savior, sent by God," to "bring light and life, good will and peace." The Jews call him "a lying prophet," arguing that their "Messiah . . . Comes not to bless the nations of the earth." In "might and regal pomp," he will "appear," and wielding "his sword God's chosen will avenge" us on "our enemies." The patriarch Joseph thanks Jehovah for making Jews "A Chosen People," but adds that their "sceptre" will "fade" when the "Messiah" brings "Salvation . . . into the world."[135]

Images of Jews improved in late-eighteenth- and early-nineteenth-century western European belles lettres, for the same reasons and in the same ways as in the theater. The Age of Reason inhibited demonization and encouraged humanitarian perspectives which expanded sympathy for Jews and other minorities. Although a number of works conveyed a better view of the Jew, routine fictional portrayals, such as Fagin in *Oliver Twist* and other figures and themes in English, French, and German literature, cast Jews as rogues.[136] Such villains also regularly appeared in American prose and poetry. Two early national novels, *The Algerine Captive* and *Modern Chivalry,* typed Jews as unscrupulous or ridiculous.

In title, topic, and treatment of Jews, *The Algerine Captive* (1797), the fourth published American novel, was similar to *Slaves in Algiers.* Like Rowson's play, Tyler's picaresque satire on the seizure of Americans by Barbary brigands used a popular subject with an exotic atmosphere to castigate Jews. Unlike Tyler's biblical dramas, *The Algerine Captive* rebuked contemporary Jewry, and its popularity (four editions by 1816) brought this detraction to a far wider audience. Rowson and Tyler also shared the strategy of presenting contrary yet consanguine major characters. Contrast between good and bad Jews became a cliché in fiction that was not rabidly anti-Semitic. Although pairing moral with immoral Jews is not in itself a sign of bigotry, this schema often does indicate derogation.

Evil and virtuous Jews are usually, as in *Slaves in Algiers,* exemplified in father and daughter. Tyler, however, distinguishes between father and son. Adonah Ben Benjamin helps an imprisoned American physician, Updike Underhill, purchase his freedom from the Algerian pirates. Underhill cures Ben Benjamin's son of fever, but the young man then steals the money Underhill has left with his father and betrays the doctor into reenslavement.[137]

Tyler also makes the directly anti-Semitic accusation that Jews are "too wilfully blind to see the accomplishment of their prophecy in the person of our Saviour" and delusionally worship a Judaic Messiah. The well-born and well-to-do New Englander also scourges this "cunning race" for "compensat[ing] themselves for the loss of Palestine by 'engrossing the wealth and often the luxuries of every other land.'" No longer expecting a "heavenly king" to "re-possess them of the holy city," and conquer "their enemies," they "solace themselves with a Messiah whose glory is enshrined in their coffers. Rigidly attached to their own custom, intermarrying among themselves," they are "content to be apparently wretched and despised, that they may wallow in secret wealth."[138]

Hugh Henry Brackenridge's *Modern Chivalry,* the earliest literary work of the rustic west (then the Allegheny Mountain territory in Pennsylvania), was published in installments between 1792 and 1815 and reprinted thirty-eight times by 1857. The first best-selling novel by a native author, it surpassed the success of *The Algerine Captive.*[139] Both books belonged to the genre of picaresque, satirical adventure, the two markedly resembled each other, and their authors also had much in common, both being legal scholars and state supreme court justices, respectively in Pennsylvania and Vermont.

Both also debased Jews in their fiction. From a rationalist outlook, the Democratic-Republican Brackenridge impaled grasping lawyers, blackguard journalists, corrupt officials, ignorant Irishmen, greedy peddlers, Methodist preachers, and social and intellectual puffery. Jews were incidental targets in this political and philosophical burlesque of American values, manners, and types; they drew less ridicule, for example, than did hypocritical politicians or Irish-Americans. Nevertheless, references to them were always pejorative. The initial installment of *Modern Chivalry* contained a poem against literary critics which included a shaft aimed at "The Rabbin and the Talmudist," who "Fought . . . About the pentateuch of Moses; / Their tales, the wildest stuff, God knows is." Having dispatched Judaism, in Enlightenment fashion, as a superstitious creed, Brackenridge scoffed at contemporary believers. An installment of 1804 recounted, in dialect, the reaction of a Jew watching a peddler begging for customers: "It is all de love of de monish, said a Jew. His conscience is monish. I go anoder way to from exchange dish morning." The following year's edition mentioned the folk maxim, "Don't like to be as rich as a Jew."[140]

Jews were not regular subjects in American literature, an indifference suggesting their relatively calm reception in the young nation. As created by successors of Tyler and Brackenridge, Jews were generally minor characters in secular works. In fiction with religion as a major theme, Christianity was preferred, but Judaism was not ordinarily despised. A staple of American folklore and a recurrent item in missionary organs, "The Converted Jew" benignly rendered Christian triumphalism. A version published in 1821 in the *Methodist Review* and later in the *Magazine of the Dutch Reformed Church* tells of an orthodox Jewish widower who moves from London to Ohio with a beautiful, refined, and intelligent daughter. On her deathbed, the daughter asks her father, as a token of his love, to accept Jesus because the Messiah revealed himself during her illness and promised to save her soul. After her death, the Jew, who has taught his child to revere Mosaic Law, adopts Christianity.[141]

Henry Ruffner, a Presbyterian minister, religious historian, and president of Washington College (later Washington and Lee University), conceived an uncommonly sympathetic treatment of Jews. Belonging to an increasingly rare species, southern abolitionists, Ruffner publicly opposed slavery. His penchant for defending the oppressed also expressed itself in two short novels against anti-Semitism, early contemplations of the problems of mixed marriage. *Judith Bensaddi* and *Seclusaval* were published in 1839 in the *Southern Literary Messenger,* a leading cultural periodical in that region, and were reviewed in northern and southern journals. They were set in western Virginia, where Ruffner lived all his life. Judith Bensaddi is the standard fictional Jewess, beautiful, dark, romantic, refined, noble, and a Christian proselyte. She and her lover eventually overcome regional prejudices and are united in matrimony. Levi, the sole unattractive Jewish character, is a stock Jewish rogue. An old, small, shriveled, sharp-visaged, rapacious swindler, he impoverishes Judith's father.[142]

"The Converted Jew" and Ruffner's books were, at worst, marginally anti-Semitic. At the opposite pole in religious fiction was Sarah Pogson Smith's savage remonstrance *Zerah, the Believing Jew.* Originally published in 1838, to raise funds for a Protestant church building in the Mississippi Valley, it was reissued in 1857, according to the author, to foster charity in young people. Whatever benevolence Smith hoped to induce certainly was not directed toward Jews. *Zerah* unstintingly glorifies Christianity and damns Israel at the time of Jesus and the apostles. Christ's followers are invariably sublime; Jehova's worshippers are inveterate wretches who delight in murder and lesser forms of vengeance against Christians. Good Jews convert or, like Paul, are evil before apostasy redeems them. As usual in Christian apologetic and homiletic literature, death is central. Retributively deserved by Jewish antagonists, it is an inspirational fulfillment, especially in martyrdom, for Christian protagonists.

Historic Israel is the nominal villain in this saga of early Christianity's trials and triumph. Smith's rhetoric reveals, however, that her real grievance is with enduring Judaism. The novel's hero, Zerah, is a Jewish convert to Christianity. Sanballad, Zerah's cruel, treacherous nemesis, has a "demoniac gaze." He tells Zerah, "take a Jew's vengeance, thou dastardly *Christian.*" Alemeth, Abishai, and Sanballad, the primary Jewish ogres, lust after either Rachel or Petronilla, Zerah's first and second wives, and seek to betray and kill them and their husband and destroy Christianity. Alemeth and Abishai fail in their vengeful pursuit of Petronilla, (the daughter of the apostle Peter), but Sanballad is instrumental in arranging the slaying of Rachel, by edict of the Sanhedrin, for turning Christian. These fanatics emblematize Jewish wickedness. A scene in which Hebrews dispute that Jesus is the Resurrection and the Life shows "the malignity of the Jews." The "Unhappy Jews" stone Peter's wife, Perpetua, to death, though she warns them not to "add to your condemnation." In "destroying those of your nation who cannot . . . close their eyes to *truth* . . . I pray that the dreadful malediction ye called upon yourselves, '*His blood be upon us, and upon our children,*' may not be awfully verified." But "blindness prevailed" and "all was duly fulfilled: *destruction* and *dispersion. Yet still* they look for him, who *was* with us."[143]

Bitterness was rarer in poetry, even in religious verse, than in prose. But excoriation issued from an unexpected source, John Pierpont's collection *Airs of Palestine,* whose original publication in 1816 put him in the front rank of American poets. Six editions were printed by 1876. Pierpont displayed only occasional and mild deprecation in his textbooks, and other references to Jews in this volume, in "Airs of Palestine" (1816), "Christmas Hymn" (18??), and an untitled Christian hymn (1837), conveyed little or no hostility, but his poem "Jerusalem" (ca 1839), which first appeared in the 1840 edition, was exceptionally execrative. For rejecting the "crown of truth," "Jerusalem" now "bearest" its "cross," an "iron yoke is on [its] neck" and "blood is on [its] brow." Christological recrimination reverberated with Old Testament prophetic admonishment of Israel. Moslem dominion was the latest visitation of "the blood rod" that "long hath scourged, Thou city of our God! . . . Jerusalem, thy prayer is heard . . . HIS BLOOD IS ON THY HEAD!"[144]

Jewish subjects, naturally scarcer in secular than in religious fiction, were insultingly presented there as well. One unfortunate example appeared in a perennially popular novel by James Fenimore Cooper, America's foremost novelist from the 1820s until the advent of Nathaniel Hawthorne and Herman Melville, and its first internationally acclaimed belletrist. Cooper seldom mentioned Jews, and his lone antagonistic portrayal of them occurred in *The Bravo,* written in 1830, published in 1831, dramatized by R. P. Smith in 1837, and reprinted thirty-eight times, exclusive of various editions of Cooper's collected works, by the early 1900s. *The Bravo* was set in Renaissance Venice rather than the American wilderness, but its romantic plot was a staple of Cooper's writings.

A jeweler and merchant, Hosea, the bad Jew in *The Bravo,* is introduced with a description that reflects prejudice tempered with awareness that Jews were not solely responsible for their disposition: "The flowing dress, the grey and venerable beard, the noble outline of features, the quick, greedy, and suspicious eye, with an expression of countenance that was, perhaps, equally marked by worldly sagacity, and feelings often rudely rebuked, proclaimed a Hebrew of the Rialto." The sliver of sympathy is deepened by a contrast between Venetian segregation of non-Catholics and American religious tolerance. Hosea is portrayed as a moneylender charging exorbitant rates to profligate Venetian nobles. But Hosea is "a rogue, rather than a villain," and when he is accused of avaricious cunning, echoes of Shylock's protest against victimization (Hosea is pat-terned on Shakespeare's usurer), humanize him. "It is its sole defence against the wrongs of the oppressor," Hosea retorts. "We are hunted like wolves, and it is not surprising that we sometimes have the ferocity of the beasts you take us for."[145]

Notwithstanding these extenuations, Hosea has stereotypical vices. He looks at an expensive ring with "glittering eyes." A wise and upright Venetian senator warns that "the young hopes of Venice must not be left to waste their substance in unweary bargains with the gainful race." And Cooper notes that the "Hebrew" left "with a manner in which habitual cupidity and subdued policy completely mastered every other feeling."[146]

Jews played lesser but more spitefully drawn roles in works by other authors. Willis was much harder on Jews in "The Gypsy of Sardis" (1836), a narrative about a platonic love affair in contemporary Constantinople, than in *Tortesa.* A minor character is "one of the obsequious Jews who swarm about the pier as interpreters." He "laughed, as Jews do since Shylock, at the misfortunes of his oppressors."[147] Despite these remarks, the novella can be categorized as casually anti-Semitic. The interpreter is not evil and the Turkish characters are shadier.

Another unpleasant Jew in a cameo part is Mr. Isaacs in *The Adventures of Harry Franco* (1839), a satire of life in Manhattan by Charles F. Briggs, a New York newspaper and magazine editor. Isaacs has a long nose, black hair and eyes, and "broad lips screwed up like the mouth of a tightly drawn purse." He is stooped and "his dress has a second hand appearance." The sly Jew cheats the hero in a business transaction.[148] Here, too, anti-Semitism is not a central motif. Isaacs appears only briefly, and other ethnic types are also caricatured. Nevertheless, the narrative presages a subgenre in American anti-Semitic writing: accounts of the ugly, Jewish skinflint-swindler in the guise of a Manhattan merchant.

The Potiphars in *Morton's Hope* (1839) represent another new negation of the Jew, one rapidly gaining notoriety in life and literature. The novel was written by John Lothrop Motley, better known as a diplomat and a historian of Holland, and based on his student years in Germany after graduation from Harvard. The upstart image of the Jews drawn by this Boston Brahmin emerged as gradual emancipation opened opportunities in politics, business, and society in Europe and America. Formerly humiliated as peddlers, pawnbrokers, and petty shopkeepers, Jews would now also be subjected to contempt as rapacious lords of finance. Moses Potiphar, patriarch of a wealthy Jewish family in Germany, is a "large greasy looking plebian, a fat vulgar looking man." Besides being physically repulsive, Moses is a cowardly banker and speculator who, "with few scruples," has amassed a fortune. His Jewish friend is "a little sneaking bald-headed man," a "little blackguard," "a money lender."

Moses's daughter, Judith, is highly attractive, but in a sensual flamboyant style rather than the refined innocence of earlier fictional Jewish daughters. She is "handsome" with "glossy hair," a full mouth, and a voluptuous shape that "accorded well with her Eastern origin."[149] The Jewess as *arriviste,* already a conceit of European fiction when she surfaced in *Morton's Hope,* projected a hint of dissoluteness comporting with her father's or husband's commercial corruption and the Jewish male's designs on Christian female purity. This exotic femme fatale, an intrusive, immoral sexual threat, symbolized the Jews' alleged invasive pollution of the established social order.

Jews have greater impact and the "Jewish question" is more profoundly addressed in Theodore Sedgwick Fay's *Sidney Clifton; or Vicissitudes in Both Hemispheres* (1839). Nevertheless, the assessment of contemporary Jews in *Sidney Clifton* is less favorable than might be expected from Fay's explicit objection to anti-Semitism and appreciation of the Jew's "constan[cy] to his faith," and "melancholy grandeur." Although Israel's "former glory" sheds "undying lustre" on its descendants, "the holy zeal" has "long been quenched," and "sublime conceptions of an Isaiah and a Jeremiah no longer glow in the bosoms of their successors."[150]

In characterization as well as commentary, Fay sought to balance negative and positive images of Jews. Isaac Samuel, gray, old, wrinkled, bowed, and shabby, "presented a striking illustration of the fearful inroads that iron hearted avarice makes upon the frame and spirit of its worshippers . . . inordinate pursuit of gain was forever to prey upon his spirit." In an "exercise of the usurer's cupidity," he compels debtors to pay outrageous prices for cheap goods. The "wily and grasping Israelite," however, has a beautiful, innocent young daughter. Rachel Samuel is tragically enamored of Edward De Lyle, a cad who hopes through her love to avoid repaying a loan from her father. Unaware of their relationship, Isaac ruthlessly harasses Edward and thus indirectly causes Rachel's death. Driven mad by grief and desire for revenge, he kills Edward and commits suicide.[151]

Embodying good and evil in separate characters, rather than combining them as different facets of the same person, prevented Fay from achieving as subtle or rounded a conception as Cooper's Hosea. Recapitulating the gender distinction of *Slaves in Algiers,* Fay, like Rowson, degrades Jewish patriarchy by isolating the bad father from the good daughter. In this common characterization, love for his daughter is the Jew's one redeeming quality and when, as often happens, she dies or leaves him to marry the Christian hero, he either converts or remains wicked and hence bereft of human companionship.

~

Deeper in the national consciousness than depictions in journalism or literature lay images expressed in charms, aphorisms, hymns, ballads, songs, tales, and other folklore. Here were visceral reactions passed on in the workplace, the field, the kitchen, and the nursery, from generation to generation, between friends and playmates, and within families. Unguarded by the rules of restraint, evidence, reason, or politeness that disciplined public discourse, private and informal communication not only nourished socially respectable grievances against Jews as miserly, covetous connivers. It also preserved primitive obsession with a people labeled Christkillers, Christian haters, ritual murderers, sorcerers, and lascivious, bloodthirsty creatures with horns, tails, and other devilish peculiarities.

These impressions, rooted in colonial times and renewed by successive waves of immigrants, spread with advancing settlement. An old adage that since Hebrews allegedly spat at Christ during the crucifixion, "Spit into your hat, if you meet a cross-eyed Jew, and you will be very lucky," circulated in Adams County, Illinois, an area populated between 1820 and 1840 by farmers of northern and western European stock. "Pork is poison because it came from a Jew," went another Adams County aphorism, "meaning a Jew was turned into a hog."[152]

A hoary figure from the mythic past was poetically summoned to personify modern, as well as traditional, defects of his people. The grim destiny of Israel was described in "The Wandering Jew" (1833): a "sad momento of bright days," he survived Israel's "glory and her fall," her "lasting ruin and disgrace." For denying the suffering Christ, the wanderer lamented, the "mark of Cain is on my brow," an "Eternal emblem of my doom." The "lonely deathless man," long "doomed" to "this cold world" as "a stranger in a stranger's land," represents the exilic plight of the unrepentant Jews. The versifier also ascribes modern Hebraic vices to the inheritors of divine retribution: "Beneath the dreadful ban of God, / Judea's sons are scattered now," the "blasted wreck of former days— / And to the god of mammon bow."[153]

Folklore creatively modified received opinions to fit new situations and American culture. One such innovation, associating Jews with Yankees, started about 1820, first in conversation and then in print and on the stage. The relation between the one stereotype, a carryover from Europe, and the other, a new myth in a new nation, came about because both popularly signified acquisitive, acute, and aggressively venal traders and shopkeepers.[154]

Another mixture of old and modern was a lithograph of 1837 depicting a store with a sign, "Shylock Graspall Licensed Pawnbroker."[155] The traditional image of the greedy Jewish usurer surfaced in what for America were recent techniques in disseminating anti-Semitism. This early pictorialization and corruption of a surname to hyperbolize distasteful Jewish traits prefigured an epidemic of similar sketches in turn-of-the-century American humor magazines like *Life* and *Puck*.

"Moses Mordecai and Co. inform their friends and the world," began an even earlier (1808) anticipation of post–Civil War ridicule of crooked Jewish entrepreneurs, "that they have opened their Universal Ware and General Business Office, at the sign of Noah's Ark, No. 777, Mt. Ararat, Salem, where they tender their services in every possible business whatever." For "sale and barter," the proprietors offered bad bonds and checks, shares in dubious banks and insurance companies, and "counterfeit money."[156]

Negative images of Jewish businessmen prejudiced behavior toward Jews who engaged in commerce. Another ancient stock figure projected from Gentile hostility and fear, the Jewish peddler, was not only unpleasantly caricatured but sometimes placed in jeopardy. A German itinerant trader traveling through Delaware in 1835 was told that if he were Jewish he would be arrested for peddling without a license.[157]

Suspicion and contempt, aloofness and alarm, permeated all types of commentary on the Jews. Vilification was unexceptional and, therefore, randomly and often casually applied. Rebecca Samuel Alexander, an Episcopal proselyte, noted in 1791 that respectable New Yorkers and Philadelphians of German stock were anti-Semitic. A generation later, the Manhattan patrician Charles King, a former Federalist, recently failed merchant, and future president of Columbia College, announced that the Jew was "deficient" in patriotic "attachment" to "the soil of his nativity or residence." A letter of 1806 to the editor of the *Alexandria* [Virginia] *Daily Advertiser* complained that, because of a visit of Indians to Congress, ladies had to sit in "amongst Jews, Infidels and Negroes, . . . among the dingy group." So regularly were Jews lumped with infidels and Turks or some other pariah enclave that Morton Borden entitled his history of American anti-Semitism *Jews, Turks, and Infidels*. The renowned Unitarian minister, abolitionist, and peace and temperance reformer Samuel J. May remembered about growing up in Boston in the early 1800s that "children of my day were taught . . . to dread, if not despise Jews." Philip Minis, of a prominent Jewish family of Savannah, Georgia, shot dead a state legislator who called him a "damned Israelite" and a "damned Jew." A jury acquitted Minis, however, for fighting a duel to defend personal and religious honor.[158]

Routine vituperation reflected habitual distrust and distaste for, and distance from, Jews. "All Christian sects enjoy in America an entire liberty. The Jews have the exercise of their religion only," noted M. Otto, the French minister to the United States, in 1786. "It would be very remarkable if this people, after having suffered the contempt of all ages and nations, should succeed in taking part in the affairs of government. But . . . prejudices are still too strong to enable Jews to enjoy the privileges accorded to all their fellow citizens." Henry M. Brackenridge, lawyer, judge, journalist, historian, politician, and son of the novelist, shared this assumption. "Most of us have been taught from earliest infancy to look upon them as a depraved and wicked people," he told the Maryland Assembly in 1819, while serving in that body and addressing it on behalf of the "Jew bill." Our "minds" have been fixed in "unchristian hatred to a portion of our fellow citizens." New York's *German Correspondent* reported in 1820 that the "Jews are not generally regarded with a favorable eye, and 'Jew' is an epithet which is frequently uttered in a tone bordering on contempt." The newspaper further noted that "prejudices against the Jew exist here and subject them to inconveniences from which other citizens of the United States are exempt."[159]

As often happens in historical phenomena, conflicting patterns coexisted and every defamation can be countered with an affirmation. Ambivalence meant ambiguity. Thus Otto also mentioned that Jews ran for state offices and that in "several of the constitutions, it is enough to recognize a God to enter the assembly."[160]

Negative attitudes might not dictate hostile behavior if individuals had divided feelings or were loyal to American values of pluralism and liberty. Pogroms, massive boycotts, and anti-Semitic demagogues, organizations, and political parties, which plagued past and future generations of European Jews, were absent from the young republic. Even open invitations to discriminate did not inevitably bring adverse treatment. Jews sometimes held public office in breach of laws requiring test oaths; Sabbath observance statutes varied in stringency and were often only intermittently enforced; Noah lost an election in which animosity against his religion had an impact, but other Jewish candidates successfully ran for government office. The worst consequences of Jew hatred never befell American Jews, and even "normal" anti-Semitism was muted. Although Jews were not assaulted, they were insulted; they competed politically and commercially, but faced barriers and constraints unconfronted by white Protestants. Lesser victims of deprivation, humiliation, and violence than were blacks, Indians, and Catholics, Jews also suffered as an outgroup. Nevertheless, the era from 1780 to 1840 was a halcyon interval for Jews in America. Such good times would not come again for more than a century.

# ~ 5
# Mid-Century Crisis

American impressions of Jews worsened considerably between 1840 and 1865. A stereotypical *parvenu,* aggressively climbing the social ladder and flaunting material success in awkward and flamboyant opulence, rapidly became an anti-Semitic convention. The customer-duping, pinchpenny Manhattan Jewish merchant, usually a Chatham Street clothier, also underwent transition from suggestion to stereotype. In this quarter-century, too, relatively mild disparagement of earlier times rigidified and became more severe. These developments, coinciding with turmoil over slavery, disunion, and war, contributed to incidents of violent and systematic discrimination that recalled perils not faced by Jews in America since early provincial settlement. In the crucible of sectional conflict was forged modern American anti-Semitism.

## Europe

Jews in western and central Europe gradually acquired citizenship or benefited from loosening of old restraints. Substantial progress was made in England, where in the 1840s the first hereditary title was awarded to a Jew and Jews were permitted to hold municipal offices. In the next decade British Jews exercised full suffrage, served on juries, and became eligible for membership in the House of Commons. During the 1860s they were admitted to Oxford and Cambridge. Complete emancipation, except for entry into the House of Lords (1885), came in 1871, when Jews were allowed to hold state offices and Parliament repealed discriminatory public oaths and declarations. French Jews won full legal rights in 1846.[1]

Attainment of equality was slower and more problematic in central Europe. Between Napoleon's exile and the Revolution of 1848, German and Austrian Jews gained stature in culture, politics, and banking and trade. Young Germany, a group of intellectuals containing several converted Jews, sought to rejuvenate nationalism by agitating for democracy and against Christian restraint and doctrine. Disproportionately represented in revolutionary ranks, Jews in 1848 won citizenship in most German states and Austria. Prussian policy remained exclusionary, although constraints did begin to diminish there during the 1840s. Total emancipation was granted in the 1860s in Austria and the North German states and in 1871 throughout the newly unified Reich.[2]

In 1838–1840 Hungarian Jews were granted unlimited residential mobility, but developments in eastern Europe generally departed from those in the north and west. Blood libels, increasingly doubted in the west, circulated with unabated credibility in Romania, Russia, and Poland. Russian Emperor Nicholas I (1825–1855) attempted to forcibly convert Jews by conscripting them into the army. He also renewed medieval prohibitions against Jews' employing Christian servants and building synagogues near churches, and the medieval custom of censoring and burning Jewish books for alleged anti-Christian content. Legal restraints eased in the early years of the reign of Alexander II (1855–1881), permitting rich and educated Jews to leave the Pale and enter government service. But improvement stopped with the Polish insurrection of 1863, when, as usual, Jews suffered from civil turmoil. Pogroms started in 1871, just as Austria, Germany, Sweden, and Switzerland unconditionally emancipated their Jewish populations.[3]

Liberalization enabled Jews to enlarge their role in national and local communities, but sparked an ominous reaction. Resistance against freedom for Jews, derived from and supported by conventional Christian theology and institutions, also incorporated a secular dimension whose most dangerous form proved to be racism.

Modern anti-Semitism fully emerged between the 1870s and the 1890s, not coincidentally as Jews attained de jure equality, but the hatred of Jews that would culminate in the Holocaust had taken shape several decades earlier. The crisis of 1848 provoked anti-Jewish riots in France, Germany, Polish territory annexed by Prussia, and what today are Hungary and the Czech and the Slovak republics. Opponents of republican insurgency, such as conservative Junkers and Catholics, labeled Jews subverters of civil order and enemies of Christianity. Defenders of royalty and Christianity accused Jews of victimizing Christians through control of modern finance. Thus emerged dual depiction of the Jew as property-destroying revolutionary and property-amassing tycoon.[4]

Jews were also identified, from the left as well as the right, as an obstacle to national development. During the 1848 uprising in Hungary Lajos Kossuth and other nationalists opposed Jewish rights out of traditional belief that Jews were outsiders and exploiters of Hungarian peasants. Nationalist resentment also flourished because Jews, feeling protected in the conglomeration of peoples in the Hapsburg domains, were the sole ethnic group committed to the unity of the Empire. Hungarian and German patriots, resisting Austrian sovereignty, accordingly attacked Jews. Many of Franz Josef's subjects, loyal or rebellious, also thought that Jews supported the empire because the Rothschilds and other Jewish bankers were its financiers.[5]

From Napoleonic conquest through the 1860s adherents of Young Germany and subsequent German liberal nationalists, like their Enlightenment predecessors, judged Judaism to be superstitious and primitive. They blamed Jews for not assimilating to German culture and, like Junkers and other reactionaries, accused Jews of exploiting the German people, using the Rothschilds as evidence of cosmopolitan (that is, antinational), despoiling Jewry. These complaints intensified in the 1840s in Germany, and in the 1860s in Austria, with an upsurge of envy of Jews' economic advances and fear that freedom for Jews would increase competition in commerce, the crafts, and the professions.[6]

Greater danger stemmed from romantic, volkish nationalism and its inevitable development into racial nationalism, which designated the Jew the unassimilable alien. Uniting emergent nationalism with pagan legend, medieval myth, resentment of modernism, and the new biology of evolution and genetics, volkish ideology transformed the Jew from outsider to outcast, from redeemable to intransigent foe. In England the new Jew hatred was inhibited by political stability and institutionalized antiauthoritarianism; in France it was combatted by republican sentiments and traditional, Catholic anti-Semitism. Hence it attained its purest form in Germany. Racial anti-Semitic ideology unfolded in a series of antinomies. Worthy traits were interrelated and incarnated in the upright citizen and the true nation. Their opposites, the marks of degeneracy, were also interrelated and personified by the Jew, nemesis and contradiction of the good citizen and the virtuous country. On the right (in both senses) side were the legatees of the pagan and medieval past. Rooted in blood, land, and inherited culture and social standing, they descended from simple, solid, clean, courageous, faithful, traditional, emotional warrior-peasant stock. These Aryans were organic citizens of the Second and Third Reichs by dint of patrimonial relationship to the First Reich. They were confronted by the Jew, their antipodal enemy, who was modern, cosmopolitan, atomistic, restless, rational, skeptical, and spurious. An aloof, calculating, urban, ghettoized businessman, a deflowerer of blond maidens and thus a defiler of Aryan or Nordic blood, the Jew introduced philistine, degenerate foreign culture. The eternal intruder was corrupt, cowardly, anomic, materialistic, and competitive. The Jew as bourgeois archetype and international capitalist joined with the Jew as anarchic and communistic world conspirator to corrode the racial and only healthy basis of national and western civilization.[7]

Racialism emerged as a creditable outlook in Europe during the 1850s and 1860s. Although Count Joseph Arthur de Gobineau, chief founder of the racist school of social interpretation, personally admired the Jews when he wrote *The Inequality of Human Races* (1854), his followers turned his ideas against this people. *Inequality* posited a "Jewish type" shaped by "race" and thus fundamentally unchangeable by environmental and historical "modifications" and unassimilable.[8]

As he aged, Gobineau grew more anti-Semitic, convinced of Aryan superiority, and attracted to the cult of Odin. In these respects he resembled his friend Richard Wagner, the artistic genius of German nationalism. Pagan and medieval legends reverberated in Wagner's operas, and mythic Aryan heroes marched through these epics. The composer became a confirmed racist and anti-Semite; by 1850 hostility permeated his private references and public writings on Jews. The "cultured Jew" was the arch-villain in Wagner's contribution to the interminable nineteenth-century German debates over the "Jewish question." Alienated from "our [German] essence," the "Jewish intellect" is "reflective" not "instinctive," foreign to "the folk source" and "its life-bestowing inner-organism," and racially imprisoned in a pecuniary and parasitical aesthetic. "Judaism is the evil conscience of our modern civilization."[9]

French Republican nationalists, roughly counterparts of the German liberals, also denounced Judaism. The historian Jules Michelet, a defender of the Revolution and the uprising of 1848, in the enormously popular *The People* (1846), called Jews usurers who "terrorize" debtors and, as masters of "the local money market," exact "a pound of flesh" from French manufacturers desperate for capital. Operating "everywhere," controlling "the funds of every [European] state," the upstarts, out of "vanity," over-confidence, and avidity for status and dominion, incurred "political risks" by controlling "kings" and "mingl[ing] with the aristocracy." Michelet also discerned, as did German nationalists, "a Jewish prejudice against nature" and hatred for the nation in which they lived.[10]

Liberals and radicals were not as extensively or virulently anti-Semitic as right-wing Christians or religious or secular nationalists. But even moderate leftists often considered Judaism an atavistic creed. Nearly all socialists and liberals, like their Age of Reason forebears, demanded absorption of Jews in a national state, or, more radically, in a socialist society; a spiritually genocidal imperative voiced only by extreme anti-Semites in reactionary Christian or nationalist circles. Right and left agreed, too, in attacking Jews for being ruthless, parasitic, warmongering capitalists who oppressed workers and peasants, funded tyrants, and bled countries.

French utopian socialists—Fourier and his disciples from the 1820s and 1830s, Saint Simonians in the 1840s and 1850s, and Proudhon and his followers in the Second Empire—judged Jews by these princip-les.[11] German radicals harbored similar views. The young left-wing Hege-lians Ludwig Feuerbach, Bruno Bauer, and Karl Marx accused Judaism of being "egoistic." Wilhelm Marr, an early racist anti-Semite who in the 1870s would coin the term "anti-Semitism," as a revolutionary democrat in the 1840s rebuked rich Jews and blamed German Jews for the failure of 1848. Jewish-born Ferdinand Lassalle, leader of the General Work-ingmen's Association (1863), denigrated Jewish liberals and businessmen. His successors and other officers of the organization were also anti-Semitic.[12]

Radical socialism, at least in its Marxist strain, and Christianity have striking similarities. Marxism dwells upon the class struggle more than the utopian outcome of proletarian victory. Christianity is only slightly less concerned with conflict than with fulfillment. Both ideologies also claim moral superiority and triumph over their respective progenitors, capitalism and Judaism. At the same time, they derive their identity by defining their creators as antithetical, indomitable opponents. Perhaps Communism, like Christianity, had an oedipal resentment at its core. Both revolutionary movements have argued that their parental antecedent, if not destroyed, or at least defeated, would eliminate them.

These convergences may bear on another mutual belief—anti-Semitism. Marx, whose father converted from Judaism to Christianity, resorted to street slurs like "Jew-boy" and ridiculed Jewish noses and "a nastily Jewish physiognomy." Lassalle, an adversary, was a "Jewish-Nigger," as "proved by his cranial formation and [curly] hair."[13] In "On the Jewish Question" (1843), the messiah of modern communism propounded the secular socialist precept that the "Jewish problem" would vanish when religion disappeared.

An objection to Judaism that crossed ideological lines was the accusation of "aloofness" derived from Enlightenment sources of Marxian ideology. The Christian version of this complaint was that Jews stubbornly withheld themselves from the universal society of saved souls. Enlightenment *philosophes*, a source of Marxian ideology, felt that Jews shunned the light of reason. Anti-Semitic nationalists and racists thought Jews incapable of joining any Gentile community. Marx likewise interpreted the Jews' belief that they were the Chosen People as an excuse for "abstaining on principle from participation in historical movement" and abjuring "the general future of mankind."[14]

As conventionally debated, the "Jewish question" addressed matters of whether, when, or how much freedom should be given to resident Jews. For Marx, however, "political rights" were irrelevant: "by acquiring financial power," the "Jew has emancipated himself in a Jewish way." Marx placed in a new context the rationalistic indictment that the worst of Christianity derived from its Judaic roots. Since "money has become a world power," the "practical Jewish spirit has become the practical spirit of Christian nations. The Jews have emancipated themselves insofar as the Christians have become Jews." Marx also agreed with reactionary-romantic nationalists: the "nationality of the Jew is the nationality of the merchant, of the money-man," hence "the Jewish religion" has "contempt for theory, for art, for history." Thus intertwined in Marx's thought were Enlightenment blaming of Judaism for deficiencies of Christianity, romantic nineteenth-century anti-Semitism, and radical vituperation of Jewish entrepreneurship.[15]

"On the Jewish Question" was not an isolated diatribe. In "The Holy Family" (1845) and other writings, Marx abused Jews and their creed. Alternating between theoretical and vulgar denunciation, he associated Judaism with "the spirit of usury," called Jews "speculators and jobbers," and claimed that "every tyrant [is financially] backed by a Jew." Anti-empirical caricature of his religious heritage contradicted Marx's philosophical premises. Along with Jew haters on the right (and several on the left), he fantasized a global "Jewish organization of loanmongers" that "amassed" immense "fortunes": the "wrongs and sufferings thus entailed on the people and the encouragement thus afforded to their oppressors still remain to be told."[16] Ahistorically ignoring Judaism's long precedence of capitalism, he claimed that cabalized *Judentum* emiserated the masses, encouraged war, and impoverished nations.

Friedrich Engels was not as indefatigably hostile but disliked the same supposedly Jewish traits. English businessmen oppressing their workers, in *The Condition of the Working-Class in England in 1844* (1845), were like "bartering Jews." In *The Peasant War in Germany* (1850), Engels declared that Jewish "usury then as now sucked the blood of the peasants of Alsace." Like Marx, he saw distasteful "Jewish" attributes in Lassalle. It "is disgusting to see how he is always trying to push his way into the world of the upper classes," wrote Engels. "He is a greasy Jew disguised under brilliantine and flashy jewels."[17]

Racists and Christians differed over whether Jews could be redeemed. On other issues, such as ritual murder, reactionary anti-Semites of both types agreed. Eastern European Orthodox Christianity was particularly obsessive, but blood libel also agitated western and central parts of the continent. The murder of a priest in Damascus in 1840 invigorated French and German anti-Semitism. Paul Lawrence Rose has pointed out that the Damascus Affair revived, especially in Germany and central Europe, the association of Judaism, blood libel, and cannibalism. According to Rose's analysis, Molech now merged with Mammon, the demon of blood sacrifice, reincarnated as crucifier and ritual murderer, with the bloodsucking capitalist.[18]

Jewish phantoms sometimes assumed a more benign form. Novels about the Wandering Jew proliferated in the nineteenth century, particularly between 1840 and 1860. Eugene Sue's best-seller *The Wandering Jew* (1844–45) portrayed the character as a sorrowful old man for whom death brings the peace he has craved through the ages. Although gentle and noble, the eternal outcast nonetheless deserves punishment for tormenting the Savior. The Jew, though not here demonized, is nonetheless an alien, occult figure.[19]

Assailment of rationality, science, industry, cities, finance capitalism, and cosmopolitanism was vented in appeals to folk, tribe, blood, and instinct, in worship at the shrines of Gothic deities, and in glorification of legendary feudal heroes, and often in a belief in the occult. For many fighters against the modern temperament, the Jew embodied what they feared and hated. If they mystified their own past, so they mystified, often in a diabolical way, the Jew.

## America

### The Favorable Response

Citizens and observers of the American scene, then and now, who have made sectarian equality a republican imperative, might find this aspiration fulfilled by certain aspects of the treatment of Jews during the middle period. In 1842 Rhode Island removed the test oath, leaving New Hampshire and North Carolina the only states disqualifying professing Jews from holding public office.[20]

An expanding Jewish presence in public office provided further proof of progress. David Yulee and Judah P. Benjamin, respectively in 1846 from Florida and 1852 from Louisiana, were the first Jews in the U.S. Senate. Yulee had previously changed his name and renounced his heritage; thus Benjamin was the first self-acknowledged Jewish senator. Between 1840 and 1865 Jews went to Congress from Texas, Maryland, Alabama, and Pennsylvania. Schenectady, New York, Galveston, Texas, and several South Carolina towns elected Jewish mayors, and South Carolina and Louisiana had Jewish lieutenant governors. Numerous Jews served in state legislatures and as municipal administrators and councilors.[21]

Elimination of test oaths and election to public posts affirmed Jewish civic legitimacy, as did a Richmond rabbi's opening prayer at a Virginia House of Delegates session of 1849. Although a rabbi had spoken at the Virginia Constitutional Convention of 1829, this was the first blessing of a Jewish clergyman over a state legislature. In 1861 another spiritual leader from the same congregation prayed before a House of Delegates meeting.[22]

As in the earlier period, Jews received reassurances from political leaders. President John Tyler told a Baltimore Jew in 1843 that America promoted creedal equality. Liberty of conscience, he said, underwrote other freedoms and guaranteed that Jews would not be "downtrodden" as "in other regions." Tyler assured another Jew that in referring to the nation as "a Christian people" he did not mean to exclude Jews from a national day of prayer, and that he felt "profound respect" for the wisdom and morality of Judaism. An identical declaration of Christian nationhood by President James Buchanan in 1858 brought forth an identical reassurance.

Buchanan wrote a Milwaukee rabbi that he was an "advocate of religious liberty," held "many of your persuasion" in "the highest personal regard" and "never intended . . . any reflection on the Jews." Senator Lewis Cass expressed the same sentiments in 1854 in presenting to the Senate a protest from Jewish citizens against a treaty with Switzerland that excluded American Jews from trading rights and privileges in some cantons. Cass praised the United States for its religious tolerance, its role as a haven for oppressed Jewry, and the "law-abiding conduct" of its Jewish citizens.[23]

Other political actions, novel in themselves or in context, opened new routes of acceptance. In the 1840s Governor William Aiken of South Carolina went further than Tyler and Buchanan, excising Christian passages in a day-of-prayer proclamation issued by his predecessor. In a similar spirit the Virginia legislature in 1849 allowed Jews to work without penalty on Sunday. A year later the Philadelphia Democratic party organization repudiated its nominee for country treasurer after his anti-Jewish feelings became known. When the New York legislature in 1852 asked Albany clergymen to select candidates for chaplain, the ministers neither invited the rabbi of the Jewish congregation, Isaac M. Wise, to their meeting nor included him on the list. But the state senate agreed with Wise's insistence on being nominated and, over the objections of the pastors, unanimously appointed him the first Jewish chaplain of an American legislature. In another first, in 1860 a rabbi gave the invocation (partly in Hebrew) at a session of the U.S. House of Representatives.[24]

Another departure from tradition was that in the 1840s and 1850s prominent Jewish political figures like Benjamin and Yulee rarely suffered abuse of their religious heritage. The nativist movement, then leading the opposition to ethnic and religious minorities, railed against "Papists" and foreigners, but rarely attacked, and sometimes attracted, Jews. Louis Levin, a Know-Nothing congressman from Philadelphia from 1845 to 1851, was an ardent anti-Catholic and immigration restrictionist. Another Jew became vice president of the American Party Club in Nashville during the 1856 presidential election. The historian of the nativists and the Jews saw no "anti-Jewish prejudice" among leaders of the movement and little animosity at the local level.[25]

Even during the Civil War, a time of a nationwide storm of anti-Semitism, Jews made civic gains. Successively Confederate attorney general, secretary of war, and secretary of state, Benjamin was the second most powerful civil official in the Confederacy, second only to Jefferson

Davis. Quartermaster and surgeon generals of the South's army were Jewish, and Yulee served in the Confederate congress. Uriah Phillips Levy, promoted to commodore in 1860, was the earliest Jew to achieve flag rank. During the war Jews served as officers, as in all previous armed conflicts, but no longer was it rare, on either side, for them to be colonels, and some, unprecedentedly, became brigadier generals. In 1862 Congress authorized commissioned Jewish chaplains in the armed forces, a year after Catholic priests were accorded this privilege.[26]

Abraham Lincoln, who asked Congress to amend the act of 1861 that reserved the chaplaincy to Christians, resisted wartime abuse of Jews. He rescinded Ulysses S. Grant's expulsion of Jews from his command, pardoned several Jewish deserters, regularly promoted and decorated Jewish officers, and visited dying Jewish soldiers. Lesser officials also defended Jews. The American consul general in Frankfurt, in an 1863 letter to *Harper's Weekly,* praised the Rothschilds, a family frequently alluded to as epitomizing clandestine Jewish financial chicanery and dominance; he said they and other German Jews supported the Union, opposed slavery, and refused to fund the rebels.[27]

Civic and legal resolution of disputes between Jews and Christians over religious matters was the ultimate test of tolerance. Such conflicts arose between Catholics and Jews in St. Louis in 1858 and in New York in 1859. These confrontations were possibly inspired by the Mortara case of 1858, in which Edgar Mortara, a young Jewish child in Rome, was kidnapped by papal order to be raised in the Vatican because he had been baptized by his Catholic nurse. This incident had an American analogue when Captain Paulson Dietrich, a Jew, died in a Catholic hospital in St. Louis. Shortly before his death, Dietrich was baptized without his consent. The priest in charge of the hospital would not discuss the case or allow visitors to see the dying man. Protests elicited no concessions from the archdiocesan archbishop, and Dietrich was interred in a Catholic cemetery. The local Jewish congregation appealed to the mayor, who ordered reburial in a Jewish cemetery. Another interfaith controversy occurred when a nurse in New York attempted to kidnap and baptize a Jewish child. A local judge ordered that the youngster be returned to the parents.[28]

Widespread antipathy toward Catholicism made the St. Louis and New York outcomes inconclusive indicators of interfaith parity. A Protestant-Jewish confrontation before the Philadelphia Court of Common Pleas in 1851 furnishes stronger evidence that Jews in religious conflicts with Christians would not be denied equal justice. In an earlier trial Warder

Cresson, scion of a prominent Philadelphia Quaker family and the first American Consul in Jerusalem, had been declared mentally incompetent to handle his property and business affairs. Cresson's estranged wife, an Episcopal proselyte, together with their children charged him with insanity. The jury decided against Cresson because he had converted to Judaism and wished to spend his fortune on rebuilding a Hebrew temple in Palestine. Back in court in 1851, his attorney argued that anti-Semitism was the basis of the earlier finding, and the judge told the jury that religious belief was not evidence of derangement. The jury acquitted Cresson and local newspapers praised the verdict for defending religious freedom. Cresson then divorced his wife, married a Jew, and moved permanently to Jerusalem.[29]

In business, as in politics, progress mainly proceeded along routes already delineated in previous periods. Jews belonged to economic elites emergent at the founding or Americanization of such cities as New Orleans, Los Angeles, San Francisco, and Santa Fe. As general entrepreneurs in young, relatively undifferentiated communities, they pioneered key ventures in trade, transportation, manufacturing, real estate, and banking. Even in older places like Baltimore, Richmond, Charleston, Philadelphia, and New York, where social distinctions rigidified with time, Jews increased their role as directors and officers of prestigious firms. They were presidents of the Gas and Light Company of Charleston, directors of South Carolina's largest and most patrician banks, and chief executives of the Philadelphia Company for Insurance. In many places Jews attained local prominence, but in New York several achieved national and international repute. August Belmont and Company became an influential Wall Street investment firm in the 1840s because its founder was the Rothschilds' American agent. In the next decade J. and W. Seligman attained importance in commercial banking. Belmont and the Seligmans aided the North during the Civil War.[30]

Although social acceptance was a more elusive goal than political or economic advancement, Jews had yet to encounter massive exclusion from elite organizations, hotels, and neighborhoods. In this respect antebellum American Jewry regrettably faced the past rather than the future. The late-nineteenth-century upsurge of anti-Semitism did not prevent Jews from continuing to overcome discrimination in politics and, somewhat less steadily, in business, but it would take a century to regain their former social status.

Voluntary associations of varying status and function, as in previous generations, admitted Jews. In Philadelphia they were officers in the

American Philosophical Society, the Philadelphia Academy of Fine Arts, the Academy of Natural Sciences, the patrician Philadelphia Club, and leading charity organizations. Richmond Jews held commensurate posts in upper-class militia companies, social clubs, and eleemosynary societies. Jews in Charleston were presidents of the Charleston Antient Artillery Company and officers of other genteel social and benevolent institutions. A Chicago Jew captained a volunteer fire company. Jews and Gentiles in that city attended the same festivities and parties, and the municipal government allowed Jewish charities to use city property for fundraising. Similar acceptance of Jews took place in early Milwaukee, St. Paul, Los Angeles, New Orleans, and Atlanta. No other antebellum Jew equaled the celebrity of August Belmont. He was admitted to New York's premier club, the Union Club, in 1848, four years before Benjamin, another nonpracticing Jew. Belmont also celebrated the most brilliant intermarriage of the era (his bride was the daughter of the blueblood Commodore Matthew C. Perry) with the most fashionable wedding of the 1849 New York social season.[31]

Jews won renown in law and medicine and studied at prestigious colleges. Benjamin, a luminary of the Louisiana bar, made a fortune defending business magnates. Jews headed the University of Maryland Medical Faculty in 1857–58 and between 1848 and 1852 served as treasurer of the American Medical Association. Yale appointed its first Jewish faculty member in 1844, and four years later the first Jew graduated from its medical school.[32]

Aspirations to political equality and professional and social recognition were possible because many Americans believed in liberty and tolerance as a national principle and/or held favorable opinions of Jews. In Albany, New York, in the 1840s, when a trial attorney moved that Jewish witnesses be disqualified because the court should discount the sworn testimony of any Jew, the local rabbi, supported by Christian lawyers, denounced the attorney, who then apologized for falsely accusing Jews of endemic perjury. As in earlier eras, Gentiles demonstrated positive feelings by attending, and donating to, synagogue dedications and Jewish philanthropic events and community dances. Local public figures and newspapers and national journals like the *North American Review* and *Harper's Weekly* lauded Jews for steadfastness to their creed, successful adaptation to America, good citizenship, altruism, intelligence, sobriety, and care of their own and other dependents.[33] Such sentiments promoted federal government action on behalf of Jews in three significant international events, the Damascus affair of 1840, negotiations for a commercial treaty with Switzerland in 1850, and the Mortara case in 1858. Advocacy of Jewish interests abroad, however, could be easier than defense against domestic infringements.

When Jews in Damascus were charged with ritual murder, several suspects were tortured and sentenced to be hanged, and Jews in that city were mobbed. Philadelphia Jews held a protest meeting, and prominent Protestant pastors spoke at the meeting or in other ways offered their support. At a mass meeting in Charleston sponsored by the mayor and attended by the Catholic archbishop of Charleston and Protestant clergymen, the assemblage denounced the treatment of Damascus Jews and resolved that ritual murder was not part of Judaism and communicated this resolution to the president and American ambassadors. Van Buren and his secretary of state instructed the consul in Alexandria and the minister to Turkey to try to obtain a fair trial for the defendants and to halt attacks on Jews in Damascus.[34]

President Millard Fillmore objected to discrimination against American Jews in the 1850 commercial treaty with Switzerland, and the Senate refused ratification. Newspapers in many cities protested against the treaty and subsequent exclusion of American Jews from trading in some cantons. But there were limits to the federal government's commitment to protect its Jewish citizens abroad, let alone to act against oppression of those from other countries. The exclusionary provision in the treaty was enforced in 1857, when an American Jew was prevented from trading in a Swiss canton, yet Buchanan's administration did not abrogate the agreement.[35] Economic interest, not hostility toward Jews, motivated the government to acquiesce in foreign discrimination against its citizens, but the result was to distinguish, at least in this case, between Gentile and Jewish Americans, to consign the latter to a lesser status, and to leave unprotected their civil rights.

The secular press and Protestant journals sided with Jews in the Mortara *cause célèbre*. According to the historian of the American reaction to this incident, the latter were motivated less by pro-Jewish sentiment than by anti-Catholicism and a desire not to compromise missions to the Jews. Buchanan and Secretary of State Cass sympathized with the Jews, and protest meetings in Albany, Chicago, and San Francisco were attended by clergymen and politicians.[36]

The Civil War outburst of bitterness did not obliterate good will to Jews and dedication to religious freedom. Several newspapers during that time expressed esteem for Jews and/or condemned anti-Semitism, approved of a Jewish chaplaincy, and opposed Grant's excluding Jews from his command.[37]

Affirmation also appeared in literature, where, as in other respects, America recapitulated European developments. Although Jewish characters in fiction and on the stage were conventionally ridiculous or antagonistic, the softening trend begun in the eighteenth century persisted into the nineteenth. Sue depicted the Wandering Jew with dignity and sympathy. Dickens, perhaps making amends for Fagin, made *Our Mutual Friend* (1864–65) a plea for tolerance and a tribute to Jewry. The book featured a good Jew—the dignified, generous, and compassionate Mr. Riah, confidante and rescuer of the heroine—and portrayed outspoken anti-Semites as louts.[38]

The great antebellum tragedians on the American stage, Junius Brutus Booth and Edwin Forrest, acted Shylock compassionately. Some contemporary plays also portrayed Jewish characters positively. *Leah, the Forsaken*, adapted from a German play by Augustin Daly, a legendary figure in the American theater, opened in Boston and New York in 1862 and was regularly performed for another forty years. The setting of this phenomenal success, a rare direct onslaught on anti-Semitism, is an eighteenth-century Austrian village. Nathan, an apostate Jew, has left his father to die of starvation and torments Leah and other members of his foresaken religion. Proud, noble Leah is unfortunately betrothed to Rudolf, a weak, disloyal Christian who capitulates to family and village pressure against intermarriage. In the final scene Nathan is arrested for murdering an elderly Jew. After betraying Leah and wedding a Christian, Rudolf redeems himself by exhorting the emperor to allow Jews to live in the village. Exposing Nathan's criminal deeds and forgiving Rudolf and the villagers who have oppressed her, Leah leaves for America with other Jews. *Harper's Weekly*, editorially reviewing the play, praised the production for denouncing hatred of Jews.[39]

Positive or neutral images of Jews appeared with greater frequency in verse than in plays, possibly because theatrical productions were aimed at a wider audience and large profits might result from an appeal to popular prejudice. New England fireside poets John Greenleaf Whittier and Henry Wadsworth Longfellow were awed by Old Testament and medieval Hebrews. Whittier, in "The Crucifixion," did not blame Jews for the death of Jesus.[40]

Among other mid-century belletrists, Lafcadio Hearn appreciated the "touching" rite of an orthodox Jewish funeral and argued that false and offensive Jewish stereotypes on the French stage encouraged anti-Semitism. William Cullen Bryant celebrated free America, where "the Jew worships unmolested in his synagogue." On a more intimate note, Margaret Fuller in 1845 told her German Jewish lover: "I have long had a presentiment, that I should meet—nearly—one of your race, who would show me how the sun of today shines upon the ancient temple."[41]

Novels, also aimed at a large audience, were probably closer to plays than to poetry in depictions of Jews. Positive characterizations nevertheless surfaced in popular fiction. With the publication of *Julian* (1841), which was reprinted nine times by 1865, Rev. William Ware completed his trilogy on the plight of Jews and early Christians in the Roman Empire. In *Zenobia* and *Aurelian,* Ware portrayed Jews of New Testament times as benignly as possible from a traditional theological perspective. Jews and Judaism are shown even more favorably in *Julian,* where the hero is reprimanded for assimilating to Roman ways and denying his heritage. Pontius Pilate is vicious to the Israelites, an oppressed people bravely defending their faith. Julian ultimately regains his religious identity and leads the Jewish resistance to Rome. Although Ware considers the religious and political elite of Israel responsible for the death of Christ, he repudiates universal Jewish guilt. The Jews regret Christ's death but, steadfast in their own faith, doubt his divinity. Ware shows a respect for Judaic commitment that is rare in Christian fiction: Julian, drawn to Christianity, remains a Jew.[42]

Another attractive major Jewish character appeared in John Richter Jones's novel *The Quaker Soldier* (1858). The Polish-born pawnbroker Solomon Isaaski speaks in stereotypic Jewish dialect and is short and fat. Isaaski nevertheless makes unpaid loans to the Continental cause so that independence will emancipate his people and demonstrate to the world that in a free nation they become worthy citizens, indistinguishable from other inhabitants. He also finances the rescue of the hero's kidnapped sister.[43]

### Anti-Semitism

American attitudes toward Jews during the middle period were not unconditionally benevolent, nor did treatment of Jews steadily improve. In fact Jews often encountered benign and forbidding circumstances simultaneously during the two decades leading to the explosion of civil war.

### Politics

Sovereignty scattered among federal, state, and local authorities contributed to the variation in treatment experienced by American Jewry. In

1835, a few years before Rhode Island repealed the test oath, the North Carolina convention to amend the state constitution refused to do so, instead substituting Christian for Protestant, enabling Catholics to hold public office. North Carolina Jews tried again in 1858 and 1861, without success, to have the oath repealed. During debates in the legislature, restrictionists justified their policy by charges that Jews were unproductive and dishonest. In a familiar example of American ambivalence, Jews sometimes served in public office despite legal prohibition. In New Hampshire, too, the constitutional convention of 1852 failed to overturn the requirement that only Protestants could be legislators. Not until 1868 in North Carolina and 1876 in New Hampshire could Jews legally hold office.[44]

Local differences also influenced elections. Jews were victorious in many races, but Leon Silverman, the 1859 Democratic candidate for Wisconsin state treasurer, ran far behind his party's defeated ticket, according to both Republican and Democratic newspapers, because he was Jewish. The German-born Silverman lagged everywhere, but especially in predominantly German-American districts. While Judaic identity did not determine other contests in the 1850s, attempts were made to discredit several Jewish candidates. Opponents of a candidate for the South Carolina senate reminded voters that he was Jewish. A politician at a Democratic rally for the New York mayoralty campaign of 1856 accused the U.S. District Attorney of appointing a Jewish Republican as his assistant. In 1856 a Philadelphia German-language paper claimed that presidential nominee John Charles Fremont had Jewish parents.[45]

America rightly congratulated itself, and Jewish citizens considered themselves fortunate, that scattered and minor incidents of electoral anti-Semitism did not seriously impede their political aspirations. A paradox in American history, however, is that the more reviled Catholics could precede Jews, as in North Carolina, in eligibility for public office. No Jew sat in a nineteenth-century federal cabinet, but a Catholic, Attorney General Roger B. Taney, was appointed in 1831. Seven Catholics antedated the first Jew in the national cabinet.[46]

Inconsistent response toward Jews can be traced in the different and changing reputations of the most prominent Jewish national figures, Noah, Belmont, Benjamin, and Yulee. Noah, who died in 1851, was the *bête noire* of Jacksonian and middle-period bigots; during the antebellum years Belmont received substantially less criticsm and Yulee and Benjamin largely escaped religious slurs. Civil turmoil, however, intensified attacks on Belmont's foreign birth, Rothschild tie, and Jewish descent, and as

America plunged into internecine conflict, Yulee and especially Benjamin faced a fusillade of epithets about their origins.

Two factors other than timing may account for the particularly harsh vilification of Noah. The first is that, unlike Yulee, Benjamin, and Belmont, he did not suppress his roots. Noah married a Jew, spoke at synagogues, joined Jewish organizations, defended Jews and Judaism, and sought to found a Jewish homeland in upstate New York. His biographer rightly concludes that he aspired to lead American Jewry.[47]

Noah's bitterest critic was James Gordon Bennett, publisher of the *New York Herald,* notorious among colleagues for ribald journalism and combative egomania. In a *Herald* editorial of 1844 ridiculing Noah's dream of a Jewish homeland in Grand Island, New York, Bennett's invective, as usual, passed beyond personal insult to ethnic diatribe. Jerusalem itself, claimed the *Herald,* would not dislodge Jews from Chatham Street. The "gilded balls will still mark the entrance to dim and dingy repositories of penury and vice—Rothschilds will still lean against the pillars of the Stock Exchange." In the last year of Noah's life, a *Herald* tirade seethed with anti-Semitic references to second-hand clothing retailers, unrepentant cads, and ostentatious *nouveaux riches.* Bennett and his wife were insulted "without . . . remorse or penitence on the part of the Jew," when Noah belittled their impact on Vienna society. The *Herald* doubted "whether Mordecai M. Noah and his better half, with all the fat feathers, and false jewelry she could muster, the first from the sausage stalls of Washington market, the latter from the old clo' shops of Chatham row, could have made a better show."[48]

The second factor that may explain the particularly harsh slurs directed at Noah is that his career centered in New York. Around 1830 that city displaced Charleston in having the largest number of Jewish residents and New York Jews became the chief victims of anti-Semitism. In Chapter 4 I took issue with the assumption that population size or growth alone heightened hostility. In any case, while rapidly increasing, Jewish representation in the total population remained minuscule. An estimated 15,000 dwelled in the United States in 1840; twenty years later the number was between 150,000 and 200,000. Although this expansion spectacularly outpaced that of the national population, in 1860 Jews still made up less than 1 percent of the 30 million Americans.

But Jewish demography in New York City had special conditions. During the 1830s protracted decline was sensationally reversed. The Jewish share of the city's population fell from about 2.5 percent in 1695 to about 0.3 percent in 1825, when approximately 500 Jews lived there. The number and percentage climbed to 2,000 and 0.7 in 1836, 7,000 and 2.2 in 1840, to 16,000 and 3.1 in 1850, to 33,000 and 4.7 in 1855, and to 40,000 and 4.7 in 1860.[49] Proliferation, however, may not account for New York's rising animosity. Jews were far better received in Charleston than in New York, although in 1820 they constituted 5 percent of white Charlestonians after more than tripling in number and doubling in share of the population between 1790 and 1820.[50] Thus mere numerical presence or visibility does not independently determine the reaction toward Jews.

Type of presence and visibility, however, can have a significant influence. Many Charleston Jews came from families that had lived there for generations. Addition of Jewish residents in New York came largely from abroad. Most Jews living in New York in 1860 had arrived after the Panic of 1837, and nearly one-third had come from Germany, with Polish immigrants not far behind. The newcomers tended to perpetuate their European experience of residing and working in their own neighborhoods. The Jewish population of Charleston, in contrast, stabilized after 1820 without a major influx of recent immigrants. Often descended from old clans that had grown up with the city, Charleston's Jews were rarely labeled alien upstarts or intruders. In New York, however, Chatham Street clothing dealers, or Jews in poor blocks in the Lower East Side or in richer districts in upper Greenwich Village and the West Side, were isolated enclaves who often spoke, dressed, and behaved in ways alien to the native majority.[51]

Demographic and structural developments that stimulated anti-Semitism in New York might have brought Belmont, Noah's successor as the premier local and national Jewish celebrity, greater abuse than his predecessor. When the banker came on the scene in the 1840s the Jewish enclave was undergoing unprecedented growth. Belmont, unlike the Philadelphia-born Noah, was a German immigrant, a Rothschild agent, and a power on Wall Street and in the Democratic party. Better than Noah, he fit the anti-Semitic mold of the Jewish financial manipulator seeking mastery over a Christian nation. Affluent and socially ambitious, he also better matched the image of the Jew as intrusive *arriviste*.

Despite such disadvantages, Belmont was less scorned, at least until the war. He probably owed this kinder reception to assimilation. Rothschild connections and German origins were partially overcome by Belmont's never belonging to a synagogue, marrying, worshipping, and bringing his children up in an elite Episcopal church, wedding an aristocratic Gentile, and becoming a high society ornament. Nor was the Rothschild association as deleterious as it might have been later in the century. Antebellum references to that family did not yet conjure up a cabal of Jewish bankers grasping at global control. Americans at that time showed greater curiosity about the clan's wealth and relationships than its purported aggrandizement and the media respectfully noted extensive Rothschild charity. *Harper's Magazine* in 1858 described Rothschild as "the most powerful man in the world" without insinuation about his morality or his creed.[52]

The Manhattan press, strident toward Noah, in the 1850s treated Belmont with some forbearance. An 1852 *New York Times* editorial drew attention to the banker's European and Rothschild associations and disagreed with his alleged promotion of foreign interests, but omitted his Jewish past. If any newspaper publisher at that time perceived Belmont as an arch foe, it was Horace Greeley, crusader against slavery, ardent Whig, and paladin of organized labor and the impoverished—causes that placed him in diametrical opposition to the banker. Several editorials in Greeley's *New York Tribune* did indeed call Belmont a foreign meddler in American politics and an instrument of aristocratic European interests and the Rothschilds. But the high-toned, idealistic Greeley never stooped to the gutter journalism of Bennett and thus did not directly taunt Belmont as a Jew. Two bitter editorials, however, castigated Belmont for supporting 1852 Democratic presidential nominee Franklin Pierce. In "Austria and the Money-Lenders for Pierce," Belmont was "this agent of the great usurer [Rothschild] who fattens on nations." A few months later, the *Tribune* again named him a Rothschild agent "spending European money, contributed by the manufacturing capitalists and bankers of the Old World to break down or keep down their American rivals in the struggle for American markets."[53] Although the *Tribune* overtly ignored the Jewishness of Belmont and the Rothschilds, for its prevalently middle-class, well-educated readers Greeley's innuendoes probably had the same impact on the reputation of Jews as did Bennett's tantrums about Noah upon buyers of the *Herald.*

Any reticence about Belmont's origins vanished in the Civil War epidemic of scapegoating, in which slander tended to focus on alleged malpractice in finance and trade. Since Belmont was one of the best-known American Jews, the foremost Jewish banker, and a leader in a party accused of "Copperheadism," he was a particular anti-Semitic target.

"What a scandal that an election should be carried by the money of a German Jew (his name is Schoenberg), the agent of the Rothschilds," carped the ex-Whig statesman and Harvard College president Edward Everett in his journal upon learning that Belmont had paid some expenses for the 1864 presidential campaign. Politicians and journalists publicly attacked the banker and the faith he had long left. The Republican *Chicago Tribune* asserted that "the Democratic presidential candidate, General George McClellan, has entered into a plot with the Rothschilds," the "heaviest holders of Confederate bonds in Europe," and that with "his election, a dishonorable peace will be patched up so that the United States will have to assume the debt of the bogus government at Richmond!" The *Tribune* made Belmont the bridge between these sinister foreign speculators and their American object: "This is the reason why Belmont spent so much money to have McClellan nominated. He was the only man named for the Presidency that the foreign Jew could manipulate." An editorial in the same issue, "The Shent per-Shent Democracy," used theatrical Yiddish dialect to connect Belmont, "the agent of a foreign money power," with Judaism. A speaker at a War Democrats convention held shortly before election day also savaged Belmont for representing the foreign "monied aristocracy" in leading the peace-seeking McClellanites. "There is not a people or government in Christendom in which the paws, or fangs, or claws of the Rothschilds are not plunged to the very bottom of the treasury." Mimicking a German-Jewish accent, the orator explained to "Mr. Belmont" that his masters wanted to lend to America because it is "able to pay shent per shent." But "we did not want to borrow, and Jews have got mad," and are "hammering at our stocks, and expanding gold wherever they could get an opportunity." Variations on the theme of traitorous, rapacious Jewish capitalists sounded in the *New York Herald,* the *Manchester* [New Hampshire] *Weekly Mirror,* the *Vincennes* [Indiana] *Weekly Gazette,* an oration at the Philadelphia Union League, and a Republican address at Cooper Institute in Manhattan.[54]

Yulee and Benjamin suffered less antebellum opprobrium than did the New Yorkers Noah and Belmont. The mid-century South attracted fewer immigrants, including German Jews, than did many parts of the North. Hence its white minorities were likelier to be long entrenched in local communities. For this reason, political anti-Semitism seems lower in the South, as evidenced by the section having the first governor, the first U.S. senators, and the first American cabinet officer of Jewish stock.

Among the four mid-century luminaries of Jewish descent, Yulee endured the least religious hostility. Perhaps not coincidentally, he went the farthest in denying his antecedents. Upon entering the Senate, he changed his name from Levy, married a Christian, and joined a Presbyterian congregation. Not satisfied with conversion, the West Indian–born Yulee disputed his Jewish background by claiming descent from a Moroccan prince.[55]

His only consistent prewar detractor seems to have been John Quincy Adams, who was also annoyed by Noah and other Jewish politicians. In Adams's diary during the 1840s Yulee was the "Jew delegate from Florida," the "alien Jew delegate from Florida," and the "squeaking Jew delegate from Florida." This introduction usually preludes ridicule of Yulee's legislative proposals. Adams called another Jewish colleague in the Congress, Representative Albert G. Marchand of Pennsylvania, "a squat little Jew-faced rotundity."[56]

War subjected Yulee, like Belmont and Benjamin, to greater execration. After he and Benjamin left the Senate to join the rebellion, they were linked as "the Children of Israel" who defected to the Confederacy. "Mr. Benjamin of Louisiana is the disunion leader in the U.S. Senate," intoned the Brahmin-patronized *Boston Evening Transcript* during Secession winter (1861). "Mr. Yulee of Florida, whose name has been changed from the more appropriate one of Levy or Levi, has always been one of the hottest leaders of the ultra fire-eaters." Does "this peculiar race—the old Catholics used to call them 'accursed'—having no country of their own, desire that other nations shall be in the same unhappy condition . . .?" Through "its principal men," this "'stiffed-necked generation' . . . lead[s] in attempting to destroy a Constitution which has been to them an Ark of refuge and safety." The future U.S. president Andrew Johnson, then an ardent Unionist-Democratic senator from Tennessee, voiced similar reproval. "There's that Yulee," he told Charles Francis Adams, Jr., "the contemptible little Jew who wants Florida to secede."[57]

Of the nationally prominent Jews, Benjamin encountered the least peacetime bigotry. One biographer notes that the future Confederate secretary of state met with little prejudice during the 1840s and another that the earliest attack on his religious origin came in 1858. Antebellum acceptance was promoted by the benign response toward Jews in Benjamin's city and state. In New Orleans, as in Charleston, Jews were welcomed in elite social circles. They became members of exclusive clubs, boards of managers at upper-class balls, and stewards of the Jockey Club. During the 1850s in Louisiana Jews served in the state senate and America's first Jewish lieutenant governor took office. Gentile clergymen asserted that New Orleans before the Civil War was a secular community where Christianity was unimportant and evangelical Protestantism was minimal. The historian of New Orleans Jewry found only one attack on Jews in local newspapers from the beginning of American rule until the early 1840s, and concluded that distaste was probably weaker there than in any large city in the country. New Orleans was a cosmopolitan center with a diverse ethnic population, and its political leaders sought support from all white groups.[58]

When war started, however, Benjamin became the most despised major American figure of Jewish descent and, unlike Yulee and Belmont, was abominated by both sides. Belmont was correctly, and not always maliciously, called a Rothschild agent. Benjamin, on the other hand, was spuriously identified with Judas Iscariot, the archetypal betrayer in Christian mythology. Forsaking Washington for Richmond provoked accusations of Jewish infidelity. Insults played on Benjamin's first name: in an 1860 Alabama political campaign he was called that "infamous Jew . . . Judas P. Benjamin." Almost a decade after Appomattox, Henry S. Foote, a former governor of Mississippi and member of the Confederate Congress, described Benjamin as having a perpetual "smile as bland and insinuating as that which may be supposed to have sat upon the face of Judas Iscariot when he was betraying the Savior of the world with a kiss."[59]

Benjamin suffered attacks even from those who praised or defended other Jews. Although Foote was an anti-Semite, he lauded Louis Levin, a congressional colleague of the 1840s, whom he noted as a Jew, for courage, chivalry, geniality, and generosity. U.S. Senator Henry Wilson, a fiery Massachusetts abolitionist, introduced the bill to allow rabbis to become military chaplains. But he told the Senate in 1861 that Benjamin's "heart was in this foul and wicked plot" to "overthrow the Government of his adopted country, which gives equality of rights even to that race that stoned Prophets and crucified the Redeemer of the World."[60]

Andrew Johnson similarly condemned Benjamin. After denouncing Yulee, he said to Charles Francis Adams, Jr., "There's another Jew—that miserable Benjamin! He looks on a country and a government as he would on a suit of old clothes. He sold out the old one; and he would sell out the new if he could in so doing make two or three millions." "Toward Jews," thought Adams, Johnson "felt a strong aversion."[61]

Benjamin was also a target of William Gannaway Brownlow, a Methodist preacher and ex–Know Nothing and a Tennessee Unionist who published the *Knoxville Whig*, which had the largest readership in the state. Like his fellow Jew-hating journalist Bennett, Brownlow was a self-righteous egotist with a special revulsion for prominent Jews. The one obsessed about Noah and the other about Benjamin. Brownlow had a personal grievance against Benjamin, who had banished him from the South in 1862 as a Union sympathizer. "He threatened to hang me, and I expected no more mercy from him than was shown by his illustrious predecessors toward Jesus Christ," said Brownlow in a speech at a Nashville Methodist chapel shortly before his forced exit from Tennessee. A "little pilfering Jew," Brownlow called Benjamin, "one of the tribe who murdered the Savior, and, ever since they parted his raiment at the crucifixion, have been dealing in ready-made clothing." Later that year, at a meeting of Cincinnati Methodist preachers, Brownlow reviled "that little contemptible Jew—Judas Benjamin" for ordering him from the Confederacy. The fugitive subsequently became Reconstruction governor of, and senator from, his home state.[62]

Benjamin was a metaphor for Jewish corruption and betrayal. Complaining that "foreign [mercantile] houses, mostly Jews," in southern ports were the lifeline of the rebellion, General Benjamin F. Butler, a Massachusetts politician turned commandant of New Orleans, swore that they "deserve to receive at the hands of this government what is due to the Jew Benjamin . . ."[63]

Southerners expressed similar feelings. The politically and socially well connected diarist Mary Chesnut recorded that Benjamin was called "Mr. Davis's pet Jew," and "very cheap, &c&c." An army officer in North Carolina during the Union blockade blended libels of avarice and cowardice: many "gentlemen of strongly Jewish physiognomy were to be met with on the streets in very delicate health," but "still in hot pursuit of the 'Monish.'" The "unctuous and oleaginous Confederate Secretary of State . . . provided for 'his people,'" by giving them "papers" to "keep them out of the army." When "the conscript officer became very zealous," they "fled away to Nassau and Bermuda."[64]

Vilification of Belmont and Benjamin reflected the upsurge of political anti-Semitism during the war. Was this development an abrupt departure from a benign norm or the culmination of steadily increasing hostility during the middle period? Imputed Jewish origins had long been an issue for some candidates for public office.[65] Given the tiny number of Jews in pre–Civil War America and the fragment who undertook electoral campaigns, the frequency of these allegations is striking.

No dramatic increase, particularly in view of the rapid rise in the Jewish population, occurred in the 1850s in these charges or in their effect on the outcome of political contests. While local Wisconsin newspapers attributed the defeat of the Jewish candidate for state treasurer in 1859 to his religion, that same relation had was also been considered a cause of Noah's 1820 defeat in the New York City sheriff race. Elections, however, are rarely decided by a single factor.

Consistent with American ambivalence regarding Jews, the impact of anti-Semitism varied locally. Bigotry may have been crucial in the Wisconsin contest. Three years later, however, a German Jewish Democrat from Detroit, running for the Michigan legislature, got more votes than any native-born local candidate, although the city's German-Republican press raised the issue of his religion.[66]

Political luminaries, however, did become more apt than in previous periods to insult Jews. In the Senate, Daniel Webster displayed what might indulgently be called ethnic insensitivity, using "Jew" as a verb meaning to cheat. In a court case of 1844 in which his clients contested the will of Stephen Girard, who had founded a college for white orphans and specified in his will that Christian clergymen could not teach there, Webster argued before the Supreme Court that "the Christian religion" was "the foundation of civil society" and "the law of the land." His plea for the ethical and civic imperative of Christianity demeaned Judaism: "When little children were brought into the presence of the Son of God, he did not send them first for lessons in morals to the schools of the Pharisees or to the unbelieving Sadducees, nor to read the precepts and lessons phylacteried on the garments of the Jewish priesthood."[67]

Justice Joseph Story, in delivering the Court's majority opinion upholding Girard's will, nevertheless stated in agreement with Webster that "the purest principles of morality" were in "the New Testament." Story also lumped "Judaism," with "Deism, or any other form of infidelity." He even recognized "Christianity" as "part of the common law of" Pennsylvania, if not broadly construed to negate Girard's exclusion of Christian clergy, at least in the "qualified sense, that its divine origin and truth are admitted, and therefore it is not to be maliciously and openly reviled and blasphemed against, to the annoyance of believers or the injury of the public."[68]

Other prominent figures also criticized Jews. The 1857 American party candidate for governor of Georgia charged that unlimited immigration would give Jews the same power and rights as Gentiles. Oliver Larkin, U.S. Naval Agent in California during the 1840s and a member of the California Constitutional Convention of 1858, assigned Jews and Christians different "looks" and "feelings." Jews had noses "like a hawk's bill" and their eyes "appear to both look down or across the Nose." Anticipating racialism, he believed that physiognomy determined moral destiny: "A city composed widely of Jews, could never subsist. They must be scatter'd about among the Christians, where they can cheat to their heart's delight."[69]

Grudges did not necessarily manifest themselves in discriminatory behavior. John Quincy Adams's malice was confided to his diary; in public he praised Jewish charities and uncandidly denied that he had belonged to a society for the conversion of the Jews. No evidence exists that Larkin's animus influenced his official actions. The Georgia gubernatorial nominee expressed intolerance publicly, but his party targeted Catholics as the enemy. Story and Webster may have considered Christianity part of the law of the land, but attempts to amend the Constitution to this effect, even amid wartime Christian fervor, universally failed. Nor did Story's construction of Christianity and common law prevent him from rejecting Webster's plea that excluding ministers from Girard's school was anti-Christian and, therefore, unconstitutional.[70]

In some cases, however, prejudice did result in discrimination. In South Carolina, a state relatively enlightened regarding Jews, Governor James Hammond in 1844 proclaimed the first Thursday in October "a day of thanksgiving, humiliation, and prayer" and exhorted "our Citizens of all denominations" to offer "devotions to God the Creator and his Son Jesus Christ, the Redeemer of the world."[71] When Presidents Tyler and Buchanan affirmed Christian nationhood they reassured Jewish protesters of their respect for religious liberty and Judaism. Hammond, however, would not conciliate the more than one hundred South Carolina Jews who petitioned against the proclamation's exclusion of their creed. The governor replied that he had not realized that "Israelites, Deists, Atheists," and other Carolinians "denied the divinity of Jesus Christ." But had he "known he wouldn't have changed the Proclamation or has no apology to make for it now." Intransigence was justified because America was "a Christian land" and Hammond the "magistrate of a Christian people." He accused the "Israelites" of trying to "intimidate one man and extract from him a confession and an apology under the apprehension of their fierce and unrelenting hostility." Did Jewish opposition, he asked, stem from "inheriting the same scorn for Jesus Christ which instigated their ancestors to crucify him . . ."?[72]

This bigot nevertheless grasped the dilemma of Jews in a nation with a Christian majority and culture: How to act and be accepted as full citizens without surrendering their heritage? He recognized that Jews "wished to be included in the same public devotion with the Christians," but rage and bias made him distort their petition. To "make that invitation acceptable to them," he declared, he "must exhort a Christian People to worship after the manner of the Jews. The Constitution forbids me to 'discriminate' in favour of the Christians; and I am denounced because I have not 'discriminated' in favour of the Israelites." Hammond made the standard anti-Semitic retort to a demand for equal treatment. By refusing to accept civic subordination to Christianity, thus incurring resentment from the majority, Jews distanced themselves from the community and further weakened their precarious position: "[I]n fulminating your wrath at me, you have exhibited a temper which in the end may be more painful to yourselves than it can be for me."[73] The governor was immovable, but his successor issued a new proclamation for this day that eliminated the parts objectionable to Jews.

Hammond defended his position with the old argument that "laws recognizing the Christian Sabbath did not violate the [state] Constitution." As in the past, Sunday laws were not always justified by judicial dicta of "decent observance" of the Lord's day "in a Christian community," though South Carolina and Pennsylvania supreme court opinions of 1848 announced this principle. In some cases legislation was upheld on grounds that a day of rest promoted good health and social order. If secular arguments prevailed, the prohibitions burdened orthodox Jews. If Christianity was acknowledged as fundamental to the state constitution and hence made the civic creed, however, all Jews were implicitly separated from or required to demonstrate fealty to a community designated as belonging to a religion in which they could not participate. Christian nationhood so conceived hindered Jews from exercising citizenship.[74]

Sunday laws were intermittently passed and enforced from early republican times, but the most blatant case of potential prejudice behind them emerged in an 1855 California assembly debate on barring business on the sabbath. House Speaker William W. Stow, an American party representative, railed that Jews "ought to respect the laws and opinions of the majority." They "came here to make money and leave as soon as they had effected their object." Since they "intended or hoped to settle in their 'New Jerusalem,'" he favored "a tax upon them" as "a prohibition to their residence amongst us. The Bible lay at the foundation of our institutions, and its ordinances ought to be covered and adhered to in legislating for the state." The *Los Angeles Star* reprimanded Stow for his tirade, and the impact of his rage remains uncertain, but the bill prohibiting business on Sunday passed in 1858. Although it remained law until 1882, like many such restrictions it went virtually unenforced.[75]

Anti-Semitic attitudes did sometimes result in discrimination. No prominent American Jew more bitterly experienced the connection between personal belief and public policy than did Commodore Uriah Phillips Levy. In 1855, after a career marred by six court martials, two dismissals from the service, and a duel in which his opponent died—all primarily caused by slurs against Levy's religion—he was dropped from the naval officer list. Two years later a naval court of inquiry heard his plea for restoration. "I perceived a strong prejudice in the service against Captain Levy," stated Secretary of the Navy George Bancroft in a deposition to the court, "in a considerable part, attributable to his being of Jewish persuasion." Bancroft had denied Levy "a command" because I "endeavored, in fitting out ships, to have some reference to that harmonious co-operation which is essential to the highest effectiveness."[76] Levy's troubles prefigured severer anti-Semitism in the armed forces during the Civil War.

~

During the Civil War, statements of politicians and government officials and civil and military actions reverberated with anti-Semitism. Heretofore desultory, prejudice now became habitual—even epidemical. Cabinet officers, congressmen, and generals, in antebellum years relatively tolerant or guarded, increasingly vilified Jews, and anti-Jewish attitudes more often influenced public policy and action.

Jews were mainly condemned as greedy, unpatriotic businessmen. "The mania for sudden fortunes made in cotton, raging in a vast population of Jews and Yankees scattered throughout this whole country," said Assistant Secretary of War Charles A. Dana in 1863, has "corrupted and demoralized the army." Cotton "is brought in from beyond our lines, especially by the agency of Jewish traders, who pay for it ostensibly in Treasury notes, but really in gold." The Illinois Republican congressman Elihu Washburne called Grant's banishment of Jews "the wisest order yet made." Your "order touching the Jews has kicked up quite a dust among the Israelites," he wrote the general from Washington. "They came here in crowds and gave an entirely false construction to the order and [Gen. Henry W.] Halleck revoked it." When Henry L. Cleveland, the chief of U.S. detectives at Memphis, was acquitted of charges of robbery, extortion, and bribery, he claimed that "the [military] court was satisfied it was a malicious prosecution gotten up by the Jews whom I had detected in smuggling." Col. Lafayette Baker, the head of the detective bureau of the war department, imagining a Jewish conspiracy, went beyond routine remarks about commercial wrongdoing. He labeled B'nai B'rith a "secret organization" and said it "had secret ramifications in the South and was helpful to traitors."[77]

Confederate officials matched their northern counterparts in malice. Derogation began at the top. "The large majority of those engaged in the [cotton] trade were foreigners," insinuated President Jefferson Davis in a speech to the Confederate House of Representatives in 1864. They "accumulate rapid fortunes, while depreciating our currency and exhausting our country of the productions which form its most valuable resources for needful supplies during the war." Before the same body, Davis later slightly shifted his accusations but not their object. Blockade-running "gains" were "monopolized by foreigners, free to engage in commerce at their pleasure while our citizens were engrossed in the sacred duty of defending their homes and liberties, and therefore unable to compete for the trade."[78]

Some lower officials did not hide behind code words like "foreigners." "It was notorious that our land has been recently deluged with foreign Jews," was the Confederate congressional record of remarks by Henry S. Foote. He "believe[d] that this influence had been effected by a mysterious process." Foote, now a representative from Tennessee, succumbed to the paranoid essence of anti-Semitism: "At least nine-tenths of those engaged in trade [in the Confederacy] were foreign Jews, spirited here by extraordinary and mysterious means." He suspected that "this swarm of Jews" was officially "permitted in many cases to conduct illicit traffic with the enemy," and he demanded a halt to Jewish immigration, claiming that "if the present state of things were to continue, the end of the war would probably find nearly all the property of the Confederacy in the hands of Jewish shylocks."[79]

Robert Hilton of Florida supported his congressional colleague's suggested policy for "foreigners," who "swarmed here as the locusts of Egypt. They ate up the substance of the country, they exhausted its supplies, they monopolized its trade. They should be dragged into military services." Blaming Jews for "high prices" and "unnatural and factitious depreciation of our currency," he saw them "flocked as vultures to every point of gain." William P. Chilton of Alabama and the South Carolina aristocrat William Porcher Miles likewise condemned Jews in the Confederate Congress.[80]

A clerk in the Confederate war department, John Beauchamp Jones, kept a diary—which was published in 1866—that bristled with invective.

A September 1861 entry claimed of Jews: "Having no nationality, all wars are harvests for them." In 1862 and 1863 Jones repeatedly described Jews as "profiteering," "extortioners," engaging in "illicit trade," and trading with the enemy. This noncombatant, who secured a safe government sinecure for his nephew, also accused "Jews," in January 1864, of dodging military service by "fleeing from Richmond with the money they have made." Despairing the noble cause in a February 1864 entry, he merged themes of flight, cowardice, and betrayal by charging that "five Jews . . . absconded to avoid military service in the Confederate States, no doubt they imparted all the information they could to the enemy."[81]

In the North, the chief culprits in the campaign against the Jews, Butler, Grant, and William Tecumseh Sherman, were top-ranked military commanders. Butler in 1862 accused New Orleans "army contractors, principally Jews" of making "fortunes by the war"; he "suppose[d that] another Jew—one Judas—thought his investment in the thirty pieces of silver was a profitable one, until the penalty of treachery reached him."[82]

Agitation centered in Grant's theater of operations in the west and was inflamed, if not inspired, by the general himself. Sherman, Grant's second-in-command, took a dim view of Jews even before the war. "Individuals may prosper in a failing community such as San Francisco," he wrote in 1858, "but they must be Jews, without pity, soul heart or bowels of compassion." Many have suspected that Sherman himself lacked these gentle qualities. As Memphis commandant in 1862, he discovered that Jews there showed no improvement over their brethren in San Francisco. The "commercial enterprise of the Jews" enabled them to make obscene profits in the cotton trade. Sherman also grumbled that Tennessee "swarm[s] with dishonest Jews who will smuggle [to the enemy] powder, pistols, percussion caps, etc., in spite of all the guards and precautions we can give."[83]

As Grant worked up to dismissing Jews from his command, he and his officers voiced systematic and extreme prejudice. In December 1861 a lieutenant warned that "smuggling" in Illinois and Indiana was "done . . . chiefly by Jews." Grant told a brigadier in July 1862 that "Jews should receive special attention" in "contraband" searches of "speculators." A few months later he telegraphed a general that "Israelites especially should be kept out" of Tennessee and ordered a colonel to remove Jews from trains because "they are such an intolerable nuisance. That the Department [of Tennessee—Grant's command] must be purged for [sic] them." A few days before issuing his order excluding Jews from his command, Grant wrote

Sherman that "in consequence of the total disregard and evasion of orders by the Jews my policy is to exclude them so far as practicable from the Dept." He explained to the assistant secretary of war that his proscription was necessitated "by Jews and other unprincipled traders" violating "Specie regulations of the Treasury Dept." Jews must be expelled because they "come in with their Carpet sacks in spite of all that can be done to prevent it."[84]

Grant's animus climaxed in the exclusion of Jews from his theater of operations. General Order No. 2, issued on December 8, 1862, mandated that "cotton-speculators, Jews and other Vagrants having not honest means of support, except trading upon the miseries of their Country . . . Will Leave in twenty-four hours or they will be sent to duty in the trenches." But this edict barred only Jews who engaged in forbidden activities. Nine days later it was superseded by General Order No. 11. Part I stated that "Jews, as a class, violating every regulation of trade established by the Treasury Department, and also Department orders, are hereby expelled from the Department [of the Tennessee]." Part II gave the Jews twenty-four hours "to leave, and anyone returning after such notification, will be arrested and held in confinement until an opportunity occurs of sending them out as prisoners." Part III barred Jews from "application for trade permits."[85] Resembling a Czarist ukase more than an American governmental decree, Grant's order was the severest attempted official violation—civil or military, federal, state, or local—of the rights of Jews in the history of this nation.

Henry W. Halleck, the army chief of staff, was also bigoted. He wrote Grant in 1864 about "numerous enemies" in "Jew traders & cotton speculators." After Lincoln revoked Grant's General Order No. 11, Halleck thought, probably erroneously, that a more viable policy would have been to ban Jewish peddlers, but not all Jews.[86]

Although the president immediately countermanded Grant's injunction, in November 1863 Maj. Gen. Stephen A. Hurlbut issued an order forbidding fourteen Jewish clothing houses in the Memphis area from selling military clothing and requiring them to send their goods back across the front line. Two non-Jewish firms were exempted from Hurlbut's order. Long after the controversy ended, Grant and his generals still expressed suspicion and contempt. A corps commander referred to "a Jew spy" in an 1864 communication to his chief. The previous year Grant had complained that Sherman "had almost to force a passage" on the railroad, while "Jews" generally "find no difficulty in going where they please."[87]

How widespread was anti-Semitism in other armies? A Jewish soldier in the Army of the Potomac reported in 1862 that he encountered a single anti-Semitic incident and that the perpetrator was reproached by Gentile soldiers. In contrast, Private Max Glass of the 8th Connecticut volunteers wrote Butler in 1864 that his comrades tormented him for being Jewish.[88]

Anti-Semitism in the South erupted in a mode somewhat contrary to that of the North. Confederate persecution was more characteristic of civil than military organizations. Hostility, however, was by no means absent in the armed forces. A Jewish colonel appointed by the war department to head a Texas regiment, ridiculed by his men and subjected to the indignity of having his horse's tail shaved, gave up his command. The colonel of an Alabama regiment tried to stop the promotion of a Jewish captain, and a brigadier said of Benjamin, "a grander rascal than this Jew does not exist in the Confederacy."[89]

More numerous and explosive official displays of prejudice occurred in southern local governments, invariably in small, backwater towns. An 1862 public meeting called in Thomasville, Georgia to discuss the "unpatriotic conduct" of Jewish merchants, resolved to prevent German Jews from visiting the village and to banish its Jewish residents. Similarly motivated, a grand jury in Talbotton, Georgia, brought in a presentment against "evil and unpatriotic conduct of the representatives of Jewish houses." Alarmed by this finding, Lazarus Straus and his sons, the sole Jewish storekeepers there, moved to Columbus. (They later owned Macy's department store in New York.)[90]

~

Political anti-Semitism extended beyond party strife and government action. Reform movements blossoming between the 1820s and the Civil War aspired to shape public policy. By the late 1840s the most important of these were nativism and abolitionism. While the former crusaded mainly against Catholics and Irish immigrants, several prominent members of the Know-Nothing party evinced anti-Semitic sentiments. Abolitionist leaders opposed proscriptive laws against aliens, protested persecution of Jews, and criticized a proposed constitutional amendment to affirm the divinity of Jesus, but a residue of anti-Semitism existed in the movement.[91]

Theodore Parker, the foremost abolitionist clergyman, detested the American party and all forms of religious and ethnic discrimination, but was not free of prejudice. Parker, professed "affection for this mysterious people, for ages oppressed" and "thought of the service they had done mankind and the reward they got!" He abhorred attempts to convert Jews, who "in true religion" ranked "above the Christians." Admiration and liberalism, however, clashed with narrower impulses. While praising "Jewish almsgiving," Parker noted that benevolence was "the distributive virtue of that people, as thrift is the cumulative virtue (and an evil odor their cumulative and distributive vice, chronic and progressive with the children of Israel)." This apostle of abolitionism expressed uglier prejudices as well. The "Hebrews had a pretty savage conception of God," their "intellect was sadly pinched in those narrow foreheads," and they "were also lecherous." In the present, he claimed, they "incline to despotism; they know no other government." Attributions of past evil culminated in blood libel: "They were . . . always cruel. I doubt not they did sometimes kill a Christian baby at the Passover or the anniversary of Haman's famous day!"[92]

Edmond Quincy joined his distant cousin John Quincy Adams in anti-Semitic convictions. Quincy was a Boston Brahmin by birth, belief, and demeanor, an officer of the Massachusetts and American Anti-Slavery Societies, editor of the Massachusetts *Abolitionist,* and a contributor to the *Liberator.* "It would be difficult even for American Christians to match this Jew for meanness and servility," wrote Quincy of proslavery Democrat Noah in an 1848 issue of the *Liberator.* "We think none the worse of a man for being a Jew, but we must say, that if this Judge [Noah] be a fair specimen of the race, it is no wonder they have been an insulted and despised people."[93]

Despite editorial criticism of religious prejudice and opposition to a Christian amendment to the Constitution, the *Liberator* flayed Noah with an anti-Semitic savagery that matched the *Herald* assault. Frequent disagreements between Noah and the abolitionists spurred William Lloyd Garrison in 1842 to call him "a Jewish unbeliever, the enemy of Christ and of liberty." Seven years later, Noah was "the miscreant Jew" and the "lineal descendant of the monsters who nailed Jesus to the cross between two thieves," a "scurrilous" and "foul . . . protect[or of] this traffic in human beings," a "Shylock [who] will have his 'pound of flesh' at whatever cost."[94] Garrison's private correspondence indicates that his comments in the *Liberator* arose from ingrained belief. During the 1850s he repeatedly identified ancient and modern Jews with despicable behavior. He informed the Hungarian nationalist Kossuth that to refuse to get involved in the American slavery controversy "is to be guilty of Jewish exclusiveness." Northern ministers insufficiently opposed to slavery made themselves "applicable to all the righteous denunciations of the prophets to the oppressive and obdurate Jews." The Pennsylvania Anti-Slave Society was reminded: "Like the ancient Jews, our feet run to evil, and we make haste to shed innocent blood, our lips have spoken lies, our tongue hath muttered perverseness; we conceive mischief, and bring forth iniquity."[95]

Like many abolitionists, Garrison participated in a number of causes. Before the crusade against slavery monopolized his energy, he championed pacifism and temperance. Lydia Maria Child was another emancipationist active in several endeavors. In addition to enlisting in the same movements as Garrison, Child was involved in education reform, prison reform, and feminism. She also edited abolitionist newspapers and wrote fiction. Like other antislavery leaders who attacked Jews, Child was capable of sympathy for them as well. She regretted persecution by Christians and was grateful to Israel for discovering monotheism.[96]

Child was a scholar of the history of religion and other theological topics, but she voiced conventional objections to Judaism. Since they appeared in *Letters from New-York*, a best-seller in the 1840s, her opinions reached a considerable audience. The differences between Judaism and Christianity were "shadow and substance, type and fulfillment," blindness and light, vengeance and forgiveness, law and love, superstition and salvation, past and present. At services in 1841 in a New York synagogue, she found "the ceremonies . . . strange and bewildering; spectral and flitting; with a sort of vanishing resemblance to reality; the 'magic lantern of the Past!'" But her reverie was abruptly terminated. The "representatives of the Past walked before me, not in the graceful oriental turban, but the useful European hat. It broke the illusion completely." Child still dreamed that Jews would grasp the true faith.[97]

Massachusetts Senator Henry Wilson was another moderately anti-Semitic abolitionist and social reformer: a spokesman for the poor and the workingman, he supported free public schools and libraries, elimination of property requirements for government office, and exemption of workers' tools from taxes. An example of the ambivalence of many antislavery leaders, he both defended and denigrated Jews.[98] The attitudes of Wilson, Garrison, and their ilk show that faith in human perfectibility and indignation over oppression did not guarantee in mid-nineteenth-century America, any more than among contemporary European champions of the downtrodden or later generations of radicals in both continents, universal immunity against bigotry.

Antislavery and other movements to redeem humankind throbbed with Christian fervor, and several abolitionists dubious about Jews—Quincy,

Childs, and Parker—were staunch Unitarians. Garrison, as in other ways, defied easy categorization but at times vented a New Testament wrath against Jews. These figures regarded bondage as an anti-Christian act—a sin against God. An "evangelical Protestant tradition" and "a fiercely Protestant morality," asserts the historian Ronald Walters, impelled the "religious crusade" to end slavery. The righteousness that inspired abolitionists to battle for the Lord on behalf of southern blacks, however, also could stir them against Judaism and, partly on creedal grounds, against proslavery Jews like Noah.[99]

## Business and Economics

Since the modern image of the Jew—greedy skinflint, rapacious financier, parasitical and unproductive speculator, upstart millionaire, extortionate moneylender, sneaky trader, and scurvy second-hand clothing dealer— was of an engulfer and devourer of wealth, it is little wonder that anti-Semitism in the economic realm surpassed that in politics.[100] Some economic discrimination, such as Sabbath legislation, was at worst marginally anti-Semitic. Other persecution reflected direct hostility, but, like Sunday closing laws, was local, incidental, and reminiscent of previous difficulties. Typical of such animosity were complaints against Jewish firms made by Gentile competitors. In an Urbana, Ohio, newspaper in 1843, Weaver and Bros. called a merchant a swindling Jew. During the Civil War several Christian merchants and firms, including Lorenzo Whitney of Dixon, Illinois, and Lyman and Cooledge of St. Louis, claimed that Jewish rivals flouted trade regulations with impunity and got preferential treatment from the army.[101]

Another type of behavior, still rare enough to be peripheral and incidental, heralded future problems for Jews. "No Jews wanted here," warned a New York newspaper ad for painters in 1849. Although the Atlanta agent of the Southern Mutual Insurance Co. was Jewish, the Georgia firm in 1857 instructed its employees not to issue policies to potential clients of questionable financial standing and specifically mentioned "Jews without real estate property." Proscriptive want ads and insurance company bias, by the late nineteenth century, were highly damaging weapons of economic prejudice.[102]

Systematic commercial discrimination against Jews began in the 1840s, a time when their political disabilities were declining, or at least not advancing. Institutionalized business hostility had not been imposed since

New Amsterdam, but in the antebellum era Dun and Bradstreet inaugurated a national campaign of credit discrimination. Organized suppression worsened during the war and culminated in the sole, except for intermittent enforcement of Sabbath legislation, official opposition to Jewish economic activity. Mounting prejudice also triggered a rare case of violence against Jewish storekeepers.

Historians have extensively examined Dun and Bradstreet records on Jewish entrepreneurs from the 1840s to the 1870s. The original credit-rating agency, Dun and Bradstreet (1841) evolved from a firm founded by Lewis Tappan, an evangelical Christian merchant in New York. Tappan also helped establish the New York and American Anti-Slavery Societies, was active in the American Bible Society and the American Board of Commissioners for Foreign Missions, and supported the revivalist Charles Grandison Finney. In the company he founded, Tappan aspired to use credit screening to apply his Christian uplift philosophy to business transactions. Many of the his credit investigators shared both his spiritual and commercial outlooks. These respected WASP attorneys, bank clerks, merchants, and public officials transmitted biographical data and assessments about the net worth, reliability, probity, and business experience of firms and proprietors in their communities.[103]

Students of this topic agree that evaluations of Jewish businessmen were prevalently prejudiced. Credit ratings introduced them as "Hebrew," "Israelite," "Jew," or "appears to be a Jew." Dun and Bradstreet agents cautioned that Jews were secretive, duplicitous, and untrustworthy and, therefore, that data were difficult to obtain and weaknesses were hidden. When a Jewish firm was deemed sound, its prosperity was often attributed, as with I. H. Heinsheimer & Co. in Burlington, Iowa, in 1851, to "money making and money saving characteristics of his race," or contradictorily to traits exempting the owner from the defects of his people. Bigotry prompted conclusions about creditworthiness contrary to estimations of the firm's assets and profits or the debt record of the local Jewish commercial enclave. "An Israelite in fair standing," was the judgment of one reporter, "but have no confidence in him." Another proprietor was considered "Responsible now, but is a Jew; there is no telling how long he will remain so." Reports on Jewish merchants in Buffalo during the 1850s routinely referred to Judaic unreliability and other vices, yet David Gerber discovered that of Jewish businessmen who failed there in that decade, 61 percent paid debts promptly, 27 percent paid slowly, and only 10 percent defaulted.[104]

Representative of the reports are the following comments: about Moses Bloom of Cincinnati, in 1863: "Very sharp Israelite . . . bound to have the best of a bargain if possible and to be dealt with cautiously." About Joseph Schwartz of Middletown, Missouri, in 1849: "A German Jew and does a small business. No one has any idea how long he will continue to do business here or where he will be a year hence. Tricky . . . slippery German." Lazarus and Leon Bloom, partners in a drygoods store in Clinton, Louisiana, in 1853 were "as reliable as Jews are generally." Their competitor Michael Frank, in 1849, was "a Jew generally, but of the more decent kind." Ohio merchant Samuel Loeb, in 1850, was a "Jew, should deem it especially before crediting to have some evidence of his responsibility." Four years later he was: "Close fisted and Jewish in his disposition, trust him with some condition."[105]

Gerber's analysis of credit reports on Jews in Buffalo leads him to conclude that these ratings reflected stereotypes of Jews as secretive, deceptive, and skillful economic predators. Gerber also claims that recent entry of foreign Jews into the city tended to make them marginal businessmen with insufficient capital and frequent bankruptcy. Under these circumstances, caution in trusting them would have been a realistic strategy. This assertion, however, is contradicted by Gerber's findings about Jewish debt repayment, and is weakened by unfavorable evaluations of Jews in places like San Francisco, a new city where all groups were newcomers. Moreover, Gerber shows that Irish and German shopkeepers were assessed differently from Jews. Germans were considered safe due to stolid, conservative, and thrifty habits. Irish were thought risky because of inadequate funds, impulsiveness, ineptitude, and inebriation. When Jews displayed traits identical to other minorities they were not given the same meaning. Thrift, a virtue in Germans, in Jews denoted miserliness. Finally, as Gerber reasons, Jewish failure, as well as success, was considered, unlike reverses suffered by Germans and Irish, the result of immorality rather than incompetence. Hence impressions of Jews were worse than even negative aspects of images of other groups.[106]

Dun and Bradstreet descriptions of Jewish merchants further distanced an already alienated group from the host community and, as historians of this subject maintain, complicated capital accumulation. Jewish proprietors in Lousiana bought from all suppliers of goods, but usually borrowed money from Jews. Since Jews experienced difficulty in drawing on Gentile sources of credit, they fell back on relatives and other Jewish bankers and associates. Dun and Bradstreet sometimes recognized the dual credit system. A peddler, one agent in Cincinnati declared, obtained advances from "brethren" for "reasonable bills . . . but his Gentile acquaintances require cash." Hoffheimer Bros., another Cincinnati agent said, "stand better with Jews than Gentiles . . . those of their faith in the same trade say they have made considerable money." Such remarks imply a dim awareness on the part of some investigators that bigotry might distort their judgments.[107]

Denial of credit made life more difficult, but did not halt the progress of American Jewry. Dun and Bradstreet operations in Buffalo during the 1850s and in Louisiana between 1840 and 1875 indicate, however, that middle-period economic hostility had greater force than other contemporary forms of bigotry. Jews fully participated in the social and political life of antebellum Louisiana. In Buffalo the major ethnic friction involved Yankees and Irish Catholics, and, as in Louisiana, Jews received no public criticism and were often termed good citizens. In both places, however, acceptance of Jews did not extend to commercial matters.[108]

Economic discrimination intensified during the Civil War. Grant's exclusionary orders were lone, if short-lived, federal government repression of Jewish businessmen. On the Confederate side, smaller persecutions surfaced in Georgia towns. In addition to previously discussed incidents, there were outbreaks of violence against Jewish traders. Women in one Georgia town raided Jewish owned stores at gunpoint and accused the proprietors of price inflation, speculation, and profiteering. Looting of Jewish-owned shops in Richmond in the autumn of 1863 drove local rabbi Maximilian J. Michelberger to defend the virtue of Jewish merchants in a sermon to his congregation.[109]

## Education

In this period, as earlier, many textbooks did not mention Jews or presented Old Testament Israelites favorably by associating American settlers in the New World with the Hebrews wandering through the wilderness to their promised land, the Federal Constitution with the Mosaic Code, or George Washington with Moses.[110]

Accounts of Jews since the coming of Christ, on the other hand, continued to be at best neutral and often negative. An example of the different treatment accorded ancient and later Jews is in the immensely popular *Introduction to the American Common-School Reader and Speaker* (1844), an anthology that went through fifteen editions by 1861. One selection made an analogy between settlers of the American West and Hebrews struggling to reach Israel. But "The Blind Man Restored to Sight," excerpted from the Gospel of John, depicted biblical Israel, and by extension modern Jews, as wrongheaded fanatics who cast Christ's followers out of their synagogues.[111]

*A System of Modern Geography* (1843) was another public school book with both neutral and nasty reports on Jews. *System* was in its eighth edition by 1864 and had many reprints in the 1870s and 1880s. "Christian nations" and the coming world dominance of their creed were touted. The discussion of "Barbary" balanced the oppression of its Jews against the wealth they gathered in trade. Remarks on Poland, however, elicited no sympathy for that country's Jews: "They are industrious, but crafty, and carry on all the trade and commerce of the country."[112]

Two popular texts first published in 1857 did not balance their criticism of Jews with any neutral or positive references. *The Progressive Fourth Grade Reader,* reissued in 1864 and twice more in 1866, included the passage from *The Merchant of Venice* in which Shylock demands a pound of flesh in payment for his loan to Antonio. Jews are portrayed as greedy and cruel and the lesson asks of the pupils: "What is said of the Jews as a people?" In another selection, E. P. Weston's, "Paul at Rome," a stanza has the apostle "Battling the hate of the envenomed Jews." *The National Pronouncing Speller,* aimed at all primary classes and was republished seven times by 1874, included a "dictation exercise" in which pupils were to improve their spelling and pronunciation by copying this sentence: "The selfish Jew, in his splendor, would not give a shekel to the starving shepherd."[113]

A more egregious identification of Jews with parsimony appeared in *The American Reader* (1840), designed for advanced classes in primary and high schools and academies. "Economy," the topic of Lesson 24, was illustrated by a poem of the same title satirizing the behavior of "Mistress Levi" after her son, Moses, "rushing up to obtain the foremost seat" for the performance of a play, falls into the orchestra pit and dies. The versifier sees this outcome as a hilarious comeuppance for a pushy Jew "In imitations of the ambitious great." After a "hysteric blast" the mother, "being with a saving knowledge blessed," pleads, in the conventional ridiculous dialect, with the theater manager: "Sher, I miss haf de shilling back, you know, / As Moses haf nat see de sho." The son represents the Jew as aggressive outsider, but his mother exemplifies the more despicable money-mad Jew. For this people, grief never takes precedence over cash.[114]

Derision of Jewish accents, rare in textbooks but invariable in the theater, fiction, magazines, and other popular media, was not of recent origin. Since sixteenth-century Germany, Yiddish had been regarded as a patois of thieves, tricksters, and outsiders. As with many imputations of Jewish inferiority, ridicule barely concealed fear. Yiddish was mocked, but it was also considered a dialect of secrecy, evil, corruption, conspiracy, and the undermining of Christian authority. Partly for these reasons, Joseph II of Austria's Edict of Toleration banned the use of Hebrew and Yiddish in commerce, and the Prussian Edict of Emancipation (1812) mandated that Jews use French or German in business and legal documents. During the Age of Reason Yiddish was also criticized as an obstacle to assimilation. Denigration of Jewish speech patterns emphasized the Jew's position as the eternal alien, the Wandering Jew, unable to absorb the language and customs of the country in which he lives, and correspondingly elevated native speech as a sign of in-group status. Jews might attain citizenship and even public office, but an unbridgeable gap announced itself every time they spoke, a gap between historical interlopers and citizens whose native ancestry harmonized with the mother tongue and all other aspects of the national way of life.[115]

Nowhere were Jews subjected to such prolonged, and rarely to such harsh, assault than in the *McGuffey Readers*. Sales of these inculcations of middle-class morality, Christian piety and missionism, and the gospel of wealth by 1870 totaled approximately 47 million. The preface to *McGuffey's Newly Revised Eclectic Fourth Reader* (1848), justifying use of scriptural passages because America is "a Christian country," showed that these texts were committed to Christian indoctrination and supremacism.[116]

Biblical selections, as in the pre-1840 Readers, accented the sinfulness and displacement of Israel. The New Testament parable "Jesus and the Blind Man" noted that the parents of the man whose sight was restored "feared the Jews: for the Jews had agreed already, that if any man did confess that he was Christian, he should be put out of the synagogue." Questions accompanying this lesson stressed Jewish interolance and resistance: "[W]hy were not the Jews convinced by them that he came from God? How did the Jews treat the man whose sight was restored? Why did they put him out of the synagogue?" *McGuffey's Rhetorical Guide; or, Fifth Reader* (1844) presented the New Testament account of "Paul's Defense before King Agrippa" (Acts 26), in which the organizer of the new creed blames the Jews for trying to kill him because he proclaims what "the prophets and Moses did say should come."[117]

Excerpts from the Bible were buttressed by commentary to indoctrinate school children in Hebraic transgressions and devalue Judaism. Jean-Jacques Rousseau seems out of place in McGuffey's didacticism, but he was enlisted in the *Revised Eclectic Fourth Reader* to contrast the Old and New Testaments: "The Jewish authors were incapable of the diction, and strangers to the morality, contained in the gospel, the marks of whose truth are so striking."[118]

All stages of their history were presented to discredit Jews, but the Readers focused on the crucifixion. "We saw the very faces of the Jews; the staring, frightful distortions of malice and rage" sermonized William Wirt's blind preacher in an account of the Savior's death included in the *Revised Fourth Reader*. In the version included in *McGuffey's New Fifth Eclectic Reader* (1866), the same character spoke the same line and a listener responded as follows: "my soul kindled with a flame of indignation; and my hands involuntarily and convulsively clinched." Rousseau's comment that Jewish writers could not match the language and ethics of the Gospels was echoed in Lesson 80, "The Scriptures and The Saviour," but now in an even more negative context. In Roman times, the Chosen People were steeped in "the most licentious fanaticism." The death "of Jesus, expiring in torments, outraged, bedeviled and execrated by a whole nation, is the most horrible that could be feared." But "Jesus in the midst of excruciating torture, prayed for his merciless tormentors."[119]

McGuffey also chided descendants of the ancient Hebrews. The *Revised Fourth* and *Fifth Eclectic* Readers featured Shylock's "pound of flesh" speech. Although the later volume mentioned that Massachusetts Bay Colony government and law derived from the Mosaic Code, contempt for Jews was more savage and frequent here than in any earlier Reader and nearly every other schoolbook.[120] In pedagogical publications as well as in economic and political life, anti-Semitism exploded during the war.

On one occasion Jews protested the use of texts that accused them or their ancestors of murdering the Messiah. The Citizens Committee of New York (1843), composed of Jews, asked that *Conversations on Common Things, Murray's English Reader, Lessons for Schools, Taken from the Holy Scriptures,* and the Bible and other books be withdrawn from the schools for instilling Christian ideology and wrongful guilt for the crucifixion. *Conversations* (1824) was a best-selling (sixty editions by 1869) "Guide to Knowledge" for schools and families. Its author was Dorothea Dix, a committed Unitarian who would become a legend in the reform movement as a founder of modern treatment of the insane. The protesters objected to the book's final "conversation," which celebrated the perfection and triumph of Christ and remonstrated that "the gospel was first sent to them [the Jews], but they, with the exception of a few disciples, rejected its precepts, and ignominiously crucified their Saviour."[121]

*The English Reader* (1799), by Lindley Murray, a Quaker minister and prior to McGuffey the best-selling American textbook writer, surpassed 200 editions by 1842 and continued to be frequently reissued through the 1850s. It included references to "our blessed Redeemer" and "our Lord" and the selection of "Paul's Defense before Festus and Agrippa" (Acts 26). The appearance of such christocentric material in a public schoolbook, as in the case of *Conversations,* upset Jewish parents and pupils.[122]

*Lessons for Schools* (1818–19), by Stephen Grellet and William Allen, was reprinted four times by 1865 and adopted by school systems in New York and other cities and in Europe. Grellet was a Quaker minister, a missionary and a social reformer who opposed slavery and labored to improve conditions for the poor. Published by the American Sunday-School Union, *Lessons* was an evangelical tract designed to impart Christian doctrine to young minds. Material in this anthology came from the scriptures, and the complainants objected to claims that the Old Testament preluded the New, that Christ was the son of God and the true Messiah, and that Christianity brought salvation while Judaism was a misdirected relic. In addition, the Jews were bothered by excerpts blaming them for the betrayal and ordeal of Jesus and for persecution of his followers.[123]

Trustees of the common schools of Manhattan's Fourth Ward, where the protest originated, recommended removal of the offending books. A board of education committee appointed to investigate the matter then overruled the trustees. The committee quoted arguments of Judges Story and Kent to assert that "the Christian religion is in fact the religion of this state," as affirmed in Sunday statutes, the New York Constitution, and the Common Law, and that Christianity was indispensable to civic virtue and stability. "Even the Jews," it said in its report, "cannot have the same privileges as those who embrace the Christian religion." Although "offering civil and religious liberty to the oppressed of other nations," America privileged Christianity. If "Jews, on coming into a Christian country, find institutions at variance with, or opposed to their own particular views," the report huffily concluded, "your committee do not perceive that they have any just ground for complaint, or that they can reasonably ask that such institutions be changed for their convenience."[124]

Judaism was deprecated in colleges as well as in common schools. William C. Larrabee, a Methodist Episcopal minister and a professor at Indiana Asbury University, in the 1840s and 1850s uplifted the souls of undergraduates with lectures on historical and scientific proofs of biblical inerrancy. While conceding Old Testament principles to be "greatly in advance of the age," Larrabee maintained that "Mosaic law was ceremonial, and restricted in application to the Jewish people and to the ante-Christian age. Its purpose was specific and temporary, and when it served that, it passed away."[125]

## Religion

Theological detraction of Judaism did not change in substance or form from previous decades, but the social and religious context was modified in a way that led to unprecedented hostility. Outbreaks of sectarian zeal and strife, reflective of social crises, as usual boded ill for Jews. Sectional conflict resulted in denominational schism: between 1837 and 1845 disagreement over slavery split the Methodists, Baptists, and Presbyterians into northern and southern sects. A group of abolitionists founded the American Missionary Society (1844) in opposition to the American Board of Foreign Missions, which the dissidents regarded as sinfully vague on emancipation.[126] The Panic of 1857 and the imminent disintegration of the Union heightened anxiety and brought on a wave of evangelical Christianity. Frustration bred by adversity generated a collective rage, which, as in other times and places, was projected onto the Jews.

The religious revival begun amid the recession of the late 1850s quickened into a millennial crusade as economic disaster gave way to fratricide. Between 1855 and 1865 the largest Protestant sects, Methodists, Baptists, Presbyterians, and Evangelical Lutherans, augmented their memberships respectively by 22, 22, 28, and 34 percent. The three next-largest, Congregationalists, Episcopalians, and Universalists, showed even bigger growth. The steepest increases were in evangelical churches, who in 1855 had 70 percent of all Protestants.[127]

Religious passion dramatically intensified during the war. Between 1861 and 1864 the Union and Confederate governments each declared nine days of national prayer. Southerners fasted and prayed to God for deliverance. Seven of the northern days were for "National Prayer and humiliation" and the remainder for "Thanksgiving, Praise [of God] and Prayer." This spirit of civic sanctification inaugurated the national Thanksgiving holiday. Calls for supplication and gratitude reflected the widespread interpretation, epitomized by Lincoln but shared by the South, of the conflict as signifying God's vengeance upon a country overcome by sin. For northerners, the crime was slavery.[128]

Chastisement by combat culminated in the redemption of a corrupt community at an American Armageddon. "Battle-Hymn of the Republic," the northern anthem composed in 1862 by Julia Ward Howe, yet another ardent abolitionist critical of Jews, proclaimed a militant Messiah who "loosed the fatal lightening of His terrible swift sword," a "fiery gospel, writ in burnished rows of steel," and a "Hero" to "crush the serpent [the Confederacy] with his heel." Apocalypse ended at Appomattox and jeremiads of humiliation, penance, and forgiveness gave way, in the North, to celebrations of thanksgiving and triumph. Amid the millennial joy of victory over disunion and slavery, however, the eschatology of the Civil War was completed by Lincoln's assassination. Like Christ on the Cross, the president was martyred on Good Friday—in another sacrificial act of atonement bringing salvation to an erring Christian community.[129]

Christological interpretations of the war and of Lincoln's death abounded in the North, but no one surpassed the president in seeing the rebellion as a divine punishment and trial or in feeling that he battled for the Lord at Armageddon. Lincoln's transformation from antebellum skeptic to profound believer epitomized the evangelization of the North during the Civil War.[130]

Few Americans had their president's capacity for spiritual exaltation; hence rising religious fervor manifested itself in contention more than in compassion, in judgmentalism more than in justice, and in ritual more than in radiance. While Lincoln's proclamations and other public actions bore no hint of creedal exclusiveness, the National Reform Association (1863) mounted the most determined effort in American history to amend the Constitution to affirm Christ's sovereignty and the divine imperative of his law. The U.S. Christian Commission, wartime alter ego of the Young Men's Christian Association (1851), sent 1,375 clergymen to army camps, where they gave spiritual guidance, consoled the sick and wounded, conducted revivals, admonished sinners, and proselytized lapsed Christians, skeptics, and Jews. Along with the American Bible and American Tract societies, the volunteer ministers distributed millions of Bibles and other Christian literature to the troops. Their equivalents in the opposing trenches, the Bible Society of the Confederacy and the Evangelical Tract Society, embarked on a similar crusade.[131] Militant Christianity, armed for an internecine conflict consecrated as a millennial struggle, not only aggravated the rift between North and South but exacerbated an older confrontation between Christian and Jew.

Although new challenges for Christianity sometimes resulted in new levels of hostility toward Jews, most middle-period anti-Semitism showed continuity with the past. In the conversion movement, the American Society for Meliorating the Condition of the Jews (ASMCJ) continued to admonish against anti-Semitism, glorify biblical Israel, and note Christianity's obligation to Judaism, the Jews' miraculous survival in the diaspora, and their future return to grace. Admiration, however, mixed with traditional resentment. In 1842 the ASMCJ's president, Rev. W. C. Brownlee, lauded the Jews for the usual reasons but declared that "they neglected the great salvation; and now they are homeless and desolate." Their misery, as well as their deliverance, was God's "vindicating justice."

Zeal for apostates did not diminish during the war, as evinced by attempts of Christian chaplains in army hospitals to convert Jewish soldiers. The religious quickening that accompanied national division also revealed itself in the post-1850 revival of the ASMCJ, the advent of the American Baptist Society for Evangelizing the Jews (1844) and a similar organization among the Presbyterians (1858), the establishment of a Jewish mission in 1861 by the Evangelical Synod of North America, and the emergence of various nondenominational conversion agencies.[132]

Renewal amid crisis also brought, as in other interactions between Christians and Jews, a harsher tone in the proselytizing movement. Missionaries to Jews at Smyrna, Turkey, in 1856 and 1857 and in Jaffa and Jerusalem in 1857, looked upon their potential flock as "rude, mercenary," "deceitful," and "lazy," regarded attempts to fulfill the prophetic return of Jews to Christ as "a hopeless affair," and concluded that they had "miserably failed." Proselytizers at home were equally strident, if less pessimistic. The chief secretary of the Presbyterian General Assembly and some colleagues in 1849 issued a manifesto to Jews demanding that they join the Presbyterian Church and announcing that missionaries would visit Jewish families to accomplish this purpose.[133]

Tradition also ruled in didactic literature for Christian children. The American Tract Society (1825) sent its publications—158 million copies of them in its first thirty years of existence—clergy, and lay agents throughout the country to the sick and the poor, to ordinary families, and later to army camps to promote moral uplift and religious conversion and rejuvenation. Among its publications was *Scripture Lessons for the Young* (1849), by Harvey P. Peet, president of the New York Institution of the Deaf and Dumb. This book, like all Society distributions, needed the approval of the Committee on Publication, a body composed of evangelical ministers. In Lesson 27 the "Jews clamored for his death; and Pilate, to please them ordered him to be crucified." In Lesson 28 the "Jews . . . nailed him to the cross" and "Many of the Jews reviled him." In Lesson 30 the "Jews hated the Christians, and persecuted them." The "Jews have been scattered among all nations, because they disobeyed God and rejected Christ."[134]

Sermons and denominational periodicals delivered the same message. A preacher at a Sunday church service in Charleston in 1846 told his parishioners that although Christ's "claims upon the Jews, to their gratitude was perfect; . . . they persecuted, tortured and crucified him. How great their sin!" They "thought he blasphemed their law, their God, they tried him by their common custom, and condemned him to the common death of a felon." The editor of the *Free Presbyterian* declared in 1854 that Jews could atone for the crucifixion only by conversion to Christianity, and the *Christian Intelligencer,* an organ of the Dutch Reformed church, referred in 1857 to "the fanatical Jew," a "bigot" who killed the Messiah and still hates Christianity.[135]

A particularly flagrant example of Jew-baiting in organized Christianity appeared in 1855 in the *Churchman,* the official Episcopalian publication. Its editors were enraged. A "blaspheming Jew," an "infuriate infidel," had "charge[d] Christians with 'misrepresenting' and 'vilifying' what he insolently calls his 'sacred belief,'" and had designated Christians persecutors of Judaism and "malicious, bigoted hypocrites." Piously and anxiously indignant, the *Churchman* responded: "If Judaism be the truth, Christianity is a lie. If, as the Jew contends, the Messiah is not yet come then . . . Christ is an imposter, and Christians are miserable dupes." Christian unease evoked this command: "Every sincere Christian *must* repudiate their [the Jews'] blasphemy and unbelief, and *must* refrain from having fellowship with them as blasphemers and unbelievers. Theirs is 'an evil heart of unbelief.'" The *Churchman* went on to issue the traditional "condemnation," saying that the "Jews . . . 'denied the Holy One and the Just, and desired a murderer to be granted unto them'—crying out, the while, those awful words, 'His blood be upon us, and upon our children.'"[136]

Liberal Christianity, too, nurtured detractors of Judaism. As indicated by the rancor of Edmond Quincy, Theodore Parker, Lydia Maria Child, and Julia Ward Howe, Unitarianism had absorbed from its Enlightenment precursors not only their optimistic rationalism but their cavils against Judaism. From 1825 through the Civil War, Unitarianism dominated theology at Harvard and formulated the prayers, and perhaps stimulated the anti-Semitism, of upper-class Boston. Not only social reformers displayed anti-Semitic attitudes; among Unitarian testifiers to defects in Judaism were William Ellery Channing, who became an abolitionist only much later in life, the Worcester Catechism, which considerably antedated the heyday of reform movements and antislavery agitation, and Harvard president James Walker, a social and political conservative.[137]

To their earlier reprovals of Judaism could be added the judgment of Abiel Abbott Livermore, a follower of Channing and a professor of biblical languages and literature at Harvard Divinity School. Possibly at mid-century the leading Unitarian interpreter of the New Testament, Livermore asserted Christianity's "succession to Judaism" and associated the latter with vengeance, guilt, and hatred for and violence against Christianity. He delivered his indictment in describing Paul before that apostle's embrace of Christ. As "a Jew," he "tasted the guilt of that passion and the force of that prejudice" against Christians. With "inhuman bigotry he 'breathed out threatenings and slaughter against the disciples of the Lord' . . . The very existence of the Christian Church was endangered by this arch-enemy."[138]

Some clergyman vented their animosity in secular recrimination. The future Episcopal Bishop of San Francisco proclaimed from an Albany pulpit in 1846 that Jews were Germans falsely calling themselves Jews for business purposes.[139]

New conflicts exacerbated traditional belligerence. Catholics and Jews avoided disputes until the Mortara affair in 1858 provoked worldwide outcry by Jews and Protestants against the papal role in the kidnapping. Except for James A. McMaster, editor of the *New-York Freeman's Journal and Catholic Register,* Catholic writers and publications unqualifiedly defended Rome, and many accused the other religions of trying to destroy Catholicism. "In the Mortara case," maintained the *Catholic Mirror,* the official organ of the bishops of Baltimore and Richmond, "an immense proportion" of critical journals "in France and Germany belong to Jews. Hebrews and Protestants will hunt in couples when Popery is on foot."[140]

This early American assertion of Jewish control over the press antici-pated twentieth-century anti-Semitic accusations. The *Guardian,* a weekly published by the Society of St. Vincent de Paul at Louisville, also mar-shaled modern and traditional anti-Semitic arguments on behalf of Mortara's baptism. Its editorials included conventional criticism: Protestants manipulated the controversy to persecute the true faith. Catholics historically protected Jews. Baptism saved the young Mortara's soul and undoing his salvation by returning him to his parents was a crime against the boy, Christianity, and God. The Mortaras should blame themselves because they violated a church edict not to employ Gentile servants, a decree meant to prevent the taking of Jewish children away from their parents. The magazine repeated untruths with which official Catholicism justified its position: The boy had reached the age of religious discretion; Mrs. Mortara was an apostate Jew and her son was baptized along with her, hence there had been no kidnapping and forced conversion; the parents were reconciled to their son's change of creed and were thinking of becoming Catholics.

The Mortara case presaged graver disagreements that would arise, starting in the 1930s, between Catholics and Jews over foreign and domestic issues, and the *Guardian's* counteroffensive mobilized an anti-Semitic canard, initially heard during the French Revolution, that would reverberate in the twentieth-century rumor of an alliance between world Jewry and world Communism. In this case the association of Judaism with radicalism linked Jewish resistance to the kidnapping with proponents of the democratic, anticlerical Risorgimento. The "complaint did not come from the parents," claimed the *Guardian,* "but from certain Mazzinian Jews of Piedmont, who were no doubt playing second fiddle to that arch-conspirator and arch assassin Mazzini."[141]

The *New York Tablet,* another Catholic weekly, repeated the rationalizations that the Mortaras had broken the law against having Christian servants and that mother and son had been baptized together. In real life, as in fiction, the Jew was depicted as an unredeemable reprobate while the Jewess inclined toward the true faith. The *Tablet* also parroted the charge that Jews, "Protestants, Pagans and Nothingarians" eagerly "pounce on any charge against Catholicity." It added that nowhere had the Jews been better treated than in Rome. "With the acquisitive instinct of their race, they have turned the indulgence of the Pontiffs to the best account and have in many instances made fortunes by it."[142]

Acrimony crested in the foremost American Catholic publication, the *Pilot,* the official periodical of the Boston archdiocese. "Jews of Europe and America" express "their hatred of the Catholic Church and their disrespect for the Sovereign Pontiff," contended one irate editorial. After "the Jewish mob pronounced a malediction upon their misguided race, 'His blood be upon us and upon our children,'" the "kindness of those who have taken pity upon them," has "been unable to effect their deliverance." Inheritors of Israel's villainy "have controlled the wealth of the world for more than a thousand years—indeed, money would seem to be a part of the curse which has pursued them so relentlessly." Apart from "enmity excited against them as the descendants of those who crucified our Lord, they have been hated by all classes of people as usurers are always hated."[143]

The Mortara frenzy quickly subsided, and relations between Jews and Catholics resumed civility that would last until the 1930s, when more protracted and tragic rifts would emerge. Meanwhile, between Jews and Protestants, old conflicts continued and new ones emerged.

Protestant resentment manifested itself even in such triumphs of tolerance and equity as Warder Cresson's acquittal, the invocation in Congress given by a rabbi in 1860, and the commissioning of Jewish military chaplains. In the Cresson case, although the court found in 1851 that religious beliefs were not a factor in determining insanity and that Cresson was not deranged, it reversed an 1848 decision that had gone against him because of his attraction to Judaism.[144]

Controversy over the Congressional prayer by Rabbi Morris Jacob revealed more basic grudges against Jews. The Washington correspondent of the *New York Herald* thought that the occasion advanced religious liberty in America, but heard these remarks from the audience: "Going to pray for ten percent a month." "The next thing we shall have" is "a pawnshop in the basement" of the House of Representatives. The irascible bigot William Brownlow, publisher of the *Knoxville Whig,* was appalled that a government assembly had been addressed by a clergyman of "the people who killed Christ." He told readers of the *Whig* that this spectacle proved "that a majority of the present Congress are about prepared to sell their interest in Christ's atonement."[145]

Objections also came from Catholic and mainstream Protestant journals. A Baltimore Catholic paper protested any devotions in Congress not addressed to God through his Son. The *Freeman,* a Protestant magazine, regarded the invocation as a "monstrous sin." According to the *Churchman,* the "infidel among its [Congress's] constituency [now] has the same right to have religious Services," a fact that entails "official rejection of Christianity by the Legislature of the Country"; the "highest council of the nation" now "sees no difference of any consequence between Truth and Falsehood." Honoring a "priest" from that "benighted and erring" people, was "evil in the sight of God" and put the nation at risk of divine punishment.[146]

Progress in civic and religious parity for Jews stirred resistance in 1861 to allowing Jews to become chaplains in the armed forces. Delegates at a YMCA meeting held in Washington to consider this matter spoke out against broadening the military ministry, and in September a YMCA worker forced the resignation of a Jewish chaplain in a Pennsylvania regiment, serving unofficially in that capacity, by reporting that he assumed a pastoral role. An editorial in the *Presbyter*, a Presbyterian publication, did not quarrel with the commissioning of Universalist and Catholic chaplains because these "denominations at least call themselves Christians." But "Jews regard Jesus of Nazareth as an imposter, a deceiver, and one worthy of every term of reproach." Should "this bill become a law," the "government would, in effect, say that one might despise and reject the Savior of men, and thus trample under foot the son of God . . . and yet be a fit minister of religion."[147]

Popular Christian rituals concerning the trial and death of Christ, a blend of folklore and theology, also infernalized Jews. After the Mexican War, the Yaqui Indians brought to New Mexico from Latin America the old custom of lighting fires at the coming of spring, a custom that had come to be associated with Easter. At this rite an effigy of Judas was burned in a consecrated bonfire. The spectacle was often accompanied by anti-Semitic abhorrence of Judas for delivering Jesus to the Jews for crucifixion. An analogous Easter ritual took place in southern California during Mexican and early American rule. The Saturday of Glory ended Easter week with the trial and execution of Judas, accused of "being a cheat, a vagabond, a Jew, and worst of all, a gringo."[148]

Blood libels circulated far less frequently in America than in Europe and Asia and even more rarely brought retribution. There were exceptions, however. On Yom Kippur eve in 1850, a mob of five hundred, mostly Irish immigrants and including several policemen, burst into a house in Brooklyn occupied by Jewish families and their synagogue, and wrecked the premises because of a rumor that its inhabitants had killed a Christian girl for the holy day feast. This was the first acting out in America of blood libel fears. A subsequent instance ended more tragically in Atlanta in 1913 when Leo Frank was lynched for the murder of a Christian employee, despite clear evidence that the young girl had been killed by another employee, a black janitor. On another Yom Kippur eve, in 1928, a four-year-old girl vanished from a small town in upstate New York. A local rabbi was interrogated at the police station, at the behest of the mayor, regarding alleged blood guilt in Judaism. Before the girl was found unharmed, a state trooper questioned Jewish merchants about the use of human blood in their holy day services and the Ku Klux Klan, backed by a menacing mob of several hundred, searched Jewish-owned stores for her body.[149] In blood libel incidents, as in so many other features of anti-Semitism, the middle period initiated or foreshadowed later developments.

## Secular Culture

America was not immune to the anti-Semitic virus infecting all Christian lands. The central themes of theological Jew hatred, guilt for deicide and for subsequent unrepentant repudiation of the Redeemer, were relentlessly instilled through both religious and secular culture. Sermons, Sunday school lessons, and denominational publications included secular and sectarian agitation against Jews. Mundane media likewise combined Christian and worldly anti-Jewish stereotypes. Emphasis, not substance, distinguished religious and secular conveyance of bigotry. The former tended toward spiritual and traditional, and the latter toward materialistic and modern, derogation.

The *New York Herald* was an extremely strident and implacable anti-Semitic voice among newspapers, merging contemporary prejudices against Noah, Chatham Street retailers, and the Rothschilds with medieval mythology. A page one story in 1850 blamed Jews for the Damascus blood libel of 1840. According to the *Herald,* Father Tommasio and his servant had been killed by "fanatics [who] use human blood to moisten their unleavened bread." Cynical, sensational urban journalism decreed that "Rothschild"—to avoid the universal "shame, the dishonor, and the ignominy it would entail upon the Jewish nation—used all his influence to prevent an investigation of the matter." The "Rothschilds and the Jewish nation" brought "the gold and jewels" of "the [Damascus] Jews" to bribe the French consul. "One of the Jewish accomplices," however, confessed "this murderous sacrifice on the altar of religious atrocity" and thus "exposed all the mysteries of the Thalmud [sic] until then concealed from all the other religions."[150]

A few Know-Nothing newspapers also, if less regularly and hysterically, inveighed against the Jews, but antebellum bigotry was more prominent in magazines.[151] Defamation ranged from elaborate discussions to sarcastic epigrams, short stories, and references and appeared in respectable journals as well as in lighter, and even vulgar, periodicals.

No antebellum American publication rivaled the *North American Review* for serious intent and scholarship. It ranked with Harvard College and the Athenaeum in the intellectual pantheon of proper Boston. An evaluation of Judaism in a review of Benjamin D'Israeli's *Tancred* in an 1847 issue, therefore, indicated customary, possibly prevalent, Brahmin attitudes toward Jews. The anonymous reviewer saw "syllogistic completeness" in "idolaters of ceremony and tradition" becoming "venders of old clothes," in "descendants" of those who "kneel[ed] before the golden calf" now being "the money-changers of Europe." The transition from superstition to commerce proceeded from "the Jewish mind" being bound to "corrupt Hebraic gloss" instead of liberated by "absolute truth." Choosing the trite over the true, "Jews" were unable to "behold clearly the countenance of their first great lawgiver, for the brightness that encompassed it" and "much less could they discern the more purely effulgent lineaments of Jesus."[152]

*Harper's Weekly,* a middle-brow magazine combining political commentary with fiction and pictorial engravings, based in New York and achieving a spectacular circulation of over 100,000 during the Civil War, was less severe toward Jews. An editorial of 1859 asserted that they wanted to assimilate and become Christians and were industrious, shrewd, enlightened, and successful in commerce and the professions. In these otherwise meritorious qualities, however, lurked a potential danger to the nation. "Their future in this country, as in Europe, [consequently] is a problem which is well deserving of sober thought."[153]

Scolding of Jews in respectable journals signified genteel contempt. The sculptor William Wetmore Story, son of the Supreme Court justice, joined his fellow Boston patricians Edmond Quincy and John Quincy Adams in venting distaste. "She was wretchedly supported by a set of dirty Jews," Story wrote to James Russell Lowell when the French-Jewish actress Rachel came to Boston in 1855. "She was jewier than ever and tried to skin a flint in Boston."[154]

Story's New York social peer, the lawyer and civic leader George Templeton Strong, also patronized Jews. "Had anyone suddenly ejaculated . . . 'Farmer's Loan and Trust Co. has just executed an incoherent assignment!'" he observed of a concert attended mostly by Jews, "the announcement would have had an appalling effect on the hook-nosed and black-whiskered congregation." Visiting a synagogue in 1855, Strong remarked that "the people" pray "in discord unspeakable, like eager bidders at a sale of stocks." He was amazed that "their worship should be so utterly unlike that of any Christian culture I ever witnessed."[155]

Unlike the more serious publications, the *Spirit of the Times,* an early chronicle of sports, literature, and the stage, substituted sarcasm for contemplative degradation. An 1845 issue contained a story about pushy, conniving Chatham Street old clothes dealers and their "little, fat, greasy children." In 1848 the magazine offered a joke about "Two old Jewish clothesmen" who steal coats and are caught by the owners. The culprits, called "rabbies," are punished by having their beards glued together. Issues during the 1850s featured tales of Jews being outsmarted in trading trickery, swindling a synagogue out of money, and masquerading as nobles in crooked gambling schemes, as well as slurs about Jewish clothing store owners, especially Chatham Street sharpies. These fictional characters were further stigmatized by having crooked noses and speaking a jaw-breaking parody of Yiddish.[156]

Jews were similarly ridiculed during the 1850s in the *Knickerbocker,* a monthly produced by the New York literary set of Washington Irving, devoted—with a light touch—to arts and belles lettres. Jokes featured Jews, sometimes termed "a relative of Shylock," being outsmarted by Gentiles, speaking gibberized Yiddish, and prizing an "old gharment." An editorial assured readers that the Academy of Music directors "are not groveling speculators; they are not Jews; but sober, Christian gentlemen." A poem represented Jews praying to Jehovah for "Real shining dollars." In a humorous anecdote in an 1860 issue Hebrews were "a contriving and cunning set" who tormented Christ in Jerusalem.[157]

Ethnic humor frequently reflects intergroup tension, but if laughter displaces animosity it reduces friction. When Jews become the butt of jests, however, wit aggravates conflict by directing laughter to reinforce and disseminate hostility. Comic slurs, therefore, confirmed and informed Gentile opinion of Jews and underscored their status as an outcast group.[158]

In scattered references in other publications, most based in New York, Jews were caricatured as shoddy *arrivistes,* knavish peddlers fortunately outwitted by their would-be victims, fraudulent Wall Street brokers, cheating Chatham Street clothiers, and miserly pawnbrokers. They were lumped with Yankees as sly skinflints, singled out as Shylocks and sons of Judas, and stereotyped by physical ugliness, particularly long, hooked noses.[159]

Among the demeaning devices was a harbinger of future invective in the *Police Gazette,* a magazine of lurid crime reports, sports articles (particularly boxing), and Victorian versions of *Playboy* centerfolds in the form of provocatively posed vaudeville, stage, and burlesque beauties. An 1860 issue warned readers that "German Jews are active as receivers of stolen goods." Many "are professional lifters, burglars, and swindlers." Although these were now conventional objections, another slander would later became an onerous burden for Jewish proprietors: "Those in business find it difficult to effect an insurance upon their stock because of the frequency with which fires occur in their stores and the suspicious circumstances attending them."[160]

Another standard degradation of Jewish businessmen appeared in J. Ross Browne's *Crusoe's Island* (1864). In its fourth edition by 1872, Browne's memoir of life in Mexico and California in the 1840s and 1850s featured a hook-nosed, dirty, Yiddish-accented, crooked Jewish peddler who allegedly tried to rob the author.[161]

A new venue for anti-Semitic debasement was the minor literary genre of guidebooks to New York City, which first appeared in the 1840s, when Chatham Street was becoming the center of the German Jewish retail clothing market. After acidly attributing aggressive salesmanship to Jewish storekeepers, the well-known New York journalist and fiction writer Cornelius Mathews, who had also reviled Jews in the *Spirit of the Times,* noted in *Pen-And-Ink Panorama of New York City* (1853): "The old red men scalped their enemies, the Chatham Clo' men skin theirs."[162]

George G. Foster's *New York in Slices* (1848), originally serialized in the *Tribune* and by 1860 in its sixth edition, depicted these merchants as "insinuating," intrusive, and unreliable. "Chatham-street" was "the gathering-place of gullibility, the metropolis of shams," a place of a "miserable speculating, under the pretence of cheap utility, upon the avarice, the weakness, and the ignorance of its customers." Foster also described a group of Wall Street speculators, "many of them with the Israelitish nose so proverbial for smelling out a good thing in embryo or a bad one just beginning to taint." Pawnbrokers in his book talked in absurdly accented Yiddish and ignored the pleas of widows and orphans forced to part with their loved ones' possessions. Leeches on human tragedy, they exacted "usurious interest," which earned one dealer the title of "the old Shekelite."[163]

Foster berated another type of Jewish trader in *New York by Gas-Light* (1850), the most popular of the antebellum urban guidebooks. In the notorious neighborhood of "Five Points" are "'fences,' or shops for the receipt and purchase of stolen goods . . . kept entirely by Jews." Presiding over these "squalid and dirty" dens, Abraham's progeny manifest the "elasticity of flesh, the glittering eye-sparkle," and "the hook of the nose which betrays the Israelite as the human kite formed to be feared, hated and despised, yet to prey upon mankind."[164]

Jews were derogated in descriptions of New York by literary luminaries as well as guidebook hacks. Walt Whitman, poetic celebrator of vital, comprehensive brotherhood, nevertheless, in his prose sketch "Broadway" (1856), mentioned "dirty looking German Jews," harking their wares "with a sharp nasal twang and flat squalling enunciation to which the worst Yankee brogue is sweet music."[165]

German-language publications also defamed Jews, tapping the undercurrent of contempt present since colonial times in Americans of German descent. During the 1840s several newspapers accused Jews of trading dishonestly, avoiding manual labor, and deceiving Christians. This reflected an intensification of animosity; although a pale preliminary of post–Civil War bigotry, hostile acts increased during the middle period. In addition to German-American opposition to Jews' running for state office in Michigan in 1856 and Wisconsin in 1859, in the 1830s a German immigrant in Charleston put up a billboard attacking a Jewish candidate. The first recorded anti-Jewish act in Baltimore occurred in 1855 when another immigrant harassed a Jewish peddler with the German anti-Semitic cry of "Hep-Hep."[166]

The deteriorating relationship between Jews and Gentiles of German extraction provoked an act of Jew hatred reminiscent of burial-plot incidents in the provincial era. In Brooklyn in 1849, a group of German-Americans prevented the interment of a Jew on land the Jews had bought for a cemetery. Wielding clubs, guns, and stones, the attackers disrupted the funeral and wounded several mourners.[167]

During the Civil War magazines continued to insult Jews, but the major vehicle of obloquy was now the newspaper. Newspaper recrimination was more currently topical and less discursive than that in the periodicals. If the latter revealed the generic bedrock of American anti-Semitism, the former manifested the recurrent historical phenomenon of a dramatic upsurge of prejudice triggered by a specific event.

Neither in frequency nor in content of anti-Semitic remarks did magazines significantly depart from the previous decade. The *Knickerbocker* perpetuated spiteful sketches, including jokes about Chatham Street retailers who spoke a ridiculous dialect. A story in an issue of 1862 conjured "the howling dervishes of the Note-Shaver and the Israel-blu-light clergymen of Old Clo-denomination." *Harper's Weekly* combined antebellum with topical reproofs. "Most of the heavy speculators were Jews," expostulated an editorial on a gold panic of 1863. They "cut miserable figures as they rushed to and fro, foaming at the mouth, cursing with impotent rage Old Abe and Secretary Chase, who had brought this ruin on the house of their fathers."[168]

Harper's Weekly's sister journal, Harper's New Monthly Magazine, a literary and illustrated publication, in 1865 made traditional anti-Jewish invective the theme of two jokes, one recounted in the usual dialect. Of severer import was the regression of the monthly from its antebellum position as an outspoken foe of anti-Semitism.[169]

Confederate magazines mirrored the aspersions of their federal counterparts. Southern Punch, based in Richmond and self-consciously modeled on its London namesake, alternated jibes (as in "Jew Shirts") with editorial vituperation. Among the latter were commentary on "Jew and Yankee extortioners," the "dirty, greasy Jew peddlar" whose wartime chicanery transforms him into a "strut[ting] . . . millionaire," and "Shylocks" who "ran up the prices upon many necessities to from 500 to 3000 per cent, upon the consumers."[170]

Magazine comments were a mere sprinkle of gall compared to the cascade that flowed from reports, editorials, and letters in Union and Rebel newspapers. The December 20, 1862, issue of the Richmond Examiner was typical. A letter on page one, subtitled "The Jews' Harvest" and signed "A Soldier," grumbled that the city's Jewish clothiers exploited scarce supplies and pressing demand to exact exorbitant prices: "specimens" of the "accursed race . . . fatten upon the calamities of the very people who are giving them a home." Conversely, Jews "are few indeed in the army, unless as camp followers, where they can follow their natural occupation." The soldier listed other common suppositions: "they are unproductive, . . . did any one ever see a Jew mechanic, a Jew farmer, or a Jew producer of any kind?" Jewish businessmen were like "Judas," by blood and creed belonging to "the extortioners of the world." An editorial repeated these accusations. Along with the rich and other foreigners, Jews avoided "conscription" by "denying their allegiance to the country" of their birth or pretended adoption. The Examiner sneered at "unkempt Israelites in our marts, . . . fat and gaudy non-conscripts who wait behind of the counters of the extortioner. Every auction room is packed with greasy Jews."[171]

The Southern Illustrated News, also published in the Confederate capital, similarly editorialized about Jews. Foreigners and Jews were destroying the South through currency speculation. "All that the Jews possess is a plentiful lot of money, together with the scorn of the world, . . . since the time they were driven out of the Temple until now, for them money has been country."[172]

Northern newspapers decried the same treachery, peculation, and parasitism. The war correspondent of a Dubuque, Iowa, paper claimed that every commissary officer in one division was a money-grubbing German Jew or a relative with the same purpose. An Associated Press reporter in New Orleans had an even uglier reaction. "The Jews of New Orleans and all the South ought to be exterminated," he thundered. "They run the blockade, and are always to be found at the bottom of every new villainy." A *Detroit Commercial Advertiser* journalist discovered that "the tribe of gold speculators" who "create distrust of the government" are "exclusively . . . hook-nosed wretches." They "speculate on disasters, and a battle lost to our army is chuckled over by them, as it puts money in their purse."[173]

Outrageous slander drew protests from Jews and a few dissenting journals. Congregations Beth Shalome and Beth Ahabah in Richmond resolved that "our character as Jews and good citizens" was "repeatedly and grossly assailed in public prints, etc." In the North, Simon Wolf, an important Jewish political figure, in 1864 wrote the *New York Evening Post,* objecting to press portrayals of Jews as copperheads, cheaters, cowards, military shirkers, and corrupt businessmen, and to the designation by religion of any Jew involved in shady activities. Simon's letter drew support from several northern papers. "We publish on our first page a heartfelt protest of Mr. Wolf," editorialized the *Evening Post,* "against the flippant and contemptuous phrases which the newspapers often use in speaking of the Israelites." Wolf's protest also elicited sympathy from the *Washington Chronicle.*[174]

Epithets and lies that passed as newspaper reportage and commentary both reflected and stimulated hatred. A Virginian told a British traveler that Jews increased the value of greenbacks because they traded with the northern enemy. Atlanta Jews, too, were called disloyal speculators. In addition to looting of Jewish-owned shops, a rock was thrown into the window of a Richmond synagogue. Bigotry was rampant among northern troops stationed in Memphis. A Jewish jeweler in that city noted that unscrupulous store owners of all ethnic affiliations were regularly labeled "swindling Jews" by victims who had never met a Jew and confused Irish and Dutch merchants with Jews.[175]

Slander was denounced and Jewish honesty and loyalty were defended by Jews themselves and, more important, by a Confederate chaplain, an

Atlanta grand jury and citizens of that city, and newspapers in Charleston, Augusta, and Richmond. Indignation was also expressed in northern dailies in Cincinnati, San Francisco, Washington, New York, Springfield, Illinois, and Franklin, Indiana.[176] Yet the need for vigorous protest and the numerical disparity between defenders and attackers among the people and the press revealed the dangerous outbreak of war-bred anti-Semitism.

~

Representation of Jews as disreputable was routine, as well, in plays, poetry, and prose. The main difference from the literary past was a tremendous accretion of stereotypes and references—multiplication, not invention, distinguished the middle period from former times.

James Pilgrim's *Yankee Jack* (1852) brought the sole new type of Jew to the stage. Kizer, a minor character in this "nautical drama," is a mercenary, probably dishonest, and faintly repugnant tavernkeeper. A stock stage Jew, Kizer is nevertheless the first American Jew presented in the American theater. Comically anxious and absurd, the tavernkeeper mangles English with an imputed Yiddish accent and worries about profit.[177]

*Yankee Jack* was one of Pilgrim's more obscure efforts. Another play with a Jewish villain, by a far better known author, Julia Ward Howe's *The World's Own* (1857), also had a brief stage life. Produced in New York and Boston in 1857, the romantic melodrama, set in eighteenth-century Italy, scandalized audiences and received poor reviews because its heroine suffered no permanent agony as a result of being seduced. Howe struck a blow for independent womanhood but showed less sympathy for another oppressed group. Jacob, "a noted usurer," has a small, but vile, role. A "mine of shrewdness" and "a serviceable imp," he is hired by a wicked queen to kidnap the hero's child. The queen's unrequited love for the hero, Count Lothair, whose reckless gambling has made him Jacob's debtor, drives her to this misdeed.[178]

Traditional fare, especially *The Merchant of Venice*, had a greater impact than did new productions in strengthening prejudice against Jews. Shylock, mythic Judaic evil personified as an aloof, cunning, clannish, cruel, underhanded, desiccated, legalistic, stubborn, Christian-hating, and vengeful moneylender, drove theatergoers to tantrums. The *Buffalo Courier*, reviewing a Memphis production of the 1850s, reported that during "the Trial scene, a man jumped upon the stage and wrenched the knife from Mr. B[uchanan]'s hand, under the impression that the whole was real life."

A member of an audience at a different time and place, witnessing the same actor in the same role, "became so enraged that he arose in his seat and cursed the Jews aloud, so that the whole house heard."[179]

By the 1860s Shylock had debuted as a comical figure. In George M. Baker's *The Peddler of Very Nice* (1865), a popular sketch written for amateur acting groups and published five times by 1894, the trial scene was burlesqued and Shakespeare's pawnbroker was now also an old clothes man and a greenbacker. Associating Shylock with current issues and characters was not an exclusively comedic strategy. Edwin Booth, America's greatest tragedian of the second half of the nineteenth century, detested the character and his people and compared Shylock to the Rothschilds, the Belmonts, Benjamin, and Jay Gould (who was often incorrectly labeled Jewish).[180]

Sarcastic doggerel abounded in popular periodicals, but condemnation in serious verse focused not on sardonic shafts but on guilt and salvation, and its topic was messianic martyrdom not Chatham Street cheating. Episcopal Rev. William Croswell mildly formulated a classical rebuke in "The Synagogue" (1842). Impressed with the splendor and beauty of the temple service and the women in the congregation, Croswell expected the eventual conversion of the Jews. "That on their harden'd hearts the veil," he prayed, "Might no longer be dark."[181]

The same plea came more angrily from the Virginian Robert Tyler, a son of President Tyler and a politician and future Confederate official, in *Ahasuerus* (1842). Since the 1820s Americans had avidly read European books about Ahasuerus, and Sue's *Wandering Jew* was a best-seller when published here in 1845. Domestic novelists immediately took up this theme, advising Jews to overcome stubbornness, vengeance, and materialism and forsake a wrongheaded creed.[182]

Tyler's retread rendition of the legend made Ahasuerus stand for Jewish selfishness, cruelty, tormenting of the Messiah, diaspora punishment, and millennial return. Christ, expiring in agony, conveyed a harsh judgment upon the Jews. The "mad multitude" mocked him with "hisses, sneers and fiendish jests and cries." Ahasuerus's assault on the beleaguered Redeemer came from "hate and malice to mankind" that "proud Satan's halls might grace." His hand "held a dagger red with blood" and "[r]apine and blood and lust" throbbed in "his iron face." Driven by "his cruel heart," he struck Jesus, who responded: "Ahasuerus tarry till I come." After the crucifixion, the Temple and the Holy City were destroyed. "Livid despair shrunk up their [the Israelites'] withering hearts." The Hebrews "smote" each other "with a maniac hand," or "baring to the steel their raging breasts, / Quench'd fear and madness both in their own blood."[183]

Unlike Tyler's monster, David Hoffman, a Baltimore attorney, legal scholar, and law professor, presented the more usual persona of a benign, forlorn, and remorseful outcast. In *Chronicles Selected from the Origins of Cartaphilus, the Wandering Jew* (1853), he conceived the semi-apparitional figure as a vehicle for proselytizing Jews and depicting the world from early Christianity to the Middle Ages. Compounded of romantic fiction, historical narrative, and Christian doctrine, the three-volume homily features an account of the crucifixion, the destruction of Jerusalem, and the diaspora less savage and condemnatory than that in *Ahasuerus*. This tamer version nonetheless contrasts Pilate and the Roman soldiers with the "more brutal and fiendish of the Jewish multitude, who more specially sought his [Jesus'] death." Readers are further reminded that the Romans will be a greater "scourge" to the Jews when Hebraic "iniquity (now nearly full) shall soon overflow." Jerusalem's consequent "desolation" is punishment for its "crime" of "DEICIDE." *Chronicles* ends with Cartaphilus (perhaps not coincidentally the name of Pilate's doorkeeper), in the ninth century C.E., angry that his people stubbornly refuse salvation, and "loathing the attempt of our Talmudic doctors to silence such a truth."[184]

This Christian legend evolved from Genesis, where Cain smites Abel and is sentenced by God to a life of itinerancy. Cain and Ahasuerus/Cartaphilus have much in common: Both are responsible to God alone for their sin, which involves violence, or at least cruelty, but is fundamentally defiance of God. The wrathful older brother kills his gentle younger sibling; the Wandering Jew, symbolizing the elder-brother faith of Christianity, abuses the gentle Messiah of the younger-brother faith. These prototypes wreak havoc because of rage and jealousy over God's preferring their victims to themselves. Cain and Ahasuerus/Cartaphilus become peripatetic outcasts, like other members of their creed punished by exile from their home—and from all communities—for defying God's will. Despite this transgression the Lord spares their lives so that they may exemplify his retribution for willful disobedience. Several versions of the tale of the Wandering Jew mark him on his forehead (like Cain, but with a flaming cross) and even call him Cain.[185]

The myth also had New Testament antecedents. In the Gospels a bystander strikes Christ on the road to Golgotha and Christ remarks that some present will tarry on earth until he returns.[186] According to some versions, the condemned smiter is called Malchus, also the name of the servant of the high priest of Israel. More indirect reference may be to Moloch and Molech. As discussed in Chapter 2, Malchus-Moloch-Molech recalls the Christian abjuration of Judaic animal sacrifice, and by extension, of crucifixion and ritual murder.[187]

The visibility of the Wandering Jew coincided with crises in Jewish and Christian history. The myth attained its complete form in the eleventh century, a time of eschatological turbulence. Dogma asserted that the Second Coming would occur in 1000 C.E., and citings of the melancholy figure were inspired by popular belief in the imminence of the Last Judgment, to be followed by the Kingdom of Glory on earth. European Christendom anxiously awaited the Antichrist to launch the apocalypse that would end in salvation. The oldest reports of the Wandering Jew identified him as the Antichrist, despite the theological and folkloric representation of Cartaphilus as emblemizing a worn-out forlorn Judaism, while the Antichrist signified a Judaism that was still formidably rebellious. The earliest known written account of the legend appeared in England in 1228, soon after the exile of Jews from Britain. No mention of it between the thirteenth and the fifteenth centuries has been recorded. The Wanderer surfaced again at the beginning of the sixteenth century (now frequently called Ahasuerus, the name of the King of Persia in the Book of Esther) and the initial modern text was a German pamphlet of 1602. The resurgence of the legend coincided with the banishment of Jews from Iberia and most German cities and with the advent of the Reformation.[188]

During the nineteenth century, the Wandering Jew was a promethean persona of the Romantic epoch, a secular and/or Christian symbol of western man as unredeemed and unintegrated—restless and rootless. In Germany especially he represented the demand that Jews assimilate to a Christian or national ethos and thus lose their separate identity. Although the legend reflected contemporary cultural currents, its essence remained unchanged. The wanderer embodied the collective, intergenerational sequence of sin, guilt, repentance, and penance for rejecting Jesus. Divine retribution for deicide conjoined in him with the divine mercy of final salvation. In a less grandiose vision just as critical to Christianity, the hero (or antihero) of the story personifies the survival of afflicted and aged Jewry as indispensable witness to Christian truth and triumph.[189]

Less frequently, as in Tyler's *Ahasuerus*, the wanderer is unremorseful, unreconciled, and unregenerate. Here he incarnates the Christian view of Jewry as obdurately blind and immoral and therefore scattered, suppressed, and suffering. Whether the wanderer is penitent or impudent, the myth confirms the Christian view of order and existence. Jesus is portrayed in the Christian (and sometimes Judaic) image of Jehovah as a vengeful deity and Jewish law as an eye-for-an-eye code of retaliation. The correlative of this Christ ("Vengeance is Mine, I will repay, saith the Lord," Rom. 12:19) is Ahasuerus *cum* Cain. Christianity, however, also promises the world, the Jews, and Ahasuerus a compassionate Savior who restores the outcasts, succors the wounded, saves the sinners, and redeems history.[190]

A respected antebellum author showed little better aptitude than did the tendentious reiterators of the Wandering Jew myth in depicting guilt, betrayal, and crucifixion. Nathaniel Hawthorne's "The Star of Calvary" (1845), originally published in a religious gift-book, typified Christian poetry in such volumes. Shopworn verses and sentiments limned the role of the Jews in the killing of the Son of God: "Behold O Israel! behold it is no human" that "you have dared to crucify . . . It is your king."[191]

Nathaniel Parker Willis, who expressed a casual and muted anti-Semitism in "The Gypsy of Sardis," delivered a relatively mild and conventional remonstrance in "Christ's Entrance into Jerusalem." Unaware of Jesus's divinity, the Jews ridicule him. In "The Leper," Willis retold a New Testament parable attesting to the superiority of Christianity over Judaism. Denied refuge in the Temple because his illness is seen as a mark of Jehovah's disfavor, a leper is cured by the Messiah and becomes a Christian. As Ahasuerus rejects the wounded Savior and as two Jewish priests refuse to help the wounded victim of a robber in Christ's parable of the good Samaritan (Luke 10:30–37), so their coreligionists spurn another sufferer—acts juxtaposing pitiless, egotistical Judaism to Christian altruism.[192]

Anti-Semitism in prose varied little from the preceding era but appeared more often and sometimes in new genres. Prejudice emanated from the works of America's greatest novelists, from contemporary best-sellers, from recently emergent genres, such as fiction of local and regional color and business novels, and from miscellaneous books, stories, and sketches.

Aversion can be traced in Hawthorne's prose as well as his poetry. Fascinated by a beautiful woman, in whom he discerned Jewish features, "I felt a sort of repugnance, simultaneously with my perception that she was an admirable creature." Visiting a synagogue in Rome in 1858, Hawthorne thought "it was dirty, and had an odor not of sanctity." In the same year and city he viewed Albrecht Dürer's "Christ Disputing with the Doctors," in which "was represented the ugliest, most evil-minded, stubborn, prag-

matical, and contentious old Jew that ever lived under the law of Moses."
Hawthorne was even more disgusted by "the Ghetto whose thousands of
Jews are crowded within a narrow compass, and lead a close unclean and
multitudinous life, resembling that of maggots when they overpopulate a
decaying cheese." Hawthorne's son Julian, also a writer, was more bluntly
anti-Semitic in his fiction.[193]

Herman Melville, the other master of the antebellum American novel,
was more outspokenly anti-Semitic in his writing than Hawthorne. Visiting Palestine in 1856–57, he had "little doubt, [that] the diabolical land-
scapes," over the "great part of Judea must have suggested to the Jewish
prophets, their ghastly theology." Christian devaluation of Judaism also
appeared in Melville's fiction. In *Pierre* (1853), Christ's "teachings seem
folly to the Jews . . . because he carried that Heaven's time in Jerusalem,
while the Jews carried Jerusalem [mundane] time there."[194]

More often, Melville's hostility was expressed in contemporary secular
terms. A sympathetic character in *The Confidence Man* (1857) defends
Indians by decrying comparisons of them with Austrian treaty-breakers,
New York rowdies, murderers, "or a Jew with hospitable speeches, coz-
ening some fainting stranger into ambuscade, there to burk him." In
*Redburn* (1849), Melville fashioned out of American pride in its ethnic
pluralism a secular parallel to Christian universalism vs. Judaic egotism.
"We are not a narrow tribe of men with a bigoted Hebrew nationality—
whose blood has been debased in the attempt to ennoble it, by maintaining an exclusive succession among ourselves." Our "blood" is a
"thousand noble currents all pouring into one. We are not a nation, so
much as a world."[195]

Melville also employed the cliché of the Chatham Street operator. Well-
ingborough Redburn, a poor rustic youth recently arrived in New York
was on Chatham Street with his rifle, "when a curley-headed little man
with a dark oily face, and a hooked nose, like the pictures of Judas Iscariot
called to me from a shop." With "a peculiar accent," an obsequious
manner, and concealed "eagerness," the pawnbroker offers a fraction of its
worth. At a second pawnshop a "hooked nosed" man rudely argued with a
woman and child over the value of a family jewel and they "shrank out of
the door" with a pittance. The establishment is run by three "hook-nosed"
Jews who fence stolen goods and quote an even lower price for Redburn's
rifle. At the novel's end the Jewish trader is a simile for dock hustlers, who
"glitter upon you an eye like a Jew's or a pawnbroker's," as they ply sailors
with overpriced wares.[196]

Melville's images—the long, crooked nose, sharp eyes, and dark complexion—disclose revulsion for Jews. Middle Eastern origins initially accounted for the association of Jews with dark hair and skin. Ironically, as Ashkenazis became genetically indistinguishable from other European peoples, darkness and blackness increasingly became metaphors for moral and personality defects ascribed to Jews. Physical darkness symbolized spiritual blindness. From the late seventeenth century, Jews were described as swarthy and black. After 1850, in America and abroad, their supposed color indicated an undesirable genotype, simultaneously a product and a sign of crossbreeding, inbreeding, ugliness, filth, and sexual and other disorders, particularly melancholia. The dark Jew became equated with the supposed racial degeneracy of "mongrelization." The large "Jewish nose," also a genetic-racial mark of Jewish otherness, hideousness, and avarice, was identified by modern extreme anti-Semites with the allegedly long Jewish penis as emblems of Jewish lewdness.[197]

Midway between masterpieces by Hawthorne and Melville and forgotten best-sellers lies Harriet Beecher Stowe's *Uncle Tom's Cabin* (1851–52). The enduring fame of this American classic owes less to literary genius than its sentimental morality, its shocking innovations of making a black man a hero and treating African-Americans as total human beings, and its impact on the coming of the war. The book sold 10,000 copies in the first week after publication and 300,000 in America alone in the first year. Stowe then turned *Uncle Tom's Cabin* into a play, which had enormous and lasting popularity on the stage.[198]

Like many other antislavery activists with a religious background (her father and brothers were celebrated ministers and opponents of bondage), Stowe lacked sympathy for Jews. She gave her character Marks, the slave catcher, standard traits of the reprobate Jew: a "peering, mousing expression about his keen black eyes," a "long nose . . . eager to bore into the nature of things," "a dry, cautious acuteness," "a long, thin hand, like a raven's claw." Matching his menacing visage is his mission to capture the runaway heroine and her son. The amoral, antiblack Marks is the sole member of the search party untouched by their plight. Stowe not only singles Marks out but compounds the condemnation by assigning him conventional deficiencies of physical cowardice and mercenary underhandedness.[199]

Anti-Semitism also surfaced in several contemporary best-sellers of dimmer literary and moral distinction and briefer renown. George Lippard's *The Quaker City*, a sensational tale of vice in Philadelphia, was serialized in the *Saturday Evening Post* in 1844 and subsequently published in book form and then staged in New York. It sold more than 175,000 copies in the U.S. within five years of its publication. The historian of best-selling American fiction placed *The Quaker City* alongside *Uncle Tom's Cabin* on his list of all-time best-sellers. *Godey's Lady's Book* in 1849 called Lippard "the most popular writer of the day." Lippard's book was a Gothic-porno-graphic narrative of corruption, crime, murder, torture, madness, seduction, and prostitution, and was vigorously attacked as degenerate. A peripheral and comparatively mild figure in *The Quaker City*, Gabriel Von Gelt, a forger, thief, and swindler, has an aquiline nose and large, brilliant, intense eyes. "Jew, was written on his face." Von Gelt speaks in stage Yiddish and his name is the Yiddish word for money, a commodity to which he forms a stereotypically ardent attachment.[200]

If Lippard pandered to prurience, Joseph H. Ingraham, an Episcopalian rector and author of eighty novels and adventure stories, aspired to elevate. Nevertheless, Ingraham's writings attained even greater popularity than those of Lippard and Stowe. Of the three best-selling antebellum authors, Ingraham was most preoccupied with Jews and Judaism. In *The Gypsy of the Highlands* (1843), the New York pawnbroker Jacob Gold-schapp has "restless and sharp" dark eyes, a nose "like the beak of an eagle," and a "thin-lipped" mouth—a physiognomy stereotypically "expressive of avarice." According to literary norm, Jacob lives with a beautiful daughter in outwardly shabby but inwardly resplendent quarters. The "wily Jew," "old miser," and "repleted leech" sucks "blood" from his victims and ruins his child by seeking to marry her off for a fortune.[201]

Ingraham created a less reprehensible Jew in *The Clipper Yacht* (1845). Like Goldschapp, Enoch Moloch is a greedy, cunning moneylender with a luxurious abode in a run-down building and a beautiful and dependent relative, this time a niece. All ends happily, however: Moloch's vengeful cruelty is attributed to Christian persecution and stops without permanent damage done anyone when his pride is satisfied and the anti-Semite who humiliated him apologizes.[202]

Another Yiddish-speaking, wicked Jewish usurer, Osias, appears in *Ramero* (1846). Ingraham gives Osias the same traits as the other Jewish merchants—cupidity, deception, and frugality—but Judaic evil is severer in this tale. Osias holds a mortgage on land desired by the church: Jewish finance threatens Christianity. Goldschapp and Moloch exploited indi-viduals, not Christian institutions. In *Ramero* Ingraham leaves no doubt about the connection between personal and ethnic vice. The "Jews were grasping everywhere for lands"; Osias exemplifies the endemic greed of his people.[203]

Upon becoming a clergyman Ingraham turned from adventure tales to epistolary religious romances. He wrote three books on the Israelites to foster "popular interest" in "Hebrew history," promote Bible reading, and "lead the devout reader to the Cross as the only solution to the mystery of this present life, and the true key to that of the world to come." Written first, but last in the "author's plan," *The Prince of the House of David* (1855) "illustrates the decadence of Hebraic power" through the suffering of Christ. *The Pillar of Fire* (1859), a narrative of Moses and the exodus, "unfolds its beginning; while its final culmination is" *The Throne of the House of David* (1860), the story of David and Solomon.[204]

These accounts of Israel and its encounters with the Messiah and his followers were colossal successes. Between 1859 and 1865 seven editions of *Pillar of Fire* were published by presses in Boston, New York, Philadelphia, and London, and *The Throne of David* became a best-seller of the 1860s. *The Prince of the House of David* had even greater impact, becoming a popular gift for girls, a staple of Sunday schools and village libraries, and the most popular American religious novel. During the 1850s over 225,000, and by 1930 between 4 and 5 million, copies were sold, surpassing the grand total of *Uncle Tom's Cabin*.[205]

Focusing on Old Testament rather than contemporary times softened Ingraham's feelings about Jews. Moderation was also induced by his hope of winning Jewish converts. Ingraham dedicated this trilogy to the scattered children of Judea in the hope that they would "follow the Light of the Cross" to "the real Canaan, under the true Joshua, Jesus, the son of Abraham, who also was the son of God." He commends the Jews before the coming of Jesus as courageous, noble, virtuous, and handsome. The greater the distance from the present, the higher the praise. In *Pillar of Fire,* where the Hebrews are delivered from Egyptian bondage, they are unstintingly glorified.[206]

Doubts begin with *The Throne of the House of David,* when David's and Solomon's triumphs erode Israel's spiritual foundation. Though still bold, warlike, dignified, intelligent, and comely, the Hebrews are cruel and vengeful toward their enemies and ungrateful toward their heroes. They are attracted to worldly splendor, are tribal instead of universal in their creed, and worship a punitive rather than forgiving deity. Far more often than in *Pillar of Fire, Throne of David* construes Old Testament history and prophecy to forecast the coming of the Messiah—who will fulfill the Chosen People by saving them from sin. More ominous is the prediction that the Jews will betray God, commit "gross iniquity," and lose their temple and kingdom. Ingraham was referring to the Babylonian captivity, but implied that wickedness and destruction in the first exile foreboded greater Hebraic evil and reprehension.[207]

Ironically, the advent of the Prince of Peace and his message of mercy enraged many Christians against Jews. Accordingly, Hebrews in *The Prince of the House of David* are devoted to luxury and to ritual, cruel, and vengeful—the last three traits also ascribed to their Jehovah. The betrayal and killing of Jesus bring death, destruction, and dispersal of Israel. "Our worship," thunders a rabbinical jeremiad, "is as a sepulchre to conceal the rottenness within." Almost literally recapitulating the Gospels, Ingraham holds the Jewish leaders primarily responsible, but also blames the entire people, for the trial and torment of Jesus and his followers. Roman soldiers "rescued him from the terrible rage of the Jews." Pilate would free Christ but for "fear of the vengeance of the Jews," who "cry for his blood." When "the Jews sen[d] up a cry of unmingled ferocity and vindictiveness," Pilate observes: "These Jews have become madmen with rage, and demand a sacrifice." Dismayed "at sacrificing to the hatred of the people an innocent man," the proconsul receives a chilling reply from "all the people": "Ay! on us and on our children rest the guilt of his blood." The next day a black cloud hangs over Jerusalem, the ground trembles, and the Hebrews realize that "retribution of God's vengeance upon our city and nation has just begun." Israel is encoiled in "veils of woe" as the "Lord in his anger" desanctifies the once-Chosen People. The "punishment of thine iniquity is accomplished, O Daughter of Zion." After Calvary, "the Jews are as bitter against the followers as against their Master."[208]

Emma Dorothy Eliza Nevitte Southworth, the most popular female author in American fiction, joined the other best selling novelists in debasing Jews. In common with many contemporaries and successors, Southworth alternated between positive and negative presentations of Jews. Sympathetic portrayals appeared in *Miriam, Avenger* (1855) and *Self-Raised* (1863). Southworth's bias therefore reveals itself in description rather than ascription. The pawnbroker in *Bridal Eve* (1864), is "a little, dark, hook-nosed, gimlet-eyed man" who speaks exaggerated Yiddish. When the needy heroine exchanges a ring for cash, "old Issachar pounc[es] . . . upon the jewel, and glar[es] upon it with ravenous eyes" and cheats her of its true value. Another unpleasant Jew, in *Allsworth Abbey*

(1865), a saleswoman in a second-hand clothing shop, tricks a poor girl into parting with garments at a niggardly price.[209]

Anti-Jewish sentiments also flourished in the middle period in several new types of fiction, chiefly the New York and business novels that respectively emerged in the late 1830s and the 1840s. Manhattan had the largest Jewish community and Jewish enterprises, and commercial stereotyping was a basic mode of degradation. Consequently, in portrayals of Jews the New York and business genres considerably overlapped. Precursors of literary realism and frequently written by journalists, these novels often focused on seedy aspects of Gotham life. The New York novel was the contemporary fictional equivalent of the New York guidebook.

Charles F. Briggs, writing under the pen name Harry Franco, drew on his experience as a New York journalist and merchant in *Bankrupt Stories* (1843). Mr. Jacobs, a money-grubbing thief, blackmailer, forger, and murderer, is a major rogue in this tale of corrupt New York merchants. Jacobs is called "the Iscariot wretch" and an "Israeltish devil," and his victims are in "this villain Jew's clutches."[210]

Walter Barrett, another former New York merchant turned journalist and novelist, also employed a pseudonym, Joseph Scoville. In *Clarence Bolton* (1852), a novel of New York that stressed commercial dealing, Barrett indirectly deprecated Jews by having one character make "thousands by playing Shylock, advancing money . . . at enormous interest, secured sometimes by personal jewelry." What was indirect in *Clarence Bolton* became blatant in *Vigor* (1863), another narrative of business and social life in New York. This work also belonged to yet another popular genre, the lurid tale, and, like *The Quaker City,* was widely condemned for indecency. *Vigor* was dedicated to James Gordon Bennett, Barrett's journalistic hero. The novel's depiction of despicable Jews and sensational vice made the dedication entirely appropriate. Mining an old but increasingly fashionable vein of bigotry, Barrett made Nordheim, a Dutch Jew who becomes a Manhattan merchant, "one of the worst libertines." Nordheim ignores his own sixteen-year-old wife and compulsively ruins married women and poor teenagers. He lures the latter into prostitution by offering money, in one case buying a daughter from her parents. Jews and whores had been associated in popular culture for at least a hundred years, both deemed debauched deviants who spread venereal diseases and exchanged sex for money. Even in bed, the Jew's true passion was profit.[211]

Jews were less central in another account of the seedy struggle for riches and pleasure in New York, *The Miser's Heir* (1854) by Peter Hamilton

Myers. A minor character in the book is an old clothes man and money-lender "whose features and occupation proclaimed him a Jew, and whose speech told that he was a German, was sitting spider like in the back part of his den, watching for prey." When not bilking customers in his store, the "sharper" imposes outrageous interest rates upon debtors.[212]

More bad Jewish traders appeared in *A Week in Wall Street* (1841), a satire of duplicity in the financial district, written by Frederick Jackson, a self-confessed failure in speculative ventures there. Underhanded investors include "Solomon Single-eye" and "Jacob Broker." One dealer looks like "King Saul," and Wall Street profiteers are out for a "pound of flesh."[213]

New York was not the only setting for the business novel. John Beauchamp Jones previewed his wartime anti-Semitism in stories about pioneer merchants in Missouri, where the future Confederate clerk grew up and embarked on a brief commercial career. The menacing outsider in *The Western Merchant* (1849) is Moses Tubal, a Jewish peddler from Indiana "with a prominent nose," "small sparkling eyes," and a Yiddish accent that mangles his adopted tongue. Tubal sells stolen and defective goods, fakes bankruptcy, and counterfeits business documents to crush honest, Christian merchants and pile up profits. Such duplicity is described as "characteristic of the peddling Jews." They "trade upon the productions of others (they never create or produce anything), and cheat the Christians with their own wares." Jones refashioned an old European fabrication as Shylock on the frontier: the Jew as alien intruder, parasite-predator, sinister manipulator, and subverter of American pioneer ideals. In his wartime diary, Jones would reinvoke this image of the Jew as treacherous despoiler. After the war, in America and abroad, Shylock was transformed into a more systematic and comprehensive and therefore more reprehensible villain. He became Rothschild, Svengali of an international Jewish financial conspiracy that cheated innocent, industrious farmers, workers, and tradesmen and plundered upright Christian nations.[214]

In Jones's *Life and Adventures of a Country Merchant* (1854) a Dutch Jew, Rhino, preys on Christian retailers in Missouri. Rhino, like Tubal, talks in ridiculous Yiddish, hawks damaged and smuggled goods, undersells honest competitors, and declares bankruptcy to avoid creditors. Hinting at a postwar stereotype, Rhino burns his goods to collect an insurance payment.[215]

Jones also derogated Jews in in *The Winkles* (1855), in which the major theme is not business but a Jesuit-Papal plot against democratic Protestant America. A secondary character in this Know-Nothing novel is Abraham

Laban, a wealthy and greedy Jewish pawnbroker called "Great Nose." A gross materialist, he refuses to buy a poem because "I pursue my business to amass riches" and not to support "men of genius."[216]

Jews continued to be insulted in older genres such as the aristocratic novel. The Boston Brahmin Edmond Quincy fortified the literary pretensions and anti-Semitism of his class with *Wensley* (1854), a narrative of nineteenth-century rural New England gentry. Its chief rogue is the forger and dissembler Aaron Abrahams, who as a commissary officer in the Revolutionary War fraudulently seized money and goods desperately needed by American troops. In creating Abrahams, Quincy proved he could be as anti-Semitic in his fiction as in antislavery articles in the *Liberator*.[217]

Theodore Sedgwick Fay's *Countess Ida* (1840), a story of European intrigue, also revealed contempt for Jews. One villain, "Old Abraham," is a usurer who hires an even more vile Jewish assassin to protect his investments. The unnamed killer, ugly and Polish born, wears the traditional gabardine of the eastern European Jew. Fay's attitude emerges in casual simile as well. "You have smitten as the Jew smote the savior," says one character, criticizing another for trying to provoke a duel by striking his adversary.[218]

Even fiction without deliberate rancor toward Jews sometimes perpetuated widely accepted slurs. No Jew is defamed in B. Perley Poore's *The Mameluke* (1852), but Mordecai, a rich Smyrna merchant, is "bowed down by the weight of tyranny and the everlasting sin of his race."[219]

In psychological terms, the myriad manifestations of anti-Semitism issued from suspicion, fear, and loathing inscribed in the consciousness of western civilization for two millennia. Folk effusions of these deeply embedded feelings were revitalized in the United States by the waves of European immigrants and diffused to Native Americans and African-Americans evangelized by Christianity.

Iniquitous expressions such as "Christ killer," "Judas," and "Shylock" became general, as well as anti-Jewish, synonyms for betrayal, parsimony, heartless greed, and unscrupulous commerce. Sometimes accompanying the epithets were alarming or ridiculous personifications, again non-Jewish as well as Jewish, of the associated traits. These personifications, however—the crafty pawnbroker, the loan shark, the pushy clothing salesman, the sly peddler—were more confined to Jews than were the linguistic labels.

The vocabulary of derision, here and abroad, included the neologism "to Jew," a designation of sharp and/or shady business dealing. An early example appeared in "Jewing and Chewing," a sardonic sketch in a New York publication of 1824: "*Due and dues* should be prounounced *Jew* and *Jews,* and you at once have the *origin* of the Jews, and the term 'Jewing,'" asserted the anonymous author. "That people's love of pelf is proverbial; and their art and perseverance in getting others in debt, or having great sums *due* from them, and making money by *sharp* dealing, very naturally gives that process the name of *Jewing,* and the practiser that of *Jew.*" This term did not allude solely to Jewish depredation. In 1861, the *Knicker-bocker* accused northerners of merchandizing their souls in pathological pursuit of gain: "dollar-hunting even to a proverb; out Jewing the Jew." Identical complaint came from across the lines. The *Southern Illustrated News,* in 1863, castigated "Gentiles," who "out-Jewed the Jews in pulling to pieces the Confederacy and amassing wealth thereby."[220]

The antebellum southwestern humorist George Washington Harris used "jew" as an American colloquialism. I "gin ole man Collins my note ove hand fur a hundred dollars, jew in year arter date," says a character in his short story "Rare Ripe Garden Seed." The debtor must "pay two hundred dollars 'bout the fust ove October, for hit'll be jew jis' then." Anti-Semitism in this slang word was blunter when applied to negative Jewish stereotypes. Harris contributed sketches to the *Spirit of the Times,* that delator of Jewish defects. "Why don't we have a Society for Ameliorating the Condition of the Jewed?," queried an 1844–45 issue. "That is the question which 'one who buys his clothes in Chatham Street,' asks us to propound."[221]

By the 1850s the pejorative use of "jew" was so widespread that *Harper's Magazine* criticized its identification with selfishness and meanness. *Harper's* later had second thoughts: "You know people who 'Jew you down,'" said an article of 1866. The "children of Abraham have always been, and still are, notorious for jewing folks down—hence they are called Jews."[222]

Thus connoted, or in related definitions, "jew" became part of the English lexicon, included well into the twentieth century in dictionaries and thesauruses. The earliest American citation may be in the 1830 edition of *Johnson's and Walker's English Dictionaries Combined,* which lists under the heading "Jew" another widely used construction: "As rich as a Jew. A proverbial phrase."[223]

New usage combined with older, peculiarly American references in an early example of the colloquialism "to jew." A South Carolinian in 1818 noted that "all Jews and worse than Jews—[are] Yankees, for a Yankee can

Jew a Jew directly." This remark early linked Jews and Yankees as shrewd, unprincipled traders.[224]

Proverbial slurs were also perpetuated, if in more formal English, in fairy tales. *Mother Goose* was a colonial best-seller in 1719, but its phenomenal popularity dates from about 1830. By 1947 an estimated 2.5 million copies had been sold, making the rhyme book one of the seven all-time best-sellers in this country. In one story, "Old Mother Goose," "Jack sold his gold egg" to "a rogue of a Jew," who "cheated him out of / The half of his due." Shortly thereafter, "The Jew and the Squire" sneaked "behind his back" to "belabor / The Sides of poor Jack." Eventually, "The Jew got the goose," which "he vowed he would kill" and "His pockets to fill."[225]

*Household Tales,* which rivaled *Mother Goose* in popularity, was an anthology of German peasant stories, compiled in 1812 and 1815 by Jakob and Wilhelm Grimm and first published in America in 1861. At least 300,000 copies were bought in that decade. Like *Mother Goose,* this collection drew upon medieval folklore and was mostly read by, or to, young children. Both the English and the German tales denigrated Jews. In "The Good Bargain" the Grimms tell of a Jew who passes bad coins but is outsmarted by a peasant he seeks to swindle. "The Jew among the Thorns" is about a rich Jew who "fleeces" people to obtain wealth. As often happens in folktales about Jews, the hero tricks the culprit into parting with his purse. In addition, the hero forces the swindler to admit before a judge that he stole the money in the purse. In the properly happy ending, "The judge then ordered the Jew to the gallows to be hanged as a thief."[226]

Anti-Semitism spread to new areas and peoples colonized by mid-century European immigrants and their descendants. Passion Plays and the burning of Judas were adapted by Mexicans and Indians in California and the Southwest. "King John and the Bishop," originally a British ballad transported to New England, also went west, following the Mormons to Utah. "The Savior for thirty bright pieces was sold," went one verse. "Among the false Jews so brazen and bold, / twenty-nine pieces is your just due," for "I think he's one piece better than you." Another case of cultural diffusion, "A Tale Told Too Often," representing Jews torturing and murdering a Christian child to mock Christianity, journeyed from fifth-century Syria to medieval England and then to America. This blood libel last surfaced in an anonymous pamphlet published in the 1930s in California. Modern slurs also reappeared on the frontier and in comic as well as tragic form. "But he stuck to me like a Jew to a customer," observed a tale anthologized in *Frontier Humor* (1895).[227]

Religious and secular songs and stories were also a source of black anti-Semitism. Evangelical Negro spirituals, from Christian and African-American contexts, glorified the Hebrews' escape from bondage but condemned them for crucifying the Lord. "And de Jews and de Romans had him hung," is a line in "Cry Holy," sung by African-American troops during the Civil War. "De Jews kill po' Jesus" was a lyric in another southern black religious folk song. In African-American jokes told in Alabama, Louisiana, and Mississippi, Jews steal money from the graves of their dead coreligionists.[228]

～

American anti-Semitism assumed its modern contours, if not its subsequent intensity and scope, from the late 1830s through the Civil War. Traditional prejudices were joined by newer forms of bigotry to create increasingly frequent anti-Jewish images and actions. The Civil War was the first national ordeal of American Jewry. This crisis brought to a climax developments in the immediate past and heralded more perilous times to come.

Throughout American history Jews have experienced a gradual expansion of rights, culminating in substantial present-day equality. These gains, however, generated anti-Jewish sentiment; advances toward parity brought mounting resistance. The significant and rising antebellum hostility toward Jews documented in this book is therefore confirmed by the contrary but coextant reality—the movement of American Jewry toward equality.

# ~ Epilogue

America's response to the Jews, while less hostile than that of Europe, replicated the European reaction in many respects. On both continents during the mid-nineteenth century, Jews progressed toward economic and political equality, and on both continents this advance generated growing resistance. At this time, the advent of racialism and the identification of the Jews as parvenus, rapacious capitalists, and revolutionaries set the course of anti-Semitism. That course proceeded similarly everywhere in the West, rising from the 1860s, reaching a peak in the 1930s and 1940s, and declining after World War II.

American and European anti-Semites also had much in common, in particular a propensity for criminal behavior. Between 1893 and 1915, 140 members of anti-Semitic groups in France and Germany, including several leaders, were convicted of libel, slander, and defamation. Perjury and forgery produced two great turn-of-the-century anti-Semitic scandals: the Dreyfus affair (1894) in which Alfred Dreyfus, a Jew and a French military officer, was falsely convicted of selling secrets to the Germans; and the *Protocols of the Elders of Zion* (1903), a publication fabricated by the Russian secret police but purporting to be a report of a conference of Jewish leaders on the progress of their plot to destroy Christian civilization and rule the world. On this side of the Atlantic, Telemachus Thomas Timayenis, America's most dedicated nineteenth-century anti-Semite, sold confidential information, slandered a Greek diplomat, and reputedly stole from his own publishing company—the house that brought out his novels and other anti-Jewish books. The rank and file of the Ku Klux Klan in the

1920s regularly resorted to libel, larceny, and lynching. In the next decade Fritz Kuhn, head of the German-American Bund, was imprisoned for stealing Bund funds, and William Dudley Pelley, founder and commander of the Christian American Patriots (the Silver Shirts), was sentenced for peddling worthless stock.[1]

In spite of their similarities, American and European anti-Semitism differ in fundamental ways. Jews in the United States escaped the tragic fate of those in France, Germany, and the Austro-Hungarian Empire primarily by not becoming key targets in the struggles to create a nation. American Jews were not enmeshed in basic controversies over whether the emerging state should break from the past or emulate it, be a republic or a monarchy, be a Christian or a secular commonwealth. As a rule, the kind of paganized, feudalistic, clerical, and romantic reactionary turbulence that endangered Jews in Europe did not threaten them in this country.

In the United States blood libel was rare, but in Germany 120 such accusations were reported in anti-Semitic newspapers between 1891 and 1900 and two cases went to court in 1891 and 1892, and in the Austro-Hungarian Empire twelve trials for ritual murder convened between 1867 and 1912. No anti-Semitic riots took place in America, as they did in France in 1898-99 and in Germany in 1880-81, 1891, and 1900.

Henry Ford and his *Dearborn Independent* were a tepid anti-Semitic force compared to Edouard Drumont, the leading anti-Dreyfusard and popularizer of anti-Semitism in France, and his *La Libre Parole*. There was no American equivalent of the Dreyfus case, which made French Jews the storm center of monarchist-Catholic *ancien régime* insurgence against a republic and its regicidal, rationalistic, revolutionary heritage. No major American politicians openly courted an anti-Semitic vote, as did Karl Lueger, a conservative Christian mayor of Vienna. No popular journals or organizations committed to anti-Jewish agitation—parties, leagues, or nationalist, agrarian, professional, student, business and other associations—appeared in late-nineteenth-century America as they did in Europe.

Catholicism and Protestantism in the United States, again in contrast to Europe, did not pulsate with anti-Semitic rancor. Here rose no equivalent of European Christian leftist bigotry as exemplified by Berlin court chaplain Adolf Stoecker, who in the 1880s turned his pro-worker Christian Social Party into an anti-Semitic organization; or of the clamor of priestly support for Drumont and the anti-Dreyfusards. Drumont, a nastier bigot than Stoecker, avowed socialism yet attracted support from the church as he scourged Jews as Christkillers, ritual murderers, Catholic haters, ruthless capitalists, and racial degenerates. American racist anti-Semitic ideologues did not achieve the esteem accorded Houston Stewart Chamberlain and his acolyte Alfred Rosenberg in Germany and Austria. And no American radicals raged against Jews in the manner of Fourier and Marx, or of leftists like Ernest Henrici and his Social Reichsparty who fused socialism with racial anti-Semitism.[2] Since these forces, institutions, movements, and figures had pale or no American correspondence, their unspeakable culmination—the Holocaust—did not happen here.

The failed attempts of Timayenis to publish an anti-Semitic magazine or launch an anti-Jewish movement illustrate the comparative weakness of anti-Semitism in the United States. Timayenis had been born and raised in Turkey, another sign that this bigotry was better nurtured abroad than at home. The Ku Klux Klan, until the 1930s the nation's primary hate group, before the Depression raged chiefly against fellow Protestants it deemed morally and politically errant, blacks allegedly defying its caste code, and Catholics.[3]

Anti-Semitism was also rare in American socialist circles. An exception was the radical theorist and journalist Laurence Gronlund, who said in *The Cooperative Commonwealth* (1884) that "Judaism . . . best expressed that special curse of our age, *Speculation,* the transfer of wealth from others to themselves by chicanery without giving them an equivalent." But he was grateful to "Judaism" for the "noble Jews" Marx and Lassalle, leaders in the "battle against this very Judaism." Gronlund's prejudice, like Timayenis's, had foreign roots: he had immigrated to the United States from Denmark as a young man. Another anomalous left-wing attack on Jews came from Jack London, who belittled "Ghetto Socialists" of New York City and introduced anti-Semitism as a minor theme in his later novels. Gronlund and London, however, did not compulsively hate Jews.[4]

Racist theoreticians here also showed milder repugnance for Jews than did their European counterparts. Although several eminent American eugenicists approved of the Nazi biological purity program, the foremost proponents of eugenics, racialism, and restriction of immigration— Edward Alsworth Ross, Charles B. Davenport, David Starr Jordan, and Madison Grant, author of racialism's American bible, *The Passing of the Great Race* (1916)—lumped Jews with Christian newcomers from southern and eastern Europe and diluted derogation of Jews with some favorable references. Even extremists in the movement, like Lothrop Stoddard, who sympathized with Third Reich genetics and believed that Bolshevism sprang from racial degeneracy and innate Jewish radicalism, were less rabid about Jews and Judaism than Chamberlain and not nearly as vicious as Rosenberg, Hitler's top racial ideologist.[5]

The attraction to the occult felt by many European anti-Semites, an interest that comported well with their demonization of Jews, was largely lacking in America. French and German books in the late 1860s alluded to a Jewish-satanic plot to rule the world. Drumont, who mongered in *La Libre Parole* medieval and modern diabolization of Jews, believed in spiritualism, magic, seers, prophets, and palmistry. Jules Langbehn, a founder of the German volkish movement, was a mystic who regarded Jews as racial incubators of modern materialism, mechanization, and rationality. A melange of racial anti-Semitism, volkish nationalism, pagan and medieval longings, and occult enthusiasms also permeated the Nazi leadership. Hitler, Himmler, and their underlings variously subscribed to magic, fortune telling, astrology, reincarnation, and spiritualism. Such fantasies were rare among American anti-Semites. The one prominent exception was Pelley, who believed in mysticism and astrology and was convinced that he had experienced a brief out-of-life episode. The lack of supernatural predilections among the Americans combined with less strident theological anti-Semitism in U.S. churches to inhibit infernalization of Jews.[6]

A unique aspect of the American anti-Semitic impulse was its association with native reform movements. Prejudice that surfaced in Populism and among the Social Gospellers expressed itself in stereotyped rebuke of grasping traders and deceitful financiers, or of Judaism as an inferior creed infused with hatred for Christianity. These were routine grudges throughout the western world, but they now appeared in ideological and institutional contexts peculiar to America. American Social Gospellers were not counterparts of Christian Socialists in France and Germany, and, in any case, they bore less animosity toward Jews. Similarly, American farmers were not counterparts of European peasants. Hence their organizations, unlike the Second Reich's Agrarian League (1893) and Central German Peasant Association (1891), were not primarily or programmatically anti-Semitic.[7]

~

American anti-Semitism, when viewed on its own apart from that of Europe, shows considerable continuity. The radical, in various guises as strike agitator, communist conspirator, and bomb-throwing revolutionary, was the only sinister anti-Jewish stereotype that emerged after the Civil War. But this incarnation of subversion was prefigured in the earlier stereotype of the Jew as rebel against spiritual and secular rectitude and order.

The post-World War I resurgence of religious anti-Semitism in America illustrates a basic contention of this book: the continuing power of Christian bigotry. This development, occurring in a nation exceptional for freedom of worship and equality for Jews and long after religion had ostensibly been replaced by racism as the main inspiration of anti-Jewish attitudes, is persuasive evidence of the traditional, christological basis of anti-Semitism in the United States.

Until the 1920s and 1930s Catholicism was the most detested creed in the Protestant-dominated national culture. During these decades, however, Christian America came to view Jews as the extreme antagonist. Henry Ford's anti-Semitic onslaught in the 1920s in the *Dearborn Independent*, which featured a reprint of the *Protocols of the Elders of Zion,* heralded this switch. At that time the Ku Klux Klan still worried more about Catholics, but a decade later it fervently joined the campaign against Jews. Gerald Winrod, a Catholic-baiter in the 1920s, muted this sentiment after 1935 and by 1939 called for a united Christian patriotic front to stop a Jewish thrust toward global rule. Although most members of the fascistic Silver Shirts were Protestant, that hate group neither openly opposed the church nor banned Catholics from its ranks.[8]

The influence of Christianity during the climactic years of Jew hatred is obvious from the backgrounds of the chieftains in the anti-Semitic movement of the 1930s and 1940s: Winrod, the founder and leader of the Defenders of the Christian Faith, was, like his father, an evangelical preacher. Gerald L. K. Smith, who played the same role in the Christian Nationalist Crusade, followed his father and grandfather as a minister in the Disciples of Christ. The charismatic radio figure Charles E. Coughlin was a populistic Catholic priest. Pelley alone of the leading bigots was not a clergyman, but his father was a Methodist minister.

Christian rage against Judaism was significant in shaping the outlook of the hate peddlers. Father Coughlin's main grievances were the monetary system and communism, but he perceived them as outgrowths of the sinister Jewish denial of the Messiah. Winrod, a dispensationist, also cast the Jew as the villain in the drama of salvation: The world conspiracy of the Elders of Zion was a satanic scheme to dethrone God and Christianity. Marxism, the Soviet revolution, the Federal Reserve System, and the Depression were additional Jewish collaborations with Satan.[9]

Pelley, the most rabid hatemonger, dreamed of a "Christian Commonwealth." Like Winrod and Coughlin, he fantasized a Jewish alliance with Russia to destroy Christian civilization and mixed modern with traditional hatred of Jews. The Silver Shirt leader claimed that the Sanhedrin Christ-killers now led the Jewish drive for world rule and that Jewry was a "synagogue of Satan." Going far beyond traditional Christian doctrine, he denied the Jewish origin of Christ and God's initial choice of the Jews over other peoples. He asserted that Jesus was the "outstanding 'Jew-baiter' of his day" and that "Christianity and anti-Semitism are synonymous."[10]

Smith, who turned anti-Semitic a decade after Coughlin, Winrod, and Pelley, reiterated their condemnation of a union of Jewish capitalists and communists bent on global rule. Jesus and Moses were the alternatives and enmity toward Jews signified "fellowship with Jesus Christ." Smith concluded his career as a leader of bigotry by staging an annual Passion Play at a place in Arkansas fittingly christened Mt. Oberammergau. Starting in 1968, it featured the standard themes of such productions—Pilate's reluctance, scheming Sanhedrin, Jewish responsibility for the crucifixion, and inherited Jewish guilt.[11]

Leaders had followers and ideology inspired action. Catholic-Jewish brawls flashed along the boundaries between Jewish and Irish neighborhoods in northern cities, chiefly New York and Boston. Violence was provoked by the Christian Front (1938) and Christian Mobilizers (1939), Coughlin's devoted anti-Semitic thugs. Many priests, especially from the Brooklyn diocese, belonged to or supported these organizations. The *Brooklyn Tablet*, the American Catholic weekly with the largest circulation, rallied around Coughlin and the Front and attacked Jews. American monastic and other Catholic periodicals deplored Jewish tribalism and aloofness in comparison with Christian altruistic inclusiveness and lambasted the Jews for killing the Savior and, out of blood guilt, wreaking vengeance upon his worshippers.[12]

Similar tirades could be found, particularly before *Kristallnacht*, in the Protestant press and in the words of ministers and theologians. The loudest came from conservative and evangelical sects and denominations of preponderantly German or Russo-German extraction. Mennonites, for example, mostly Russo-German Americans in Kansas and Iowa, avidly supported Winrod. But not all anti-Semitic attacks emanated from the Bible Belt and the inner-city parish. The *Christian Century*, a spokesman of liberal Protestantism, with the largest number of subscribers among Protestant weeklies, relentlessly assailed the Jews.[13]

Conventional Christian slurs fueled the eruption of anti-Semitism in America. *Bible History* (1869), by Richard Gilmour, Bishop of Cleveland, a text widely used in Catholic schools in the 1930s, received a papal benediction and recommendations for parish and parochial school teaching from two American cardinals, twelve archbishops, and sixteen bishops. It portrayed a "faithless and thankless people," stained by the blood of the Messiah as evidenced by the eclipse of their creed by Christianity, the desolation of Israel, and their estrangement until "the end of time." Similar derogation was equally, if more politely, expressed in *A Catholic Dictionary*, published in 1931 and in its eighth edition by 1943.[14]

Contempt for Jews also permeated American Protestant tracts. A 1943 Lutheran catechism contrasted "Ceremonial" and "Political" Mosaic law with the higher "Moral Law" of the New Testament. It dwelled upon the "wickedness of the Jews," manifested in the crucifixion, which "brought about the destruction of Jerusalem" and "cursed themselves and their children." Perfidious Jewry, justly and perpetually chastened for its perversity; and arid Judaism, antiquated, legalistic, ritualized, and lacking Christian universality, empathy, and spirituality—these images frequently appeared in the teaching materials of other Protestant sects, in sermons and theological treatises, and even in secular textbooks.[15] In 1942 this outlook, particularly inculcation about deicide, impressed the head of psychological research at the Menninger Clinic as an "important factor" in instilling anti-Semitism in children.[16]

Christological recrimination also echoed down in African-American anti-Semitism. A black teacher, growing up as a Pentecostal in New Jersey in the 1960s, repeatedly heard that "Jews killed Christ." An "attitude of antagonism or distrust toward Jews was bred in us from childhood," declared the novelist Richard Wright; "it was part of our cultural heritage." James Baldwin, the son of a minister in the Abyssinian Baptist Church and in his youth a minister himself, asserted that "the traditional Christian accusation that the Jews killed Christ" shaped "the Negro's ambivalent relation to the Jew." This charge, the subject of many sermons by his pastor, was "neither questioned nor doubted." It was followed by a "catalogue of their subsequent sins and the suffering visited upon them by a wrathful God," thus making Jews signify "all infidels of white skin who have failed to accept the Savior."[17] As has so often happened in America, however, acrimony mixed with admiration. African-Americans, like the New England Puritans, empathized with the people of Exodus. As the Puritans identified with the Israelites who braved the wilderness en route to the Promised Land, African-Americans identified with the Israelites in bondage in Egypt.

~

Christianity has a powerful anti-Semitic impulse, America is a Christian country, and America is anti-Semitic. The truth of this syllogism has been empirically demonstrated throughout this book. But the argument, as has also been here documented, is not a smooth sequence of premise to conclusion. Christianity also has benign and neutral attitudes toward Jews, and its sentiments toward them have considerably varied over time and place. Moreover, religious feelings about Jews have always been affected, for better or for worse, by secular factors. It may be contended that if the United States had not been a Christian nation it would have accepted Jews more wholeheartedly. But it may also be claimed that because Christianity in the United States was uniquely shaped by American religious and secular circumstances, Jews have been better treated here than in any other western Christian land.

# ～ Notes

## 1. The Anatomy of Anti-Semitism

1. See Gavin Langmuir, *Toward a Definition of Antisemitism* (Berkeley and Los Angeles: University of California Press, 1990), pp. 131–133, 306–308, 324–328, and *History, Religion, and Antisemitism* (Berkeley and Los Angeles: University of California Press, 1990), pp. 298–305, 344–346.

2. Claude Lévi-Strauss, *Structural Anthropology* (1963; New York: Anchor Books, 1967), pp. 223–224, 231–234; Sander L. Gilman, *Difference and Pathology: Stereotypes of Sexuality, Race and Madness* (Ithaca and London: Cornell University Press, 1985), pp. 27–33.

3. For discussions of economic anti-Semitism: J. O. Hertzler, "The Sociology of Anti-Semitism through History," in *Jews in a Gentile World: The Problem of Anti-Semitism,* ed. Isacque Graeber and Steuart H. Britt (New York: Macmillan, 1942), pp. 89–92; Talcott Parsons, "The Sociology of Modern Anti-Semitism," ibid., pp. 113–114, 117; Ellis Freeman, "The Motivation of Jewish-Gentile Relationships," ibid., p. 172; Robin Williams, "Changes in Value Orientation," ibid., p. 345; George E. Simpson and J. Milton Yinger, *Racial and Cultural Minorities: An Analysis of Prejudice and Discrimination* (New York: Harper and Row, 1972), p. 288; Rudolph M. Loewenstein, *Christians and Jews* (New York: Delta Books, 1951), pp. 87–88; Gordon Allport, *The Nature of Prejudice* (Cambridge, Mass.: Addison-Wesley, 1954), pp. 122–123, 212; Jean-Paul Sartre, *Anti-Semite and Jew* (1948; New York: Schocken Books, 1970), pp. 23–28, 67–69, 93–95, 99, 127–129; Werner J. Cahnman, "Socio-Economic Causes of Anti-Semitism," *Social Problems,* 5 (July 1957): 22–26.

4. For discussion of political and nationalistic anti-Semitism: Allport, *Prejudice,* pp. 194–196, 212, 250–252, 406; Loewenstein, *Christians and Jews,* pp. 48–49, 55–56, 67, 72, 78–79, 87–88; Simpson and Yinger, *Minorities,* pp. 302–308; W. D. Rubinstein, *The Left, the Right and the Jews* (London: Croom Helm, 1982), pp. 72–79, 84–85, 226–227; Erich Kahler, *The Jews among the Nations* (New York: Frederick Ungar, 1967), p. 93; Paul Lawrence Rose, *Revolutionary Antisemitism in Germany from Kant to Wagner* (Princeton: Princeton University Press, 1990); Langmuir, *History, Religion,* pp. 304–341; Julius Carlebach, *Karl Marx and the Radical Critique of*

*Judaism* (London: Routledge and Kegan Paul, 1978); Hertzler, "Sociology of Anti-Semitism," pp. 75, 77, 80–81, 89–93, 97; Parsons, "Sociology of Modern Anti-Semitism," pp. 107, 113–117; Sartre, *Anti-Semite,* pp. 23–28, 82–88, 93–95, 127–129, 133–136; Otto Fenichel, "Elements of a Psychoanalytic Theory of Anti-Semitism," in *Anti-Semitism: A Social Disease,* ed. Ernst Simmel (New York: International Universities Press, 1946), p. 30; Benjamin Halpern, "Anti-Semitism in the Perspective of Jewish History," in *Jews in the Mind of America,* ed. Charles H. Stember et al. (New York: Basic Books, 1966), pp. 274–275, 280–282; Alfred D. Low, *Jews in the Eyes of the Germans from the Enlightenment to Imperial Germany* (Philadelphia: Institute for the Study of Human Issues, 1979); Jacob Katz, *Out of the Ghetto: The Social Background of Jewish Emancipation, 1770–1870* (Cambridge, Mass.: Harvard University Press, 1973), and *From Prejudice to Destruction: Anti-Semitism, 1700–1933* (Cambridge, Mass.: Harvard University Press, 1980); Shmuel Almog, "Nationalism and Antisemitism in Modern Europe: 1815–1845," in *Antisemitism through the Ages,* ed. Almog (Oxford: Pergamon Press, 1990), pp. 1–23; Arthur Hertzberg, *The French Enlightenment and the Jews* (New York: Columbia University Press; Philadelphia: Jewish Publication Society of America, 1969); Robert F. Byrnes, *Anti-Semitism in Modern France: The Prologue to the Dreyfus Affair* (New York: Howard Fertig, 1969), 2 vols.; Stephen Wilson, *Ideology and Experience: Anti-Semitism in France at the Time of the Dreyfus Affair* (London and Toronto: Associated University Presses; Rutherford, N.J.: Fairleigh Dickinson University Press, 1982); Hannah Arendt, *The Origins of Totalitarianism* (1958; New York: Meridian, 1972), pp. 45–50; Paul W. Massing, *Rehearsal for Destruction: A Study of Political Anti-Semitism in Imperial Germany* (New York: Harper and Bros., 1949); Robert S. Wistrich, *Socialism and the Jews: The Dilemmas of Assimilation in Germany and Austria-Hungary* (London and Toronto: Associated University Presses; Rutherford, N.J.: Fairleigh Dickinson University Press, 1982); George L. Mosse, *Germans and Jews* (New York: Howard Fertig, 1970); Celia S. Heller, *On the Edge of Destruction: Jews of Poland between Two World Wars* (New York: Columbia University Press, 1977); Salo W. Baron, *The Russian Jew under Tsars and Soviets* (London and New York: Macmillan, 1964); John Higham, *Send These to Me: Jews and Other Immigrants in Urban America* (New York: Atheneum, 1975), pp. 116–195, and "American Anti-Semitism Historically Reconsidered," in *Jews in the Mind of America,* ed. Stember et al., pp. 237–258; Morton Keller, "Jews and the Character of American Life Since 1930," ibid., pp. 259–272; Williams, "Changes," ibid., pp. 345–348; Dennis H. Wrong, "The Psychology of Prejudice and the Future of Anti-Semitism in America," ibid., pp. 331–334; Michael N. Dobkowski, *The Tarnished Dream: The Basis of American Anti-Semitism* (Westport, Conn.: Greenwood Press, 1979); Oscar Handlin, *Race and Nationality in American Life* (Boston and Toronto: Little, Brown, 1957), pp. 54, 67, 71–95, 176–177, and "American Views of the Jew at the Opening of the Twentieth Century," *Publications of the American Jewish Historical Society,* 40 (June 1951): 323–344; *Anti-Semitism in American History,* ed. *David Gerber* (Urbana and Chicago: University of Illinois Press, 1986); Benjamin Halpern, *The American Jew: A Zionist Analysis* (New York: Theodore Herzl Foundation, 1956); Carey McWilliams, *A Mask for Privilege: Anti-Semitism in America* (Boston: Little, Brown, 1948); Morton Borden, *Jews, Turks, and Infidels* (Chapel Hill and London: University of North Carolina Press, 1984); Seymour Martin Lipset and Earl Raab, *The Politics of Unreason: Right-Wing Extremism in America, 1790–1970* (New York, Evanston, London: Harper and Row, 1970), pp. 6–7, 10–15, 92, 114, 166.

5. For historical, theological, anthropological, and psychological studies of Christian anti-Semitism: J. Talmon, "European History—Seedbed of the Holocaust," *Midstream,* 19 (May 1973): 3–25; Melvin M. Tumin, *An Inventory and Appraisal of Research on American Anti-Semitism* (New York: Freedom Books, 1961), pp. 142–144; Allport, *Prejudice,* pp. 248–250; Loewenstein, *Christians and Jews,* pp. 30–31, 40–47, 90–103, 404–423; Theodore Isaac Rubin, *Anti-Semitism: A Disease of the Mind* (New York: Continuum, 1990), pp. 53, 56–66, 70–71, 81–82, 98–99, 114; Halpern, *American Jew,* pp. 43–58, 113–114, and "Anti-Semitism in the Perspective," pp. 275–280; Fenichel, "Elements of a Psychoanalytic Theory," pp. 13–14, 19–21, 24–29; Ernest Simmel, "Anti-Semitism and Mass Psychopathology," in *Social Disease,* ed. Simmel, pp. 54–62; Bernhard Berliner, "On Some Religious Motives of Anti-Semitism," ibid., pp. 79–84; Sartre, *Anti-Semite,* pp. 39–50, 67–69; Rose, *Revolutionary Antisemitism,* pp. 23–54; Langmuir, *Toward a Definition,* pp. 11–15, 58–62, 104–106, 109–111, 131–133, 211–222 270, 300, 303–309, 329, 333, 347, and *History, Religion,* pp. 18–44, 279–305; Rosemary Ruether, *Faith and Fratricide: The Theological Roots of Anti-Semitism* (New York: Seabury Press, 1974); Thomas Indinopulos and Roy Owen Ward, "Is Christology Inherently Anti-Semitic?" *Journal of the American Academy of Religion,* 45 (June 1972): 190–210; John M. Oesterreicher, *Anatomy of Contempt: A Critique of R. R. Ruether's "Faith and Fratricide,"* Institute of Judaeo-Christian Studies, Paper no. 4, Fall 1975 (South Orange, N.J.: Seton Hall University, 1975), pp. 1–24; *The Wandering Jew: Essays in the Interpretation of a Christian Legend,* ed. Galit Hasan-Rokem and Alan Dundes (Bloomington: Indiana University Press, 1986); Ruth Mellinkopf, *The Mark of Cain* (Berkeley and Los Angeles: University of California Press, 1990); Norman Ravitch, "The Problem of Christian Anti-Semitism," *Commentary,* 73 (April 1982): 41–52; Peter L. Berger, *The Sacred Canopy: Elements of a Sociological Theory of Religion* (Garden City, N.Y.: Doubleday, 1967), pp. 69–71, 76–79; Ernest A. Rappaport, *Anti-Judaism: A Psychohistory* (Chicago: Perspective

Press, 1975); Hyam Maccoby, *The Sacred Executioner: Human Sacrifice and the Legacy of Guilt* (New York: Thames and Hudson, 1982); Sigmund Freud: *Moses and Monotheism* (New York: Vintage Books, 1939); Fred Gladstone Bratton, *The Crime of Christendom: The Theological Sources of Christian Anti-Semitism* (Boston: Beacon Press, 1969); Norman Cohn, *Warrant for Genocide: The Myth of the Jewish World-Conspiracy and the Protocols of Zion* (New York: Harper and Row, 1967); Franklin H. Littel, *The Crucifixion of the Jews* (New York: Harper and Row, 1975); Conrad Henry Moehlman, *The Christian-Jewish Tragedy: A Study in Religious Prejudice* (Rochester, N.Y.: Leo Hart, 1933); Dagobert D. Runes, *The Jew and the Cross* (New York: Philosophical Library, 1965); Jules Isaac, *The Teaching of Contempt* (New York: Holt, Rinehart and Winston, 1964); Reinhold Niebuhr, *Pious and Secular America* (New York: Charles Scribner's Sons, 1958), pp. 86–112; Theodore F. O'Dea, "The Changing Image of the Jew and the Contemporary Religious Situation: An Exploration of Ambiguities," in *Jews in the Mind of America,* ed. Stember et al., pp. 304–307.

6. See references in note 5.

7. See Alexander Bein, "The Jewish Question in Modern Anti-Semitic Literature: Prelude to a Final Solution," in *The Catastrophe of European Jewry,* ed. Yisrael Gutman and Livia Rothkirchen (Jerusalem: Yad Vashem, 1976), pp. 79–80; Uriel Tal, "Anti-Christian Anti-Semitism," ibid., pp. 91–96, 118–119; Jacob L. Talmon, "Mission and Testimony: The Universal Significance of Modern Anti-Semitism," ibid., pp. 149, 154–159; Loewenstein, *Christians and Jews,* pp. 103–06.

8. T. W. Adorno et al., *The Authoritarian Personality* (New York: Harper and Row, 1950); *Social Disease,* ed. Simmel; Nathan W. Ackerman and Marie Jahoda, *Anti-Semitism and Emotional Disorder* (New York: Harper and Bros., 1950); Rubin, *Disease of the Mind.*

9. Douglas W. Orr, "Anti-Semitism and the Psychopathology of Everyday Life," in *Social Disease,* ed. Simmel, pp. 85–95; Simmel, "Mass Psychopathology," pp. 35–44, 51–53; Fenichel, "Elements of a Psychoanalytic Theory," pp. 13–14; Else Frenkel-Brunswick and R. Nevitt Sanford, "The Anti-Semitic Personality: A Research Report," in *Social Disease,* ed. Simmel, pp. 96–124; Adorno et al., *Authoritarian Personality;* Loewenstein, *Christians and Jews,* pp. 30–31, 40–43; Simpson and Yinger, *Minorities,* p. 288; Ackerman and Jahoda, *Anti-Semitism and Emotional Disorder,* pp. 5–6, 16–18, 29–73; Bruno Bettelheim, "The Dynamism of Anti-Semitism in Gentile and Jew," *Journal of Abnormal and Social Psychology,* 42 (April 1947): 153–168; Leo Lowenthal and Norbert Guterman, *Prophets of Deceit* (Palo Alto, Calif.: Pacific Books, 1970); Rubin, *Disease of the Mind,* pp. 18–20.

10. Roger Brown, *Social Psychology* (New York: Free Press; London: Collier-Macmillan, 1965), p. 510.

11. Ibid., pp. 477–546; Tumin, *Inventory,* pp. 28–29; Bohan Zawadski, "Limitations of the Scapegoat Theory of Prejudice," *Journal of Abnormal and Social Psychology,* 43 (April 1948): 127–141; Gardner Lindzey, "An Experimental Examination of the Scapegoat Theory of Prejudice," ibid., 45 (April 1950): 296–309; Donald Weatherly, "Anti-Semitism and the Expression of Fantasy Aggression," ibid., 62 (March, 1961): 454–457; Langmuir, *Toward a Definition,* pp. 322–333; Higham, *Send These to Me,* pp. 174–177.

12. Lipset and Rabb, *Politics of Unreason,* pp. 241, 261–264, 399.

13. Higham, *Send These to Me,* pp. 174–175.

14. For discussions of ethnocentrism, xenophobia, scapegoating, and the targeting of Jews see: Fenichel, "Elements of a Psychoanalytic Theory," pp. 12–15; T. W. Adorno, "Anti-Semitism and Fascist Propaganda," in *Social Disease,* ed. Simmel, pp. 126–128, 133; Tumin, *Inventory,* pp. 128, 143, 151–152; Loewenstein, *Christians and Jews,* pp. 50–52; Lowenthal and Guterman, *Prophets of Deceit,* pp. 24–25, 33–77, 81–86, 97, 101–102; Langmuir, *Toward a Definition,* pp. 315–349; Sartre, *Anti-Semite,* pp. 30–35; Charles V. Glock et al., *Adolescent Prejudice* (New York: Harper and Row, 1975), pp. 39, 110–117; Hertzler, "Sociology of Anti-Semitism," pp. 68, 74–75, 80–83, 89–93, 97; Parsons, "Sociology of Modern Anti-Semitism," pp. 107, 113–117; Robert LeVine and Donald T. Campbell, *Ethnocentrism: Theories of Conflict, Ethnic Attitudes and Group Behavior* (New York and London: John Wiley and Sons, 1972); Henry Tajfel, "Cognitive Aspects of Prejudice," *Journal of Social Issues,* 25 (Autumn 1969): 79–97, and *Differentiation between Social Groups: Studies in the Social Psychology of Intergroup Relations* (London, New York, San Francisco: Academic Press, 1978); Joshua A. Fishman, "An Examination of the Process and Function of Stereotyping," *Journal of Social Psychology,* 47 (Feb. 1956): 27–64; David Brion Davis, "Some Ideological Functions of Prejudice in Ante-Bellum America," *American Quarterly,* 15 (Summer 1963): 115–125, and *The Fear of Conspiracy: Images of Un-American Subversion from The Revolution to the Present* (Ithaca: Cornell University Press, 1971); Richard Hoftstadter, *The Paranoid Style in American Politics and Other Essays* (New York: Alfred A. Knopf, 1965), pp. 29–39, 60–61; Harold E. Quinley and Charles Y. Glock, *Anti-Semitism in America* (New York: Free Press, 1979), pp. 172–176, 190–197; Lipset and Raab, *Politics of Unreason,* pp. 6–7, 14–16, 23, 92, 117, 123–129, 156–157, 166, 172–176, 220–221, 240–264, 277–281, 292, 360–361, 399, 495–496.

## 2. Historical Outsider

1. This account of Jewish-Christian interaction in antiquity draws on the following studies: Menahem Stern, "Antisemitism in Rome," in *Antisemitism through the Ages,* ed. Shmuel Almog (Oxford: Pergamon Press, 1988),

pp. 16–25; Wayne A. Meeks and Robert L. Wilken, *Jews and Christians in Antioch in the First Four Centuries of the Common Era* (Missoula, Mont.: Scholars Press, 1978), pp. 4–5; J. N. Sevenster, *Roots of Pagan Anti-Semitism in the Ancient World* (Leiden: E. J. Brill, 1978), pp. 6–8, 14–20, 50–218; John G. Gager, *The Origins of Anti-Semitism: Attitudes toward Christianity in Pagan and Christian Antiquity* (New York and Oxford: Oxford University Press, 1983), pp. 39–112, 127–130; Peter Garnsey, "Religious Toleration in Classical Antiquity," in *Persecution and Toleration: Studies in Church History*, vol. 21, ed. W. J. Sheils (London: Basil Blackwell, 1984), pp. 2, 9–12, 25; Ralph Marcus, "Antisemitism in the Hellenistic-Roman World," in *Essays on Antisemitism*, ed. Koppel S. Pinson (New York: Macmillan, 1965), pp. 11–13, 18–19, 23–24; James Parkes, *The Conflict of the Church and the Synagogue: A Study in the Origins of Anti-Semitism* (1934; New York: Atheneum, 1960), pp. 10–13, 16–19, 22–23; Ernest L. Abel, *The Roots of Anti-Semitism* (Cranberry, N.J.: Associated University Presses, 1975), pp. 51–52, 57–59, 68–111, 139–148; Léon Poliakov, *The History of Anti-Semitism* (New York: Vanguard Press, 1965–1974), vol. 1, pp. 8–9, 12; Salo Wittmayer Baron, *A Social and Religious History of the Jews* (New York: Columbia University Press; Philadelphia: Jewish Publication Society of America, 1952–1983), vol. 1, pp. 188–195; vol. 2, pp. 90–98, 102–105; Edward H. Flannery, *The Anguish of the Jews* (New York: Macmillan, 1965), pp. 11–13, 18–19, 23–24; Erich Kahler, *The Jews among the Nations* (New York: Frederick Ungar, 1967), pp. 96–99; Friedrich Heer, *God's First Love: Christians and Jews over Two Thousand Years* (New York: Weybright and Talley, 1970), pp. 16–19; Rosemary Ruether, *Faith and Fratricide: The Theological Roots of Anti-Semitism* (New York: Seabury Press, 1974), pp. 22–63. For excerpts of pagan views of Jews: Molly Whittaker, *Jews and Christians: Graeco-Roman Views* (Cambridge: Cambridge University Press, 1984), pp. 22, 26, 34, 44–45, 61–63, 68, 72, 76–77, 79–83, 85, 88, 90–91, 108–109, 113–115, 118–120, 122–124. For a review of the scholarly literature: William Klassen, "Anti-Judaism in Early Christianity: The State of the Question," in *Anti-Judaism in Early Christianity: Studies in Christianity and Judaism*, no. 2, ed. Peter Richardson (Waterloo, Ontario: Canadian Corporation for Studies in Religion, 1986), part 1: pp. 1–15; John C. Meagher, "As the Twig was Bent," in *Antisemitism and the Foundations of Christianity*, ed. Alan T. Davies (New York: Paulist Press, 1979), pp. 1–26.

2. Thomas Idinopulos and Roy Owen Ward, "Is Christology Inherently Anti-Semitic?" *Journal of the American Academy of Religion*, 45 (June 1972): 200–202; John M. Oesterreicher, *Anatomy of Contempt: A Critique of R. R. Ruether's "Faith and Fratricide,"* Institute of Judaeo-Christian Studies Paper no. 4 (South Orange, N.J.: Seton Hall University Press, 1975), pp. 21–24; *Anti-Judaism*, ed. Richardson, pp. 15–216.

3. Garnsey, "Religious Toleration," pp. 2–7.

4. See Ruth Mellinkopf, *The Mark of Cain* (Berkeley and Los Angeles: University of California Press, 1981); *The Wandering Jew: Essays in the Interpretation of a Christian Legend*, ed. Galit Hasan-Rokem and Alan Dundes (Bloomington: Indiana University Press, 1986).

5. See Gavin I. Langmuir, *Toward a Definition of Antisemitism* (Berkeley and Los Angeles: University of California Press, 1990), pp. 6–7, and *History, Religion, and Antisemitism* (Berkeley and Los Angeles: University of California Press, 1990), p. 20.

6. Garnsey, "Religious Toleration," pp. 9–10.

7. References for the last two paragraphs: Idinopulos and Ward, "Christology," 70, 200–203, 209–210; Gager, *Origins of Anti-Semitism*, pp. 16–24, 35, 113–120, 134–195; David Rokeah, "The Church Fathers and the Jews in Writings Designed for Internal and External Use," in *Antisemitism through the Ages*, ed. Almog, pp. 45–46, 51–55, 62–65; Jeremy Cohen, "The Jews as Killers of Christ in the Latin Tradition, from Augustine to the Friars," *Traditio*, 39 (1983): 5–6; Langmuir, *History, Religion*, pp. 20, 205–207.

8. Oesterreicher, *Anatomy of Contempt*, pp. 18–21.

9. Gager, *Origins of Anti-Semitism*, pp. 8, 39–63; Stern, "Antisemitism in Rome," pp. 26–27.

10. Langmuir, *History, Religion*, pp. 18–44, 279–305, and *Toward a Definition*, pp. 11–14, 58–62, 109–111, 131–133, 211–222, 303–309.

11. Idinopulos and Ward, "Christology," 198–199, 209; Oesterreicher, *Anatomy of Contempt*, pp. 4–6, 8–15, quote p. 8. Among the New Testament passages cited on behalf of these arguments are 1 Cor. 2:7–8; Rom. 9:2–36; 11:1, 23–25, 27–28, 30–32; Phil. 3:6; Luke 23:24; Acts 3:17. For analyses that do concede some theological anti-Judaism in the New Testament see *Anti-Judaism*, ed. Richardson, pp. 15–216; Langmuir, *Toward a Definition*, pp. 59, 75, 109–111, and *History, Religion*, pp. 18–44, 279–305. Polarities of the debate are epitomized by Indinopulos, Ward, and Oesterreicher vs. Ruether, *Faith and Fratricide*. Moderate positions, qualifiedly sympathetic to Ruether, are in *Antisemitism and Foundations*, ed. Davies.

12. See note 11; Douglas R. A. Hare, "The Rejection of the Jews in the Synoptic Gospels and Acts," in *Antisemitism and Foundations*, ed. Davies, pp. 29, 36–38.

13. Indinopulous and Ward, "Christology," 198; Oesterreicher, *Anatomy of Contempt*, p. 7; an argument for the authenticity of the passage is John C. Hurd, "Paul Ahead of His Time: 1 Thess. 2:13–16," in *Anti-Judaism*, ed. Richardson, pp. 21–36.

14. Oesterreicher, *Anatomy of Contempt*, p. 7.

15. Ibid.

16. Idinopulos and Ward, "Christology," 198. Passages supporting this contention are Rom. 1:17; 3:21; 7:12; 10:3; 11:28. For positions between the apologists

and Ruether: Hurd, "Paul Ahead of His Time," pp. 21–36; Lloyd Gaston, "Paul and the Torah," in *Antisemitism and Foundations,* ed. Davies, pp. 48–67.

17. For other examples of Paul's view on Jewish law: Rom. 3:1–31; 7:1–25; 10:1–21; Heb. 8:6–7, 13.

18. For similar punitive statements: Rom. 2:5–6; Matt. 8:12–13; 12:30, 32. For other discussions of anti-Semitism in the Gospels: Hare, "Rejection," pp. 29–46; John T. Townsend, "The Gospel of John and the Jews: The Story of a Religious Divorce," in *Antisemitism and Foundations,* ed. Davies, pp. 72–88; John T. Pawlikowski, "The Historicizing of the Eschatological: The Spiritualizing of the Eschatological: Some Reflections," ibid., pp. 155, 164–165; Douglas John Hall, "Rethinking Christ," ibid., pp. 167–169.

19. Oesterreicher, *Anatomy of Contempt,* pp. 15–17. For different views of the Church Fathers: Meeks and Wilken, *Jews and Christians,* pp. 85–126; Rokeah, "Church Fathers," pp. 60–65; Kenneth R. Stow, "Hatred of the Jews or Love of the Church: Papal Policy toward the Jews in the Middle Ages," in *Antisemitism through the Ages,* ed. Almog, p. 72; David P. Efroymson, "The Patristic Connection," in *Antisemitism and Foundations,* ed. Davies, pp. 98–114.

20. John Chrysostom, "Homily 1" (386), in Meeks and Wilken, *Jews and Christians,* pp. 86–87, 92–93, 96, 98, and "Homily 8" (387), ibid., p. 122, and *Homilies on the Gospel of Saint John and the Epistle to the Hebrews: A Select Library of the Nicene and Post-Nicene Fathers of the Christian Church,* ed. Philip Schaff (New York: Charles Scribner's Sons, 1906), vol. 14, p. 515. For other examples of Chrysostom's venom, *Commentary on Saint John the Apostle and Evangelist* (ca. 390), in *The Fathers of the Church* (Washington, D.C.: Catholic University of America Press and Consortium Books, 1947–1983; hereinafter cited as *Fathers*), vol. 33 (1956), pp. 33, 38, 72, 82, 88–89, 91, 99, 121, 168, 210, 233, 280–286, 290, 300, 302–303, 306–309, 313, 316–319, 322–327, 342–344, 346, 361, 363, 372, 375, 382, 389, 404–412, 449, 462; vol. 41 (1962), pp. 3, 7–8, 12–13, 17–22, 24–29, 31, 55, 66–74, 76–82, 100, 103, 106–115, 140–142, 150, 152–159, 180, 205–208, 215, 222, 235–237, 276–277, 286, 292, 332, 399–340, 367–369, 394, 409–413, 417–423, 427, 429–430, 434–435, and *Discourses against Judaizing Christianity* (ca. 386–387), in *Fathers,* vol. 68 (1979), pp. 4, 11–12, 24–25, 36, 38, 67, 81, 84, 92–93, 98–100, 130–132, 149, 151, 162, 174, 221, and *On the Incomprehensible Nature of God* (ca. 386–389), in *Fathers,* vol. 72 (1982), pp. 63, 71–72, 178, 194, 233–235, 273–274, 295.

21. St. Jerome, *Jerome's Commentary on Daniel,* (Grand Rapids, Mich.: Baker Book House, 1958), pp. 131–133, 136, 138–139, 146.

22. St. Jerome, *The Homilies of Saint Jerome,* in *Fathers,* vol. 48 (1964), pp. 31, 244, 255, 259, 262, 339, cf. pp. 94–95, 100, 215, 240, 261, 267, 405, 409, and "The Dialogue against the Pelagians" (415), in *Dogmatic and Polemical Works,* in *Fathers,* vol. 53 (1965), p. 342, and *Selected Letters of Saint Jerome*

(London: William Heinemann, 1930), pp. 53, 217, 275, 357, 451, and *The Letters of Saint Jerome,* ed. Thomas Comerford Lawler (Westminster, Md.: Newman Press; London: Longmans, Green, 1963), pp. 55, 69.

23. St. Ambrose, *Theological and Dogmatic Works,* in *Fathers,* vol. 44 (1962), pp. 13, 21, 38, 97, 135, 159, 197–198, 273, 276, 300–301, and *Seven Exegetical Works,* in *Fathers,* vol. 65 (1971), pp. 11, 120, 198, 221, 227–230, 234–237, 246, 257, 336, 375–377, 391, 414, and *Letters,* in *Fathers,* vol. 26 (1954), pp. 10–11, 13–16, 148, 251, 390–392.

24. Aurelius Augustine, *The City of God* (Edinburgh: T. and T. Clark, 1909), vol. 2, pp. 277–279, 281, 405–412. For Augustine's influence on the Middle Ages: Cohen, "Jews as Killers," 22.

25. The Roman laws are in Amnon Linder, *The Jews in Roman Imperial Legislation* (Detroit: Wayne State University Press, 1987); quotes pp. 59, 127, 148, 171, 258, 329–330; other scurrilious references to Jews on pp. 59–61.

26. *The Seven Ecumenical Councils of the Undivided Church, Their Canons and Dogmatic Decrees, Together with the Canons of All the Local Synods Which Received Ecumenical Acceptance,* ed. Henry R. Percival (Oxford: n.p., 1900), pp. 151, 278; Linder, *Imperial Legislation,* pp. 179–180.

27. R. M. De Lange, *Origen and the Jews: Studies in Jewish-Christian Relations in Third-Century Palestine* (Cambridge: Cambridge University Press, 1976).

28. Gager, *Origins of Anti-Semitism,* pp. 118–120; Langmuir, *Toward a Definition,* pp. 70–75; *Seven Ecumenical Councils,* ed. Percival, pp. 151, 278; Rokeah, "Church Fathers," pp. 51–55; Linder, *Imperial Legislation,* pp. 285, 288, 291; Abel, *Roots,* pp. 148–161; Meeks and Wilken, *Jews and Christians,* pp. 25, 30–35; Edward A. Synan, *The Popes and the Jews in the Middle Ages* (New York: Macmillan, 1965), pp. 11–13, 18–19, 23–24; Heer, *God's First Love,* pp. 33–43, 48–49; Baron, *Social and Religious History,* vol. 2, pp. 180–181, 187–189; Ruether, *Faith and Fratricide,* pp. 117–196; Raphael Patai and Jennifer P. Wing, *The Myth of the Jewish Race* (New York: Charles Scribner's Sons, 1975), pp. 103–104; Poliakov, *History of Anti-Semitism,* vol. 1, pp. 25–27; Flannery, *Anguish,* pp. 29–39, 44–63, 66–68; Marcus, "Hellenistic-Roman World," pp. 86–89; A. Roy Eckardt, *Your People, My People: The Meeting of Jews and Christians* (New York: Quadrangle Books, 1974), pp. 14–18; Jacob S. Raisin, *Gentile Reactions to Jewish Ideas* (New York: Philosophical Library, 1953), pp. 355–374; Fred Gladstone Bratton, *The Crime of Christendom: The Theological Sources of Christian Anti-Semitism* (Boston: Beacon Press, 1969), pp. 41–90; Alan T. Davies, *Anti-Semitism and the Christian Mind: The Crisis of Conscience after Auschwitz* (New York: Herder and Herder, 1969), pp. 54–59, 69.

29. Cohen, "Jews as Killers," 3–25; Langmuir, *Toward a Definition,* pp. 204–205; Norman Ravitch, "The Problem of Christian Anti-Semitism," *Commentary,* 73 (April 1982): 44.

30. Ernest A. Rappaport, *Anti-Judaism: A Psychohistory* (Chicago: Perspective Press, 1975), p. 4.

31. Ruether, *Faith and Fratricide,* p. 143.

32. Hyam Maccoby, *The Sacred Executioner: Human Sacrifice and the Legacy of Guilt* (New York: Thames and Hudson, 1982), pp. 172–175.

33. Robert Bonfil, "The Devil and the Jews in the Middle Ages," in *Antisemitism through the Ages,* ed. Almog, pp. 97–98; Peter Berger, *The Sacred Canopy: Elements of a Sociological Theory of Religion* (Garden City, N.Y.: Doubleday, 1967), pp. 69–71.

34. Sigmund Freud, *Moses and Monotheism* (New York: Vintage Books, 1939), pp. 108, 111–112, 175–176. See also E. Isaac-Edersheim, "Ahasver: A Mythic Image of the Jew," in *Wandering Jew,* ed. Hasan-Rokem and Dundes, pp. 204–206; Langmuir, *Toward a Definition,* p. 322; Maccoby, *Sacred Executioner,* p. 161; Rappaport, *Anti-Judaism,* p. 283; Rudolph Loewenstein, *Christians and Jews* (New York: Delta Books, 1951), pp. 30–31, 40–43, 90–102; Gordon W. Allport, *The Nature of Prejudice* (Cambridge, Mass.: Addison-Wesley, 1954), pp. 248–249; Norman Cohn, *The Pursuit of the Millennium* (New York: Oxford University Press, 1970), pp. 85–87, and *Warrant for Genocide: The Myth of the Jewish World-Conspiracy and the Protocols of Zion* (New York: Harper and Row, 1967), pp. 256–267; Otto Fenichel, "Elements of a Psychoanalytic Theory of Anti-Semitism," in *Anti-Semitism: A Social Disease,* ed. Ernest Simmel (New York: International Universities Press, 1946), p. 29; Bernhard Berliner, "On Some Religious Motives of Anti-Semitism," ibid., pp. 79–83; J. L. Talmon, "European History—Seedbed of the Holocaust," *Midstream,* 19 (May 1973): 3–25.

35. Berliner, "Religious Motives," pp. 79–83; Loewenstein, *Christians and Jews,* pp. 30–31, 40–43.

36. Freud, *Moses,* pp. 110–111, 168, 175–176; Loewenstein, *Christians and Jews,* pp. 30–31, 40–43; Fenichel, "Elements of a Psychoanalytic Theory," p. 43; Cohn, *Warrant for Genocide,* pp. 256–267, and *Pursuit of the Millennium,* pp. 86–87; Talmon, "European," 3–25; Rappaport, *Anti-Judaism,* p. 283.

37. Freud, *Moses,* p. 116; Sander L. Gilman, *The Jew's Body* (New York and London: Routledge, 1991), pp. 91–96, 155, 157–158, 231.

38. Freud, *Moses,* pp. 110–111, 170–176; Talmon, "European History," 3–25; Cohn, *Warrant for Genocide,* pp. 256–267, and *Pursuit of the Millennium,* pp. 86–87; Loewenstein, *Christians and Jews,* pp. 30–31, 404–443.

39. Maccoby, *Sacred Executioner,* pp. 98–103; Joseph L. Gaer, *The Legend of the Wandering Jew* (New York: Mentor Books, 1961), pp. 75–78; Paul Rose, *Revolutionary Antisemitism in Germany from Kant to Wagner* (Princeton: Princeton University Press, 1990), pp. 45–47, 53.

40. Maccoby, *Sacred Executioner,* pp. 143–144.

41. Ibid., pp. 122, 127–129, 131–133, 135–136.

42. Ibid., p. 117.

43. Freud, *Moses,* p. 110, and *Totem and Taboo* (1913; New York: W. W. Norton, 1950), pp. 153–154.

44. Cohn, *Pursuit of the Millennium,* pp. 78–90; Maccoby, *Sacred Executioner,* pp. 172–173.

45. See Langmuir, *Toward a Definition,* p. 322; Carl J. Jung, "The Importance of Dreams," in *Man and His Symbols,* ed. Jung (1964; New York: Dell, 1968), pp. 3–12, 41–42, 83–94.

46. This examination of early Christian anti-Semitism is informed by Cohn, *Pursuit of the Millennium,* pp. 29–35, 77–90, and *Warrant for Genocide,* pp. 256–267; Davies, *Anti-Semitism and Foundations,* pp. 54–59, 69; Bratton, *Crime of Christendom,* pp. 11–90; Raisin, *Gentile Reactions,* pp. 355–374; Eckardt, *Your People,* pp. 8–18; Flannery, *Anguish,* pp. 29–39; Parkes, *Conflict of Church and Synagogue,* pp. 95–106, 126, 375–376; Heer, *God's First Love,* pp. 33–43; Abel, *Roots of Anti-Semitism,* pp. 148–181; Talmon, "European History," 3–25; Loewenstein, *Christians and Jews,* pp. 30–31, 40–47, 90–103, 404–443; Freud, *Moses,* pp. 108, 110–111, 116, 168, 170–176, and *Totem,* pp. 153–154; Berliner, "Religious Motives," pp. 79–83; Fenichel, "Elements of a Psychoanalytic Theory," p. 43; Allport, *Prejudice,* pp. 248–249; Franklin H. Littell, *The Crucifixion of the Jews* (New York: Harper and Row, 1975); Conrad Henry Moehlman, *The Christian-Jewish Tragedy: A Study in Religious Prejudice* (Rochester: Leo Hart, 1933); Dagobert D. Runes, *The Jew and the Cross* (New York: Philosophical Library, 1965); Jules Isaac, *The Teaching of Contempt* (New York: Holt, Rinehart and Winston, 1964); Reinhold Niebuhr, *Pious and Secular America* (New York: Charles Scribner's Sons, 1958), pp. 86–112; Galit Hasan-Rokem, "The Cobbler of Jerusalem in Finnish Folklore," in *Wandering Jew,* ed. Hasan-Rokem and Dundes, p. 127; Isaac-Edersheim, "Ahasver," pp. 200–202; Rappaport, *Anti-Judaism,* pp. 1–4, 80, 283; Berger, *Sacred Canopy,* pp. 69–71, 76–79; Langmuir, *Toward a Definition,* pp. 104–111, 322; Ravitch, "Christian Anti-Semitism," 43–44; Gager, *Origins of Anti-Semitism,* pp. 16–21, 24, 28–31, 113–120, 134–195; Rokeah, "Church Fathers," pp. 39–67; Bonfil, "Devil and the Jews," pp. 97–98; Stow, "Hatred," pp. 72–76; Cohen, "Jews as Killers," 1–27; Jeremy Cohen, *The Friars and the Jews: The Evolution of Medieval Anti-Judaism* (Ithaca: Cornell University Press, 1982), pp. 19–24; Gaer, *Legend of the Wandering Jew,* pp. 75–78; Rose, *Revolutionary Antisemitism,* pp. 45–47, 53; Maccoby, *Sacred Executioner,* pp. 98–103, 113–114, 117, 122, 127–152, 172–175; Ruether, *Faith and Fratricide,* pp. 64–182.

47. Bernard S. Bachrach, *Early Medieval Jewish Policy in Northern Europe* (Minneapolis: University of Minnesota Press, 1977), pp. 7–123; Robert Chazan,

*European Jewry* (Berkeley and Los Angeles: University of California Press, 1987), pp. 31–37; Langmuir, *Toward a Definition*, pp. 75–83; R. I. Moore, *The Formation of a Persecuting Society: Power and Deviance in Western Europe, 950–1250* (Oxford: Basil Blackwell, 1986), pp. 13–19, 27, 81–85.

48. Bachrach, *Early Medieval Jewish Policy*, pp. 7–26; Patai and Wing, *Myth of the Jewish Race*, pp. 103–104; Parkes, *Conflict of Church and Synagogue*, pp. 347–370; Abel, *Roots of Anti-Semitism*, pp. 206–215; Flannery, *Anguish*, pp. 73–76; Baron, *Social and Religious History*, vol. 3, pp. 33–45; *Seven Ecumenical Councils*, ed. Percival, pp. 561–598.

49. Bachrach, *Early Medieval Jewish Policy*, pp. 11–18, 59–63, 67–68, 80, 106–107, 120–123, 130–133, 136, 139; *Seven Ecumenical Councils*, ed. Percival, pp. 370, 561, 598.

50. Bachrach, *Early Medieval Jewish Policy*, pp. 98–102; "Tract of Agobard to Louis the Pious and the Palace Bishops," in Kenneth R. Stow, "Agobard of Lyons and the Medieval Concept of the Jew," *Conservative Judaism*, 29 (Fall 1974): 58–65.

51. Bachrach, *Early Medieval Jewish Policy*, pp. 102, 110–114, 119–124, 130–131, 139.

52. Ibid., pp. 9–10, 16–18, 35–37.

53. Moore, *Persecuting Society*, pp. 8, 12–19; Langmuir, *History, Religion*, pp. 289–290; Chazan, *European Jewry*, pp. 31–39.

54. Chazan, *European Jewry*, pp. 31–39; Lester K. Little, *Religious Poverty and the Profit Motive in Medieval Europe* (Ithaca: Cornell University Press, 1978), pp. 42, 46–47; Moore, *Persecuting Society*, pp. 29, 32–33; Poliakov, *History of Anti-Semitism*, vol. 1, pp. 36–46; Baron, *Social and Religious History*, vol. 4, pp. 43, 47.

55. Baron, *Social and Religious History*, vol. 4, pp. 9–12; Heer, *God's First Love*, pp. 64–67; Moore, *Persecuting Society*, p. 19; Langmuir, *History, Religion*, pp. 289–290, and *Toward a Definition*, pp. 87–92, 117–128; Cohen, *Friars and the Jews*, pp. 249–250.

56. Moore, *Persecuting Society*, pp. 8–9, 29, 32, 39–42; Langmuir, *Toward a Definition*, pp. 128–133; Little, *Religious Poverty*, pp. 47–48; Heer, *God's First Love*, pp. 64–67; Baron, *Social and Religious History*, vol. 4, pp. 10–12; Salo Wittmayer Baron, *The Russian Jew under Tsars and Soviets* (New York and London: Macmillan, 1964), pp. 5–8.

57. Jonathan Riley Smith, "The First Crusade and the Persecution of the Jews," in *Persecution and Toleration*, ed. Sheils, pp. 51–72; Chazan, *European Jewry*, pp. 53–105, 137; Moore, *Persecuting Society*, pp. 29–31, 117–121; Langmuir, *History, Religion*, pp. 289–293, and *Toward a Definition*, pp. 86–89; Baron, *Social and Religious History*, vol. 4, pp. 94–116; Flannery, *Anguish*, pp. 90–92; Cohn, *Warrant for Genocide*, p. 22; Malcolm Hay, *Europe and the Jews: The Pressure of Christendom on the People of Israel for 1900 Years* (Boston:

Beacon Press, 1961), pp. 37–38; James Parkes, *Antisemitism* (Chicago: Quadrangle Books, 1964), pp. 63, 66–67; Patai and Wing, *Myth of the Jewish Race,* pp. 83–84; Heer, *God's First Love,* pp. 64–67.

58. Chazan, *European Jewry,* pp. 64–68, 81, 88–89; Smith, "First Crusade," pp. 56–58; Langmuir, *History, Religion,* pp. 290–293.

59. Langmuir, *History, Religion,* pp. 289–291, and *Toward a Definition,* pp. 93–94; Smith, "First Crusade," pp. 58–72; Chazan, *European Jewry,* pp. 63–65, 68–75, 99–105.

60. Chazan, *European Jewry,* pp. 53, 82–84, 88–99, 137, 195–196, 200–211; Smith, "First Crusade," pp. 53–54, 61–62, 65–66; Moore, *Persecuting Society,* pp. 117–121, 147–153; Langmuir, *Toward a Definition,* pp. 93, 96–99.

61. Langmuir, *History, Religion,* pp. 291–292, and *Toward a Definition,* pp. 303–304; Chazan, *European Jewry,* pp. 211–214.

62. Chazan, *European Jewry,* pp. 169–179, 189–191; Moore, *Persecuting Society,* pp. 31–32; Little, *Religious Poverty,* pp. 48–49; Zefira Entin Rokeah, "The State, the Church and the Jews in Medieval England," in *Antisemitism through the Ages,* ed. Almog, p. 112; Flannery, *Anguish,* pp. 92–94, 117; Poliakov, *History of Anti-Semitism,* vol. 1, pp. 48–50; Baron, *Social and Religious History,* vol. 4, pp. 81, 124–127; vol. 9, pp. 201–211; vol. 11, p. 211; Cecil Roth, *A History of the Jews in England* (Oxford: Clarendon Press, 1941), pp. 19–25, 90; Hay, *Europe and the Jews,* pp. 41–44.

63. Patai and Wing, *Myth of the Jewish Race,* p. 111; Hay, *Europe and the Jews,* pp. 54–57; Heer, *God's First Love,* pp. 64–67; Synan, *Popes and the Jews,* pp. 81, 94; Langmuir, *Toward a Definition,* pp. 89–92, 117–127; Moore, *Persecuting Society,* pp. 8–9, 144–145.

64. Cohen, *Friars and the Jews,* pp. 28–32.

65. Hans Mayer, *Outsiders: A Study in Life and Letters* (1976; Cambridge and London: MIT Press, 1982), p. 273; Moore, *Persecuting Society,* pp. 98, 105–106; Langmuir, *Toward a Definition,* p. 305; Werner J. Cahnman, "Socio-Economic Causes of Anti-Semitism," *Social Problems,* 5 (July 1957): 24.

66. For this and the previous paragraph: Flannery, *Anguish,* pp. 95–97; Baron, *Social and Religious History,* vol. 4, pp. 75–76, 81, 87–89, 154–164, 183–185, 200–205; Heer, *God's First Love,* p. 84; Joshua Trachtenberg, *The Devil and the Jews: The Medieval Conception of the Jew and Its Relation to Modern Anti-Semitism* (New Haven: Yale University Press, 1943), p. 190; Poliakov, *History of Anti-Semitism,* vol. 1, pp. 76–81, 115–119; Synan, *Popes and the Jews,* pp. 94, 222; Moore, *Persecuting Society,* pp. 33–34, 42–43, 85–89; Langmuir, *Toward a Definition,* pp. 140–166, 184, 305–306; Little, *Religious Poverty,* pp. 54–57; Cahnman, "Socio-Economic Causes," 22–24, 26.

67. Moore, *Persecuting Society,* pp. 105–106; Langmuir, *History, Religion,* pp. 105–106; Rose, *Revolutionary Antisemitism,* pp. 44–50; Cahnman, "Socio-Economic Causes," 22–24, 26.

68. Moore, *Persecuting Society*, pp. 33–34, 42–43; Langmuir, *Toward a Definition*, pp. 142–166, 184; Baron, *Social and Religious History*, vol. 11, pp. 211–212; Poliakov, *History of Anti-Semitism*, vol. 1, p. 79; Hay, *Europe and the Jews*, p. 75.

69. Chazan, *European Jewry*, pp. 180–182.

70. Hermann Sinsheimer, *Shylock: The History of a Character or the Myth of the Jew* (London: Victor Gollancz, 1947), pp. 71–82; Edgar Rosenberg, *From Shylock to Svengali: Jewish Stereotypes in English Fiction* (Stanford: Stanford University Press, 1960), pp. 22–25; Trachtenberg, *Devil and the Jews*, pp. 188–195; Loewenstein, *Christians and Jews*, pp. 87–88; Little, *Religious Poverty*, pp. 52–53; Moore, *Persecuting Society*, pp. 38–39.

71. Maccoby, *Sacred Executioner*, pp. 131–133; Langmuir, *Toward a Definition*, pp. 329–330; Little, *Religious Poverty*, pp. 52–53.

72. Moore, *Persecuting Society*, pp. 117–121; Maccoby, *Sacred Executioner*, p. 166.

73. Langmuir, *Toward a Definition*, pp. 58–62.

74. Ibid., pp. 213, 242–244; Little, *Religious Poverty*, pp. 51–52; Moore, *Persecuting Society*, pp. 36–37; Rokeah, "State, Church, and Jews," pp. 104–106; Roth, *Jews in England*, pp. 9, 13, 24, 55–57, 78; Trachtenberg, *Devil and the Jews*, pp. 124–155; Poliakov, *History of Anti-Semitism*, vol. 1, pp. 56–64; Baron, *Social and Religious History*, vol. 4, pp. 135–138; vol. 11, pp. 146–157; Hay, *Europe and the Jews*, pp. 117–139; Flannery, *Anguish*, pp. 98–100.

75. Trachtenberg, *Devil and the Jews*, pp. 124–155; Ernest Simmel, "Anti-Semitism and Mass Psychopathology," in *Social Disease*, ed. Simmel, pp. 56–62; Maccoby, *Sacred Executioner*, pp. 104–106, 152–164; Rappaport, *Anti-Judaism*, pp. 95–97, 114.

76. Maccoby, *Sacred Executioner*, pp. 155–164.

77. Ibid., pp. 153–155; Langmuir, *Toward a Definition*, pp. 270, 278–281; Moore, *Persecuting Society*, p. 37; Brian Babbington, "Little Sir Hugh: An Analysis," in *The Blood Libel Legend: A Casebook in Anti-Semitic Folklore*, ed. Alan Dundes (Madison: University of Wisconsin Press, 1991), pp. 76–77; Magdalene Schultz, "The Blood Libel: A Motif in the History of Childhood," ibid., pp. 293–295.

78. See Bernard Glassman, *Anti-Semitic Stereotypes without Jews: Images of the Jews in England, 1290–1700* (Detroit: Wayne State University Press, 1975), pp. 15–19; Baron, *Social and Religious History*, vol. 4, p. 141; Flannery, *Anguish*, pp. 90–100; Hay, *Europe and the Jews*, pp. 117–139; Harold Fisch, *The Dual Image: The Figure of the Jew in English and American Literature* (New York: KTAV, 1971), pp. 20–21; Montague Frank Modder, *The Jew in the Literature of England to the End of the Nineteenth Century* (Philadelphia: Jewish Publication Society of America, 1939), pp. 12–13; Rosenberg, *Shylock to Svengali*, pp. 22–25.

79. Cohn, *Warrant for Genocide,* p. 21; Baron, *Social and Religious History,* vol. 11, pp. 164–174; Poliakov, *History of Anti-Semitism,* vol. 1, pp. 58–59; Trachtenberg, *Devil and the Jews,* pp. 108–123; Rappaport, *Anti-Judaism,* p. 109; Langmuir, *Toward a Definition,* pp. 13–14, 307–308, and *History, Religion,* pp. 300–303; Maccoby, *Sacred Executioner,* pp. 155–161; Little, *Religious Poverty,* p. 52; Moore, *Persecuting Society,* p. 38.

80. Langmuir, *Toward a Definition,* pp. 13–14, 307–308, and *History, Religion,* pp. 300–303; Rappaport, *Anti-Judaism,* p. 109; Maccoby, *Sacred Executioner,* pp. 155–161.

81. Cohn, *Warrant for Genocide,* p. 261; Baron, *Social and Religious History,* vol. 11, pp. 158–164; Mordechai Bruer, "The 'Black Death' and Antisemitism," in *Antisemitism through the Ages,* ed. Almog, p. 140.

82. Little, *Religious Poverty,* pp. 50, 53–54; Moore, *Persecuting Society,* pp. 38–39, 64–65, 88–91, 117–121, 144–145; Bonfil, "Devil and the Jews," pp. 94–98; Langmuir, *History, Religion,* pp. 298–305; Joseph Reider, "Jews in Medieval Art," in *Essays on Antisemitism,* ed. Pinson, pp. 94–101.

83. Little, *Religious Poverty,* p. 53; Bonfil, "Devil and the Jews," pp. 94–98; Moore, *Persecuting Society,* pp. 64–65; Baron, *Social and Religious History,* vol. 11, pp. 135–138, 229–231; Poliakov, *History of Anti-Semitism,* vol. 1, pp. 104–106, 115, 134–137, 141–149; Trachtenberg, *Devil and the Jews,* pp. 44–80; Heer, *God's First Love,* pp. 87–88, 92; Glassman, *Anti-Semitic Stereotypes,* pp. 32–34; Parkes, *Antisemitism,* pp. 67–68; Sigmund Altman, *The Comic Image of the Jew: Explorations of a Pop Culture Phenomenon* (Rutherford and Teaneck, N.J.: Fairleigh Dickinson University Press, 1971), pp. 172–173; Reider, "Jews in Medieval Art," pp. 94–101.

84. Maccoby, *Sacred Executioner,* pp. 155–161; Langmuir, *History, Religion,* pp. 298–305; Baron, *Social and Religious History,* vol. 10, pp. 69, 90.

85. Langmuir, *Toward a Definition,* pp. 294–295, 306–309, and *History, Religion,* pp. 298–305; Sinsheimer, *Shylock: The History,* pp. 32–33; Cohn, *Warrant for Genocide,* p. 21.

86. Baron, *Social and Religious History,* vol. 11, pp. 120, 201–211; Roth, *Jews in England,* p. 13; Rokeah, "State, Church, and Jews," p. 101.

87. Baron, *Social and Religious History,* vol. 3, pp. 194, 212–213, 219; Poliakov, *History of Anti-Semitism,* vol. 1, pp. 303–308; Flannery, *Anguish,* pp. 122–131.

88. Moore, *Persecuting Society,* pp. 33–34, 38, 117–121; Chazan, *European Jewry,* pp. 183–186; Stow, "Hatred," p. 81; Bruer, "Black Death," pp. 141–142; Synan, *Popes and the Jews,* pp. 98–100, 114–115, 119–120, 132–133; Poliakov, *History of Anti-Semitism,* vol. 1, pp. 58, 110–111; Baron, *Social and Religious History,* vol. 10, p. 58; vol. 11., pp. 40–41, 232–233; Hay, *Europe and the Jews,* pp. 70–74; Thomas Aquinas, *The Summa Theologica* (London: Burns, Oates and Washbourne, 1922–1924), vol. 9, pp. 134–135, 145, and "On the Government of Jews: Letter to the Duchess of Brabant" (ca. 1270) in

*Aquinas: Selected Political Writings,* ed. A. P. D'Entreves (Oxford: Basil Blackwell, 1965), p. 85.

89. Baron, *Social and Religious History,* vol. 5, pp. 5–6; vol. 11, pp. 268–270; Poliakov, *History of Anti-Semitism,* vol. 1, pp. 69–72, 139–140; Kahler, *Jews among the Nations,* pp. 50–51; Trachtenberg, *Devil and the Jews,* pp. 170–187; Hay, *Europe and the Jews,* pp. 108–109; Moore, *Persecuting Society,* pp. 6–9; Langmuir, *Toward a Definition,* pp. 273–276; Cohen, *Friars and the Jews,* pp. 34–42, 103–170, 249–264.

90. Moore, *Persecuting Society,* p. 6; Cohen, *Friars and the Jews,* pp. 249–264.

91. Moore, *Persecuting Society,* pp. 6, 103–106, 234–236; Heer, *God's First Love,* pp. 72–74; Poliakov, *History of Anti-Semitism,* vol. 1, pp. 64–74; Kahler, *Jews among the Nations,* pp. 50–51; Hay, *Europe and the Jews,* pp. 75–87; Flannery, *Anguish,* pp. 101–102; Synan, *Popes and the Jews,* pp. 87–89, 93–106, 221–222, 226–227, 234–236; Chazan, *European Jewry,* pp. 180–182; Stow, "Hatred," pp. 81–82.

92. Aquinas, *The Summa Theologica,* Questions 98–108, in *Basic Writings of St. Thomas Aquinas,* ed. Anton Regis (New York: Random House, 1945), vol. 2, pp. 806–979, and *The Summa Theologica* (1922–1924 edit.), vol. 9, pp. 128, 130–131, 134–135, 140–143, 145; vol. 11, pp. 96, 175; vol. 12, p. 39; vol. 16, pp. 288, 291–293, 296, 302, 304–309; vol. 19, pp. 267, 273, and "On the Government of Jews," pp. 85, 87, 89, 95, quote p. 85; Hay, *Europe and the Jews,* p. 91; Baron, *Social and Religious History,* vol. 10, pp. 143–144, 160–161; Trachtenberg, *Devil and the Jews,* p. 34.

93. Cohen, "Jews as Killers," 1–27, and *Friars and the Jews,* pp. 14–15, 23–27, 47–50, 254–264; Edwards, "Mission and Inquisition," pp. 140–143.

94. Baron, *Social and Religious History,* vol. 5, pp. 6, 10–11, 156; vol. 9, pp. 62–67, 87; vol. 10, p. 60; Poliakov, *History of Anti-Semitism,* vol. 1, pp. 69–72; Kahler, *Jews among the Nations,* p. 51; Hay, *Europe and the Jews,* pp. 107–108; Trachtenberg, *Devil and the Jews,* pp. 178–179; Roth, *Jews in England,* pp. 54–55; Synan, *Popes and the Jews,* pp. 108, 111–112; Cohen, *Friars and the Jews,* pp. 62–86, 96–97, 125–126, 166–167, 242, 257–260; James Edwards, "Mission and Inquisition among *Conversos* and *Moriscos* in Spain, 1250–1550," in *Persecution and Toleration,* ed. Sheils, p. 140; Langmuir, *History, Religion,* pp. 295–305.

95. Cohen, *Friars and the Jews,* pp. 64–79, 242, 257–260, and "Jews as Killers," 24–27; Edwards, "Mission and Inquisition," p. 140; Little, *Religious Poverty,* p. 50; R. Edelmann, "Ahasuerus, the Wandering Jew: Origin and Background," in *Wandering Jew,* ed. Hasan-Rokem and Dundes, p. 3.

96. Cohen, *Friars and the Jews,* pp. 78, 82–84, 96–99; Rokeah, "State, Church, and Jews," p. 113; Poliakov, *History of Anti-Semitism,* vol. 2, pp. 141–142; Baron, *Social and Religious History,* vol. 9, pp. 71–87; Roth, *Jews in England,* pp. 42–43, 76–79.

97. Baron, *Social and Religious History*, vol. 10, p. 143; Roth, *Jews in England*, pp. 42–43, 76–77; Rokeah, "State, Church, and Jews," pp. 113–114; Yosef Hayim Yerushalmi, *Assimilation and Racial Antisemitism: The Iberian and German Models* (New York: Leo Baeck Institute, 1982), pp. 6, 10; Cohen, *Friars and the Jews*, pp. 37–38.

98. Yerushalmi, *Assimilation*, p. 6; Cohen, "Jews as Killers," 24–27, and *Friars and the Jews*, pp. 14, 37–38; Edwards, "Mission and Inquisition," pp. 141–143.

99. Patai and Wing, *Myth of the Jewish Race*, pp. 79–80; Baron, *Social and Religious History*, vol. 4, pp. 154–164; vol. 5, pp. 125–128, 131–137; vol. 9, pp. 24–42, 75, 94–95, 131–132; vol. 11, pp. 106–110; vol. 13, pp. 5–6, 10–11; Trachtenberg, *Devil and the Jews*, pp. 170–187; Kahler, *Jews among the Nations*, pp. 50–51; Roth, *Jews in England*, pp. 40–43, 76–79; Rokeah, "State, Church, and Jews," pp. 112–114; Cohen, *Friars and the Jews*, pp. 42–44, 86; Yerushalmi, *Assimilation*, p. 7; Edwards, "Mission and Inquisition," pp. 141–143.

100. Aquinas, *Summa*, vol. 9 (1922–1924 ed.), pp. 140–141; vol 2 (1945 ed.), p. 943; Trachtenberg, *Devil and the Jews*, pp. 190–191; Flannery, *Anguish*, pp. 101–102; Roth, *Jews in England*, p. 42; Hay, *Europe and the Jews*, pp. 86–87, 91; Poliakov, *History of Anti-Semitism*, vol. 1, pp. 76–77; Baron, *Social and Religious History*, vol. 4, pp. 75–76, 205–206; vol. 9, pp. 36–37, 50–51; vol. 12, pp. 133–134, 138–140, 143–147, 151–153, 155–156, 165–169, 172–174, 193–197; Synan, *Popes and the Jews*, pp. 334–335; Innocent III, to the King of the Franks, and to the Count of Nevers, ibid., pp. 222, 227; Rokeah, "State, Church, and Jews," pp. 112–113; Langmuir, *Toward a Definition*, pp. 140–141, 305; Chazan, *European Jewry*, pp. 180–182.

101. Rokeah, "State, Church, and Jews," p. 102; Roth, *Jews in England*, pp. 35–37, 44–50, 55, 66–68, 72, 79, 84–85, 98–102.

102. Chazan, *European Jewry*, pp. 188–191; Poliakov, *History of Anti-Semitism*, vol. 1, pp. 76–81, 115–119; Baron, *Social and Religious History*, vol. 4, pp. 76–78, 81, 87–88, 183–185; vol. 9, pp. 193–226; vol. 10, pp. 9, 67–91, 94–95, 106–107, 112, 123, 140, 184–186, 198, 211, 213–214; vol. 12, pp. 30–31, 35, 43, 45, 52–54, 59–62, 66–67, 72, 101, 103–104, 110–111, 151, 168; vol. 13, pp. 127–128, 151, 155–156, 160, 165–166, 169, 172–174, 193–197, 200–235; Cohen, "Jews as Killers," 1–27, and *Friars and the Jews*, pp. 14, 34–35, 245; Moore, *Persecuting Society*, pp. 33–34, 39–44, 88–89, 105–153.

103. Moore, *Persecuting Society*, pp. 105–106.

104. Baron, *Social and Religious History*, vol. 9, pp. 193–226; vol. 10, pp. 9, 57–91, 172–174, 187; vol. 11, pp. 223, 232–233, 268–270; vol. 12, pp. 33–34, 45, 57, 59–60, 66–67, 72, 101, 103–104, 110–111, 138–140, 143–147, 151–153, 193–197; Roth, *Jews in England*, pp. 36, 56, 59, 61–62, 90; Poliakov, *History of Anti-Semitism*, vol. 1, pp. 76–81, 115–117.

105. Baron, *Social and Religious History,* vol. 11, pp. 213–215, 219–221, 225; Kahler, *Jews among the Nations,* p. 65; Poliakov, *History of Anti-Semitism,* vol. 2, p. 149.

106. Cohen, *Friars and the Jews,* pp. 47–50, 90–91.

107. Baron, *Social and Religious History,* vol. 10, pp. 36, 66, 90, 107, 112–114, 227–228; Moore, *Persecuting Society,* pp. 37–38; Langmuir, *Toward a Definition,* pp. 238–242, 264–268; Rokeah, "State, Church, and Jews," pp. 108–110; Cohen, *Friars and the Jews,* pp. 42–44.

108. Baron, *Social and Religious History,* vol. 10, pp. 9, 13, 19–20; vol. 11, pp. 164–174, 268–280; Poliakov, *History of Anti-Semitism,* vol. 1, pp. 99–100; Hay, *Europe and the Jews,* pp. 144–149; Kahler, *Jews among the Nations,* p. 65; Trachtenberg, *Devil and the Jews,* pp. 108–123; Little, *Religious Poverty,* p. 52; Moore, *Persecuting Society,* p. 38; Langmuir, *Toward a Definition,* pp. 273–275, 307–308, and *History, Religion,* pp. 300–301.

109. Langmuir, *History, Religion,* pp. 300–301, and *Toward a Definition,* pp. 307–308; Little, *Religious Poverty,* p. 52; Moore, *Persecuting Society,* p. 38.

110. Trachtenberg, *Devil and the Jews,* pp. 97–108; Moore, *Persecuting Society,* pp. 147–153; Poliakov, *History of Anti-Semitism,* vol. 1, pp. 104–107, 115, 149–153; Cohn, *Warrant for Genocide,* p. 261; Heer, *God's First Love,* pp. 87–88; Baron, *Social and Religious History,* vol. 9, pp. 81–83, 89–90; vol. 10, pp. 35–36, 69, 90; vol. 11, p. 281; Kahler, *Jews among the Nations,* pp. 65–66; Bruer, "Black Death," pp. 140, 143, 147–149; Sander L. Gilman, *Difference and Pathology: Stereotypes of Sexuality, Race and Madness* (Ithaca and London: Cornell University Press, 1985), pp. 151–152.

111. Poliakov, *History of Anti-Semitism,* vol. 1, pp. 99–103, 108, 110–114, 117–122; vol. 2, p. 149; Parkes, *Antisemitism,* pp. 67–68; Cohn, *Pursuit of the Millennium,* p. 87, and *Warrant for Genocide,* p. 251; Salo Wittmayer Baron, "Medieval Folklore and Jewish Fate," in *Jewish Heritage Reader,* ed. Lily Edman (New York: Taplinger, 1967), p. 180, and *Social and Religious History,* vol. 10, pp. 10, 19–20, 36; vol. 11, pp. 268–270, 281; Flannery, *Anguish,* pp. 109–110; Kahler, *Jews among the Nations,* pp. 65–66; Heer, *God's First Love,* pp. 89–90; Hay, *Europe and the Jews,* p. 143; Langmuir, *Toward a Definition,* pp. 307–308, and *History, Religion,* p. 301; Bruer, "Black Death," pp. 139–140, 149; Chazan, *European Jewry,* p. 211.

112. Langmuir, *Toward a Definition,* pp. 307–308, and *History, Religion,* p. 301; Bruer, "Black Death," pp. 141–150; Chazan, *European Jewry,* p. 211.

113. See references listed in note 82.

114. Trachtenberg, *Devil and the Jews,* pp. 12–31, 196–216; Baron, "Medieval Folklore," pp. 178–179, and *Social and Religious History,* vol. 9, pp. 100–103; vol. 11, pp. 122–191; Poliakov, *History of Anti-Semitism,* vol. 1, pp. 124–136, 166–189, 340–343; Altman, *Comic Image,* pp. 172–173; Glassman, *Anti-Semitic Stereotypes,* pp. 22–41, 58–59; Modder, *Jew in the*

*Literature,* pp. 12–16; Rosenberg, *Shylock to Svengali,* pp. 22–24; Fisch, *Dual,* pp. 15–22; Charles C. Lehrmann, *The Jewish Element in French Literature* (Rutherford, N.J.: Fairleigh Dickinson University Press, 1971), pp. 38–39, 43–45, 47–49; Geoffrey Chaucer, "The Prioress' Tale," in *The Canterbury Tales: A Selection* (New York: Signet, 1969), pp. 217–225; Little, *Religious Poverty,* pp. 50–51.

115. Reider, "Jews in Medieval Art," pp. 94–101; Trachtenberg, *Devil and the Jews,* pp. 46–48; Poliakov, *History of Anti-Semitism,* vol. 1, pp. 134–137, 144; Heer, *God's First Love,* pp. 80–82; Baron, "Medieval Folklore," p. 180; Altman, *Comic Image,* pp. 172–173; Bonfil, "Devil and the Jews," pp. 94–95; Little, *Religious Poverty,* pp. 50–51; Yerushalmi, *Assimilation,* p. 5; Moore, *Persecuting Society,* p. 44.

116. Roth, *Jews in England,* p. 40; Trachtenberg, *Devil and the Jews,* pp. 44–46, 180; Glassman, *Anti-Semitic Stereotypes,* p. 16; Baron, *Social and Religious History,* vol. 9, pp. 24–26; vol. 11, pp. 96–106; Poliakov, *History of Anti-Semitism,* vol. 1, p. 65; vol. 2, p. 167; Bonfil, "Devil and the Jews," p. 98; Rokeah, "State, Church, and Jews," p. 113; Mellinkopf, *Mark of Cain,* pp. 97–98.

117. Baron, *Social and Religious History,* vol. 5, pp. 133–134; vol. 9, pp. 24–26; vol. 10, pp. 125–126, 134–135, 153, 158; vol. 11, pp. 78–87; Trachtenberg, *Devil and the Jews,* p. 187; Roth, *Jews in England,* pp. 42–43; Patai and Wing, *Myth of the Jewish Race,* pp. 106–107, 111–114, 123–125; Kahler, *Jews among the Nations,* pp. 50–51; Rokeah, "State, Church, and Jews," p. 112.

118. Baron, *Social and Religious History,* vol. 9, pp. 32–36; vol. 10, pp. 123, 140, 153; vol. 11, pp. 87–96; Poliakov, *History of Anti-Semitism,* vol. 1, p. 153; Patai and Wing, *Myth of the Jewish Race,* pp. 85, 87–88, 106–107; Kahler, *Jews among the Nations,* p. 51; Flannery, *Anguish,* pp. 145–147.

119. Baron, *Social and Religious History,* vol. 11, pp. 51–52.

120. Langmuir, *Toward a Definition,* pp. 163–166, 170–175, 183–194; Gindo Kisch, "The Jews in Medieval Law," in *Essays on Antisemitism,* ed. Pinson, pp. 103–108; Moore, *Persecuting Society,* pp. 39–42.

121. Langmuir, *History, Religion,* p. 304, and *Toward a Definition,* pp. 140–146, 184; Cohen, *Friars and the Jews,* p. 15; Moore, *Persecuting Society,* pp. 144–145.

122. Moore, *Persecuting Society,* p. 44; Rokeah, "State, Church, and Jews," pp. 113–114; Baron, *Social and Religious History,* vol. 10, pp. 112–114; vol. 12, pp. 138–140, 143–147; Roth, *Jews in England,* pp. 84–86; Poliakov, *History of Anti-Semitism,* vol. 1, p. 78; Hay, *Europe and the Jews,* pp. 141–142; Cohen, *Friars and the Jews,* pp. 42–44.

123. Moore, *Persecuting Society,* p. 43; Poliakov, *History of Anti-Semitism,* vol. 1, pp. 79, 115–117; Hay, *Europe and the Jews,* pp. 142–143; Baron, *Social and Religious History,* vol. 10, pp. 57–58, 69–70, 73; vol. 11, pp. 219–223; vol. 12, pp. 138–140, 143–147; Langmuir, *Toward a Definition,* pp. 140–146.

124. Poliakov, *History of Anti-Semitism,* vol. 1, pp. 117–121; Baron, *Social and Religious History,* vol. 10, pp. 9, 13, 19–20, 246–265, 278, 281–282.
125. Rokeah, "State, Church, and Jews," pp. 102–103, 112–114; Yerushalmi, *Assimilation,* pp. 6, 10; Edwards, "Mission and Inquisition," pp. 140–143; Michael Glatzer, "Pablo de Santa Maria on the Events of 1391," in *Antisemitism through the Ages,* ed. Almog, pp. 129–133; Baron, *Social and Religious History,* vol. 10, pp. 143–144, 146, 153, 172–174; vol. 11, pp. 225–233; Poliakov, *History of Anti-Semitism,* vol. 2, pp. 149–150, 157–167; Flannery, *Anguish,* pp. 131–133; Patai and Wing, *Myth of the Jewish Race,* pp. 106–107; Heer, *God's First Love,* pp. 98–99.
126. Flannery, *Anguish,* pp. 122–127; Poliakov, *History of Anti-Semitism,* vol. 2, pp. 303–308; Baron, *Social and Religious History,* vol. 9, pp. 24–26, 36–37, 54, 94, 132–192; vol. 11, pp. 249–262.
127. For general assessment of the adversity of medieval Jewry see: Kisch, "Jews in Medieval Law," pp. 103–108; Ruether, *Faith and Fratricide,* pp. 198–214; Baron, *Social and Religious History,* vol 5, pp. 125–137; vol. 9, pp. 5–6, 9–13, 94, 100–103, 130–135; vol. 11, pp. 75–121, 158–164, 190, 198–201; Cohen, "Jews as Killers," 1–27, and *Friars and the Jews,* pp. 15, 19–50, 63–100, 103–170, 242–245, 250–264; Little, *Religious Poverty,* pp. 50–58; Chazan, *European Jewry,* pp. 211–222; Moore, *Persecuting Society,* pp. 6, 29–45, 64–65, 88–91, 94, 97–99, 103, 105–153; Langmuir, *History, Religion,* pp. 294–305, and *Toward a Definition,* pp. 61–62, 131–133, 140–146, 305–309.
128. Yerushalmi, *Assimilation,* pp. 8–10; Edwards, "Mission and Inquisition," pp. 141–143; Baron, *Social and Religious History,* vol. 10, pp. 171, 184–186, 192–193, 198, 207–208, 211–214, 217; vol. 11, pp. 238–249; Patai and Wing, *Myth of the Jewish Race,* pp. 106–107; Heer, *God's First Love,* pp. 98–117; Flannery, *Anguish,* pp. 137–141; Kahler, *Jews among the Nations,* pp. 68–69; Chazan, *European Jewry,* p. 199.
129. Yerushalmi, *Assimilation,* pp. 9–28; Joseph Kaplan, "Jews and Judaism in the Political and Social Thought of Spain in the Sixteenth and Seventeenth Centuries," in *Antisemitism through the Ages,* ed. Almog, pp. 130–159; Baron, *Social and Religious History,* vol. 13, pp. 23–61, 155–156; vol. 15, pp. 160–240; Flannery, *Anguish,* pp. 137–141; Poliakov, *History of Anti-Semitism,* vol. 2, pp. 178–232, 239–241, 283–288, 293–297; Edwards, "Mission and Inquisition," pp. 143–145; Gilman, *Jew's Body,* pp. 96–101, 124–127.
130. Cohen, *Friars and the Jews,* pp. 83–84, 166; Langmuir, *History, Religion,* p. 319; Little, *Religious Poverty,* p. 52; Heiko A. Oberman, *The Roots of Anti-Semitism in the Age of Renaissance and Reformation* (1981; Philadelphia: Fortress Press, 1984), pp. 13–14, 25–31, 42; George K. Anderson, *The Legend of the Wandering Jew* (Providence: Brown University Press, 1965), pp. 27–28,

38–41; Trachtenberg, *Devil and the Jews*, p. 179; Rappaport, *Anti-Judaism*, p. 16; Edelmann, "Ahasuerus," pp. 3, 5–6.

131. Oberman, *Roots of Anti-Semitism*, pp. 31–40.

132. Altman, *Comic Image*, pp. 172–173; Rosenberg, *Shylock to Svengali*, pp. 25–36; Modder, *Jew in the Literature*, pp. 20–30; Glassman, *Anti-Semitic Stereotypes*, pp. 57–59, 64–72; Baron, *Social and Religious History*, vol. 11, pp. 123–127, 191; vol. 13, pp. 158–204; vol. 15, pp. 133–135; Sinsheimer, *Shylock: The History*, pp. 51–54, 89–91, 102–103; Flannery, *Anguish*, pp. 149–150; Christopher Marlowe, "The Jew of Malta," in *The Plays of Christopher Marlowe*, ed. Leo Kirschbaum (New York and Cleveland: Meridian Books, 1962), pp. 395–455; Shakespeare, *The Merchant of Venice*, ed. John Russell Brown (Cambridge, Mass.: Harvard University Press; London: Methuen, 1961).

133. Oberman, *Roots of Anti-Semitism*, pp. 64–75, 82, 101–167.

134. Martin Luther, *On the Jews and Their Lies* (Marietta, Ga.: Thunderbolt, n.d.), pp. 3, 8–21, 27–54, 56–60, quotes pp. 8, 51, 53; for other anti-Semitic writings see "An Appraisal of Mankind" (1543), ibid., pp. 61–63; "Warning against the Jews" (1546), ibid., pp. 63–64; "A New Preface to the Prophet Ezekiel" (1545), in *The Works of Martin Luther* (Philadelphia: Muhlenberg, 1932), vol. 6, pp. 414–419. A discussion of Luther's anti-Semitism is in Oberman, *Roots of Anti-Semitism*, pp. 101–124.

135. Oberman, *Roots of Anti-Semitism*, p. 141.

136. Ibid., pp. 41–43, 75–79, 90, 95–96, 141; Poliakov, *History of Anti-Semitism*, vol. 1, pp. 214–221; Baron, *Social and Religious History*, vol. 11, pp. 96–106, 164–174, 275–277; vol. 12, pp. 153–157; vol. 13, pp. 207–296; vol. 14, pp. 149, 157–158, 162, 168–171, 220, 234, 238, 242–251; Patai and Wing, *Myth of the Jewish Race*, pp. 112–114; Kahler, *Jews among the Nations*, p. 55; Flannery, *Anguish*, pp. 152–54; Trachtenberg, *Devil and the Jews*, p. 179.

137. Baron, *Social and Religious History*, vol. 11, p. 223; vol. 12, pp. 155–156, 165–166, 169, 172–174, 193–197; Poliakov, *History of Anti-Semitism*, vol. 1, pp. 189–190, 214–215; Patai and Wing, *Myth of the Jewish Race*, p. 111; Arthur Hertzberg, *The French Enlightenment and the Jews* (New York: Columbia University Press; Philadelphia: Jewish Publication Society of America, 1969), p. 14; Trachtenberg, *Devil and the Jews*, p. 179.

138. Baron, *Social and Religious History*, vol. 10, pp. 49–51; vol. 11, p. 280; vol. 12, pp. 64, 67.

139. Ibid., vol. 12, pp. 158–204; vol. 15, pp. 150–157, 160.

140. Ibid., vol. 10, pp. 243–246.

141. Ibid., vol. 10, p. 278; vol. 11, pp. 87–206; vol. 12, pp. 30–31, 35, 66; vol. 14, pp. 29–32, 34–43, 45, 47–49, 51–52, 56–58, 76, 82–96, 114–121, 124–147; Flannery, *Anguish*, p. 155; Poliakov, *History of Anti-Semitism*, vol.

2, pp. 317–318; Patai and Wing, *Myth of the Jewish Race,* pp. 78–79, 108–110; Kahler, *Jews among the Nations,* p. 51; Cohen, *Friars and the Jews,* pp. 83–84, 167.

142. Ceila S. Heller, *On the Edge of Destruction: Jews of Poland between the Two World Wars* (New York: Columbia University Press, 1977), pp. 14–16; Poliakov, *History of Anti-Semitism,* vol. 1, pp. 246–249.

143. Poliakov, *History of Anti-Semitism,* pp. 255–259; Heller, *Edge of Destruction,* pp. 17, 20–22, 26; James Parkes, *The Emergence of the Jewish Problem: 1878–1933* (1946; Westport, Conn.: Greenwood Press, 1970), pp. 128–129; Raphael Mahler, "Antisemitism in Poland," in *Essays on Antisemitism,* ed. Pinson, pp. 146–152; Baron, *Social and Religious History,* vol. 10, pp. 35–38; vol. 16, pp. 10–11, 13–15, 21, 32, 38, 40, 60–61, 83–85, 91, 94–99, 101–103, 106, 109, 112, 116–117, 123, 141, 145–46, 298, 301–306; Kahler, *Jews among the Nations,* pp. 63–66; Heer, *God's First Love,* p. 139; Flannery, *Anguish,* pp. 155–158.

144. Baron, *Social and Religious History,* vol. 17, pp. 116–128, and *Russian Jew,* pp. 8–10, 15, 19–21; Poliakov, *History of Anti-Semitism,* vol. 1, pp. 256–259, 275–282; Kahler, *Jews among the Nations,* pp. 63–65; Heer, *God's First Love,* pp. 140–149; Patai and Wing, *Myth of the Jewish Race,* pp. 88–90.

145. Baron, *Social and Religious History,* vol. 10, pp. 29–30; vol. 14, pp. 174–175, 179, 192–200; vol. 17, p. 115; Patai and Wing, *Myth of the Jewish Race,* pp. 85–86.

146. Robert F. Byrnes, *Anti-Semitism in Modern France: The Prologue to the Dreyfus Affair* (New York: Howard Fertig, 1969), vol. 1, p. 75; Poliakov, *History of Anti-Semitism,* vol. 1, pp. 189–190, 214–215, 236–245; vol. 3, pp. 13–14; Flannery, *Anguish,* pp. 148–149; Cohn, *Warrant for Genocide,* p. 251; Glassman, *Anti-Semitic Stereotypes,* pp. 84–85, 90–92, 100–104, 107–108, 149–151; Baron, *Social and Religious History,* vol. 15, pp. 22–73, 94–96, 140–151, 156–157, 160; Roth, *Jews in England,* pp. 145–171, 202–203.

## 3.  Ambivalence at America's Dawn

1. Bernard Glassman, *Anti-Semitic Stereotypes without Jews: Images of the Jews in England, 1299–1700* (Detroit: Wayne State University Press, 1975), pp. 76–151; Cecil Roth, *A History of the Jews in England* (Oxford: Clarendon Press, 1941), pp. 145–171, 202–203; Peter Toon, "The Question of Jewish Immigration," in *The Millennium and the Future of Israel: Puritan Eschatology 1600 to 1660,* ed. Toon (Cambridge and London: James Clarke, 1970), pp. 115–121, 124–125; J. Van Den Berg, "The Eschatological Expectation of Seventeenth-Century Dutch Protestantism with Regard to the Jewish People," ibid., pp. 137–153; Salo Wittmayer Baron, *A Social and Religious History of the Jews* (New York: Columbia University Press; Philadelphia: Jewish Publi-

cation Society of America [hereafter JPSA], 1952–1983), vol. 13, pp. 285–291; vol. 14, pp. 22–73, 125–160; Léon Poliakov, *The History of Anti-Semitism* (New York: Vanguard Press, 1965–1974), vol. 1, pp. 203–209; Erich Kahler, *The Jews among the Nations* (New York: Frederick Ungar, 1967), pp. 72–75; Haiko A. Oberman, *The Roots of Anti-Semitism in the Age of Renaissance and Reformation* (1981; Philadelphia: Fortress Press, 1984), p. 141; Myriam Yardeni, *Anti-Jewish Mentalities in Early Modern Europe* (Lanham, Md., New York, London: University Press of America, 1990), pp. 1–15, 71–72, 140–141.

2. Baron, *Social and Religious History,* vol. 15, pp. 94–96, 110–111; Poliakov, *History of Anti-Semitism,* vol. 1, pp. 189–190, 229–232, 243–245.

3. Joseph Kaplan, "Jews and Judaism in the Political and Social Thought of Spain in the Sixteenth and Seventeenth Centuries," in *Antisemitism through the Ages,* ed. Shmuel Almog (Oxford: Pergamon Press, 1988), pp. 153–159.

4. Toon, "Question," pp. 122–125; Van Den Berg, "Eschatological Expectation," p. 138; Colin Holmes, *Anti-Semitism in British Society: 1876–1939* (London: Edward Arnold, 1979), p. 2; Roth, *Jews in England,* p. 166; Baron, *Social and Religious History,* vol. 15, pp. 15, 110, 117–122, 156; Yardeni, *Anti-Jewish Mentalities,* pp. 1–70, 141–149, 201–210, 217–223.

5. Van Den Berg, "Eschatological Expectation," pp. 139–153; Holmes, *Anti-Semitism in British Society,* p. 3; Baron, *Social and Religious History,* vol. 4, p. 23; Poliakov, *History of Anti-Semitism,* vol. 3, pp. 34–36; Oberman, *Roots of Anti-Semitism,* p. 141.

6. Glassman, *Anti-Semitic Stereotypes,* pp. 136–137, 149; Baron, *Social and Religious History,* vol. 15, pp. 157–158; Poliakov, *History of Anti-Semitism,* vol. 3, pp. 205–209.

7. Baron, *Social and Religious History,* vol. 15, pp. 85–86, 108–111, 156–158; Poliakov, *History of Anti-Semitism,* vol. 3, pp. 26–33, 236–237; Arthur Hertzberg, *The French Enlightenment and the Jews* (New York: Columbia University Press, 1968), pp. 83, 218–221; Alfred D. Low, *Jews in the Eyes of the Germans from the Enlightenment to Imperial Germany* (Philadelphia: Institute for the Study of Human Issues, 1979), pp. 23–29; Edward H. Flannery, *The Anguish of the Jews* (New York: Macmillan, 1965), pp. 153–154; Yardeni, *Anti-Jewish Mentalities,* pp. 241–253.

8. Baron, *Social and Religious History,* vol. 15, pp. 158–159; Poliakov, *History of Anti-Semitism,* vol. 3, pp. 26–33; Glassman, *Anti-Semitic Stereotypes,* pp. 85–103, 136–138, 141–143, 148–149, 153–155; Hertzberg, *French Enlightenment,* pp. 8–10; Low, *Jews in the Eyes of the Germans,* p. 7; Jacob Katz, *From Prejudice to Destruction: Anti-Semitism, 1700–1933* (Cambridge, Mass.: Harvard University Press, 1980), pp. 54–62; Flannery, *Anguish,* pp. 148–150; Yardeni, *Anti-Jewish Mentalities,* pp. 1–70, 141–149, 217–223, 301–310.

9. Poliakov, *History of Anti-Semitism*, vol. 3, p. 214; Low, *Jews in the Eyes of the Germans*, pp. 18–22, 216–217; Katz, *Prejudice to Destruction*, pp. 52–54; Yardeni, *Anti-Jewish Mentalities*, 253–270.

10. Jacob Rader Marcus, *The Colonial American Jew: 1492–1776* (Detroit: Wayne State University Press, 1970), vol. 1, pp. 35–94.

11. Ibid., pp. 95–140.

12. Ibid., pp. 142–204.

13. *The Federal and State Constitutions, Colonial Charters and other Organic Laws of The United States of America*, ed. Francis N. Thorpe (Washington, D.C.: U.S. Government Printing Office, 1909): "The Charter of Maryland" (1632), vol. 3, pp. 1678–1686; "The Charter of Carolina" (1663), vol. 5, pp. 2752–2753; "Concessions and Agreements of the Lords Proprietors of the Province of Carolina" (1665), vol. 5, p. 2757; "The Fundamental Constitutions of Carolina" (1669), vol. 5, pp. 2772–2776, 2779, 2783–2784; Marcus, *Colonial American Jew*, vol. 1, pp. 343, 463–468; Jacob Rader Marcus, *Early American Jewry: The Jews of Philadelphia and the South* (Philadelphia: JPSA, 1951–1953), vol. 2, pp. 228–229.

14. "Indictment of Dr. Joseph Lumbrozo, Feb. 25, 1658, at a Provincial Court, St. Mary's Maryland," in *A Documentary History of the Jews in the United States: 1654–1875*, ed. Morris U. Schappes (New York: Schocken Books, 1971), pp. 14–15; *Archives of Maryland*, 41 (1924): 202–204; 53 (1936): 319–320, 335–336, 429, 496–498; *Publications of the American Jewish Historical Society* (hereafter *PAJHS*), 1 (1893): 25–39; Marcus, *Colonial American Jew*, vol. 1, pp. 449–451; vol. 3, pp. 1125–1126; Abraham Goodman, *American Overture: Jewish Rights in Colonial Times* (Philadelphia: JPSA, 1947), pp. 130–143; Richard B. Morris, "Civil Liberties in the Jewish Tradition in Early America," in *The Jewish Experience in America*, ed. Albert J. Karp (New York: KTAV, 1969), vol. 1, pp. 417–420; Isaac M. Fein, *The Making of an American Jewish Community: The History of Baltimore Jewry from 1773 to 1920* (Philadelphia: JPSA, 1971), pp. 7–9.

15. Peter Stuyvesant to the Amsterdam Chamber of the Dutch West India Co., Sept. 22, 1654, in *Documentary History*, ed. Schappes, pp. 1–2; Marcus, *Colonial American Jew*, vol. 1, pp. 71–81, 209–210.

16. For the documents cited in this paragraph see *Documentary History*, ed. Schappes, pp. 4–14; see also Marcus, *Colonial American Jew*, vol. 1, pp. 175–179, 218–243; Morris, "Civil Liberties," pp. 410–412, 415–416; Goodman, *American Overture*, pp. 105–107, 116–117; *PAJHS*, 5 (1897): 195; 8 (1900): 14, 28; 18 (1909): 4–9, 19–36, 58–59, 67, 73–75; 29 (1925): 52; 32 (1934): 49–51; 46 (1956): 48–50; Leon Huhner, "Asser Levy: A Noted Jewish Burgher of New Amsterdam," in *Jewish Experience*, ed. Karp, vol. 1, pp. 54–55.

17. John Megapolensis to the Classis of Amsterdam, March 18, 1655, in *Ecclesiastical Records: State of New York* (Albany: James B. Lyons, 1901), vol. 1, p. 33; Van Den Berg, "Eschatological Expectation," p. 138.

18. "The Charter of Rhode Island and Providence Plantations" (1663), in *Federal and State Constitutions,* ed. Thorpe, vol. 5, pp. 3212–3213; Marcus, *Colonial American Jew,* vol. 1, pp. 298–300, 415–417, 422–424, 427, 435–437, 501–503; Morris, "Civil Liberties," pp. 407–409.

19. John Winthrop, *Winthrop's Journal: The History of New England, 1630–1649,* ed. James K. Hosmer (New York: Barnes and Noble, 1959), Oct. 26, 1636, vol. 1, p. 196; John Norton, *Abel Being Dead, Yet Speaketh; or, The Life and Death of that Deservedly Famous Man of God, Mr. John Cotton,* (1658; Delmar, N.Y.: Scholars' Facsimiles and Reprints, 1978), p. 22; Joseph B. Felt, *The Ecclesiastic History of New England* (Boston: Congregational Library Association and Congregational Board of Education, 1855), vol. 1, pp. 262–263; vol. 2, p. 236; George A. Kohut, *Ezra Stiles and the Jews: Selected Passages from His Literary Diary Concerning Jews and Judaism* (New York: Philip Cowen, 1902), p. 4; Abraham I. Katsh, *Hebrew in American Higher Education* (New York: New York University Press, 1941), pp. 28–39; Dan A. Oren, *Joining the Club: A History of Jews and Yale* (New Haven and London: Yale University Press, 1985), p. 3; Leon Huhner, *Jews in America in Colonial and Revolutionary Times* (New York: Gertz Bros., 1959), pp. 75–76; Albert Ehrenfield, "A Chronicle of Boston Jewry: From the Colonial Settlement to 1900" (manuscript, 1963; a copy is in the library of the University of Illinois, Champaign-Urbana), p. 36; Robert St. John, *Jews, Justice and Judaism: A Narrative of the Role Played by the Bible People in Shaping American History* (Garden City, N.Y.: Doubleday, 1969), pp. 15–25; Morris, "Civil Liberties," p. 407; Marcus, *Colonial American Jew,* vol. 2, pp. 1092–1093. For similar attitudes of British Puritans see *Millennium and the Future,* ed. Toon.

20. William Bradford, *Of Plymouth Plantation: 1620–1647,* ed. Samuel Eliot Morison (New York: Modern Library, 1952), pp. 19, 47, 53, 63, 130–131, 236, 322, 329–330, 351–352; John Winthrop, "A Modell of Christian Charity," *Winthrop Papers* (Boston: Massachusetts Historical Society, 1929–1947), vol. 2, pp. 282–287; cf. Winthrop to Sir William Spring, Feb. 8, 1630, ibid., p. 204; Increase Mather, *Remarkable Providences* (1684; New York: Arno Press, 1977), p. 253; Cotton Mather, *Days of Humiliation: Times of Affliction and Disaster* (Gainesville, Fla.: Scholars' Facsimiles and Reprints, 1970), pp. 2–33, 41–42, 46–49, 51–54, 58–59, 62–69, 90–91, 103, 115–123, 146–149, 167–168, 226–231, 268, 294, 333–336, 347, 360, and *Magnalia Christi Americana: or the Ecclesiastical History of New England* (1702; New York: Russell and Russell, 1967), vol. 1, pp. 52, 81, 121, 144, 152, 404, 414, 437; vol. 2, pp. 528, 674, and for a comparison between

Hebrews and Puritans in another context see *The Present State of New England* (Boston: Samuel Green, 1690), pp. 2–9, 13–25, 30, 34–36, 40–41, 45–46.

21. John Cotton, *A Brief Exposition of the Whole Book of Canticles, or Song of Solomon* (London: J. Young, 1648), p. 119; Roger Williams, *The Complete Writings of Roger Williams* (New York: Russell and Russell, 1963), vol. 7, pp. 49, 135.

22. C. Mather, *Days of Humiliation,* p. 122; cf. *Diary of Cotton Mather* (New York: Frederick Ungar, 1957), vol. 1, p. 298; Cotton, *Brief Exposition,* pp. 194, 218; Williams, *Complete Writings,* vol. 7, p. 136; Increase Mather, *The Mystery of Israel's Salvation Explained and Applied* (London: John Allen, 1669), pp. 2, 11, 64, 175.

23. I. Mather, *Mystery of Israel's Salvation,* p. 64, cf. p. 2; C. Mather, *Diary,* vol. 1, p. 298, and *Magnalia,* vol. 1, p. 331.

24. Cotton, *Brief Exposition,* pp. 155, 218, and *God's Mercy Mixed with His Justice of His People's Deliverance in Times of Danger* (Gainesville, Fla.: Scholars' Facsimilies and Reprints, 1958), pp. 78–80; Williams, *Complete Writings,* vol. 3, p. 182; vol. 4, pp. 349, 409; vol. 5, pp. 271, 420; vol. 6, pp. 311, 244; vol. 7, pp. 249, 277; I. Mather, *Mystery of Israel's Salvation,* pp. 20–25, 27; C. Mather, *Days of Humiliation,* p. 35.

25. *Winthrop Papers,* vol. 5, pp. 55–56; vol. 2, p. 122.

26. Cotton, *Christ the Fountain of Life; or, Sundry Choice Sermons on Part of the Fifth Chapter of the First Epistle of St. John* (London: Robert Ibbitson, 1651), pp. 218, 246, "A letter of Mr. John Cottons [sic] Teacher of the Church in Boston, In New-England to Mr. Williams A Preacher There," in Williams, *Complete Writings,* vol. 1, p. 301, and "A Sermon Delivered at Salem" (1636), in *John Cotton on the Churches of New England,* ed. Larzer Ziff (Cambridge, Mass.: Harvard University Press, 1968), p. 54; C. Mather, *Magnalia,* vol. 1, pp. 204–205; vol. 2, pp. 306, 372.

27. Williams, *Complete Writings,* vol. 4, p. 137; vol. 5, p. 350; vol. 6, p. 107; vol. 7, p. 137.

28. I. Mather, *Mystery of Israel's Salvation,* pp. 7, 94, 173, 175–176. For analysis of this work and its contribution to Mather's reputation see Kenneth Ballard Murdock, *The Foremost American Puritan* (1925; New York: Russell and Russell, 1966), pp. 94–95.

29. I. Mather, *Mystery of Israel's Salvation,* pp. 11, 72, 175.

30. William Penn, "A Visitation to the Jews" (1695), in *A Collection of the Works of William Penn* (London: J. Sowle, 1726), vol. 2, pp. 848–853, quote p. 853, and "Frame of Government," in Samuel Hazard, *Annals of Pennsylvania from the Discovery of Delaware* (Philadelphia: Hazard and Mitchell, 1850), p. 573; Marcus, *Early American Jewry,* vol. 2, pp. 10, 166, and *Colonial American Jew,* vol. 1, p. 462.

31. Population estimate from Marcus, *Early American Jewry,* vol. 2, p. 293.

32. "An Action or Complaint of Major William Dyer Surveyor General Against Mordecai Campanel . . . and other Jews Born Foreign at Newport March 31, 1685," in *PJAHS*, 26 (1920): 175–176; Morris, "Civil Liberties," pp. 413–414; Marcus, *Colonial American Jew*, vol. 1, p. 316.

33. Dongan's edict in *Documentary History*, ed. Schappes, pp. 17–18; Marcus, *Colonial American Jew*, vol. 1, pp. 402–403; Goodman, *American Overture*, p. 105; *PAJHS*, 6 (1897): 96, 100–103; *Minutes of the Common Council of the City of New York: 1675–1776* (New York: Dodd, Mead, 1905), vol. 1, pp. 10, 168–169; *The Colonial Laws of New York* (Albany: J. B. Lyon, 1894–1896), vol. 1, p. 192.

34. Dongan's order and denial of the Jews' petition in *Documentary History*, ed. Schappes, pp. 18–19; *Minutes of the Common Council*, vol. 1, p. 169; *Colonial Laws of New York*, vol. 1, p. 115; *PAJHS*, 3 (1895): 41–59; Marcus, *Colonial American Jew*, vol. 1, pp. 400–402; Hyman B. Grinstein, *The Rise of the Jewish Community of New York: 1654–1860* (Philadelphia: JPSA, 1945), p. 39.

35. *Public Records of the Colony of Connecticut*, ed. J. Hammond Trumbull (Hartford: F. A. Brown, 1852), vol. 2, p. 144; Goodman, *American Overture*, pp. 25–27.

36. *The Records of New Amsterdam*, ed. Berthold Fernow (New York: Knickerbocker Press, 1897), vol. 1, pp. 290–291, 385; vol. 2, pp. 22–23, 32–33, 38, 42–43, 97–98, 124, 130–131, 136–137; Huhner, "Asser Levy," pp. 51–65; Marcus, *Colonial American Jew*, vol. 1, p. 230; vol. 3, p. 1124.

37. Peter quoted in Marcus, *Colonial American Jew*, vol. 1, p. 115; *Records of New Amsterdam*, ed. Fernow, vol. 2, pp. 416–417, 419, 424; "The Dutch Records of Kingston, Ulster County, New York: 1658–1664," *Proceedings of the New York State Historical Association*, 11 (1912): 62, 66; Marcus, *Colonial American Jew*, vol. 1, p. 230; vol. 3, pp. 1121–1122, 1126.

38. Felix Grendon, "The Anglo-Saxon Charms," *Journal of American Folklore*, 12 (1909): 185; cf. 179, 186–187; Rudolf Glanz, *The Jew in the Old American Folklore* (New York: Waldon Press, 1961), pp. 10–17.

39. Ellen Powell Thompson, "Folklore from Ireland, II," *Journal of American Folklore*, 12 (1909): 225.

40. Thomas R. Brendle and Claude W. Unger, "Folk Medicine of the Pennsylvania Germans: The Non-Occult Cures," *Pennsylvania German Society Proceedings*, 45 (1935), part 2: 175.

41. Samuel McCord Crothers, "An Hour with Our Prejudices," *Atlantic Monthly*, 93 (May 1904): 673.

42. Arthur Kyle Davis, Jr., *Traditional Ballads of Virginia* (Cambridge, Mass.: Harvard University Press, 1929), pp 400–415, and *More Traditional Ballads of Virginia* (Chapel Hill: University of North Carolina Press, 1960), pp. 229–238; Helen Hartness Flanders and Marguerite Olney, *Ballads Migrant in New England* (1953; Freeport, N.Y.: Books for Libraries Press,

1968), pp. 28–32; Florence H. Ridley, "A Tale Told Too Often," *Western Folklore,* 26 (July 1967): 153–156; Marcus, *Colonial American Jew,* vol. 3, p. 1117; Glantz, *Old American Folklore,* pp. 9–29.

43. Marcus, *Colonial American Jew,* vol. 1, pp. 229, 399–409, 415, 421–424, 427, 441, 451–454, 480, 490–508, 510, 513; Holmes, *Anti-Semitism in British Society,* pp. 2–3; Roth, *Jews in England,* pp. 166, 202–203, 252–253.

44. Michael N. Dobkowski, *The Tarnished Dream: The Basis of American Anti-Semitism* (Westport, Conn.: Greenwood Press, 1979), pp. 10–13.

45. *Ezra Stiles,* ed. Kohut, p. 26; Ezra Stiles, "The United States Elevated to Glory and Honor: A Sermon Preached Before His Excellency Jonathan Trumbull and the General Assembly of the State of Connecticut" (1783), in *The Pulpit of the American Revolution: or The Political Sermons of the Period of 1776,* ed. John Wingate Thornton (Boston: Gould and Lincoln, 1860), pp. 401–520; Charles Chauncy, "A Discourse on the Good News from a Far Country" (1766), ibid., p. 129; Samuel West, "A Sermon Preached before the Honorable Council and the Honorable House of Representatives of the Colony of Massachusetts-Bay in New England" (1780), ibid., pp. 359–361; John J. Zubly, "The Law of Liberty" (1775), *American Archives,* 4th ser., 2 (1839): 1563; Huhner, *Jews in America,* p. 143; Connecticut *Courant,* Sept. 12, 1765, p. 3.

46. Anson Phelps Stokes, *Church and State in the United States* (New York: Harper and Row, 1950), vol. 1, pp. 467–468.

47. *The Literary Diary of Ezra Stiles,* ed. F. B. Dexter (New York: Charles Scribner's Sons, 1901), vol. 1, p. 6n; vol. 2, p. 391; cf. Kohut, *Ezra Stiles,* p. 53; *Boston Daily Evening Traveller,* Sept. 16, 1754, in Ehrenfield, "Boston Jewry," p. 372; *Newport Mercury,* Dec. 5, 1763, ibid., p. 133.

48. "The Charter of Georgia" (1732), in *Federal and State Constitutions,* ed. Thorpe, vol. 7, p. 773; Goodman, *American Overture,* pp. 192–193, 195; *Jewish Experience,* ed. Karp, vol. 1, p. 74; Marcus, *Colonial American Jew,* vol. 1, pp. 421–422, 441, 443–447, 451, 454–455, 466–467, 485, 499–505, 507–508, and *Early American Jewry,* vol. 2, pp. 330–331.

49. C. Mather, *Magnalia,* vol. 2, p. 12; *Literary Diary of Ezra Stiles,* ed. Dexter, vol. 2, pp. 290–291; Ehrenfield, "Boston Jewry," pp. 90, 105, 726; Huhner, *Jews in America,* p. 172; Morris Silverman, *Hartford Jews: 1659–1970* (Hartford: Connecticut Historical Society, 1970), p. 7; Katsh, *Hebrew in American Higher Education,* pp. 18–22; Goodman, *American Overture,* pp. 21, 108; Marcus, *Colonial American Jew,* vol. 1, p. 513; vol. 3, pp. 1199, 1206–1207, and *Early American Jewry,* vol. 2, pp. 466–467.

50. Marcus, *Early American Jewry,* vol. 2, pp. 246–248.

51. Goodman, *American Overture,* pp. 126–127; *Jewish Life in Philadelphia: 1830–1940,* ed. Murray Friedman (Philadelphia: ISHI Publications, 1983), pp. 5, 291–292; Ehrenfield, "Boston Jewry," p. 140, Huhner, *Jews in Amer-*

*ica,* p. 145; Marcus, *Colonial American Jew,* vol. 3, pp. 1206–1207, and *Early American Jewry,* vol. 2, pp. 8, 244, 495–498, and *American Jewry: Documents, Eighteenth Century* (Cincinnati: Hebrew Union College Press, 1959), p. 7.

52. Huhner, *Jews in America,* p. 149; Marcus, *Colonial American Jew,* vol. 3, pp. 1148–1152, 1307–1309, and *Early American Jewry,* vol. 2, pp. 81, 265, 330, 348, 495–498, 511; Leo Hershkowitz, "Some Aspects of the New York Jewish Merchant Community," *American Jewish Historical Quarterly,* 66 (Sept. 1976): 12, 25–27.

53. Marcus, *Colonial American Jew,* vol. 3, pp. 1146–1147, 1157–1172, 1226–1227, 1234, 1298–1299, and *Early American Jewry,* vol. 2, pp. 503–507.

54. Marcus, *Early American Jewry,* vol. 2, p. 535.

55. "Minutes of the New York City Common Council," Oct. 14, 1718, Sept. 17, 1766, in *Documentary History,* ed. Schappes, pp. 19, 41; Hershkowitz, "New York Merchant Community," 13; Goodman, *American Overture,* pp. 20, 199–200; Marcus, *Colonial American Jew,* vol. 1, p. 463; vol. 3, pp. 1261–1262, 1276, 1279–1280, 1307–1309, and *Early American Jewry,* vol. 2, pp. 229, 245, 160, 165, 344–348, 518–519, 527, and *American Jewry,* p. 80; Huhner, *Jews in America,* pp. 147–149; Morris, "Civil Liberties," p. 415.

56. Marcus, *Colonial American Jew,* vol. 1, pp. 405, 408–410, 422, 424, 436–437, 441, 444, 446–447, 462–465, 470, 510; vol. 3, p. 1282, and *Early American Jewry,* vol. 2, pp. 154–156, 166, 229, 265, 330–331, 518–519, 522–526, 529–530; Goodman, *American Overture,* pp. 110–114; Morris, "Civil Liberties," p. 416; Hershkowitz, "New York Merchant Community," 13; "The Constitution of South Carolina" (1778), in *Federal and State Constitutions,* ed. Thorpe, vol. 6, p. 3250; "The Constitution of New York" (1777), ibid., vol. 5, pp. 2630, 2632, 2636–2638.

57. Marcus, *Colonial American Jew,* vol. 1, pp. 444–445, 485–490, 514, and *Early American Jewry,* vol. 2, pp. 515–516, and *American Jewry,* p. 200; Ehrenfield, "Boston Jewry," p. 113.

58. Marcus, *Colonial American Jew,* vol. 1, pp. 435–437; Morris, "Civil Liberties," p. 416; Ehrenfield, "Boston Jewry," pp. 138–140; Lopez's petition in *Extracts from the Itineraries and Other Miscellanies of Ezra Stiles, D.D., LL.D.: 1755–1794,* ed. Franklin Bowditch Dexter (New Haven: Yale University Press, 1916), p. 52; quote p. 53.

59. *Narratives of Early Carolina: 1650–1708,* ed. Alexander S. Salley, Jr. (New York: Barnes and Noble, 1911), pp. 347–348; Amherst County, Virginia petition quoted in Thomas J. Curry, *The First Freedoms: Church and State in America to the Passage of the First Amendment* (New York: Oxford University Press, 1986), p. 145; Marcus, *Early American Jewry,* vol. 2, pp. 516, 524–526.

60. James Logan quoted in Marcus, *Colonial American Jew,* vol. 3, p. 1126. For Smith see *PAJHS,* 6 (1897): 99; 46 (1956): 32–35; Morris, "Civil

Liberties," p. 416; Goodman, *American Overture*, pp. 110–111; Marcus, *Colonial American Jew*, vol. 1, pp. 409–410. For Maryland see Curry, *First Freedoms*, pp. 153, 157–158.

61. *Rivington's N-Y Gazetteer*, Sept. 8, 1774, in Marcus, *Colonial American Jew*, vol. 3., p. 1128; *Pennsylvania Evening Post*, Sept. 24, 1776, p. 476; Sept. 26, 1776, p. 479; Henry Melchoir Muhlenberg to ?, Oct. 2, 1776, in *Pennsylvania Magazine of History and Biography*, 22 (1898): 129–130; "The Constitution of Pennsylvania" (1776), in *Federal and State Constitutions*, ed. Thorpe, vol. 5, p. 3085; "The Constitution or Form of Government for the Commonwealth of Massachusetts" (1780), ibid., vol. 3, p. 1908; Isaac Backus, "A Door Opened to Liberty" (1783), in *Isaac Backus on Church, State and Calvinism: Pamphlets, 1754–1789*, ed. William G. McLoughlin (Cambridge, Mass.: Harvard University Press, 1968), p. 436.

62. Letters to *Charlestown Gazette*, Dec. 1, 3, 1778, in *Jews and the American Revolution: A Bicentennial Documentary*, ed. Jacob Rader Marcus (Cincinnati: American Jewish Archives, 1978), pp. 149–150.

63. Johannes Wollebius, *The Abridgement of Christian Divinitie*, trans. Alexander Ross (London: John Saywell, 1656), 2nd ed., pp. 24, 59, 231; Oren, *Joining the Club*, p. 4.

64. Egal Feldman, *Dual Destinies: The Jewish Encounter with Protestant America* (Chicago, Urbana: University of Illinois Press, 1990), pp. 25–29; William G. McLoughlin, *Modern Revivalism: Charles Grandison Finney to Billy Graham* (New York: Ronald Press, 1959), p. 8.

65. Jonathan Edwards, *Works of Jonathan Edwards,* ed. Stephen Stein (New Haven and London: Yale University Press, 1977), vol. 5, pp. 135, 140, 195–197, 218, 287, 292–293, 295–296, 333–334, 337, 410–411, and "Editor's Introduction," ibid., pp. 11–12, 17, 40, 47; "The Folly of Looking Back in Fleeing Out of Sodom" (1735) and "The Perpetuity and Change of the Sabbath" (n.d.), in *The Works of President Edwards* (New York: Burt Franklin, 1968), vol. 7, pp. 406, 501–519.

66. Edwards, "Notes on the Apocalypse," in *Works of Jonathan Edwards,* ed. Stein, vol. 5, pp. 218, 135, and cf. "Folly," p. 406.

67. Edwards, *The Great Christian Doctrine of Original Sin Defended* (1758), rpt. as *Original Sin*, ed. Clyde A. Holbrook (New Haven and London: Yale University Press, 1970), pp. 337, 296, cf. pp. 293–305, 335–343.

68. Ibid., p. 182.

69. "Sinners in the Hands of an Angry God" (1748), in *Jonathan Edwards: Representative Selections*, ed. Clarence H. Faust and Thomas H. Johnson (New York: American Books, 1935), p. 155; *The Journals of Henry Melchoir Muhlenberg*, ed. Theodore G. Tappert and John W. Doberstein (Philadelphia: Muhlenberg Press, 1942), Jan. 1747, vol. 1, pp. 125–126.

70. Stiles, "United States Elevated to Glory," pp. 401–403; Samuel Langdon, "Government Corrupted by Vice and Recovered by Righteousness" (1775), in *Pulpit of the American Revolution,* ed. Thornton, p. 239; Phillips Payson, "A Sermon Preached before the Honorable Council and the Honorable House of Representatives of the State of Massachusetts" (1778), ibid., p. 337; Isaac Backus, "A Short Description between the Bondwoman and the Free" (1756), in *Isaac Backus,* ed. McLoughlin, pp. 137, 144, 146–147, 149–150, 152–153, 156–157; "A Fish Caught in His Own Net" (1756), ibid., pp. 172, 181, 263, 274; "The Sovereign Decrees of God" (1773), ibid., p. 301; "Government and Liberty Described" (1778), ibid., p. 364; "Truth Is Great and Will Prevail" (1781), ibid., p. 402; "The Doctrine of Particular Election and Final Perseverance" (1789), ibid., p. 455; *Literary Diary of Ezra Stiles,* ed. Dexter, Sept. 1, 1770, vol. 1, p. 68.

71. David McClure quoted in "Lancaster in 1772," in *Papers Read before the Lancaster County Historical Society,* 5 (1901): 109; Marcus, *Colonial American Jew,* vol. 3, p. 1132.

72. *Literary Diary of Ezra Stiles,* ed. Dexter, May 31, 1770, vol. 1, pp. 53–54; Aug. 23, 1770, vol. 1, p. 65; March 21, 1777, vol. 2, p. 151; Kohut, *Ezra Stiles,* pp. 32–33.

73. Edwin Wolf 2d and Maxwell Whiteman, *The History of the Jews of Philadelphia from Colonial Times to the Age of Jackson* (Philadelphia: JPSA, 1957), p. 117; Marcus, *Colonial American Jew,* vol. 3, pp. 1226–1227, and *Early American Jewry,* vol. 2, pp. 125–128.

74. Andrew McKenzie to Joseph Miguel De St. Juan, June 7, 1753, in *Collections of the Connecticut Historical Society,* 16 (1916): 175; Marcus, *Colonial American Jew,* vol. 3, p. 1129; F. Tennent to Michael Gratz, Sept. 6, 1776, in *Documentary History,* ed. Schappes, p. 48; "Journal of James Kenny, 1761–1763," ed. John W. Jordan, *Pennsylvania Magazine of History and Biography,* 37 (1913): 33–34, 154.

75. *Philadelphia Gazette,* March 13, 1753, in *American Jewry,* ed. Marcus, p. 2.

76. Robert Rogers, *A Concise Account of North America* (London: J. Millan, 1769), pp. 59, 65–66, 191.

77. *New-York Weekly Journal,* May 8, 1749, p. 1; Marcus, *Colonial American Jew,* vol. 1, p. 316.

78. *PAJHS* 5 (1897): 202–203; Josephine Fisher, "Bennet Allen, Fighting Parson," *Maryland Historical Magazine,* 38 (1943): 320–322; 39 (1944): 49–50; Marcus, *Colonial American Jew,* vol. 3, p. 1216; "Journal of James Kenny," ed. Jordan, Dec. 24, 1761, 33.

79. Marcus, *Colonial American Jew,* vol. 1, pp. 496–499, and *American Jewry,* p. 294.

80. *The Statutes at Large: Being a Collection of All the Laws of Virginia, from the First Sessions of the Legislature in the Year 1619,* ed. William Waller Hening (1809; Philadelphia: Thomas DeSilver, 1823), vol. 3, pp. 298–299, 449–450; vol. 6, p. 359; Marcus, *Early American Jewry,* vol. 2, pp. 166–167; Myron Berman, *Richmond's Jewry: 1769–1976* (Charlottesville: University of Virginia Press, 1979), p. 35.

81. *The Colonial Records of the State of Georgia,* ed. Allen D. Candler (Atlanta: Franklin, 1904–1916), vol. 1, pp. 98–99, 149–153; vol. 2, p. 62; "Journal of the Transactions of the Trustees for Establishing the Colony of Georgia in America," Dec. 22, 1733, Jan. 5, 1734, in *Documentary History,* ed. Schappes, pp. 24–25; Malcolm Stern, "New Light on the Jewish Settlement of Savannah," in *Jewish Experience,* ed. Karp, vol. 1, pp. 74, 84–85; *PAJHS,* 1 (1893): 5–12; Marcus, *Colonial American Jew,* vol. 1, pp. 352–353, 356; vol. 3, p. 1126.

82. *New-York Weekly Journal,* May 16, 1743, p. 1; petitioners quoted in Goodman, *American Overture,* p. 197, cf. pp. 176–183, 196–197; *Colonial Records,* ed. Candler, vol. 17, p. 572; Marcus, *Early American Jewry,* vol. 2, pp. 345, 517, and *Colonial American Jew,* vol. 1, p. 471; vol. 2, p. 888; vol. 3, p. 1130.

83. Bertram Wallace Korn, *The Early Years of New Orleans* (Waltham, Mass.: American Jewish Historical Society, 1969), pp. 3, 6–8, 29–33; Marcus, *Colonial American Jew,* vol. 1, pp. 370–374.

4.   Progress and Problems in the Young Republic

1. Denis Diderot, "Philosophic Thoughts" (1746), in *Diderot's Philosophical Works,* ed. Margaret Jourdain (1916; New York: Burt Franklin, 1972), p. 49, and "Rameau's Nephew" (1774), in *Diderot: Interpeter of Nature* (New York: International Publishers, 1963), pp. 296–298, 320–321.

2. Paul Henry Thiery d'Holbach, *Good Sense; or, Natural Ideas Opposed to Supernatural* (1772; New York: Wright and Owen, 1831), pp. 77, 105, and *Superstition in All Ages* (1762; New York: Truth Seeker, 1950), pp. 123–124, 171, 216, 273–274, 291–296, 319–324, 329, quotes pp. 274, 32, and *Ecce Homo; or, A Critical Enquiry, Into the History of Jesus Christ; Being Rational History of the Gospels* (1770; London: D. I. Eaton, 1813), pp. 23–29. Voltaire, *The Philosophy of History* (1766; New York: Philosophical Library, 1965), pp. 17–18, 115, 131, 145, 158, 163–165, 172–203, 206–207, 215–216, 218–219, 225–228, 233, 242, and *The Philosophical Dictionary, The Works of Voltaire,* ed. John Morley (1764; Akron: Werner, 1905), vol. 5, p. 50; vol. 10, pp. 264, 266, 278, 280–286, 292–294, 313; vol. 38, p. 161. For the French Enlightenment and the Jews: Arthur Hertzberg, *The French Enlightenment and the Jews* (New York: Columbia University Press, 1968), pp. 280–286, 309–312; Léon Poliakov,

*The History of Anti-Semitism* (New York: Vanguard Press, 1964–1974), vol. 3, pp. 88–99, 108–115; Jacob Katz, *From Prejudice to Destruction: Anti-Semitism, 1700–1933* (Cambridge, Mass.: Harvard University Press, 1980), pp. 33–47, and *Out of the Ghetto: The Social Background of Jewish Emancipation, 1770–1870* (Cambridge, Mass.: Harvard University Press, 1973), pp. 80–103; Charles C. Lehrmann, *The Jewish Element in French Literature* (Rutherford, Teaneck, Madison, N.J.: Fairleigh Dickinson University Press, 1971), pp. 116–128.

3. Immanuel Kant, *Political Writings*, ed. Hans Reiss (Cambridge: Cambridge University Press, 1960), p. 177, and *Religion within the Limits of Reason Alone* (1792–1797; Chicago and London: Open Court, 1934), pp. 116–118, 155; Kant to K. L. Reinhold, March 28, 1794, in *Philosophical Correspondence*, ed. Arnulf Zweig (Chicago: University of Chicago Press, 1967), p. 212; Paul Lawrence Rose, *Revolutionary Antisemitism in Germany from Kant to Wagner* (Princeton: Princeton University Press, 1990), pp. 93–109; Emil L. Fackenheim, *Encounters between Judaism and Modern Philosophy* (New York: Basic Books, 1973), pp. 43–77, 89, 96, 164–165; Poliakov, *History of Anti-Semitism*, vol. 3, pp. 59–69, 175–189; Katz, *Out of the Ghetto*, pp. 80–103; Alfred D. Low, *Jews in the Eyes of the Germans from the Enlightenment to Imperial Germany* (Philadelphia: Institute for the Study of Human Issues, 1979), pp. 35–100; Nathan Rotenstreich, *The Recurring Pattern: Studies in Anti-Judaism in Modern Thought* (London: Eidenfeld and Nicholson, 1963), pp. 23–47.

4. Fackenheim, *Encounters*, p. 88.

5. Voltaire, *Philosophical Dictionary*, vol. 10, pp. 288–290; Rousseau quoted in Lester G. Crocker, *Jean Jacques Rousseau* (New York: Macmillan, 1968, 1973), vol. 2, p. 151; for Rousseau's view of Christianity: Rousseau, *Emile* (1762; London: J. M. Dent and Sons; New York: E. P. Dutton, 1948), pp. 260–261, 267–268, 279; Stephen J. Gendzier, "Diderot and the Jews," *Diderot Studies,* 16 (1973): 39–54; Kant, *Political Writings*, p. 108; Kant to Moses Mendelssohn, Aug. 16, 1783, in *Philosophical Correspondence*, p. 108; Harold Fisch, *The Dual Image: The Figure of the Jew in English and American Literature* (New York: KTAV, 1971), pp. 44–50; Edgar Rosenberg, *From Shylock to Svengali: Jewish Stereotypes in English Fiction* (Stanford: Stanford University Press, 1960), pp. 38–70; Sigmund Altman, *The Comic Image of the Jew: Explorations of a Pop Culture* (Rutherford, Madison, Teaneck, N.J.: Fairleigh Dickinson University Press, 1971), pp. 173–177; Montague Frank Modder, *The Jew in the Literature of England to the End of the Nineteenth Century* (Philadelphia: Jewish Publication Society of America [hereafter JPSA], 1939), pp. 121–122, 127–130; George K. Anderson, *The Legend of the Wandering Jew* (Providence: Brown University Press, 1965), pp. 128–160.

6. Low, *Jews in the Eyes of the Germans*, pp. 18–22, 104–108; Katz, *Prejudice to Destruction*, pp. 2, 52–54; Poliakov, *History of Anti-Semitism*, vol. 3, pp. 214–215, 219–228; Erich Kahler, *The Jews among the Nations* (New

York: Frederick Ungar, 1967), pp. 75–83; Zosa Szajkowski, *Jews and the French Revolutions of 1789, 1830, and 1848* (New York: KTAV, 1970), pp. 398–412, 920–924; Simon Schwarzfuchs, *Napoleon, the Jews, and the Sanhedrin* (London: Routledge and Kegan Paul, 1979), pp. 6–45, 124–267; Rose, *Revolutionary Antisemitism,* pp. 70, 83–87.

7. Schwarzfuchs, *Napoleon,* pp. 6–7, 16–17, 27–28; Hertzberg, *French Enlightenment,* pp. 1–2, 8–9, 238, quote p. 360; Hannah Arendt, *The Origins of Totalitarianism* (1958; New York: Meridian, 1972), pp. 11–12, 56–62; Szajkowski, *Jews and the French Revolutions,* pp. 382–384, 388–413; Poliakov, *History of Anti-Semitism,* vol. 3, pp. 214, 219–220, 226.

8. Rose, *Revolutionary Antisemitism,* pp. 57–58, 70–71, 97–127, 131–132; Julius Carlebach, *Karl Marx and the Radical Critique of Judaism* (London: Routledge and Kegan Paul, 1979), pp. 60, 77, 84, 88–90, 107–109; Shmuel Almog, "Nationalism and Antisemitism in Modern Europe: 1815–1845," in *Antisemitism through the Ages,* ed. Almog (Oxford: Pergamon Press, 1990), pp. 13–16; Kahler, *Jews among the Nations,* p. 83; Arendt, *Totalitarianism,* pp. 29–35, 45–50; Low, *Jews in the Eyes of the Germans,* pp. 216–217, 220–221, 244–250.

9. Charles Dickens, *Oliver Twist* (Oxford: Clarendon Press, 1966), pp. 50–56, 75–82, 93–95, 100–105, 114–115, 118–129, 158–172, 228, 278–287, 353–355; Modder, *Jew in the Literature of England,* pp. 99–102, 120–121; Rosenberg, *Shylock to Svengali,* pp. 37–38, 88; Lehrmann, *Jewish Element,* pp. 147–153, 158–161; Robert F. Byrnes, *Anti-Semitism in Modern France: The Prologue to the Dreyfus Affair* (New York: Howard Fertig, 1969), vol. 1, pp. 104–110; Rose, *Revolutionary Antisemitism,* pp. 25–43, 97–109, 117–125, 131–132.

10. Charles Fourier, *The Utopian View of Charles Fourier,* ed. Jonathan Beecher and Richard Bienvenu (London: Jonathan Cape, 1979), pp. 117, 122, 199, and *Selections from the Works of Fourier* (London: Swan Sonnenschein, 1901), p. 96; Szajkowski, *Jews and the French Revolutions,* pp. 1104–1107; Myriam Yardeni, *Anti-Jewish Mentalities in Early Modern Europe* (Lanham, Md., London, New York: University Press of America, 1990), pp. 271–281.

11. Schwarzfuchs, *Napoleon,* pp. 45–46, 49–53, 59, 61, 68, 80–88, 97–101, 125, 127, 141–142, 183–184; Poliakov, *History of Anti-Semitism,* vol. 3, pp. 228–231, 278–287; Norman Cohn, *Warrant for Genocide: The Myth of the Jewish World-Conspiracy and the Protocols of the Elders of Zion* (New York: Harper and Row, 1967), pp. 27–31; Low, *Jews in the Eyes of the Germans,* pp. 223–224.

12. Low, *Jews in the Eyes of the Germans,* pp. 87–92, 170–184, 200–201, 223–224; Katz, *Out of the Ghetto,* pp. 193–208, and *Prejudice to Destruction,* pp. 54–62, 76–88, 149–158; Poliakov, *History of Anti-Semitism,* vol. 3, pp. 233, 240–244, 393–397; Arendt, *Totalitarianism,* pp. 29–35, 66–67;

Almog, "Nationalism and Antisemitism," pp. 6–32, 10–16; Rose, *Revolutionary Antisemitism*, pp. 97–109, 117–125, 131–132; Carlebach, *Karl Marx*, pp. 60–64, 77, 84, 88–90, 107–109.

13. *On Christianity: Early Theological Writings by Friedrich Hegel*, ed. T. M. Knox and Richard Kroner (Gloucester, Mass.: Peter Smith, 1970), pp. 67–70, 78–79, 98–99, 139–140, 177–181, 188–191, 194–196, 198–200, 202, 208, 253, 256, 265, 268–269, 281–283, 285, 298, and *Hegel's Philosophy of Right*, ed. T. M. Knox (Oxford: Clarendon Press, 1964), pp. 184, 242; Johann Gottlieb Fichte, *Attempt at a Critique of All Revelation* (1798; Cambridge: Cambridge University Press, 1978), p. 142n; Robert Adamson, *Fichte* (Edinburgh, London: William Blackwood and Son, 1881), p. 39n.

14. Poliakov, *History of Anti-Semitism*, vol. 3, pp. 240–244, 302–305; Katz, *Prejudice to Destruction*, pp. 97–104; Arendt, *Totalitarianism*, pp. 29–35; Szajkowski, *Jews and the French Revolutions*, pp. 1028–1032; Almog, "Nationalism and Antisemitism," pp. 8, 15, 17–23; Rose, *Revolutionary Antisemitism*, pp. 85–87, 114, 126–132; Carlebach, *Karl Marx*, pp. 24, 58–59, 85–89, 103.

15. Cecil Roth, *A History of the Jews in England* (Oxford: Clarendon Press, 1941), pp. 204–265; W. D. Rubinstein, *The Left, the Right and the Jews* (London: Croom Helm, 1982), pp. 13, 182; Colin Holmes, *Anti-Semitism in British Society, 1876–1932* (London: Edward Arnold, 1979), p. 8; Stephen Wilson, *Ideology and Experience: Antisemitism in France at the Time of the Dreyfus Affair* (London and Toronto: Associated Universities Press; Rutherford, N.J.: Fairleigh Dickinson University Press, 1982), p. 169; Katz, *Prejudice to Destruction*, pp. 195–202, 210–211, 223, 231–232, 236; Low, *Jews in the Eyes of the Germans*, pp. 216–217, 223–224, 244–250; Poliakov, *History of Anti-Semitism*, vol. 3, pp. 230–231, 391–392; Paul W. Massing, *Rehearsal for Destruction: A Study of Political Anti-Semitism in Imperial Germany* (New York: Harper and Bros., 1949), pp. 3–4; Waldemar Gurian, "Antisemitism in Modern Germany," *Essays on Antisemitism*, ed. Koppel S. Pinson (New York: Conference on Jewish Relations, 1946), 222.

16. Byrnes, *Anti-Semitism in Modern France*, vol. 1., pp. 86–87; James Parkes, *The Emergence of the Jewish Problem, 1878–1939* (1946; Westport, Conn.: Greenwood Press, 1970), pp. 94–103, 128–129; Raphael Mahler, "Antisemitism in Poland," in *Essays on Antisemitism*, ed. Pinson, pp. 146–148, 151–152, 157–161; Celia S. Heller, *On the Edge of Destruction: Jews of Poland between the Two World Wars* (New York: Columbia University Press, 1977), pp. 15–17, 20–21, 26–27; Salo W. Baron, *The Russian Jew under Tsars and Soviets* (New York and London: Macmillan, 1964), pp. 15, 19–20.

17. Parkes, *Jewish Problem*, pp. 212–213; James Parkes, *Antisemitism* (Chicago: Quadrangle Books, 1964), pp. 38–39; Baron, *Russian Jew*, pp. 19–21, 29–33, 35–41; *Jews in Soviet Russia since 1917*, ed. Lionel Kochan (Oxford and

London: Oxford University Press, 1978), p. 17; Mark Vishniak, "Antisemitism in Tsarist Russia," in *Essays on Antisemitism,* ed. Pinson, pp. 121–127.

18. Arthur Goren, "Jews," in *Harvard Encyclopedia of American Ethnic Groups* (Cambridge, Mass.: Harvard University Press, 1981), p. 571; Jacob Rader Marcus, *Early American Jewry* (Philadelphia: JPSA, 1951, 1953), vol. 1, p. 3; vol. 2, p. 393; Dov Weinryb, "A Hundred Years of Jewish Immigration to America," *American Jewish Year Book,* vol. 5, ed. Menachem Ribalow (New York: Histadruth Ivrit, 1940), pp. 327–328; Jacob Lestschinsky, "The Economic Development of American Jews," ibid., vol. 7 (1942), p. 503; Ira Rosenwaike, "An Estimate and Analysis of the Jewish Population of the United States in 1790," *Publications of the American Jewish Historical Society* (hereafter *PAJHS*), 50 (Sept. 1960): 23, 30, and "The Jewish Population of the United States as Estimated in the Census of 1820," *American Jewish Historical Quarterly* (formerly PAJHS), 53 (Dec. 1963): 132, 148.

19. Howard Mumford Jones, *America and French Culture: 1750–1848* (1927; Westport, Conn.: Greenwood Press, 1973), pp. 366–369, 376–387, 400–407, 530–554; Louis Hartz, *The Liberal Tradition in America* (New York: Harcourt, Brace and World, 1955), pp. 3–86.

20. *The Federal and State Constitutions, Colonial Charters, and Other Organic Laws of the States, Territories, and Colonies Now or Heretofore Forming The United States of America,* ed. Francis N. Thorpe (Washington, D.C.: U.S. Government Printing Office, 1909), vol. 1, pp. 29, 97, 269, 271–272, 537, 544–545, 566. 568, 583; vol. 2, pp. 651, 664, 668–670, 779, 784, 786, 789, 800–801, 981, 1058; vol. 3, pp. 1274, 1277, 1286, 1382–1383, 1388, 1647, 1689–1690, 1700, 1705, 1889–1890, 1908, 1912–1914, 1918; vol. 4, pp. 1932, 1939–1940, 2035–2036, 2043, 2049, 2163, 2454, 2461–2463, 2471–2472, 2477–2479, 2481; vol. 5, pp. 2597–2598, 2630–2632, 2636–2638, 2641–2642, 2648, 2788, 2793, 2799, 2910, 3082, 3085, 3100, 3113; vol. 6, pp. 3250, 3252, 3255, 3257–3264, 3420, 3422, 3426–3427, 3437, 3536, 3542, 3547, 3739–3740, 3743, 3752, 3757, 3762, 3767, 3768–3771; vol. 7, pp. 3814, 3816, 3824–3825; Thomas J. Curry, *The First Freedoms: Church and State in America and the Passage of the First Amendment* (New York: Oxford University Press, 1986), pp. 152, 157, 221; Stanley F. Chyet, "The Political Rights of the Jews in the United States: 1776–1840," in *Critical Studies in American Jewish History: Selected Articles from American Jewish Archives,* ed. Jacob R. Marcus (New York: KTAV, 1971), vol. 2, pp. 35, 39–69; Charles R. Erdman, *The New Jersey Constitution of 1776* (Princeton: Princeton University Press, 1929), p. 54; Reba Carolyn Strickland, *Religion and the State in Georgia in the Eighteenth Century* (1939; New York: AMS Press, 1967), pp. 163–164, 177; Charles F. James, *Documentary History of the Struggle for Religious Liberty in Virginia* (Lynchburg, Va.: J. P. Bell, 1900), pp. 129–141, 263; Thomas Jefferson, "Autobiogra-

phy" (1821), in *The Writings of Thomas Jefferson,* ed. Albert E. Bergh (Washington, D.C.: Thomas Jefferson Memorial Association of the United States, 1903), vol. 1, pp. 166–167; James Madison, "To the Honorable The General Assembly of the Commonwealth of Virginia: A Memorial and Remonstrance," June 20, 1785, in *The Papers of James Madison,* ed. Robert A. Rutland et al. (Chicago and London: University of Chicago Press, 1962–), vol. 8, pp. 298–304.

21. Anson Phelps Stokes, *Church and State in the United States* (New York: Harper and Row, 1950), vol. 1, pp. 858–859; Morton Borden, *Jews, Turks and Infidels* (Chapel Hill: University of North Carolina Press, 1984), pp. 28, 141; Jackson T. Main, *The Anti-Federalists: Critics of the Constitution, 1781–1788,* (Chapel Hill: University of North Carolina Press, 1969), p. 159; *The Jews of the United States, 1790–1840: A Documentary History,* ed. Joseph L. Blau and Salo W. Baron (New York: Columbia University Press; Philadelphia: JPSA, 1963), vol. 1, p. 3.

22. *American Jewry: Documents Eighteenth Century,* ed. Jacob Rader Marcus (Cincinnati: Hebrew Union College Press, 1959), p. 73; Nathaniel Weyl, *The Jew in American Politics* (New Rochelle, N.Y.: Arlington House, 1968), p. 50; Myron Berman, *Richmond's Jewry, 1769–1976* (Charlottesville: University of Virginia Press, 1979), pp. 3, 10, 72, 90–91; Herbert T. Ezekiel and Gaston Lichtenstein, *The History of the Jews of Richmond from 1769 to 1917* (Richmond: Herbert T. Ezekiel, 1917), pp. 41, 61–63; Leon Huhner, *Jews in America in Colonial and Revolutionary Times* (New York: Gertz Bros., 1959), pp. 136–137, 185–186, 215–217, 225, 227; Henry Samuel Morais, *The Jews of Philadelphia* (Philadelphia: Levytype, 1894), p. 393; Barnett A. Elzas, *The Jews of South Carolina: From the Earliest Times to the Present Day* (1905; Spartanburg, S.C.: Reprint Co., 1972), pp. 127–128, 140–142, 189, 192–194, 202, 205, 243; Charles Reznikoff, *The Jews of Charleston: A History of an American Jewish Community* (Philadelphia: JPSA, 1950), pp. 103–104, 285–286n.

23. *American Jewry,* ed. Marcus, pp. 7, 30–32, 55; Berman, *Richmond's Jewry,* pp. 18, 73, 84, 123; Ezekiel and Lichtenstein, *History of the Jews of Richmond,* pp. 19, 21, 27–28, 35–36, 39–40; Huhner, *Jews in America,* pp. 154, 183, 225, 227; Albert Ehrenfield, "A Chronicle of Boston Jewry: From the Colonial Settlement to 1900" (manuscript, 1963; a copy is in the library of the University of Illinois, Champaign-Urbana), pp. 237, 252–253, 726, 729; Dan A. Oren, *Joining the Club: A History of Jews at Yale* (New Haven and London: Yale University Press, 1985), p. 6; *Jews of the United States,* ed. Blau and Baron, vol. 2, pp. 455–456; *Jewish Life in Philadelphia: 1830–1940,* ed. Murray Friedman (Philadelphia: ISHI Publications, 1983), pp. 5, 291; Nathaniel Burt, *The Perennial Philadelphians: The Anatomy of a Ruling Class* (Boston, Toronto: Little, Brown, 1963), pp. 262, 565; E. Digby Baltzell, *Philadelphia Gentlemen: The Making of a National Upper Class* (New York: Free Press, 1958),

pp. 276–279; Reznikoff, *Jews of Charleston,* pp. 87, 94–96, 104–105; Elzas, *Jews of South Carolina,* pp. 180, 192, 196, 143; Morais, *Jews of Philadelphia,* pp. 33, 41, 272, 286–289, 341, 403, 417–419.

24. *Jews and the American Revolution: A Bicentennial Documentary,* ed. Jacob R. Marcus (Cincinnati: American Jewish Archives, 1975), p. 244; *Jewish Life in Philadelphia,* ed. Friedman, pp. 5, 292; Morais, *Jews of Philadelphia,* pp. 19–20; Benjamin Rush to Elias Boudinot, July 9, 1788, in Lyman H. Butterfield, ed., *The Letters of Benjamin Rush* (Princeton: Princeton University Press, 1951), vol. 1, p. 470; cf. Rush to ?, April 16, 1790, ibid., p. 556.

25. Jefferson, "Autobiography," pp. 66–67; *Papers of James Madison,* vol. 8, pp. 298–304; James, *Documentary History of the Struggle,* pp. 129–141.

26. "Jefferson's Reply to the Address of the Danbury Baptist Association" (1802), in *Jews of the United States,* ed. Blau and Baron, vol. 1, p. 11; Jefferson to Joseph Marx, July 8, 1820, and to Jacob De La Motta, Sept. 9, 1820, ibid., p. 13, and to Isaac Harby, Jan. 6, 1826, ibid., vol. 3, pp. 704–705, and to Mordecai Noah, May 28, 1818, in *The Jewish Experience in America,* ed. Albert J. Karp (New York: KTAV, 1969), vol. 1, pp. 359–360.

27. John Adams to F. A. Vanderkemp, Feb. 16, 1809, in *The Works of John Adams,* ed. Charles Francis Adams (Boston: Little, Brown, 1854), vol. 9, p. 609, and to Mordecai Noah, July 31, 1818, in *Jews of the United States,* ed. Blau and Baron, vol. 1, p. 12.

28. Madison, "To the Honorable General Assembly," in *Papers of James Madison,* vol. 8, pp. 298–304, and to Jacob De La Motta, Aug. 1820, in *Jews of the United States,* ed. Blau and Baron, vol. 1, p. 14; cf. to Mordecai Noah, May 15, 1818, in *Jewish Experience,* ed. Karp, vol. 1, p. 360.

29. Curry, *First Freedoms,* p. 145.

30. "George Washington to the Hebrew Congregation in Newport, Rhode Island" (1790), in *Jews and the American Revolution,* ed. Marcus, pp. 256–257; cf. "Washington's Reply to the Hebrew Congregations in the Cities of Philadelphia, New York, Charleston, and Richmond" (1790), in *Jews of the United States,* ed. Blau and Baron, vol. 1, p. 10; "Washington's Reply to the Hebrew Congregation of the City of Savannah" (1790), ibid., p. 11.

31. Rush to Boudinot, July 9, 1788, vol. 1, p. 470; Naphtali Phillips to James McAllister, Oct. 24, 1868, in "The Federal Parade of 1788," *American Jewish Archives,* 7 (Jan. 1, 1955): 65–67; Borden, *Jews, Turks,* p. 4–5.

32. Berman, *Richmond's Jewry,* p. 130; Henry Clay to Solomon Etting, July 16, 1832, in *Jews of the United States,* ed. Blau and Baron, vol. 1, pp. 58–59.

33. Huhner, *Jews in America,* pp. 120, 183; *Jewish Life in Philadelphia,* ed. Friedman, pp. 5, 292; Morais, *Jews of Philadelphia,* pp. 19–20; *Jews and the American Revolution,* ed. Marcus, p. 244; Hyman B. Grinstein, *The Rise of the Jewish Community of New York: 1654–1860* (Philadelphia: JPSA, 1945), p. 176; Louis Harap, *The Image of the Jew in American Literature from Early Republic to*

*Mass Immigration* (Philadelphia: JPSA, 1974), p. 70; "A Protestant" (probably Rev. Charles Crawford), *Philadelphia Packet and Daily Advertiser,* Dec. 23, 1784, in *American Jewry,* ed. Marcus, pp. 136–137; Christopher Gadsden to David Lopez, 1802, in *Jews of the United States,* ed. Blau and Baron, vol. 3, p. 685, cf. Gadsden to Congregation Beth Elohim, Jan. 27, 1802, ibid., p. 684; John Henry Hobart (Episcopal Bishop of New York) to Congregation Shearith Israel, Sept. 24, 1823, ibid., p. 693; Edward Rutledge to Isaac Harby, March 17, 1827, ibid., p. 705.

34. Rosenwaike, "Estimate and Analysis," 28, 34, and "Jewish Population," pp. 136, 152; *Jews of the United States,* ed. Blau and Baron, vol. 2, pp. 455–456.

35. Memorial of the Trustees of the Congregation Shearith Israel to the New York State Legislature, drawn up by DeWitt Clinton (1811), in *Jews of the United States,* ed. Blau and Baron, vol. 2, pp. 445–446; cf. *A Documentary History of the Jews in the United States: 1654–1875,* ed. Morris U. Schappes (New York: Schocken Books, 1971), pp. 126–127. See also *Jews of the United States,* vol. 2, pp. 443–446; Jacob Hartstein, "The Polonies Talmud Torah of New York," in *Jewish Experience,* ed. Karp, vol. 2, pp. 45–63.

36. Rosenwaike, "Estimate and Analysis," 32, 35, and "Jewish Population," p. 152; Reznikoff, *Jews of Charleston,* p. 238, quotes pp. 56, 111.

37. *New York Commercial Advertiser,* Oct. 16, 1822, in *Jewish Experience,* ed. Karp, vol. 2, p. 145; editorial in the *Virginia (Constitutional) Whig,* 1829, quoted in Ezekiel and Lichtenstein, *Jews of Richmond,* pp. 55–56.

38. Editorials from the *Maryland Censor,* the *Philadelphia Freeman's Journal,* and the *Charleston Southern Patriot,* in *Jews of the United States,* ed. Blau and Baron, vol. 1, pp. 41–42, 49.

39. Hannah Adams, *The History of the Jews from the Destruction of Jerusalem to the Nineteenth Century* (Boston: John Eliot, Jr., 1812), vol. 1, pp. iii–iv, 22–30, 41–42, 206–209, 218–219, 223–224, 229–235, 269–289, 294, 297–304, 308, 315–316, 320–321, 326–334, 338, 348–352; vol. 2, pp. 47–48 63, 66, 88, 110–111, 142–144, 146, 149, 162–163, 169–170, 174–175, 178–183, 210, 214, 295, 318–321, 326–330; for biographical information on Adams see Harap, *Jew in American Literature,* pp. 27–28. S. G. Goodrich, *The Fourth Reader: For the Use of Schools* (Louisville: Morton and Griswold, 1839), p. 143; for other favorable references in schoolbooks published between 1780 and 1830 see Ruth Miller Elson, *Guardians of Tradition: American Schoolbooks of the Nineteenth Century* (Lincoln: University of Nebraska Press, 1964), pp. 59–60.

40. For favorable portrayals of Jews in German literature and theater see Poliakov, *History of Anti-Semitism,* vol. 3, pp. 162–164, 166–171; Low, *Jews in the Eyes of the Germans,* pp. 50, 87–92, 170–171. For French literature and theater see Moses Debré, *The Image of the Jew in French Literature from 1800 to*

*1908* (New York: KTAV, 1970), pp. 25, 45–85. For English literature and theater see Rosenberg, *Shylock to Svengali,* pp. 37–38; Fisch, *Dual Image,* pp. 44–50, 57–58, 72–75; Modder, *Jew in the Literature of England,* pp. 83–95, 102–104, 108–155. For the European and British stage see Ellen Schiff, *From Stereotype to Metaphor: The Jew in Contemporary Drama* (Albany: State University of New York Press, 1982), pp. 16–17.

41. Walter Scott, *Ivanhoe: A Romance* (New York: Dodd, Mead, 1928), pp. 68–76, 85–86, 88–89, 120, 131–132, 134, 230–232, 252–260, 294–300, 361, 417, 441–443, 499.

42. Schiff, *Stereotype to Metaphor,* p. 16; Toby Lelyveld, *Shylock on the Stage* (London: Routledge and Kegan Paul, 1961), pp. 39–55, 63–65; Charles H. Shattuck, *Shakespeare on the American Stage: From the Hallams to Edwin Booth* (Washington, D.C.: Folger Shakespeare Library, 1976), pp. 2–3, 34–35; Thomas Gould, *The Tragedian: An Essay on the Histrionic Genius of Junius Brutus Booth* (New York: Hurd and Houghton, 1868), pp. 73–81; Lisbeth Jane Roman, "The Acting Style and Career of Junius Brutus Booth" (Ph.D. diss., University of Illinois, 1969), pp. 3, 138–142.

43. Philip Freneau, "Robert Slender Argueth with the Parson," *Philadelphia Aurora,* Oct. 9, 1800, in *The Prose of Philip Freneau,* ed. Philip M. Marsh (New Brunswick, N.J.: Scarecrow Press, 1955), p. 435.

44. Charles Brockden Brown, *Arthur Mervyn; or, Memoirs of the Year 1793* (1799–1800; Philadelphia: J. B. Lippincott, 1859), vol. 2, pp. 167, 184–186, 204, quotes pp. 186, 204.

45. William Ware, *Letters from Palmyra: By Lucius Manlius Piso to His Friend Marcus Cartius at Rome* (1837; London: Richard Bentley, 1838; pub. in 1843 as *Zenobia; or, The Fall of Palmyra*), vol. 1, pp. 9, 13, 15, 62, 75, 87–91, quote p. 15; vol. 2, pp. 59–61, and *Aurelian; or, Rome in the Third Century* (New York: James Miller, 1866; first pub. in 1838 as *Probus; or, Rome in the Third Century*), vol. 1, pp. 218–219, 225–230; vol. 2, pp. 215–216, 235–240.

46. William Gilmore Simms, *Pelayo: A Story of the Goth* (New York: Harper and Bros., 1838), vol. 1, pp. 16–17, 82–86, 93–94, 97–98, 101, 106, 136–137, 179–180, 193; vol. 2, pp. 30, 34, 196–197, 202, 238–281.

47. Theodore Sedgwick Fay, *Sydney Clifton; or, Vicissitudes in Both Hemispheres* (New York: Harper and Bros., 1839), vol. 1, pp. 140–141; Harap, *Jew in American Literature,* pp. 20–45.

48. Rush to Julia Rush, June 27, 1787, and to Elhanan Winchester, May 11, 1791, in *Letters of Benjamin Rush,* ed. Butterfield, vol. 1, pp. 431, 581–582.

49. Jefferson to Rush, April 21, 1803, "Syllabus of An Estimation of the Merit of the Doctrines of Jesus, Compared with Those of Others," in *The Writings of Thomas Jefferson,* ed. Paul Leicester Ford (New York: G. P. Putnam's Sons, 1892–1899), vol. 8, p. 226, and to Joseph B. Priestly, April 9, 1803, ibid.,

p. 229n. For other examples of Jefferson's views see Jefferson to John Adams, Nov. 13, 1813, in *Writings of Thomas Jefferson,* ed. Bergh, vol. 13, pp. 388–389, and to Ezra Stiles, June 15, 1819, ibid., vol. 15, p. 203.

50. Jonathan Elliot, *The Debates in the Several State Conventions on the Adoption of the Federal Constitution* (1836–1859; Philadelphia: J. B. Lippincott, 1891), vol. 4, p. 199; "Address by a Watchman," (1786), in *The Complete Anti-Federalist,* ed. Herbert J. Storing (Chicago: University of Chicago Press, 1981), vol. 4, p. 232.

51. "A Journal of the Proceedings of the Convention of the State of New Hampshire Which Adopted the Federal Constitution" (1788), in *Provincial and State Papers: Documents and Records Relating to New Hampshire at Different Periods,* ed. Nathaniel Bouton (Concord, N.H.: Edward A. Jenks, 1867–1877), vol. 10, pp. 2–7, 17–18; "A Journal of the Proceedings of the Convention of the State of New Hampshire for Revising the Constitution of Said State" (1791), ibid., pp. 46, 58–62; Jeremy Belknap, *The History of New Hampshire* (1812; New York: Johnson Reprint, 1970), vol. 2, pp. 202–203, 245; Borden, *Jews, Turks,* pp. 15–19; Curry, *First Freedoms,* p. 221.

52. *Journal of Debates and Proceedings in the Convention of Delegates Chosen to Revise the Constitution of Massacusetts: Begun and Holden at Boston, November 15, 1820, and continued by Adjournment to January 19, 1821* (Boston: Boston Daily Advertiser, 1853), pp. 169–171, 187, 205–207, 613–614, 623–624, 633; quotes pp. 170, 206.

53. Isaac M. Fein, *The Making of a Jewish Community: The History of Baltimore Jewry from 1773 to 1920* (Philadelphia: JPSA, 1971), pp. 25–34; *Jews of the United States,* ed. Blau and Baron, vol. 1, pp. 33–40. The best account is Edward Eitches, "Maryland's Jew Bill," *American Jewish Historical Quarterly,* 60 (March 1971): 258–279.

54. Stokes, *Church and State,* vol. 3, p. 87; Eitches, "Jew Bill," 260, 270, 273–275, 277; *Cornerstones of Religious Freedom in America* (Boston: Beacon Press, 1950), ed. Joseph L. Blau, p. 90; Fein, *Making of a Jewish Community,* pp. 32–36; *Jews of the United States,* ed. Blau and Baron, vol. 1, pp. 41–43, 48–49.

55. Eitches, "Jew Bill," 277.

56. Ibid., 277–278; *Jews of the United States,* ed. Blau and Baron, vol. 1, pp. 52–55; Fein, *Making of a Jewish Community,* pp. 43–44.

57. *Journal of the Convention Called By the Freemen of North-Carolina to Amend the Constitution* (Raleigh: J. Gales and Son, 1835), pp. 47, 49–51.

58. James Rivington, "Preface to the American Edition," Henry James Pye, *The Democrat; or, Intrigues and Adventures of Jean Le Noir* (New York: James Rivington, 1795), vol. 1, pp. v–viii, quote p. vii; Schappes, "Anti-Semitism and Reaction, 1795–1800," *Jewish Experience,* ed. Karp, vol. 1, pp. 366–367.

59. *New York Journal,* Dec. 19, 1795, cited in Eugene Perry Link, *Democratic-Republican Societies, 1790–1800* (New York: Columbia University Press,

1942), p. 51n; Charles Nisbet to Charles Wallace, Dec. 11, 1797, in Schappes, "Anti-Semitism and Reaction," p. 387n; cf. Bertram Wallace Korn, *American Jewry and the Civil War* (Philadelphia: JPSA, 1951), p. 156; for the *Tree of Liberty,* Schappes, "Anti-Semitism and Reaction," pp. 368–369; Korn, *American Jewry,* vol. 1, p. 157.

60. Schappes, "Anti-Semitism and Reaction," pp. 386–387.

61. "The Letters of Joseph Dennie: 1768–1812," ed. Laura Green Pedder, *University of Maine Studies* (Orono: University of Maine Press, 1936), 2nd ser., no. 36, pp. xiii–xvi, 127–128, 168; quotes pp. 182, 185–186, 171.

62. John Quincy Adams, Diary, Dec. 30, 1794, in *Memoirs of John Quincy Adams,* ed. Charles Francis Adams (Philadelphia: J. B. Lippincott, 1874–1877), vol. 1, p. 58, and *Letters on Silesia* (London: J. Budd, 1804), p. 6.

63. David Hackett Fischer, *The Revolution of American Conservatism: The Federalist Party in the Era of Jeffersonian Democracy* (New York: Harper and Row, 1965), p. 164, cf. pp. 165, 225.

64. Ibid., pp. 164–165, 225; Link, *Democratic-Republican Societies,* p. 51n; Schappes, "Anti-Semitism and Reaction," pp. 369–370.

65. Quotes from Alfred D. Young, *The Democratic-Republicans of New York: The Origins, 1763–1797* (Chapel Hill: University of North Carolina Press, 1967), pp. 179, 185, 335; John Malcolm to Horatio Gates, March 24, 1790, in *Documentary History,* ed. Schappes, p. 73.

66. Nehemiah Dodge, *Discourse Delivered . . . In Honor of the Late Presidential Election of Thomas Jefferson* (Norwich, Conn.: Sterry and Foster, 1805), pp. 5–6, 10, 12, 25–26.

67. "Cursory Remarks on Men and Manners in Georgia" (1784), in Max J. Kohler, "Phases in the History of Religious Liberty in America, with Particular Reference to the Jews—II," *PAJHS,* 13 (1905): 24–28.

68. Fisher was responded to in "A Jew Broker" (probably written by Haym Solomon), *Independent Gazetteer* (Philadelphia), March 13, 1784, in *American Jewry,* ed. Marcus, pp. 41–46.

69. [Pascal Strong], "Extracts from Strong's Sermon on the Plague," *Evangelical Witness,* vol. 1 (Feb. 1823): 311–312; Jonathan D. Sarna, *Jacksonian Jew: The Two Worlds of Mordecai Noah* (New York and London: Holmes and Meier, 1981), quotes pp. 13, 44–46; Harap, *Jew in American Literature,* pp. 264–266.

70. Sarna, *Jacksonian Jew,* pp. 53–54, 78, 99, 119, 178, 62n; *New York Herald,* Nov. 18, 1837, p. 2; *Washington Globe,* Oct. 2, 1833, p. 2; Oct. 3, 1833, p. 2.

71. Abram Kanof, "Uriah Phillips Levy: The Story of a Pugnacious Commodore," in *Jewish Experience,* ed. Karp, vol. 2, pp. 200–227; Robert St. John, *Jews, Justice and Judaism: A Narrative of the Role Played by the Bible People in Shaping American History* (Garden City, N.Y.: Doubleday, 1969), pp. 138–142.

72. An 1834 carciature quoted in Rudolf Glanz, *The Jew in the Old American Folklore* (New York: Waldon, 1961), p. 196n. "How to Make the Mare Go" (1838), in *A Bicentennial Festschrift for Jacob Rader Marcus,* ed. Bertram Wallace Korn (New York: KTAV; Waltham, MA: American Jewish Historical Society, 1976), p. 30.

73. *The Letters of William Lloyd Garrison,* ed. Walter M. Merrill and Louis Ruchames (Cambridge, Mass.: Harvard University Press, 1971–1981): Garrison to Samuel J. May, Sept. 23, 1836, vol. 2, p. 178, to the editor of the (New England) *Spectator,* Oct. 20, 1837, p. 316, and other slurs in 1837, pp. 247, 281; for the comment of the editors, p. 320n.

74. Leon Huhner, "The Struggle for Religious Liberty in North Carolina, with Special Reference to the Jews," *PAJHS,* 16 (1907): 46–48. James Monroe to Mordecai Noah, April 25, 1815, in *Jews of the United States,* ed. Blau and Baron, vol. 2, p. 318; Sarna, *Jacksonian Jew,* pp. 25–28.

75. William C. C. Claiborne to James Madison, Feb. 13, 1804, in *Official Letterbooks of W. C. C. Claiborne,* ed. Dunbar Rowland (Jackson, Mich.: State Department of Archives and History, 1917), vol. 1, pp. 372–373; Bertram Wallace Korn, *The Early Jews of New Orleans* (Waltham, Mass.: American Jewish Historical Society, 1969), pp. 70–71.

76. Several sabbath laws and court decisions from the 1790s to the 1830s are in *Documentary History,* ed. Blau and Baron, vol. 1, pp. 22–27. For fuller discussion see Borden, *Jews, Turks,* p. 111–117, 125; James R. Rohrer, "Southern Mails and the Church-State Theme in Jacksonian America," *Journal of the Early Republic,* 7 (Spring 1987): 53–74; Leland Winfield Meyer, *The Life and Times of Colonel Richard M. Johnson of Kentucky* (New York: Columbia University Press, 1932), pp. 256–263.

77. William Wetmore Story, *The Life and Letters of Joseph Story* (Boston: Charles C. Little and James Brown, 1851), vol. 2, p. 8; Joseph Story, *Commentaries on the Constitution of the United States* (1833; Durham, N.C.: Academic Press, 1987), vol. 3, pp. 699, 701.

78. James Kent, opinion in *People v. Ruggles* (1811), quoted in John Theodore Horton, *James Kent: A Study in Conservatism, 1763–1847* (New York and London: D. Appleton-Century, 1939), pp. 188–189, 191; Mark DeWolfe Howe, *The Garden and the Wilderness: Religion and Government in American Constitutional History* (Chicago and London: University of Chicago Press, 1965), p. 29.

79. For a discussion of the impact of Christian anti-Semitism upon American attitudes toward Jews see Michael N. Dobkowski, *The Tarnished Dream: The Basis of American Anti-Semitism* (Westport, Conn.: Greenwood Press, 1979), pp. 9–34.

80. Ezra Stiles Ely, "The Duty of Christian Freemen to Elect Christian Rulers" (1827), in *Church and State in American History,* ed. John F. Wilson (Englewood Cliffs, N.J.: D. C. Heath, 1965), p. 97.

81. "The Doctrine of Particular Election and Final Perseverance" (1789), in *Isaac Backus on Church, State and Calvinism: Pamphlets, 1754–1789*, ed. William G. McLoughlin (Cambridge, Mass.: Harvard University Press, 1968), p. 455.

82. "An Address to the Roman Catholics of the United States of America by a Catholic Clergyman" (1784), in *The John Carroll Papers*, ed. Thomas O'Brien Hanley (Notre Dame, Ind.: University of Notre Dame Press, 1976), vol. 1, p. 129, and "The First Diocesan Synod, Third Session, Nov. 8, 1791: Concerning the Most Holy Eucharist," ibid., p. 528.

83. John D. Marsh, *An Epitome of General Ecclesiastical History* (1827; New York: A. S. Barnes, 1867), pp. 44–132, quotes are on pp. 123, 125, 131–132.

84. Ibid., pp. 134, 137.

85. Ibid., pp. 148, 163–164.

86. Ibid., pp. 165–166, 448.

87. Ibid., pp. 448–449.

88. Ibid., pp. 459–460.

89. On the Second Great Awakening and Finney's attitudes toward Jews see Egal Feldman, *Dual Destinies: The Jewish Encounter with Protestant America* (Chicago and Urbana: University of Illinois Press, 1990), pp. 60–63; Charles Grandison Finney, *Lectures on Revivals of Religion*, ed. William G. McLoughlin (1835; Cambridge, Mass.: Harvard University Press, 1960), pp, viii, xiv–xlii, lviii, quotes pp. 250–251.

90. These sentiments are expressed in the works of authors active in the movement and in the official reports of the organizations. Cf. Adams, *History of the Jews*, see pp. listed in note 39; Matthew A. Berk, *The History of the Jews from the Babylonian Captivity to the Present Time* (1842; Boston: Matthew A. Burk, 1849), pp. 5–9, 11–14, chs. 1–19; "Director's Report, 1823" of the ASCMJ, in *Jews of the United States*, ed. Blau and Baron, vol. 3, pp. 734–735.

91. *New-York Evening Post*, Nov. 5, 1822, p. 2; *Jews of the United States*, ed. Blau and Baron, vol. 3, pp. 714–757; Robert Baird, *Religion in America* (New York: Harper and Bros., 1856), p. 629; Ehrenfield, "Boston Jewry," pp. 588–590; Harap, *Jew in American Literature*, pp. 27–28.

92. Adams, *History of the Jews*, pp. 64–65.

93. Ibid., pp. 271, 320.

94. Ibid., pp. 326–332, quote p. 325.

95. Philip Milledoler, Presidential Address to the ASEJ, *Religious Intelligencer*, 1 (Jan. 25, 1817): 555–558.

96. "Directors Report, 1823," pp. 734–735.

97. John H. Livingston to Peter Wilson, ca. 1824, in *Jews of the United States*, ed. Blau and Baron, vol. 3, pp. 748–749.

98. J. Q. Adams, Diary, June 6, 1839, in *Memoirs*, vol. 10, p. 91.

99. Baird, *Religion in America*, pp. 308–315; Martin E. Marty, *Righteous Empire: The Protestant Experience in America* (New York: Dial Press, 1970), pp. 75–76.

100. *Union Questions; or, Questions on Select Portions of Scripture from the Old and New Testaments* (Philadelphia: American Sunday School Union, 1834), see cover.

101. Ibid., pp. 31, 91, 115, 117, 120, 122.

102. Harap, *Jew in American Literature,* pp. 147–148.

103. [Jarvis Gregg], *Elisama; or, The Captivity and Restoration of the Jews* (Philadelphia: American Sunday-School Union, 1835), pp. 29, 178.

104. Ibid., pp. 179–180.

105. Ibid., p. 288.

106. [Gregg], *Selumiel; or, A Visit to Jerusalem* (Philadelphia: American Sunday-School Union, 1833), p. 23.

107. Ibid., pp. 221, 125–126, 168.

108. Andrew Delbanco, *William Ellery Channing: An Essay on the Liberal Spirit in America* (Cambridge, Mass., and London: Harvard University Press, 1981), pp. 78–80; William E. Channing, "Sermon at the Ordination of Jared Sparks" (1819), in H. Shelton Smith, Robert T. Handy, and Lefferts A. Loetscher, *American Christianity: An Historical Interpretation with Representative Documents* (New York: Charles Scribner's Sons, 1960), vol. 1, p. 493, and cf. *The Works of William E. Channing* (Boston: James Munroe; New York: C. S. Francis, 1848), vol. 3, pp. 122–123.

109. James Walker, "The Day of Judgement," in *An American Reformation: A Documentary History of Unitarian Christianity,* ed. Sydney E. Ahlstrom and Jonathan Carey, (Middletown, Conn.: Wesleyan University Press, 1985), p. 310.

110. *The Worcester Catechism,* ibid., pp. 181, 192, 194–195, 197–199; bibliographical information, pp.177–178. Another discussion of Unitarian views is in Feldman, *Dual Destinies,* pp. 51–53.

111. Eliza Robbins, *American Popular Lessons* (1820; New York: R. Lockwood, 1829), p. 148.

112. John Pierpont, *The American First Class Book; or, Exercises in Reading and Recitation* (1823; Boston: Charles Bowen, 1836), pp. vi, 187.

113. Pierpont, *The National Reader* (1827; Boston: Richardson, Lord, Holbrook and Hillard et al., 1831), pp. 145–147, quote p. 147.

114. J[ohn] L. Blake, *A Geography for Children* (Boston: Lord and Holbrook, 1831), pp. 28, 56.

115. Caleb Bingham, *The Columbian Orator* (1797; Troy, N.Y.: Parker and Bliss, 1839), pp. 75–76.

116. Ibid., p. 206.

117. Denis Louis Cottineau, *Geographical Compilation for the Use of Schools* (Baltimore: John West Butler, 1806), vol. 1, p. 6.

118. Daniel Staniford, *The Art of Reading* (1802; Boston: West and Richardson, 1813), pp. 160–161, 163, 167, 169.

119. John Hubbard, *The American Reader* (1804; Walpole, N.H.: Isaiah Thomas, 1811), pp. 25, 107–108.

120. Staniford, *Art of Reading*, p. 70; *The Book of Commerce by Sea and Land, Exhibiting Its Connection with Agriculture, the Arts and Manufacturings* (Philadelphia: Uriah Hunt, 1837), p. 66.

121. A[braham] T. Lowe, *Second Class Book; Principally Consisting of Historical, Geographical, and Biographical Lessons, Adapted to the Capacities of Youth, and Designed for Their Improvement* (1825; Worcester, Mass.: Dorr and Howland, 1831), p. 72.

122. J[oseph] E[merson] Worcester, *An Epitome of History* (Cambridge, Mass.: Hilliard and Brown, 1827), p. 49.

123. Lowe, *Second Class Book*, pp. 185–189. For more on anti-Semitism in textbooks see Elson, *Guardians*, pp. 52–55, 59–60, 79, 81–85, 196.

124. Richard Mosier, *Making the American Mind: Social and Moral Ideas in the McGuffey Readers* (New York: Russell and Russell, 1965), chs. 1–6, sales estimates p. 168; John H. Westerhoff III, *McGuffey and His Readers: Piety, Morality, and Education in Nineteenth-Century America* (Nashville: Abingdon, 1978), pp. 74–110.

125. William G. McGuffey, "Lecture on the Relative Duties of Parents and Teachers" (1835), in Westerhoff, *McGuffey and His Readers*, p. 181, and *The Eclectic Third Reader; Containing Selections in Prose and Poetry, from the Best American and English Writers* (Cincinnati: Truman and Smith, 1837), p. 61.

126. "Roy's Hebrew Lexicon—Secret Conspiracy against Religion Developed," *New York Herald*, Nov. 11, 1837, p. 2.

127. *New-York Evening Post*, Nov. 5, 1822, p. 2.

128. For favorable opinion in the *Register* see Isaac M. Fein, "*Niles' Weekly Register* on the Jews," in *Jewish Experience*, ed. Karp, vol. 2, pp. 83–92, 96–101. For accusations against Jews see *Niles' Weekly Register*, 10 (Aug. 24, 1816): 429; 23 (Oct. 19, 1822): 429; 69 (Jan. 3, 1846): 284; the quote is from "Jews in Maryland," 19 (Oct. 21, 1820): 114.

129. Byrnes, *Anti-Semitism in Modern France*, vol. 1, pp. 104–110; M. J. Landa, *The Jew in Drama* (London: P. S. King and Son, 1926), pp. 120, 123, 143–150; Schiff, *Stereotype to Metaphor*, pp. 20–22; Modder, *Jew in the Literature of England*, 64–77, 120–121; Debré, *Jew in French Literature*, pp. 3–4, 19, 22; Lehrmann, *Jewish Element*, pp. 147–155. Two examples of bad Jews in French drama are Israel Ben-Manasseh, an exotic rabbi, spy, usurer, sorcerer, astrologer, and adviser to Oliver Cromwell in Victor Hugo's, *Cromwell* (1827); and an unnamed minor character in another Hugo play, *Mary Tudor* (1833). See *The Works of Victor Hugo* (Boston: Little, Brown, 1909), vol. 24, pp. 46, 136–138, 262–274, 300–305, 452–454; Sander L. Gilman, *The Jew's Body* (New York and London: Routledge, 1991), pp. 10–37, and *Jewish Self-Hatred: Anti-Semitism and the Hidden Language of the Jews* (Baltimore and London:

Johns Hopkins University Press, 1986), pp. 87–188, and "Chicken Soup, or the Penalities for Sounding too Jewish," *Shofar,* 2 (Winter 1991): 55–69.

130. Ellen Schiff, "Shylock's *Mishpocheh:* Anti-Semitism on the American Stage," in *Anti-Semitism in American History,* ed. David A. Gerber (Urbana: University of Illinois Press, 1986), p. 83.

131. John Howard Payne, *Trial Without Jury and Other Plays* (Princeton: Princeton University Press, 1940), pp. 13, 24–25, 37–38, quote p. 25. For discussion of Shylock types on the stage see Dobkowski, *Tarnished Dream,* pp. 79–80.

132. Susanna Haswell Rowson, *Slaves in Algiers; or, A Struggle for Freedom* (Philadelphia: Wrigley and Berriman, 1794), pp. 16–17; Schiff, "Shylock's *Mishpocheh,*" p. 81.

133. Nathaniel Parker Willis, "Tortesa the Usurer," in Arthur Hobson Quinn, ed., *Representative American Plays from 1762 to the Present Day* (New York: Appleton-Century-Crofts, 1953), p. 266.

134. Louis Harap, "The Image of the Jew in American Drama, 1794–1831," *American Jewish Historical Quarterly,* 60 (March 1971): 249.

135. Royall Tyler, "The Origin of the Feast of Purim; or, The Destinies of Haman and Mordecai: A Sacred Drama in Three Acts," in *Four Plays by Royall Tyler: America's Lost Plays,* ed. Arthur Wallace Peach and George Floyd Newbrough (1940; Bloomington: University of Indiana Press, 1965), vol. 15, p. 37; "Joseph and His Brethren: A Sacred Drama," ibid., p. 69; "The Judgement of Solomon: A Sacred Drama in Two Acts," ibid., p. 99.

136. Lehrman, *Jewish Element,* pp. 158–161; Byrnes, *Anti-Semitism in Modern France,* vol. 1, pp. 104–110; Debré, *Jew in French Literature,* pp. 5–6, 23–85; Poliakov, *History of Anti-Semitism,* vol. 3, pp. 156–210; Modder, *Jew in the Literature of England,* pp. 17–23, 83–155; Fisch, *Dual Image,* pp. 44–50, 57–58, 63–65, 72–75; Rosenberg, *Shylock to Svengali,* pp. 38–70.

137. Royall Tyler, *The Algerine Captive; or, The Life and Adventures of Dr. Updike Underhill, Six Years a Prisoner among the Algerines* (1797; Gainesville, Fla.: Scholars' Facsimilies and Reprints, 1967), vol. 2, pp. 177–189, 215–220.

138. Ibid., pp. 133, 167.

139. Frank Luther Mott, *Golden Multitudes: The Story of Best Sellers in the United States* (New York: Macmillan, 1947), p. 316.

140. Hugh Henry Brackenridge, *Modern Chivalry* (1792–1815; New York: American Book Co., 1927), pp. 166, 442, 570.

141. "The Converted Jew," in *Jews of the United States,* ed. Blau and Baron, vol. 3, pp. 711–713.

142. Henry Ruffner, *Judith Bensaddi: A Tale and Seclusaval; or, The Sequel to the Tale of Judith Bensaddi* (1839; Baton Rouge, Louisiana State University Press, 1984).

143. Sarah Pogson Smith, *Zerah, the Believing Jew* (1838; Charleston: W. R. Babcock, 1857), pp. 45, 49, 132, 137–138, 151–152.

144. John Pierpont, *Airs of Palestine and Other Poems* (Boston: James Munroe, 1840), pp. 333–334.

145. James Fenimore Cooper, *The Bravo: A Venetian Story* (1831; London: Richard Bentley, 1851), pp. 75, 327, 263.

146. Ibid., pp. 77, 69–70, 79.

147. Nathaniel P. Willis, "The Gypsy of Sardis," in *The Prose Writings of Nathaniel Parker Willis* (1836; New York: AMS Press, 1970), pp. 160, 177.

148. Charles F. Briggs, *The Adventures of Harry Franco: A Tale of the Great Panic* (New York: F. Saunders, 1839), vol. 2, pp. 49, 51, 141–146.

149. John Lothrop Motley, *Morton's Hope; or, The Memoirs of a Provincial* (New York: Harper and Bros., 1839), vol. 1, pp. 197–198; vol. 2, pp. 34, 63–65.

150. Fay, *Sidney Clifton*, vol. 1, pp. 140–141.

151. Ibid., vol. 1, pp. 141–144; vol. 2, p. 134.

152. Harry Middleton Hyatt, *Folk-Lore from Adams County, Illinois* (New York: Alma Egan Foundation, 1935), pp. 154, 392; Glanz, *Jew in Old American Folklore*, p. 16.

153. "The Wandering Jew," *Western Monthly Magazine,* 1 (June 1833): 273, 275.

154. Rudolf Glanz, *Studies in Judaica Americana* (New York: KTAV, 1970), pp. 338, 340–342, 345, 350, 357, and *Jew in Old American Folklore*, pp. 6–8.

155. Glanz, *Jew in Old American Folklore*, p. 49.

156. Rudolf Glanz, *The Jew in Early American Wit and Graphic Humor* (New York: KTAV, 1973), pp. 61–62.

157. Glanz, *Studies in Judaica*, pp. 59–60.

158. Rebecca Samuel Alexander to her parents, Jan. 12, 1791, in *American Jewry,* ed. Marcus, p. 52; Charles King quoted in Jonathan D. Sarna, "Anti-Semitism and American History," *Commentary,* 71 (March 1981): 44; Letter to the Editor, *Alexandria* [Virginia] *Daily Advertiser,* Jan. 1, 1806, p. 3; *Memoir of Samuel Joseph May,* ed. Thomas James Mumford (Boston: Roberts Brothers, 1874), p. 15; "Extract from the Manuscript Diary of Richard Arnold" (1832), in *Jews of the United States,* ed. Blau and Baron, vol. 1, pp. 176–177.

159. M. Otto to the Comte de Vergennes, Jan. 2, 1786, in Stokes, *Church and State,* vol. 1, p. 796; H. M. Brackenridge, "Speech on the Maryland 'Jew Bill'," in *Cornerstones,* ed. Blau, pp. 103–104; *German Correspondent,* Jan. 31, 1820, p. 6.

160. Otto to Vergennes, vol. 1, p. 296.

## 5.  Mid-Century Crisis

1. Cecil Roth, *A History of the Jews in England* (Oxford: Clarendon Press, 1941), pp. 253, 263, 265; Colin Holmes, *Anti-Semitism in British Society, 1876–1939* (London: Edward Arnold, 1979), p. 8; W. D. Rubinstein, *The Left, the Right and the Jews* (London: Croom Helm, 1982), pp. 13, 182;

Stephen Wilson, *Ideology and Experience: Antisemitism in France at the Time of the Dreyfus Affair* (London and Toronto: Associated Universities Presses; Rutherford, N.J.: Fairleigh Dickinson University Press, 1982), p. 169.

2. Paul W. Massing, *Rehearsal for Destruction: A Study of Political Anti-Semitism in Imperial Germany* (New York: Harper and Bros., 1949), pp. 3–4; Alfred D. Low, *Jews in the Eyes of the Germans from the Enlightenment to Imperial Germany* (Philadelphia: Institute for the Study of Human Issues, 1979), pp. 300–301, 307, 310–311; Jacob Katz, *From Prejudice to Destruction: Anti-Semitism, 1700–1933* (Cambridge, Mass.: Harvard University Press, 1980), pp. 175–194, 210–211, 223, 227; Julius Carlebach, *Karl Marx and the Radical Critique of Judaism* (London: Routledge and Kegan Paul, 1978), pp. 85–89, 345.

3. Robert F. Byrnes, *Anti-Semitism in Modern France: The Prologue to the Dreyfus Affair* (New York: Howard Fertig, 1969), vol. 1, pp. 76, 86–88; Katz, *Prejudice to Destruction*, pp. 231–232; Mark Vishniak, "Antisemitism in Tsarist Russia," in *Essays on Antisemitism*, ed. Koppel S. Pinson (New York: Conference on Jewish Relations, 1946), pp. 121–130; Raphael Mahler, "Antisemitism in Poland," ibid., pp. 157–161; Salo W. Baron, *The Russian Jew Under Tsars and Soviets* (New York and London: Macmillan, 1964), pp. 30, 33–41, 47–50; *The Jews in the Soviet Union Since 1917*, ed. Lionel Kochan (Oxford and London: Oxford University Press, 1978), pp. 17–18.

4. Katz, *Prejudice to Destruction*, pp. 195–202, 227–229; Hannah Arendt, *The Origins of Totalitarianism* (1958; New York: Meridian, 1972), pp. 29–35; Carlebach, *Karl Marx*, pp. 60–64, 77, 84–90, 103, 107–109; Shmuel Almog, "Nationalism and Antisemitism in Modern Europe: 1815–1845," in *Antisemitism through the Ages*, ed. Almog (Oxford, England: Pergamon Press, 1990), pp. 21–23.

5. Almog, "Nationalism and Antisemitism," pp. 21–23; Katz: *Prejudice to Destruction*, pp. 232–236; Arendt, *Totalitarianism*, pp. 42–45; Jacob L. Talmon "Mission and Testimony: The Universal Significance of Modern Anti-Semitism," in *The Catastrophe of European Jewry*, ed. Yisrael Gutman and Livia Rothkirchen (Jerusalem: Yad Vashem, 1976), p. 145.

6. Katz, *Prejudice to Destruction*, pp. 149–158, 177–184, 195–202, 208–209, 232–236, and *Out of the Ghetto: The Social Background of Jewish Emancipation, 1770–1870* (Cambridge, Mass.: Harvard University Press, 1973), pp. 199–200; Low, *Jews in the Eyes of the Germans*, pp. 244–275, 300–301, 316–320, 328–339; Uriel Tal, *Christians and Jews in Germany: Religion, Politics and Ideology in the Second Reich, 1870–1914* (Ithaca: Cornell University Press, 1975), pp. 40–65, 78–80; Arendt, *Totalitarianism*, pp. 26–45, 56–62, 66; Paul Lawrence Rose, *Revolutionary Antisemitism in Germany from Kant to Wagner* (Princeton: Princeton University Press, 1990), pp. 19–21, 359–368; Moshe Zimmerman, "From Radicalism to Antisemitism," in *Antisemitism through the Ages*, ed. Almog, pp. 245–251; Robert S. Wistrich, *Socialism and the Jews:*

*The Dilemmas of Assimilation in Germany and Austria-Hungary* (Rutherford, N.J.: Fairleigh Dickinson University Press; London and Toronto: Associated University Presses, 1982), pp. 60–61, 180–184; Léon Poliakov, *The History of Anti-Semitism* (New York: Vanguard Press, 1964–1974), vol. 3, pp. 305, 393–397; Wilson, *Ideology and Experience*, p. 107; Bernard D. Winryb, "The Social and Economic Background of Modern Antisemitism," *Essays on Antisemitism*, ed. Pinson, pp. 21, 27–30; Adolf Leschnitzer, *The Magic Background of Modern Anti-Semitism: An Analysis of the German-Jewish Relationship* (New York: International Universities Press, 1956), pp. 89–93, 125–131; Massing, *Rehearsal for Destruction*, pp. 12–13.

7. Norman Cohn, *Warrant for Genocide: The Myth of the Jewish World-Conspiracy and the Protocols of the Elders of Zion* (New York: Harper and Row, 1967), pp. 169–170, 175; Low, *Jews in the Eyes of the Germans*, pp. 108–109, 154–156, 169–184, 206–214; Katz, *Prejudice to Destruction*, pp. 185–194, 217–220; Leschnitzer, *Magic Background*, p. 136; Poliakov, *History of Anti-Semitism*, vol. 3, pp. 309–312, 380–392, 429–457, 461; Massing, *Rehearsal for Destruction*, pp. 82–84; George L. Mosse, *The Crisis of German Ideology: Intellectual Origins of the Third Reich* (New York: Universal Library, 1964), pp. 36–45, 57–58, and *Germans and Jews* (New York: Howard Fertig, 1970), pp. 34–76; Eva G. Reichman, *Hostages of Civilization: The Social Sources of National Socialist Anti-Semitism* (London: Victor Gollancz, 1950), pp. 121–171; Arendt, *Totalitarianism*, pp. 26–35, 42–45; Zimmerman, "Radicalism to Antisemitism," pp. 245–251.

8. Arthur de Gobineau, *The Inequality of Human Races* (1854; London: William Heinemann, 1915), pp. 122, 195. For Gobineau's outlook on the Jews see Michael D. Biddiss, *Father of Racist Ideology: The Social and Political Thought of Count Gobineau* (New York: Weybright and Talley, 1970), pp. 110, 115, 124–125, 229, 250, 254–255.

9. Richard Wagner, "Jews in Music," in *Wagner on Music and Drama*, ed. Albert Goldman and Evert Sprinchorn, (New York: E. P. Dutton, 1964), pp. 52–53, 55–57, 59; cf. "Opera and Drama" (1850–51), ibid., p. 112; *Letters of Richard Wagner*, ed. Wilhelm Altman (New York: E. P. Dutton; London and Ontario: J. M. Dent and Sons, 1927), vol. 1, pp. 23, 243, 255, 272, 280; vol. 2, pp. 35, 267, 297.

10. Jules Michelet, *The People*, ed. and trans. John P. McKay (1846; Urbana: University of Illinois Press, 1973), pp. 34, 65, 133, 93n.

11. Zosa Szajkowski, *Jews and the French Revolutions of 1789, 1830 and 1848* (New York: KTAV, 1970), pp. 1099, 1104–1107, 1109–1110, 1113–1117; Katz, *Prejudice to Destruction*, pp. 119–128; Wilson, *Ideology and Experience*, pp. 319–340, 737–738; Wistrich, *Socialism and the Jews*, pp. 25–28; Byrnes, *Anti-Semitism in Modern France*, vol. 1, pp. 115–125; Charles Fourier, *Selections from the Works of Fourier* (London: Swan Sonnenschien, 1901)

pp. 96, 96n; *The Utopian Vision of Charles Fourier,* ed. Jonathan Beecher and Richard Bienvenu (London: Jonathan Cape, 1975), pp. 117, 122, 199; Pierre Joseph Proudhon, *What Is Property? or, An Inquiry into the Principle of Right and of Government* (1840; London: William Reeves, n.d.), p. 253.

12. Byrnes, *Anti-Semitism in Modern France,* vol. 1, pp. 115–118; Emil L. Fackenheim, *Encounters between Judaism and Modern Philosophy* (New York: Basic Books, 1973), pp. 139–142, 145–148, 150–151; Carlebach, *Karl Marx,* pp. 99–146, 152–156, 164–184; Rose, *Revolutionary Antisemitism,* pp. 19–20, 23–24, 251–278, 296–305, 341–349, 359–360; Zimmerman, "Radicalism to Antisemitism," pp. 241–254, Letter from Wilhelm Marr to ? Hobelmann, June 4, 1862, ibid., pp. 247–249; Katz, *Prejudice to Destruction,* pp. 159–174; Poliakov, *History of Anti-Semitism,* vol. 3, pp. 421–429; Massing, *Rehearsal for Destruction,* pp. 155–156, 165–166; Low, *Jews in the Eyes of the Germans,* pp. 404–405; Wistrich, *Socialism and the Jews,* pp. 25–28, 31–34, 46–47.

13. Karl Marx to Friedrich Engels, Feb. 22, 1859, July 30, 1862, to Antoinette Philips, March 24, 1861, in *The Letters of Karl Marx,* ed. Saul K. Padover (Englewood Cliffs, N.J.: Prentice Hall, 1979), pp. 435, 456, 466; Marx, "Herr Voigt" (1860), in *Karl Marx, Frederick Engels, Collected Works* (New York: International Publishers, 1975–81), vol. 17, p. 245. For assessments of Marx's anti-Semitism see Rose, *Revolutionary Antisemitism,* pp. 296–305; Fackenheim, *Judaism and Modern Philosophy,* pp. 145–148, 150–151; Carlebach, *Karl Marx,* pp. 152–156, 164–184, 310, 349, 352, 356–359.

14. Marx, "On the Jewish Question" (1843), in *On Religion: The Karl Marx Library,* ed. Saul K. Padover (New York: McGraw-Hill, 1974), vol. 5, pp. 188–189, 191, 170.

15. Ibid., pp. 187–191.

16. Marx, "The Holy Family" (1845), in *Karl Marx, Frederick Engels,* vol. 4, pp. 109–110, and "The Italian Insurrection—British Politics" (1853), ibid., vol. 11, p. 512, and "Parliamentary Debates—The Clergy against Socialism—Starvation" (1853), ibid., pp. 522–523, and "The Loanmongers of Europe" (1855), in *On Religion,* ed. Padover, vol. 5, p. 219, and "Jewish Question," ibid., p. 191, and "The Russian Loan" (1856), ibid., pp. 221–225.

17. Friedrich Engels, *The Condition of the Working-Class in England in 1844,* ed. Florence Kelley Wischnewetzky (1845; London: Swan Sonnenschein, 1892), p. 277, and "The Peasant War in Germany" (1850), in *The German Revolution,* ed. Leonard Krieger (Chicago: University of Chicago Press, 1967), p. 56; Engels to Marx, May 11, 1857, in *Karl Marx and Friedrich Engels: Selected Letters: The Personal Correspondence,* ed. Fritz J. Raddatz (Boston: Little, Brown, 1980), p. 72, and to Marx, March 7, 1856, in *Engels: Selected Writings,* ed. W. O. Henderson (Baltimore: Penguin Books, 1967), p. 129.

18. Poliakov, *History of Anti-Semitism,* vol. 3, pp. 345–349; Rose, *Revolutionary Antisemitism,* pp. 47–50, 54.

19. Eugene Sue, *The Wandering Jew* (Chicago: M. A. Donohue, n.d.), pp. 62–63, 118–119, 139–143, 192–196, 648–651; John Gaer, *The Legend of the Wandering Jew* (New York: Mentor Books, 1961), pp. 122–131; Poliakov, *History of Anti-Semitism*, vol. 3, pp. 353–355.

20. *The Federal and State Constitutions, Colonial Charters, and Other Organic Laws of the States, Territories and Colonies Now or Heretofore Forming the United States of America*, ed. Francis N. Thorpe (Washington, D.C.: U.S. Government Printing Office, 1909), vol. 6, pp. 3223, 3231–3232.

21. Eli N. Evans, *Judah P. Benjamin: The Jewish Confederate* (New York: The Free Press, 1988), pp. 46–48; Leon Huhner, *Jews in America after the Revolution* (New York: Gertz Brothers, 1959), pp. 78–79; Bertram Wallace Korn, *The Early Jews of New Orleans* (Waltham, Mass.: AJHS, 1969), pp. 185, 206, 227; Henry Samuel Morais, *The Jews of Philadelphia* (Philadelphia: Levytype, 1894), pp. 396–397, 401, 406; *Jewish Life in Philadelphia: 1830–1940*, ed. Murray Friedman (Philadelphia: ISHI Publications, 1985), p. 292; Isaac M. Fein, *The Making of a Jewish Community: The History of Baltimore Jewry from 1773 to 1920* (Philadelphia: JPSA, 1971), pp. 23, 25; Herbert T. Ezekiel and Gaston Lichtenstein, *The History of the Jews of Richmond from 1769 to 1917* (Richmond: Herbert T. Ezekiel, 1917), pp. 30–31, 41, 61–66, 71, 209; Myron Berman, *Richmond's Jewry, 1769–1976* (Charlottesville: University of Virginia Press, 1979), pp. 128, 235–236; Stuart E. Rosenberg, *The Jewish Community in Rochester: 1843–1925* (New York: AJHS, Columbia University Press, 1954), p. 13; Albert Ehrenfield, "A Chronicle of Boston Jewry: From the Colonial Settlement to 1900" (manuscript, 1963; a copy is in the library of the University of Illinois at Champaign-Urbana), p. 418; W. Gunther Plaut, *The Jews in Minnesota: The First Seventy-Five Years* (New York: AJHS, 1959), pp. 19–20; Morris Silverman, *Hartford Jews: 1659–1970* (Hartford: Connecticut Historical Society, 1970), pp. 71, 102–104; Charles Reznikoff, *The Jews of Charleston: A History of an American Jewish Community* (Philadelphia: JPSA, 1950), pp. 285–286; Barnett A. Elzas, *The Jews of South Carolina from the Earliest Times to the Present Day* (1902; Spartanburg, S.C.: Reprint Co., 1972), pp. 190, 194, 196–197, 202–205; Louis J. Swichkow and Lloyd P. Gartner, *The History of the Jews of Milwaukee* (Philadelphia: JPSA, 1963), pp. 514–515; Max Vorspan and Lloyd P. Gartner, *History of the Jews of Los Angeles* (San Marino, Calif.: Huntington Library), pp. 17–18, 46, 49–50; Morris A. Gutstein, *A Priceless Heritage: The Epic Growth of Nineteenth-Century Chicago Jewry* (New York: Bloch, 1953), pp. 423–425.

22. Ezekiel and Lichtenstein, *Jews of Richmond*, p. 244; Bertram Wallace Korn, *Eventful Years and Experiences: Studies in Nineteenth-Century American Jewish History* (Cincinnati: American Jewish Archives, 1954), p. 114; Berman, *Richmond's Jewry*, p. 130.

23. John Tyler to Joseph Simpson, July 10, 1843, in *PAJHS*, 11 (1903): 158–159; Tyler to Jacob Ezekiel, April 19, 1841, in Ezekiel and Lichtenstein, *Jews of Richmond*, p. 118; Buchanan to Isidor Kalisch, Sept. 11, 1858, in Swichkow and Gartner, *Jews of Milwaukee*, p. 44; Cass, speech in the U.S. Senate, April 19, 1854, in Solomon M. Stroock, "Switzerland and the American Jews," in *The Jewish Experience in America: Selected Studies from the PAJHS*, ed. Abraham J. Karp (New York: KTAV, 1969), vol. 3, p. 90.

24. *A Documentary History of the Jews in the United States: 1654–1875*, ed. Morris U. Schappes (New York: Schocken Books, 1971), p. 235; *Jewish Life in Philadelphia*, ed. Friedman, p. 5; Ezekiel and Lichtenstein, *Jews of Richmond*, p. 116; Isaac M. Wise, *Reminiscences* (Cincinnati: Leo Wise, 1901), pp. 217–219; *Congressional Globe*, 29 (Washington, D.C.: John C. Reeves, 1860), 36th Cong., 1st. Sess., 1860, part 1, pp. 648–649.

25. Pierce Butler, *Judah P. Benjamin* (Philadelphia: George W. Jacobs, 1907), p. 189; Robert D. Meade, *Judah P. Benjamin: Confederate Statesman* (New York: Oxford University Press, 1943), p. 49; Henry S. Foote, *Casket of Reminiscences* (Washington, D. C.: Chronicle, 1874), p. 70; Korn, *Eventful Years*, pp. 59, 61–63, 99–101, quote is on p. 59.

26. Ehrenfield, "Boston Jewry," pp. 408, 418–420; Elzas, *Jews of South Carolina*, pp. 221–237; Reznikoff, *Jews of Charleston*, pp. 158–159; *Congressional Globe*, 32 (Washington, D.C.: Congressional Globe Office, 1862), 37th Cong., 2d Sess., 1861–62, part 1, pp. 157–158; 1862, part 4, p. 414; Bertram Wallace Korn, *American Jewry and the Civil War* (Philadelphia: JPSA, 1951), pp. 56–66; Harry Simonhoff, *Jewish Participants in the Civil War* (New York: Arco, 1963), pp. 6–9, 20–43, 91–98, 105–113, 132–140, 161–171, 183–187, 207–213; Allen Tarshish, "The Board of Delegates of American Israelites," in *Jewish Experience*, ed. Karp, vol. 3, pp. 129–130; Isaac Markens, "Lincoln and the Jews," ibid., pp. 226, 268–69.

27. Korn, *American Jewry and Civil War*, pp. 70, 125–126; Lincoln to A. Fischel, Dec. 13, 1861, ibid., p. 70; Rabbi Isaac M. Wise, Report of a Delegation to President Lincoln, Jan. 8, 1863, *The Israelite* (Jan. 16, 1863), in *Documentary History*, ed. Schappes, pp. 473–474; Markens, "Lincoln and the Jews," pp. 226, 229–230, 263–269; W. W. Murphy, letter to the editor, *Harper's Weekly*, 7 (April 25, 1863): 258.

28. Bertram Wallace Korn, *The American Reaction to the Mortara Case: 1858–1859* (Cincinnati: American Jewish Archives, 1957), p. 38; Hyman B. Grinstein, *The Rise of the Jewish Community of New York: 1654–1860* (Philadelphia: JPSA, 1945), p. 385.

29. Frank Fox, "Quaker, Shaker, Rabbi: Warder Cresson, The Story of a Philadelphia Mystic," *Pennsylvania Magazine of History and Biography*, 95 (April 1971): 148–149, 171–183.

30. Frederic Cople Jaher, *The Urban Establishment: Upper Strata in Boston, New York, Charleston, Chicago, and Los Angeles* (Urbana: University of Illinois Press, 1982), pp. 593–599, 601–603; Gunter Barth, *Instant Cities: Urbanization and the Rise of San Francisco and Denver* (New York: Oxford University Press, 1975), pp. 72–73; Vorspan and Gartner, *Jews of Los Angeles,* pp. 34–36; Peter R. Decker, *Fortunes and Failures: White-Collar Mobility in Nineteenth-Century San Francisco* (Cambridge, Mass.: Harvard University Press, 1978), pp. 116–118, 238–239; Korn, *Jews of New Orleans,* pp. 96, 115–116, 125, 225–227; Fein, *Making of a Jewish Community,* p. 17; Berman, *Richmond's Jewry,* pp. 72, 127; Elzas, *Jews of South Carolina,* pp. 185, 188, 192, 196–197, 204; Reznikoff, *Jews of Charleston,* pp. 89–90; Morais, *Jews of Philadelphia,* p. 271; Irving Katz, *August Belmont: A Political Biography* (New York: Columbia University Press, 1968), pp. 6–7, 91–115; Stephen Birmingham, *"Our Crowd": The Great Jewish Families of New York* (New York: Harper and Row, 1967), pp. 31–32, 58, 66–68, 71–76.

31. Morais, *Jews of Philadelphia,* pp. 33, 41, 272, 286–289, 298, 417; *Jewish Life in Philadelphia,* ed. Friedman, p. 5; Ezekiel and Lichtenstein, *Jews of Richmond,* pp. 35–36, 39–40, 62; Berman, *Richmond's Jewry,* pp. 18, 84, 128, 234; Leopold Mayer, "Reminiscences of Early Chicago," in *Memoirs of American Jews: 1775–1865,* ed. Jacob Rader Marcus (Philadelphia: JPSA, 1955), vol. 3, pp. 281–286; Gutstein, *Priceless Heritage,* pp. 61–64, 276–277, 312; Elzas, *Jews of South Carolina,* p. 243; Reznikoff, *Jews of Charleston,* pp. 94–97; Korn, *Jews of New Orleans,* pp. 96, 115–116, 125, 225–228; Meade, *Judah P. Benjamin,* pp. 82–84; Swichkow and Gartner, *Jews of Milwaukee,* pp. 55, 58–60; Plaut, *Jews in Minnesota,* pp. 23–24; Harris Newmark, *Sixty Years in Southern California: 1853–1913* (New York: Knickerbocker Press, 1916), pp. 203, 383; Steven Hertzberg, *Strangers within the Gate City: The Jews of Atlanta, 1845–1915* (Philadelphia: JPSA, 1978), pp. 20, 68–69; Katz, *August Belmont,* pp. 1–2, 8–9; Birmingham, *"Our Crowd,"* pp. 54–62.

32. Meade, *Judah P. Benjamin,* pp. 107–123; Fein, *Making of a Jewish Community,* p. 107; Morais, *Jews of Philadelphia,* p. 417; Dan A. Oren, *Joining the Club: A History of Jews and Yale* (New Haven: Yale University Press, 1985), p. 10.

33. Wise, *Reminiscences,* pp. 75–76; Korn, *Jews of New Orleans,* pp. 223–228; Decker, *Fortunes and Failures,* pp. 116–118, 238–239; Swichkow and Gartner, *Jews of Milwaukee,* pp. 32–33; Grinstein, *Rise of a Jewish Community,* pp. 187–189; Rosenberg, *Jewish Community in Rochester,* pp. 13, 44; Ehrenfield, "Boston Jewry," pp. 342–344, 372; Silverman, *Hartford Jews,* p. 108n15; Fein, *Making of a Jewish Community,* pp. 59, 75; Gutstein, *Priceless Heritage,* pp. 297, 323–324; Leon L. Watters, *The Pioneer Jews of Utah* (New York: AJHS, 1952), pp. 67–69; David Gerber, "Cutting Out Shylock," in *Anti-Semitism in American History,* ed. Gerber (Urbana: University of Illinois Press, 1986), pp. 210–211; *Memoirs of American Jews,* ed. Marcus, vol.

2, pp. 64–65, 67, 83–84, 284–285; Henry Lee Higginson to George Higginson, 1858, in Bliss Perry, *Life and Letters of Henry Lee Higginson* (Boston: Atlantic Monthly Press, 1921), p. 125; Pomroy Jones, *Annals and Recollections of Oneida County* (Rome, N.Y.: Pomroy Jones, 1851), p. 591; "Present State of the Jewish People in Learning and Culture," *North American Review,* 83 (Oct. 1856): 354, 357, 360–361, 365, 367–369, 373, 378–380; "Antipathy of Race and Religion," editorial, *Harper's Weekly,* 7 (Feb. 28, 1863): 130–131; "The Old Story," editorial, ibid. (Aug. 1, 1863): 482. For a selection of newspaper editorials praising Jews and denouncing discrimination see *Documentary History,* ed. Schappes, pp. 342–346, 401–405.

34. Joseph Buchler, "The Struggle for Unity: Attempts at Union in American Jewish Life, 1654–1858," in *Critical Studies in American Jewish History: Selected Articles from The American Jewish Archives,* ed. Jacob Rader Marcus (New York: KTAV, 1971), vol. 3, pp. 108–109; Joseph Jacobs, "The Damascus Affair of 1840 and the Jews of America," in *Jewish Experience,* ed. Karp, pp. 271–280; *Documentary History,* ed. Schappes, pp. 201–213; *The Jews of the United States, 1790–1840: A Documentary History,* ed. Joseph L. Blau and Salo W. Baron (New York: Columbia University Press; Philadelphia: JPSA, 1963), vol. 3, pp. 928–929, 940–943. The last two references contain correspondence between the secretary of state and the consul in Alexandria and the minister to Turkey.

35. Buchler, "Struggle for Unity," pp. 109–110; Gutstein, *Priceless Heritage,* pp. 323–324; Stroock, "Switzerland," pp. 78, 80, 85, 87–88, 93–94, 98–99.

36. Korn, *American Reaction,* pp. 40, 51–52, 54, 61–62, 68, 79–135; Fein, *Making of a Jewish Community,* p. 106; Grinstein, *Rise of a Jewish Community,* p. 431.

37. Markens, "Lincoln and the Jews," pp. 226, 229–230, 263–267; *Documentary History,* ed. Schappes, pp. 473–476; Korn, *American Jewry and Civil War,* pp. 65, 70, 125–126, 128–130, 170–173; Gutstein, *Priceless Heritage,* p. 331; Rosenberg, *Jewish Community in Rochester,* p. 16; "Antipathy of Race," 130–131; "Old Story," 482.

38. Moses Debré, *The Image of the Jew in French Literature from 1800 to 1908* (New York: KTAV, 1970), pp. 45–85; Harold Fisch, *The Dual Image: The Figure of the Jew in English and American Literature* (New York: KTAV, 1971), pp. 63–65, 72–75; Montague Frank Modder, *The Jew in the Literature of England to the End of the Nineteenth Century* (Philadelphia: JPSA, 1939), pp. 94–95, 168–169, 223–224; Low, *Jews in the Eyes of the Germans,* pp. 170–184; Charles Dickens, *Our Mutual Friend* (1864–65; New York: University Society, 1908), vol. 1, pp. 308–316, 456–459; vol. 2, pp. 2–6, 10–14, 16–20, 111, 346–350, 353–358.

39. Toby Lelyveld, *Shylock on the Stage* (London: Routledge and Kegan Paul, 1961), pp. 63–65; Thomas R. Gould, *The Tragedian: An Essay on the Histrionic Genius of Junius Brutus Booth* (New York: Hurd and Houghton, 1868),

pp. 73–81; Lisbeth Jane Roman, "The Acting Style and Career of Junius Brutus Booth" (Ph.D diss., University of Illinois, 1968), pp. 138–142; Louis Harap, *The Image of the Jew in American Literature from Early Republic to Mass Immigration* (Philadelphia: JPSA, 1974), pp. 216–218; Augustin Daly, *Leah, The Forsaken* (New York and London: S. French, 187?); "Leah," *Harper's Weekly,* 7 (March 7, 1863): 146.

40. Henry Wadsworth Longfellow, "Sandalphon," in James K. Hosmer, *The Jews* (London: T. Fisher Unwin, 1886), pp. 146–147; *The Complete Poetical Works of John Greenleaf Whittier* (Boston and New York: Houghton Mifflin, 1894), pp. 91–92, 126, 418–419, 423–426, 488.

41. Lafcadio Hearn, *Occidental Gleanings* (New York: Dodd, Mead, 1925), vol. 2, pp. 179–189; *The Prose Writings of William Cullen Bryant,* ed. Parke Godwin (New York: D. Appleton, 1901), vol. 2, p. 358; *Margaret Fuller, American Romantic: A Selection from Her Writings and Correspondence* (Ithaca: Cornell University Press, 1963), p. 202.

42. William Ware, *Julian; or, Scenes in Judea* (1841; New York: Thomas R. Knox, 1899), vol. 1, pp. 1–41; vol. 2, pp. 266–267.

43. John Richter Jones, *The Quaker Soldier; or, The British in America* (Philadelphia: T. B. Peterson and Bros., 1859), pp. 97–99, 105, 107, 548–550.

44. *Federal and State Constitutions,* ed. Thorpe, vol. 4, pp. 2490–2502; vol. 5, pp. 2793, 2799, 2806; *The Israelite,* 7 (March 22, 1861): 300–301; Leon Huhner, "The Struggle for Religious Liberty in North Carolina, with Special Reference to the Jews," *PAJHS,* 16 (1907): 46, 55–65; *Journal of the Convention Called by the Freemen of North-Carolina to Amend the Constitution of the State* (Raleigh: J. Gales and Son, 1835), pp. 47, 49.

45. *Milwaukee Sentinel,* Nov. 23, 1859, p. 2; *Michigan Journal* (Lansing) editorial, in *The Israelite,* 5 (Sept. 24, 1859): 94; Korn, *Eventful Years,* pp. 62–64.

46. Claris Edwin Silcox and Galen M. Fisher, *Catholics, Jews and Protestants: A Study of Relationships in the United States and Canada* (1934; Westport, Conn.: Greenwood Press, 1979), p. 101.

47. Jonathan D. Sarna, *Jacksonian Jew: The Two Worlds of Mordecai Noah* (New York and London: Holmes and Meier, 1981), pp. 53–54, 61–75, 119–142.

48. *New York Herald,* Oct. 30, 1844, p. 2; April 6, 1850, p. 4; for other anti-Semitic attacks on Noah see Sarna, *Jacksonian Jew,* pp. 13, 44–47, 53–54, 78, 85–86, 89, 99, 113, 119–121, 144–145, 147, 155.

49. *Encyclopedia Judaica* (Jerusalem: Encyclopedia Judaica; New York: Macmillan, 1971–1977), vol. 12, pp. 1069–1070; vol. 15, pp. 1596, 1648; Grinstein, *Rise of a Jewish Community,* p. 469.

50. See Chapter 4, note 34.

51. Reznikoff, *Jews of Charleston,* pp. 4, 12–13, 39, 176, 179, 186; Grinstein, *Rise of a Jewish Community,* pp. 23, 30, 342; Robert Ernst, *Immigrant Life in New York City: 1825–1863* (New York: Columbia University Press, 1949), p. 46.

52. Katz, *August Belmont*, pp. 1, 3, 113; "Editor's Easy Chair," *Harper's Magazine*, 17 (July 1858): 268; Rudolf Glanz, "The Rothschild Legend in America," in Glanz, *Studies in Judaica Americana* (New York: KTAV, 1970), pp. 361, 366–369.

53. *New York Times*, Dec. 19, 1852, p. 4; *New York Tribune*, Oct. 26, 1852, p. 4, and Nov. 1, 1852, p. 4; cf. editorials of Oct. 27–30, 1852.

54. Edward Everett, "Journal," Nov. 28, 1864, extracted in Paul Revere Frothingham, *Edwart Everett: Orator and Statesman* (Boston and New York: Houghton Mifflin, 1925), p. 463; *Chicago Tribune*, Sept. 10, 1864, pp. 1, 2; *New York Times*, Nov. 2, 1864, p. 1; Katz, *August Belmont*, pp. 113, 144, 146; Simonhoff, *Jewish Participants*, p. 146; Korn, *American Jewry in Civil War*, p. 160.

55. Evans, *Judah P. Benjamin: Jewish Confederate*, pp. 47–48; Huhner, *Jews in America*, pp. 78–79.

56. *Memoirs of John Quincy Adams*, ed. Charles Francis Adams (Philadelphia: J. B. Lippincott, 1874–1877), vol. 10, pp. 304, 483; vol. 11, pp. 62, 155, 162, 294, 500–502; vol. 12, p. 164.

57. "The Children of Israel," *Boston Evening Transcript*, Jan.5, 1861, p. 2; *Charles Francis Adams, 1835–1915: An Autobiography* (1916; New York: Russell and Russell, 1968), p. 94.

58. Butler, *Judah P. Benjamin*, p. 189; Meade, *Judah P. Benjamin*, pp. 49, 83; Korn, *Jews of New Orleans*, pp. 96, 115–116, 125, 221–223, 225–228.

59. Korn, *American Jewry in Civil War*, p. 158; Foote, *Casket of Reminiscences*, p 237.

60. Foote, *Casket of Reminiscences*, pp. 65–71; *Congressional Globe*, 37th Congress, 2d Sess, Part 1, pp. 156–157; 3rd Sess., part 1, pp. 245–256; for his denunciation of Benjamin, 36th Congress, 2d Sess., part 3, Feb. 21, 1861, p. 1091.

61. Andrew Johnson quoted in *Charles Francis Adams*, p. 94.

62. Selection from Brownlow's speech, in *The Israelite*, 9 (Dec. 5, 1862): 172; William Gannaway Brownlow, *Portrait and Biography of Parson Brownlow, The Tennessee Patriot* (Indianapolis: Asher, 1862), pp. 20, 46. For Benjamin's role in Brownlow's arrest and exile see Benjamin to the District Attorney of Knoxville, Tenn., (New Orleans) *Daily Delta*, Jan. 3, 1862, p. 1.

63. Butler to Edwin Stanton, Oct. 10, 1962, in James Parton, *General Butler in New Orleans* (New York: Mason Bros., 1864), p. 391.

64. *Mary Chesnut's Civil War*, ed. C. Vann Woodward (New Haven and London: Yale University Press, 1981), Feb. 13, 1862, pp. 288–289; John Jones, "Wilmington During the Blockade," *North Carolina Civil War Documentary*, ed. W. Buck Yearns and John G. Barrett (Chapel Hill: University of North Carolina Press, 1980), p. 75.

65. Korn, *Eventful Years*, pp. 62–63; *Milwaukee Sentinel*, Nov. 23, 1859, p. 2; *Michigan Journal* editorial, in *The Israelite*, 5 (Sept. 24, 1859): 94; Robert A.

Rockaway, "Anti-Semitism in an American City: Detroit, 1850–1914," *PAJHS,* 64 (Sept. 1974): 43.

66. *Milwaukee Sentinel,* Nov. 23, 1859, p. 2; *Michigan Journal,* in *Israelite,* 94; Rockaway, "Anti-Semitism in an American City," 43.

67. Sarna, *Jacksonian Jew,* p. 121; Daniel Webster, *The Christian Ministry and the Religious Instruction of the Young* (Washington, D.C.: Gales and Seaton, 1844), pp. 27, 52.

68. *Reports of Cases Argued and Adjudged in the Supreme Court of the United States: January Term, 1844,* ed. Benjamin C. Howard (Philadelphia: T. and J. W. Johnson, Law Booksellers, 1844), vol. 2, pp. 198, 200.

69. Hertzberg, *Strangers within the Gate,* p. 20; Thomas Oliver Larkin, "My Itinerary: U.S. America," (1825), in Robert J. Parker, "A Chapter in the Early Life of Thomas Oliver Larkin," *California Historical Society Quarterly,* 16 (1937): 157.

70. *Memoirs of John Quincy Adams,* Dec. 20, 1834, vol. 10, p. 191. For attempts to amend the constitution see Borden, *Jews, Turks,* pp. 58–63, 66–69; *Liberator,* 34 (Dec. 16, 1864): 204.

71. James Hammond, "Proclamation of Sept 9, 1844," in *Documentary History,* ed. Schappes, pp. 236–237.

72. Letter from the Jews of Charleston to Hammond and Hammond's reply, ibid., pp. 236–242.

73. Ibid., p. 242.

74. Ibid., p. 241; "Sunday Laws," editorial in *Sunday Times and Noah's Weekly Register,* Feb. 13, 1848, ibid., pp. 279–281; Reznikoff, *Jews of Charleston,* p. 110; Borden, *Jews, Turks,* pp. 111–116.

75. Summary of Stow's speech from the *Sacramento Democratic State Journal,* in "Anti-Jewish Sentiment in California—1855," *American Jewish Archives,* 12 (April 1960): 15–34; Justin G. Turner, "The First Decade of Los Angeles Jewry," in *Jewish Experience,* ed. Karp, pp. 75–76; Vorspan and Gartner, *Jews of Los Angeles,* p. 15.

76. Selections from the "Proceedings of a U.S.N. Court of Inquiry (1857)," in *Memoirs of American Jews,* ed. Marcus, vol. 1, pp. 84, 103–106.

77. Dana to Edwin Stanton, Jan. 21, 1863, *U.S. War Department, The War of the Rebellion: A Compilation of the Official Records of the Union and Confederate Armies* (Washington, D.C.: Government Printing Office, 1898), ser. 1, vol. 52, part 1, p. 331; Washburne to Ulysses S. Grant, Jan. 8, 1863, in *The Papers of Ulysses S. Grant,* ed. John Simon (Carbondale: Southern Illinois University Press, 1967–), vol. 7, p. 56n; Cleveland quoted in ibid., p. 380n; Baker quoted in Simonhoff, *Jewish Participants,* pp. 147–148.

78. Davis speeches of June 10 and Dec. 20, 1864, in *Official Records,* ser. 4, vol. 3, pp. 553, 949.

79. Foote's speech of Jan. 14, 1863, in *Proceedings of the First Confederate Congress, 3rd Sess.: Southern Historical Society Papers* (Richmond: William Byrd Press, 1930), new ser., vol. 9, p. 122.

80. Ibid., p. 123. For Chilton and Miles see Berman, *Richmond Jewry*, pp. 187–188; Simonhoff, *Jewish Participants*, pp. 289–290, Korn, *American Jewry in Civil War*, p. 178.

81. John Beauchamp Jones, *A Rebel War Clerk's Diary: At the Confederate States Capital* (1866; New York: Old Hickory Bookshop, 1935), vol. 1, pp. 78, 87, 128, 150, 164, 218–219, 221, 289, 369; vol. 2, pp. 117, 138, 141.

82. Butler to Edwin M. Stanton, Oct. 1862, in Parton, *General Butler*, p. 318; cf. pp. 391–392.

83. Sherman to Ellen Ewing Sherman, Sept. 18, 1858, in *Home Letters of General Sherman*, ed. M. A. DeWolfe Howe (New York: Charles Scribner's Sons, 1909), pp. 155, 229–230, and to Salmon P. Chase, Aug. 11, 1862, in *Memoirs of General William T. Sherman* (New York: Appleton, 1875), vol. 1, p. 267, and to the Adjutant-General of the Army, Aug. 11, 1862, *Official Records*, Series 3, vol. 2, p. 350.

84. All quotations from *Papers of Ulysses S. Grant*, ed. Simon: S. Ledyard Phelps to Andrew H. Foote, Dec. 30, 1861, vol. 3, p. 425; Grant to J. T. Quimby, July 26, 1862, vol. 5, p. 238, and to Stephen A. Hurlbut, Nov. 9, 1862, vol. 6, p. 283, and to Joseph D. Webster, Nov. 10, 1862, vol. 6, p. 283n, and to Sherman, Dec. 5, 1862, vol. 6, p. 394, and to Christopher P. Wolcott, Dec. 17, 1862, vol. 7, p. 56.

85. General Order No. 2, ibid., vol. 7, p. 9n; General Order No. 11, ibid., p. 58.

86. Henry W. Halleck to Grant, Sept. 30, 1864, ibid., vol. 12, p. 32n; Washburne to Grant, Jan. 8, 1863, ibid., vol. 7, p. 56n; cf. pp. 54–56n;

87. Korn, *Eventful Years*, p. 143; Hurlbut to Grant, Oct. 4, 1864, in *Papers of Ulysses Grant*, vol. 10, p. 387n; Grant to George H. Thomas, Dec. 22, 1863, ibid., vol. 9, p. 549.

88. "Sketches from the Seat of War by a Jewish Soldier," in *Documentary History*, ed. Schappes, pp. 466–467; Glass to Butler, April 12, 1864, ibid., pp. 493–496.

89. Bell Irvin Wiley, *The Common Soldier in the Civil War: The Life of Johnny Reb* (New York: Grosset and Dunlap, 1943), p. 237; Simonhoff, *Jewish Participants*, p. 290.

90. Korn, *American Jewry in Civil War*, pp. 179, 183, quote on p. 179; excerpts from the unpublished autobiography of Isidor Straus, in *Memoirs of American Jews*, ed. Marcus, vol. 2, p. 304; Simonhoff, *Jewish Participants*, pp. 190, 293, quote p. 293.

91. Louis Ruchames, in "The Abolitionists and the Jews," *PAJHS*, 42 (Sept. 1952–June 1953): 131–155, denies significant hostility toward Jews in the

movement. In a subsequent article, "The Abolitionists and the Jews: Some Further Thoughts," *A Bicentennial Festscrift for Jacob Rader Marcus* (Waltham, Mass.: AJHS; New York: KTAV, 1976), pp. 505–517, he concedes the existence of more animosity. For positive abolitionist attitudes see *Liberator,* 8 (Sept. 21, 1838): 150; 34 (Dec. 16, 1864): 204; *The Albion,* 3 (Nov. 2, 1844): 529.

92. John Weiss, *Life and Correspondence of Theodore Parker* (New York: D. Appleton, 1964): Theodore Parker, "Journal," March 1843, vol. 1, p. 214, and Parker to Dr. Francis, May 26, 1844, vol. 1, p. 236, and "Letter to the Members of the 2–8th Congregational Society of Boston" (1859), vol. 2, p. 497, and "Some Thoughts on the Charities of Boston" (1858), vol. 1, p. 397, and to Rev. David Wasson, Dec. 12, 1857, vol. 1, pp. 395–396. See also Egal Feldman, *Dual Destinies: The Jewish Encounter with Protestant America* (Urbana and Chicago: University of Illinois Press, 1990), pp. 56–59.

93. Lawrence J. Friedman, *Gregarious Saints: Self and Community in American Abolitionism, 1830–1870* (Cambridge and New York: Cambridge University Press, 1982), pp. 47–48, 53, 57; Edmond Quincy, "A Jew and a Christian," *Liberator,* 18 (Aug. 11, 1848): 126.

94. *Liberator,* 15 (May 20, 1842): 1; 19 (May 18, Sept. 21, 1849): 77, 751.

95. *The Letters of William Lloyd Garrison,* ed. Walter M. Merrill and Louis Ruchames (Cambridge, Mass.: Harvard University Press, 1971–1981), vol. 4: Garrison to Kossuth, Feb. 2, 1852, p. 160, and to Helen E. Garrison, Oct. 29, 1858, p. 595, and to the Pennsylvania Anti-Slave Society, Oct. 20, 1857, p. 493.

96. Child to Mrs. S. B. Shaw, 1859, in *Letters of Lydia Maria Child* (Boston: Houghton Mifflin, 1883), p. 141; Lydia Maria Child, *Letters from New-York* (New York: Charles Francis; Boston: James Munroe, 1843), pp. 25–26, 31, 33.

97. Child, *Letters from New-York,* pp. 12–13, 26–29, 31, 33–34, 217–218, 225.

98. For Wilson see Ray Allen Billington, *The Protestant Crusade, 1800–1860: A Study of the Origins of American Nativism* (1938; Chicago: Quadrangle, 1964), pp. 424–428.

99. Ronald G. Walters, *The Antislavery Appeal: American Abolitionism after 1830* (Baltimore and London: Johns Hopkins University Press, 1976), pp. 12–13, 33, 52.

100. On images of the grasping Jew see Michael N. Dobkowski, *The Tarnished Dream: The Basis of American Anti-Semitism* (Westport, Conn.: Greenwood Press, 1979), pp. 78–85.

101. Louis Stix, "Reminiscences Chronicled as a Recreation in His Later Years, 1821–1902," excerpted in *Memoirs of American Jews,* ed. Marcus, vol. 1, pp. 317–318; Lorenzo Whitney to Elihu B. Washburne, Nov. 14, 1863, in

*Papers of Ulysses S. Grant,* ed. Simon, vol. 9, p. 389n; Lyman and Cooledge to U. S. Grant, Aug. 8, 1863, ibid., p. 141n.

102. The ad (from another newspaper) was quoted in a *New York Sun* editorial, Mar. 17, 1849, in *Documentary History,* ed. Schappes, p. 286; Hertzberg, *Strangers within the Gate,* p. 20.

103. Peter Decker, "Jewish Merchants in San Francisco: Social Mobility on the Urban Frontier," *American Jewish History,* 68 (June 1979): 398–399, 402; Stephen G. Mostov, "Dun and Bradstreet Reports as a Source of Jewish Economic History: Cincinnati, 1840–1875," ibid., 72 (March 1983): 333–353; Korn, *Jews of New Orleans,* p. 74; Elliott Ashkenazi, *The Business of Jews in Louisiana, 1840–1875* (Tuscaloosa: University of Alabama Press, 1988), pp. 74–75, 151; "R. G. Dun and Bradstreet Credit Reports: Columbus to Cleveland, Ohio," in *Jews and Judaism in the United States: A Documentary History,* ed. Marc Lee Raphael (New York: Behrman House, 1985), pp. 34–35, 38; Gerber, "Cutting out Shylock," pp. 212–213, 218–220, 224; Bertram Wyatt-Brown, *Lewis Tappan and the Evangelical War against Slavery* (Cleveland: Case Western Reserve University Press, 1969), pp. 228–234, 241–243; Friedman, *Gregarious Saints,* pp. 71–76, 80, 85–87.

104. Mostov, "Dun and Bradstreet," 348–349; Gerber, "Cutting out Shylock," pp. 219–220.

105. Mostov, "Dun and Bradstreet," 343–344, 348–349; Ashkenazi, *Business of Jews,* pp. 74–75.

106. Gerber, "Cutting out Shylock," pp. 215–219.

107. Ibid., p. 220; Mostov, "Dun and Bradstreet," 348–353, quotes 351–353; Decker, "Jewish Merchants," 399, 402; Ashkenazi, *Business of Jews,* p. 164.

108. Gerber, "Cutting out Shylock," pp. 209–210.

109. Korn, *American Jewry in Civil War,* pp. 179, 183; Berman, *Richmond Jewry,* pp. 188–190.

110. Ruth Miller Elson, *Guardians of Tradition: American Schoolbooks of the Nineteenth Century* (Lincoln: University of Nebraska Press, 1964), pp. 59–60, 196.

111. William Russell and John Goldsbury, *Introduction to the American Common-School Reader and Speaker; Comprising Selections in Prose and Verse* (1844; Boston: Tappan, Whittemore and Mason, 1845), pp. 37, 26–27. Bibliographical data in *Dictionary of American Biography* (hereafter *DAB*), ed. Dumas Malone (New York: Charles Scribner's Sons, 1928–1988), vol. 16, pp. 299–300.

112. S. Augustus Mitchell, *A System of Modern Geography* (Philadelphia: Thomas, Cowperthwaite, 1843), pp. 50, 227, 307; *DAB,* vol. 13, p. 61.

113. Salem Town and Nelson M. Holbrook, *The Progressive Fourth Grade Reader, For Public and Private Schools* (1857; Boston: Oliver Ellsworth, 1864), pp. 418, 427; Richard G. Parker and J. Madison Watson, *The National Pronouncing Speller* (1857; New York and Chicago: A. S. Barnes, 1874), p. 66; *DAB,* vol. 14, pp. 236–237, and vol. 19, p. 544.

114. *The American Reader: Containing Selections in Prose, Poetry and Dialogue,* ed. P. H. Snow (Hartford: Spalding and Storrs; Boston: Gould, Kendall and Lincoln, 1840), p. 216.
115. See Sander L. Gilman, *Jewish Self-Hatred: Anti-Semitism and the Hidden Language of the Jews* (Baltimore and London: Johns Hopkins University Press, 1986), pp. 68–86, 120, 155–164, and "Chicken Soup, or the Penalties for Sounding too Jewish," *Shofar,* 2 (Winter 1991): 55–69, and *The Jew's Body* (New York and London: Routledge, 1991), pp. 96–101, 124–127.
116. Harvey C. Minnich, *William Holmes McGuffey and His Readers* (New York: American Book Company, 1936); John H. Westerhoff, III, *McGuffey and His Readers: Piety, Morality, and Education in Nineteenth-Century America* (Nashville, Abingdon, 1978), pp. 74–110; Richard D. Mosier, *Making the American Mind: Social and Moral Ideas in the McGuffey Readers* (New York: Russell and Russell, 1965), sales data p. 168; William McGuffey, *McGuffey's Newly Revised Eclectic Fourth Reader* (Cincinnati: William B. Smith, 1848), p. 9.
117. Ibid., pp. 185–186; William McGuffey, *McGuffey's Rhetorical Guide; or Fifth Reader* (Cincinnati: Winthrop B. Smith, 1844), p. 115.
118. *Newly Revised Eclectic Fourth Reader,* p. 191.
119. Ibid., p. 193; William McGuffey, *McGuffey's New Fifth Eclectic Reader: Selected and Original Exercises for Schools* (Cincinnati and New York: Van Antwerp, Bragg, 1866), pp. 280, 282, 284.
120. McGuffey, *Newly Revised Eclectic Fourth Reader,* pp. 228–230, and *New Fifth Eclectic Reader,* pp. 198–203, 251.
121. *Report of the Selection Committee of the Board of Education, to which was Referred a Communication from the Trustees of the Fourth Ward, in Relation to the Sectarian Character of Certain Books in Use in the Schools of that Ward* (New York: Levi D. Slamm, 1843); Floyd S. Furman, "The Jews and the Problem of Church and State in America Prior to 1881," *Educational Forum,* 15 (Jan. 1951): 335–341; Dorothea L. Dix, *Conversations on Common Things; or, Guide to Knowledge with Questions* (1824; Boston: Munroe and Francis, 1831), pp. 282, 284, 286, quote p. 282; *DAB,* vol. 5, pp. 323–325.
122. Lindley Murray, *The English Reader; or, Pieces in Prose and Verse Selected from the Best Authors* (1799; Newark, N.J.: Benjamin Olds, 1841), pp. 117–119, 139–140; *DAB,* vol. 13, pp. 365–366.
123. [Stephen Grellet and William Allen], *Lessons for Schools, Taken from the Holy Scriptures: In the Words of the Text* (Philadelphia: American Sunday-School Union, 1865), pp. 3–4, 112–140, 146, 149, 153–158, 165–167, 180–183, 254–265, 272–300; *DAB,* vol. 7, pp. 606–607.
124. *Report of the Selection Committee,* pp. 14, 7–8.
125. William C. Larrabee, *Lectures on the Scientific Evidences of Natural and Revealed Religion* (Cincinnati: L. Swormstedt and A. Poe, 1853), p. 392.

126. James H. Moorhead, *American Apocalypse: Yankee Protestants and the Civil War, 1860–1869* (New Haven: Yale University Press, 1978), pp. 16–17.

127. Ibid., pp. 20–21; Timothy L. Smith, *Revivalism and Social Reform in Mid Nineteenth Century America* (New York and Nashville: Abingdon Press, 1957), pp. 17, 20–22, 43, 45–79.

128. Elton Trueblood, *Abraham Lincoln: Theologian of American Anguish* (New York: Harper and Row, 1973), pp. 6–7, 77, 84–94; Moorhead, *American Apocalypse*, pp. 42–49; Richard N. Current, *The Lincoln Nobody Knows* ((New York: McGraw-Hill, 1958), pp. 73–74; Donald G. Jones, *The Sectional Crisis and Northern Methodism: A Study in Piety, Political Ethics and Civil Religion* (Metuchen, N.J.: Scarecrow Press, 1979), pp. 69–96; Friedman, *Gregarious Saints*, p. 217; Drew Gilpin Faust, *The Creation of Confederate Nationalism: Ideology and Identity in the Civil War South* (Baton Rouge: Louisiana State University Press, 1988), pp. 22–33, 42, 60–61, 82–83; W. Harrison Daniel, "Southern Protestantism," *Civil War History*, 5 (Sept. 1989): 277.

129. Moorhead, *American Apocalypse*, pp. 42–81, 174–178; Smith, *Revivalism and Social Reform*, pp. 232–235; Jones, *Sectional Crisis*, pp. 69–96; Daniel, "Southern Protestantism," 278–282; Stephen B. Oates, *Abraham Lincoln: The Man behind the Myths* (New York: Harper and Row, 1984), p. 4.

130. Oates, *Abraham Lincoln*, p. 188; Current, *Lincoln Nobody Knows*, pp. 72–74; Dwight G. Anderson, *Abraham Lincoln: The Quest for Immortality* (New York: Alfred A. Knopf, 1982), pp. 128, 167–169; Trueblood, *Abraham Lincoln: Theologian*, esp. pp. 8–10, 31–32, 44–45, 86–89.

131. Smith, *Revivalism and Social Reform*, pp. 76–78; Moorhead, *American Apocalypse*, pp. 65–72; Clifford S. Griffin, *Their Brothers' Keepers: Moral Stewardship in the United States, 1800–1865* (New Brunswick, N.J.: Rutgers University Press, 1960), pp. 242–252.

132. W. C. Brownlee, "Preface to the First Edition," in Matthew A. Berk, *The History of the Jews from the Babylonian Captivity to the Present Time* (1842; Boston: Matthew A. Berk, 1849), pp. 5–9, quote p. 5; cf. Rev. William Jenks, "Preface to the Second Edition" (1849), pp. 12–14; Korn, *American Jewry in Civil War*, p. 96; Robert Baird, *Religion in America* (New York: Harper and Bros., 1856), p. 629; Feldman, *Dual Destinies*, p. 73.

133. Wise, *Reminiscences*, p. 121; Herman Melville, *Journal of a Visit to Europe and the Levant, Nov. 11, 1856—May 6, 1857*, ed. Howard C. Horsford (Princeton: Princeton University Press, 1955), pp. 108n, 130n, 156–157, 157n, 159.

134. Baird, *Religion in America*, pp. 337–338; Harvey P. Peet, *Scripture Lessons for the Young* (New York: American Tract Society, 1849), pp. 84, 86, 90, 92.

135. William T. Sherman to Ellen Boyle Ewing, Jan. 31, 1846, *Home Letters*, ed. Howe, p. 32; *Christian Intelligencer* and *Free Presbyterian* quoted in Louise A. Mayo, "The Ambivalent Image: The Perception of the Jew in Nineteenth Century America" (Ph.D diss., City University of New York, 1977), pp. 20, 30.

136. "Reviling Christianity," *Churchman*, 25 (March 15, 1855): 20; cf. "Religious Liberty," ibid. (March 29, 1855): 36.

137. Feldman, *Dual Destinies*, pp. 52–53.

138. Abiel Abbott Livermore, "Essay III: The Apostle Paul," from *The Apostle Paul and the Epistle of Paul to the Romans* (1854), in *An American Reformation: A Documentary History of Unitarian Christianity*, ed. Sydney E. Ahlstrom and Jonathan S. Carey (Middletown, Conn.: Wesleyan University Press, 1985), pp. 277, 279, 289.

139. Wise, *Reminiscences*, p. 64.

140. Korn, *American Reaction*, pp. 153–155; *Catholic Mirror*, 9 (Dec. 4, 1858): 2.

141. "The Story of a Boy," *Guardian*, 1 (Nov. 13, 1858): 4; "The Mortara Persecution," ibid., (Jan. 15, 1859): 4.

142. "The Jew Story," *New York Tablet*, 2 (Nov. 6, 1858): 8; for a milder version of the Catholic position see "The Mortara Case," *United States Catholic Miscellany* 37 (Jan. 29, 1859): 231.

143. "The Jews and the Holy See," *Pilot*, 21 (Dec. 18, 1858): 4; cf. "The Mortara Abduction Case," ibid. (Nov. 27, 1858): 4; "Naturalism," ibid., 22 (Jan. 1, 1859): 4.

144. Fox, "Quaker, Shaker," 171, 175–176.

145. *New York Herald*, Feb. 5, 1860; p. 1; *Brownlow's Knoxville Whig*, Feb. 18, 1860, p. 1.

146. Korn, *Eventful Years*, p. 104; *Freeman* quoted p. 106; "Who Is the God of This Nation," *Churchman*, 30 (Feb. 11, 1960): 434.

147. Korn, *American Jewry in Civil War*, pp. 58–62; Simonhoff, *Jewish Participants*, pp. 42–43, *Presbyter* quoted on p. 42.

148. Archer Taylor, "The Burning of Judas," *Washington University Studies: Humanistic Series*, 11 (Nov. 1923): 159–186; Horace Bell, *Reminiscences of a Ranger or, Early Times in Southern California* (Los Angeles: Yarnell, Caystile and Mathes, 1881), p. 286–288, quote p. 287.

149. *Allegemeine Zeitung des Judentum* (1850), in Saul S. Freedman, *The Incident at Massena: The Blood Libel in America* (New York: Stein and Day, 1978), p. 593; Leonard Dinnerstein, *The Leo Frank Case* (New York: Columbia University Press, 1969); Hertzberg, *Strangers within the Gate*, pp. 161–162, 166–167, 174–175; *Louis Marshall, Champion of Liberty: Selected Papers and Addresses*, ed. Charles Reznikoff (Philadelphia: JPSA, 1957), vol. 1, pp. 419–421. For the 1928 case see Freedman, *Incident at Massena*.

150. *New York Herald*, April 6, 1850, p. 1.

151. Korn, *Eventful Years*, p. 60.

152. "D'Israeli's *Tancred, or the New Crusade*," *North American Review*, 66 (July 1847): 212–214.

153. Frank Luther Mott, *A History of American Magazines* (Cambridge, Mass.: Harvard University Press, 1938), vol. 2, pp. 469–476; "Jewish Prospects," *Harper's Weekly*, 3 (Nov. 19, 1859): 733.

154. Story to Lowell, Dec. 30, 1855, in Henry James, *William Wetmore Story and His Friends* (1903; New York: Grove Press, n.d.), vol. 1, p. 303.

155. *The Diary of George Templeton Strong*, ed. Allan Nevins and Milton Halsey Thomas (New York: Macmillan, 1952), vol. 1, p. 256; vol. 2, p. 231.

156. *Spirit of the Times*, 14 (Jan. 11, 1845): 544; 18 (Aug. 5, 1848): 282; 19 (Feb. 9, 1850): 605; 20 (1850–51): 85; 22 (April 3, 1852): 77; 22 (April 17, 1852): 99–100; 23 (1853–54): 303.

157. *Knickerbocker*, 36 (1850): 489–490; 42 (Sept. 1853): 322; 45 (May 1855): 551; 50 (Nov. 1857): 477; 56 (Dec, 1860): 660.

158. This analysis of anti-Semitic humor is from Sig Altman, *The Comic Image of the Jew: Explorations of a Pop Culture Phenomenon* (Rutherford, N.J.: Fairleigh Dickinson University Press, 1971), pp. 23–24, 172, 204.

159. "The Snoblace Ball," *Spectator* (1845), in Rudolf Glanz, *The Jew in Early American Wit and Graphic Humor* (New York: KTAV, 1973), p. 25; Glanz, *Studies in Judaica*, pp. 127, 143, 338, 340, 345, 350, 357, and *The Jew in Old American Folklore* (New York: Waldon Press, 1961), pp. 45–48, 125–128, 130, 132–134, 147–165, 168–169, 220n, 209n.

160. Glanz, *Studies in Judaica*, p. 148.

161. J. Ross Browne, *Crusoe's Island: A Ramble in the Footsteps of Alexander Selkirk, with Sketches of Adventure in California and Washoe* (New York: Harper and Bros., 1864), pp. 347–350, 397–400, 418.

162. Cornelius Mathews, *Pen-And-Ink Panorama of New York City* (New York: John S. Taylor, 1853), p. 166.

163. [George G. Foster], *New York In Slices* (1848; New York: W. F. Burgess, 1849), pp. 14–18, 31–32. For more on anti-Semitism in New York guidebooks see Mayo, "Ambivalent Image," pp. 188–190.

164. G[eorge] G. Foster, *New York by Gas-Light with Here and There a Streak of Sunshine* (1850; New York: M. J. Ivers, 185?), pp. 57–59.

165. Walt Whitman, "Broadway," in *New York Dissected* (New York: Rufus Rockwell Wilson, 1936), p. 123.

166. Glanz, *Studies in Judaica*, pp. 60, 67, 144–148, 228–229, 234–236; Fein, *Making of a Jewish Community*, p. 203.

167. *Sunday Times and Noah's Weekly and Messenger*, Aug. 12, 1849, in *Documentary History*, ed. Schappes, p. 293.

168. *The Knickerbocker*, 59 (March 1962): 307; 60 (Aug. 1862): 121; "The Great Panic," *Harper's Weekly*, 7 (1863): 187.

169. *Harper's New Monthly Magazine* 32 (1865–66): 401, 405; 17 (July 1858): 267.

170. *Southern Punch,* 2 (Oct. 10, 1863): 4; (Oct. 17, 1863): 2.

171. *Richmond Examiner,* Dec. 20, 1862, pp. 1–2. For newspaper attacks on Jews see Simonhoff, *Jewish Participants,* pp. 145–147; Korn, *American Jewry in Civil War,* pp. 128, 130, 158–164, 167, 177–180; Emory M. Thomas, *The Confederate State of Richmond: A Biography of the Capital* (Austin: University of Texas Press, 1971), p. 151; Berman, *Richmond Jewry,* pp. 185–186; Glanz, *Jew in Old American Folklore,* pp. 50, 100.

172. *Southern Illustrated News,* Oct. 3, 1863, p. 100.

173. *The Israelite,* 9 (Dec. 5, 1862): 172; *Detroit Commercial Advertiser* quoted in ibid., 6 (March 6, 1863): 277; Associated Press reporter quoted in Simonhoff, *Jewish Participants,* p. 146.

174. Congregations Beth Ahabah and Beth Shalome resolutions respectively of October 21 and Dec. 29, 1863, in Ezekiel and Lichtenstein, *Jews of Richmond,* pp. 246–247; Simon Wolf to the editor of the *New York Evening Post,* Nov. 20, 1864, and "The Hebrew Race," *Washington Chronicle,* editorial, Nov. 1864, in *Memoirs of American Jews,* ed. Marcus, vol. 2, pp. 223–229, quote p. 229.

175. *New York Times,* Sept. 18, 1864, p. 2; Hertzberg, *Strangers within the Gate,* pp. 25–27; Berman, *Richmond Jewry,* pp. 188–189; *Harper's Magazine,* 30 (1864–65): 131.

176. Ezekiel and Lichtenstein, *Jews of Richmond,* pp. 246–247; Berman, *Richmond Jewry,* pp. 188–190; Hertzberg, *Strangers within the Gate,* p. 27; Korn, *American Jewry in Civil War,* pp. 170–173, 180–181, 186–187; Simonhoff, *Jewish Participants,* p. 296.

177. Harap, *Jew in American Literature,* p. 211; James Pilgrim, "Yankee Jack; or, The Buccaneer of the Gulf: A Nautical Drama," 1852 (mss. on microfilm at the University of Illinois, Champaign-Urbana), Act 3, pp. 14, 20.

178. Julia Ward Howe, *The World's Own* (Boston: Ticknor and Fields, 1857), pp. 104–105, 107–108; Louisa Hall Tharp, *Three Saints and a Sinner: Julia Ward Howe, Louisa, Annie and Samuel Ward* (Boston and Toronto: Little, Brown, 1956), pp. 230–231.

179. *Buffalo Courier* review in *Spirit of the Times,* 21 (Dec. 13, 1852): 516.

180. George M. Baker, *The Peddler of Very Nice: A Burlesque of the Trial-scene in the Merchant of Venice* (1865; Boston: Walter H. Baker, 1893); Lelyveld, *Shylock on Stage,* p. 75.

181. William Croswell, "The Synagogue," in *The Poets and Poetry of America,* ed. Rufus Wilmot Griswold (1842; Philadelphia: Carey and Hart, 1848), p. 301.

182. Harap, *Jew in American Literature,* pp. 241–255.

183. [Robert Tyler], *Ahasuerus: A Poem* (New York: Harper and Bros., 1842), pp. 15–17, 20.

184. David Hoffman, *Chronicles Selected from the Origins of Cartaphilus, the Wandering Jew* (London: Thomas Bosworth, 1853), vol. 1, pp. 93, 96, 421; vol. 3,

p. 383; R. Edelmann, "Ahasuerus, The Wandering Jew: Origin and Background," in *The Wandering Jew: Essays in the Interpretation of a Christian Legend,* ed. Galit Hasan-Rokem and Alan Dundes (Bloomington: Indiana University Press, 1986), p. 4.

185. For the relationship between the myths of Cain and Abel and the Wandering Jew see Ruth Mellinkopf, *The Mark of Cain* (Berkeley and Los Angeles: University of California Press, 1981), pp. 38–40, 92, 115–116n; Gaer, *Legend of the Wandering Jew,* pp. 78–79, 202; Rose, *Revolutionary Antisemitism,* p. 53; E. Isaac-Edersheim, "Ahasver: A Mythic Image of the Jew," in *Wandering Jew,* ed. Hasan-Rokem and Dundes, p. 202.

186. Matt. 16:28; 26:50–51; Mark 9:1; 14:46–47; John 14:2–3; 18:22–23.

187. Gaer, *Legend of the Wandering Jew,* pp. 75–78; Leviticus 18:21; Rose, *Revolutionary Antisemitism,* pp. 45–47, 53; Edelmann, "Ahasuerus," p. 4.

188. Gaer, *Legend of the Wandering Jew,* pp. 11–18, 34–38, 113–144; Edelmann, "Ahasuerus," pp. 3, 5–6; Hasan-Rokem, "The Cobbler of Jerusalem in Finnish Folklore," in *Wandering Jew,* ed. Hasan-Rokem and Dundes, pp. 127, 141; Hyam Maccoby, *The Sacred Executioner: Human Sacrifice and the Legacy of Guilt* (New York: Thames and Hudson, 1982), pp. 167, 174; Ernest A. Rappaport, *Anti Judaism: A Psychohistory* (Chicago: Perspective Press, 1975), p. 81; Rose, *Revolutionary Antisemitism,* pp. 23–24; Aaron Schaffer, "The Ahasver-Volksbuch of 1602," in *Wandering Jew,* ed. Hasan-Rokem and Dundes, pp. 5–6, 27–29, 33.

189. S. Hurwitz, "Ahasver, The Eternal Wanderer: Psychological Aspects," in *Wandering Jew,* ed. Hasan-Rokem and Dundes, p. 224; Adolf L. Leschnitzer, "The Wandering Jew: The Alienation of the Jewish Image in Christian Consciousness," ibid., pp. 229–230; Hasan-Rokem, "Cobbler," pp. 127, 142; Isaac-Edersheim, "Ahasver," pp. 198–200; Maccoby, *Sacred Executioner,* pp. 167–169, 172–173; Rose, *Revolutionary Antisemitism,* pp. 23–24, 31–43, 53–54.

190. Hasan-Rokem, "Cobbler," p. 127; Maccoby, *Sacred Executioner,* p. 168; Gaer, *Legend of the Wandering Jew,* p. 151.

191. Nathaniel Hawthorne, "The Star of Calvary," in *An American Anthology: 1787–1900,* ed. Edward C. Stedman (Boston: Houghton Mifflin, 1900), p. 191.

192. Nathaniel Parker Willis, *The Poems, Sacred, Passionate, and Humorous* (New York: Clark, Austin 1850), "The Leper," pp. 6–7; "Christ's Entrance into Jerusalem," p. 34.

193. Nathaniel Hawthorne, *Passages from the English Note-Books* (Boston: Houghton Mifflin, 1870), vol. 1, April 1856, p. 18, and *Passages from the French and Italian Note-Books* (Boston: Houghton Mifflin, 1871), vol. 1, Italy, 1858, pp. 49, 82, and *The Marble Faun; or, The Romance of Monte Beni* (1860; Boston: Houghton Mifflin, 1888), p. 175; Julian Hawthorne, *Sebastian Strome*

(1880; London: Chatto and Windus, 1881), pp. 42–43, 121–125, 146, 175–179, 182–186, 195–198, 203, 252, 260–262, 279–280, 287, and *Beatrix Randolph* (Boston: James R. Osgood, 1884), pp. 70–72.

194. Melville, *Journal of a Visit,* p. 151, and *Pierre: or the Ambiguities* (1853; New York: Russell and Russell, 1963), p. 295.

195. Melville, *The Confidence Man: His Masquerade* (1857; New York: Russell and Russell, 1963), p. 195, and *Redburn: His First Voyage* (1849; New York: Russell and Russell, 1963), p. 216.

196. Melville, *Redburn,* pp. 22–23, 25–26, 250.

197. Gilman, *Jew's Body,* pp. 171–179.

198. *DAB,* vol. 18, p. 117.

199. Harriet Beecher Stowe, *Uncle Tom's Cabin; or, Life among the Lowly* (1851–1852; New York: Modern Library, 1938), pp. 78–79, 243, 245.

200. Frank Luther Mott, *Golden Multitudes: The Story of Best Sellers in the United States* (New York: Macmillan, 1947), pp. 247, 307; *DAB,* vol. 11, pp. 285–286; E. Douglas Branch, *The Sentimental Years: 1836–1860* (New York: Hill and Wang, 1962), p. 128; George Lippard, *The Quaker City; or, The Monks of Monk Hall* (Philadelphia: T. B. Peterson and Bros., 1876), pp. 30–31, 35–36, 148–149, 178, 202–203, 476.

201. *DAB,* vol. 9, pp. 479–480; Mott, *Golden Multitudes,* p. 94; Donald C. Seitz, "A Prince of Best Sellers," *Publishers' Weekly,* 110 (Feb. 21, 1937): 940; J. H. Ingraham, *The Gypsy of the Highlands; or, The Jew and the Heir* (Boston: Redding, 1843), pp. 17, 20–21, 28–30.

202. Ingraham, *The Clipper Yacht; or, Moloch, the Money-Lender* (Boston: H. L. Williams, 1845), pp. 8–9, 12, 14–15, 21, 32–33, 52, 54.

203. Ingraham, *Ramero: or, The Prince and the Prisoner* (Boston: Henry L. Williams, 1846), pp. 42–43, 48–49, 54, quote p. 49.

204. Ingraham, *The Throne of David* (Rahway, N.J.: Mershon, 1860), pp. vii–viii.

205. Mott, *Golden Multitudes,* pp. 94, 307, 320; Seitz, "Prince of Best Sellers," 940.

206. Ingraham, Preface to *The Prince of the House of David; or Three Years in the Holy City* (1855; New York: Grosset and Dunlap, 1908), p. iii, and *The Pillar of Fire; or, Israel in Bondage* (1859; Boston: Roberts Bros., 1871), dedication, and *Throne of David,* p. v, and *Pillar of Fire,* pp. 50, 103–107, 110–112, 118, 136–143, 147–148, 301, 342, 432–468, 509.

207. Ingraham, *Throne of David,* pp. 46–48, 202–212, 306–307, quote p. 309.

208. Ingraham, *Prince of the House,* pp. 226, 350, 354, 385, 391, 405, 409, 342, 378, 343, 353.

209. Mott, *Golden Multitudes,* pp. 136–142; E. D. E. N. Southworth, *Miriam, Avenger; or, The Missing Bride* (1855; Philadelphia: T. B. Paterson and Bros., 1874), pp. 538–543, and *Self-Raised; or, From the Depths* (1863; New York:

Grosset and Dunlap, n.d.), pp. 171–172, 300–303, and *The Bridal Eve* (1864; Chicago: M. A. Donahue, n.d.), p. 255, and *Allworth Abbey; or, Eudora* (1865; New York: Hurst, 1876), p. 144.

210. Charles Frederick Briggs (Harry Franco), *Bankrupt Stories* (1843; New York: John Allen, 1844), pp. 103, 188, 309–310, 322–327, 343–344, quotes p. 310.

211. Walter Barrett (Joseph Scoville), *Clarence Bolton: A New York Story, With City Society in All Its Phases* (New York: Garrett, 1852), p. 58, and *Vigor: A Novel* (New York: George W. Carleton, 1863), pp. 34, 38–44, 97, 120–121, 130–131, 136, quote p. 34; Gilman, *Jew's Body,* pp. 120–125.

212. P. Hamilton Myers, *The Miser's Heir; or, The Young Millionaire* (Philadelphia: T. B. Peterson, 1854), pp. 91–93, quote p. 92.

213. [Frederick Jackson], *A Week in Wall Street* (New York: n.p., 1841), pp. 6, 25, 144.

214. John Beauchamp Jones, *The Western Merchant* (Philadelphia: Grigg, Elliot, 1849), pp. 128, 131–143, 203, 210–211, 226–227, quotes pp. 128, 133. On post–Civil War fantasies of a Jewish financial conspiracy see Frederic Cople Jaher, *Doubters and Dissenters: Cataclysmic Thought in America, 1885–1918* (New York: Free Press, 1964).

215. Jones, *Life and Adventures of a Country Merchant* (Philadelphia: Lippincott, Grambo, 1854), pp. 308–309, 342–344, 368, 369–371.

216. Jones, *The Winkles; or, The Merry Monomaniacs* (New York: D. Appleton, 1855), pp. 32–33, 36–37, 170–172, quote p. 37.

217. Edmond Quincy, *Wensley: A Story without a Moral* (Boston: Ticknor and Fields, 1854), pp. 275–276, 282, 288.

218. Theodore Sedgwick Fay, *The Countess Ida: A Tale of Berlin* (New York: Harper and Bros., 1840), vol. 1, pp. 46–47, vol. 2, p. 248, quote vol. 1, p. 47.

219. B. Perley Poore, *The Mameluke; or, The Sign of the Mystic Tie* (Boston: F. Gleason, 1852), p. 22.

220. Roderick Roundelay (pseud.), "Jewing and Chewing," *A Little Bit of a Tid-Re-I; or a Chorus to the Times* (New York), no. 2 (May 1824): 104; *Knickerbocker,* 58 (1861): 381; *Southern Illustrated News,* 2 (Oct. 3, 1860): 100.

221. George W. Harris, "Rare Ripe Garden Seed," in *Native American Humor,* ed. Walter Blair (New York: American Book, 1937), p. 386; *Spirit of the Times,* 14 (1844–45): 506.

222. *Harper's Magazine,* 17 (July 1858): 267–268; 22 (1866): 404.

223. See *The Century Dictionary* (New York: Century, 1889), vol. 3, pp. 3230–3231; *The New American Encyclopedic Dictionary* (New York: J. A. Hall, 1906), p. 2401; *Student's Edition of a Standard Dictionary of the English Language* (New York and London: Funk and Wagnalls, 1907 and 1915), p. 388; *Webster's Collegiate Dictionary,* Merriam Series, 3rd ed. (Springfield, Mass.: G. and C. Merriam, 1934), p. 54; *Roget's International Thesaurus of*

*English Words and Phrases* (New York: Thomas Y. Crowell, 1925), pp. 587, 803, 819, 984; *Johnson's and Walker's English Dictionaries Combined* (Boston: Perkins and Marvin, 1830), p. 535. For "rich as a Jew" see Glanz, *Jew in Old American Folklore,* pp. 9–29, 40–44, 47–49, 55, 98, 101–103, 119–120, 125–128, 130, 132–134, 147–176.

224. Glanz, *Jew in Old American Folklore,* pp. 6–8, quote p. 6.

225. "Old Mother Goose," in *Mother Goose* (orig. pub. in America 1719; New York: Century, 1913), pp. 213–215; Mott, *Golden Multitudes,* pp. 28–29, 261n, 303.

226. Mott, *Golden Multitudes,* pp. 99, 308; Jakob and Wilhelm Grimm, *The Complete Grimm's Fairy Tales* (New York: Pantheon Books, 1972), pp. 54–55, 507–508; "The Jew among the Thorns," in *Grimm's Fairy Tales* (Philadelphia: J. B. Lippincott, 1902), pp. 265–279, quote p. 279; John M. Ellis, *One Fairy Story Too Many: The Brothers Grimm and Their Tales* (Chicago and London: University of Chicago Press, 1983), p. 90.

227. Lester Hubbard and Le Roy J. Robertson, "King John and the Bishop," in "Traditional Ballads from Utah," *Journal of American Folklore,* 64 (Jan.–March 1951): 44; Florence Ridley, "A Tale Told Too Often," *Western Folklore,* 26 (July 1967): 153–156; "A Substitute for the Minister," in Palmer Cox, *Frontier Humor* (Philadelphia: Hubbard, 1895), p. 147.

228. "Cry Holy," in T. W. Higginson, "Negro Spirituals," *Atlantic Monthly,* 19 (June 1867): 688; Howard W. Odum, "Religious Folk-Songs of the Southern Negroes," *American Journal of Religious Psychology and Education,* 3 (1909): 291; Arthur Fauset, "Negro Folk Tales from the South," *Journal of American Folklore,* 40 (July–Aug. 1927): 271.

## Epilogue

1. Richard S. Levy, *Downfall of the Anti-Semitic Parties in Imperial Germany* (New Haven: Yale University Press, 1975), pp. 77, 104, 159, 242–243; Norman Cohn, *Warrant for Genocide: The Myth of the Jewish World Conspiracy and the Protocols of the Elders of Zion* (New York: Harper and Row, 1967), pp. 61–66; Steven Wilson, *Ideology and Experience: Anti-Semitism in France at the Time of the Dreyfus Affair* (London and Toronto: Associated University Presses; Rutherford, N.J.: Fairleigh Dickinson University Press, 1982), pp. 75–78, 110, 116–118, 139–140, 185–186, 197–203, 699–702, 730; Malcolm Hay, *Europe and the Jews: The Pressure of Christendom on the People of Israel for 1900 Years* (Boston: Beacon Press, 1961), pp. 194–207; Hannah Arendt, *The Origins of Totalitarianism* (1950; New York: Meridian, 1972), pp. 95–117; Leonard Greenberg and Harold J. Jonas, "An American Anti-Semite in the Nineteenth Century," in *Essays on Jewish Life and Thought,* ed. Joseph L. Blau (New York: Columbia University Press, 1950), pp. 267–268, 279–283;

David M. Chalmers, *Hooded Americanism: The First Century of the Ku Klux Klan, 1865–1965* (Garden City, N.J.: Doubleday, 1965), chs. 4–42; Ralph Lord Roy, *Apostles of Discord: A Study of Organized Bigotry on the Fringes of Protestantism* (Boston: Beacon Press, 1953), pp. 101–102; Donald S. Strong, *Organized Anti-Semitism in America: The Rise of Group Prejudice During the Decade 1930–1940* (1941; Westport, Conn.: Greenwood Press, 1979), pp. 24–26, 40; Gustavus Myers, *History of Bigotry in the United States* (New York: Random House, 1943), pp. 394, 408–411.

2. The discussion of Europe is informed by the following works: Levy, *Downfall of the Anti-Semitic Parties*; Richard Gutteridge, *Open Thy Mouth for the Dumb: The German Evangelical Church and the Jews, 1879–1950* (Oxford: Basil Blackwell, 1976); George Mosse, *Crisis of German Ideology: Intellectual Origins of the Third Reich* (New York: Universal Library, 1964); Robert S. Wistrich, *Socialism and the Jews: The Dilemmas of Assimilation in Germany and Austria-Hungary* (London and Toronto: Associated University Presses; Rutherford, N.J.: Fairleigh Dickinson University Press, 1982); Friedrich Heer, *God's First Love: Christians and Jews over Two Thousand Years* (New York: Weybright and Talley, 1970); Hay, *Europe and the Jews*; James Parkes, *The Emergence of the Jewish Problem: 1878–1939* (1941; Westport Conn.: Greenwood Press, 1970); Cohn, *Warrant for Genocide*; Paul W. Massing, *Rehearsal for Destruction: A Study of Anti-Semitism in Imperial Germany* (New York: Harper and Bros., 1949); Uriel Tal, *Christians and Jews in Germany: Religion, Politics and Ideology in the Second Reich, 1870–1914* (Ithaca: Cornell University Press, 1975); Jacob Katz, *From Prejudice to Destruction: Anti-Semitism, 1700–1933* (Cambridge, Mass.: Harvard University Press, 1980); Paula Hyman, *From Dreyfus to Vichy: The Remaking of French Jewry, 1906–1939* (New York: Columbia University Press, 1979); Robert F. Byrnes, *Anti-Semitism in Modern France: The Prologue to the Dreyfus Affair* (New York: Howard Fertig, 1969); Arendt, *Totalitarianism*; Wilson, *Ideology and Experience*.

3. Greenberg and Jonas, "American Anti-Semite," p. 282; Chalmers, *Hooded Americanism*, chs. 4–42.

4. Laurence Gronlund, *The Cooperative Commonwealth* (1884; Cambridge, Mass.: Harvard University Press, 1965), p. 44; Philip S. Foner, *Jack London: An American Rebel* (New York: Citadel Press, 1947), p. 124. For anti-Semitism in London's novels see *Burning Daylight* (New York: Macmillan, 1910), pp. 142–143; *Michael, Brother of Jerry* (New York: Macmillan, 1919), p. 63.

5. David Starr Jordan, *The Human Harvest: A Study of the Decay of the Races through the Survival of the Unfit* (Boston: Beacon Press, 1907), p. 40, and *Unseen Empire: A Study of the Plight of Nations That Do Not Pay Their Debts* (Boston: Beacon Press, 1912), pp. 9–24; Edward Alsworth Ross, *The Old World in the New: The Significance of Past and Present Immigration to the American People* (New York: Century, 1914), pp. 30–31, 62, 143–167, 263, 289–290, 294,

and *Standing Room Only?* (New York: Century, 1927), pp. 313–355; Charles B. Davenport, *Heredity in Relation to Eugenics* (New York: Henry Holt, 1913), pp. 212, 216; Henry Pratt Fairchild, *Immigration: A World Movement and Its American Significance* (1913; New York: Macmillan, 1922), pp. 142–143, 269, 271, 293, 323, 362, and *The Melting Pot Mistake* (Boston: Little, Brown, 1926), pp. 112–113, 223–225; Madison Grant, *The Passing of the Great Race; or, The Racial Basis of European History* (1916; New York: Charles Scribner's Sons, 1923), pp. 16, 89–94, 222, 227, 229–230, and *The Conquest of a Continent; or, The Expansion of Races in America* (New York: Charles Scribner's Sons, 1933), pp. 225–227.

6. Cohn, *Warrant for Genocide,* pp. 34–38, 177; Hay, *Europe and the Jews,* pp. 177–200; Byrnes, *Anti-Semitism in Modern France,* vol. 1, pp. 137–145, 305–306; Wilson, *Ideology and Experience,* pp. 486–491; Mosse, *Crisis in German Ideology,* pp. 40–45, 306–07; Heer, *God's First Love,* pp. 154, 162; Roy, *Apostles of Discord,* pp. 101–102, 105–106, 142.

7. For anti-Semitism in Populism see Ignatius Donnelly, *Caesar's Column* (1890; Cambridge, Mass.: John Harvard Press, 1960); Mary Elizabeth Lease, *The Problem of Civilization Solved* (Chicago: Laird and Lee, 1895); Frederic Cople Jaher, *Doubters and Dissenters: Cataclysmic Thought in America, 1885–1918* (New York: Free Press, 1964), pp. 129–137, 139–140, 237n–238n. For anti-Semitic German agrarian organizations see Levy, *Downfall of Anti-Semitic Parties,* pp. 59–60, 87–89, 199–227; Tal, *Christians and Jews,* pp. 129–132. For anti-Semitism in the Social Gospel movement see Lyman Abbott, "God's Glory in Christ's Face," *Outlook,* 60 (Dec. 31, 1898): 1066, and "Paganism, Judaism and Christianity," ibid., 61 (Jan. 14, 1899): 107–109, and "Was Jesus Christ a Jew," ibid., 75 (June 1, 1903): 311–313; Walter Rauschenbusch, *A Theology for the Social Gospel* (1917; Nashville: Abington Press, 1978), pp. 13, 33, 82–83, 107, 110, 154, 159–162, 215–217, 248–255, 259.

8. Hiram Wesley Evans, "The Klan's Fight for Americanism," *North American Review,* 223 (March 1926): 44–48, 60–61; Leroy Percy, "The Modern Ku Klux Klan," *Atlantic Monthly,* 130 (July 1922): 124; Mark H. Elovitz, *A Century of Jewish Life in Dixie: The Birmingham Experience* (University, Ala.: University of Alabama Press, 1974), pp. 84–87; Leo P. Ribuffo, *The Old Christian Right: The Protestant Far Right from the Great Depression to the Cold War* (Philadelphia: Temple University Press, 1983), p. 119; Strong, *Organized Anti-Semitism,* p. 52.

9. Charles E. Coughlin, "Am I an Anti-Semite? 9 Addresses on Various 'Isms' Answering the Question" (1939), in *Anti-Semitism in America: 1878–1939* (New York: Arno Press, 1977), pp. 28–29, 37–65, 76–85, 94–120, and "Background for Persecution," *Social Justice* (Dec. 5, 1938), in Strong, *Organized Anti-Semitism,* pp. 61–63. On Winrod see ibid., pp. 71–78, 164–165;

Roy, *Apostles of Discord*, pp. 14, 26–39, 44–45; Ribuffo, *Old Christian Right*, pp. 98, 107–126, 249–254; O. John Rogge, *The Official German Report* (London and New York: Thomas Yoseloff, 1961), pp. 213–215.

10. Willam D. Pelley, *The Door to Revelation: An Intimate Biography* (Asheville, N.C.: Foundation Fellowship, 1936), pp. 191–196, 230, and *No More Hunger: The Compact Plan of the Christian Commonweal* (Asheville: Pelley Publishers, 1936), pp. 310–311, 14, 28–29, 39, 48, 54, 91, and *No More Hunger: An Exposition of Christian Democracy* (Asheville: Pelley Publishers, 1938), pp. 137–142, and *Forty-Five Questions Most Frequently Asked about the Jews: With the Answers* (Asheville: Pelley Publishers, 1939), pp. 14–40; Pelley quoted in Rogge, *Official German Report*, p. 436.

11. Gerald L. K. Smith, *Too Much and Too Many Roosevelts* (St. Louis: Christian Nationalist Crusade, 1950), pp. 59, 61, "Martin Luther and the Jews," *The Cross and the Flag*, 6 (Jan. 1948): 7; "Jesus and the Jews," ibid., 3–4; "We Take Our Stand" (1942), in *Anti-Democratic Trends in Twentieth-Century America*, ed. Roland L. Delmore and Raymond G. McInnis (Reading, Mass.: Addison Wesley, 1969), pp. 188–189; Calvin Trillin, "U.S. Journal: Eureka Springs, Arkansas," *New Yorker* 45 (July 26, 1969): 69–79.

12. Ronald H. Bayor, *Neighbors in Conflict: The Irish, Germans, Jews and Italians of New York City, 1929–1941* (Baltimore: Johns Hopkins University Press, 1978), pp. 24–30, 40, 46–50, 87–108, 113–116, 121, 150–166, 175–176; Strong, *Organized Anti-Semitism*, pp. 64–69; John F. Stack, Jr., *International Conflict in an American City: Boston's Irish, Italians, and Jews, 1935–1944* (Westport, Conn.: Greenwood Press, 1979), pp. 56–63, 69–73, 84–85, 91, 123–160; Alson J. Smith, "The 'Christian' Terror," *Christian Century*, 56 (Aug. 23, 1939): 1017–1019, and "Father Coughlin's Platoons," *New Republic*, 100 (Aug. 30, 1939): 96–97; "The Brooklyn Beer Hall Putsch," ibid., 102 (Feb. 22, 1940): 99; "New York Meeting," *Commonweal*, 30 (Sept. 1, 1939): 428–429; "The Hypnotized," ibid., 31 (Jan. 26, 1940): 293; Lawrence Phelan, "An Evening with the Mobilizers," ibid. (March 22, 1940): 470–473; Thomas Irwin, "Inside the Christian Front," *Forum*, 103 (March 1940): 102–108; Dale Kramer, "The American Fascists," *Harper's Magazine*, 181 (Sept. 1940): 380, 384–389; J. J. Murphy, "Catholic Anti-Semitism," *Humanist*, 4 (Summer 1944): 103–107; James Travis, "The Secret of Anti-Semitism," *Catholic World*, 156 (Jan. 1943): 422–423; Esther Y. Feldblum, *The American Catholic Press and the Jewish State, 1917–1959* (New York: KTAV, 1977), pp. 5–6, 38–77, 139, 142n, 172–173.

13. Frederick K. Wentz, "The Reaction of the Religious Press in America to the Emergence of Nazism" (Ph.D. diss., Yale University, 1954), pp. 100–273; Robert W. Ross, *So It Was True: The American Protestant Press and the Nazi Persecution of the Jews* (Minneapolis: University of Minnesota Press, 1980), pp. 5–40, 51–65, 268–269, 287–301; William E. Nawyn, *American Protes-*

*tantism's Response to Germany's Jews and Refugees, 1933–1951* (Ann Arbor: UMI Research Press, 1981), pp. 42–43, 53–54, 64, 70–71; "Demonic Germany and the Predicament of Humanity," *Christian Century,* 55 (Nov. 30, 1938): 1456–1458; "The Forbidden Theme," ibid., 58 (Sept. 24, 1941): 1167–1169; "Horror Stories from Poland," ibid., 59 (Nov. 9, 1942): 1518–1519.

14. Richard Gilmour, *Bible History: Containing the Most Remarkable Events of the Old and New Testament* (1869; Cincinnati and St. Louis: Benziger Bros., 1881), pp. 12–22, 26, 61, 65, 71, 81, 105–106, 128, 158, 162, 189–191, 211–219, 225, 238–239, 244, 251–252, 266–267; *A Catholic Dictonary,* ed. Donald Attwater (1931; New York: Macmillan, 1943), pp. 282, 286; Philip S. Bernstein, "Unchristian Christanity and the Jews," *Harper's Magazine,* 162 (May, 1931): 660.

15. *A Short Explanation of Dr. Martin Luther's Small Catechism* (St. Louis: Concordia Publishing House, 1943), pp. 44, 50, 55, 81, 83, 111, 131; Arno C. Gaebelein, *The Conflict of the Ages: The Mystery of Lawlessness. Its Origins, Historic Development and Coming Defeat* (New York: Arno C. Gaebelein, 1934), pp. 35–39, 42–44, 47, 52, 55, 78–79, 90, 95–111, 115, 146–153, 156–157, 166–169; Basil Mathews, *The Jew and the World Ferment* (New York: Friendship Press, 1935), pp. 133–169; Bernstein, "Unchristian Christianity," 661; Frank Eakin, "What Christians Teach about Jews," *Christian Century,* 52 (Sept. 18, 1935): 1173–1175; James Baldwin, *Notes of a Native Son* (New York: Dial Press, 1963), pp. 59–60; Albert Trever, *History of Ancient Civilization* (New York: Harcourt, Brace, 1939), vol. 2, pp. 468–476.

16. J. F. Brown, "The Origin of the Anti-Semitic Attitude," in *Jews in a Gentile World: The Problem of Anti-Semitism,* ed. Isacque Graeber and Steuart H. Britt (New York: Macmillan, 1942), pp. 134–135.

17. *Jerusalem Post,* July 24, 1990, p. 6; Richard Wright, *Black Boy* (1945; New York: New American Library, 1964), p. 70; Baldwin, *Native Son,* p. 59.

# ～ Index

Abel, 21, 36, 228
Abolitionists, 138, 200, 201–203, 215
Abraham, 38, 40, 56, 92, 124, 135, 140, 147, 222, 239
Act Concerning Religion (Maryland Toleration Act), 88
Adams, Charles Francis, Jr., 190, 191
Adams, Hannah, 127, 144–145
Adams, John, 123, 133
Adams, John Quincy, 134–135, 143, 146, 190, 194, 201, 220
Adams County, Ill., 167
Adorno, Theodore W., 14
*Adventures of Harry Franco,* 165
African-Americans, 6, 7, 8, 106, 111, 138, 169, 232, 238; folklore of, 97, 241; anti-Semitism of, 241, 248
Age of Reason, 5, 6, 83, 86, 100, 107, 114–116, 117, 119, 120, 121, 130, 135, 160, 161, 172, 175, 208; in America, 120, 123, 125, 215. *See also* Deism
Agobard, archbishop of Lyons, 46–47
*Ahaseurus,* 227–228, 229. See also *Wandering Jew, The;* Wandering Jew legend
Aiken, William, 178
*Airs of Palestine,* 163
Alabama, 177, 197, 200, 241
Albany, New York, 178, 182, 215
Albertus Magnus, 61
Albigensian Crusade. *See* Heresy
Alexander, Rebecca Samuel, 168
Alexander II, emperor of Russia, 171
Alexander III, pope, 64
Alexandria, Egypt, 18, 32, 182
*Alexandria Daily Advertiser,* 168
*Algerine Captive,* 159, 160–161
Alien and Sedition Acts, 133

*Allsworth Abbey,* 235–236
Alsace, France, 84, 116, 140
Ambrose, bishop of Milan, 30, 32
America: anti-immigration policy in, 6; no national established church in, 87; pluralism in, 87; a Christian country, 139–140, 173, 177–178, 194–195, 208, 212. *See also* National Reform Association
American Baptist Society For Evangelizing the Jews, 213
American Bible Society, 204, 212
American Board of Commissioners for Foreign Missions, 204, 211
*American First Class Book, The,* 150
American party, 178, 190, 191, 193, 195, 200. *See also* Nativist movement
*American Popular Lessons,* 150
*American Reader, The,* 152
*American Reader, The: Containing Selections in Prose, Poetry and Dialogue,* 207
American Revolution, 103, 112–113, 133, 135, 184, 238
American Society for Evangelizing the Jews, 145
American Society for Meliorating the Condition of the Jews, 137, 143–146, 155, 213
American Sunday-School Union, 143, 146–147, 210
American Temperance Union, 141
American Tract Society, 213–214
Amherst County, Va., 106, 124
Anglicans. *See* Church of England
Antichrist, 2, 3, 28, 30, 35, 46, 61, 62, 76, 77, 229; in America, 93, 106
Anti-Judaism, distinguished from anti-Semitism, 23–24
Antioch, Syria, 18, 29

Antiochus, IV (Epiphanes), 18
Anti-Semites: as criminals, 242–243; as believers in the supernatural, 245
*Anti-Semitism: A Disease of the Mind,* 12
*Anti-Semitism: A Social Disease,* 12
Apostles/Apostolic Age, 23, 24–28, 162, 163
Aquinas, Thomas, 30, 61, 64
Aragon, Spain, 60
Archbishop of Canterbury, 63
Arkansas, 247
Armeggedon, 2, 37, 61, 212
Army of the Potomac, 200
Artemo, Italy, 48
*Arthur Merwyn,* 128
*Art of Reading, The,* 152
Aryan, 8, 173. *See also* Nationalism; Racialism
Assembly of (Jewish) French Notables, 117
Atlanta, Ga., 181, 203, 218
Augustine, Aurelius, 30–31, 46, 51, 62
*Aurelian,* 128–129, 183
Austria, 58, 65, 77, 78, 81, 85, 116, 117, 119, 171, 172, 186, 188, 208
Austro-Hungarian Empire, 171, 243
*Authoritarian Personality, The,* 12, 14
Axis Powers, 6

Babylon, 159, 235
Backus, Isaac, 107, 109, 140, 142
Baker, George M., 227
Baldwin, James, 248
Baltimore, First Lord of (George Calvert), 87–88
Baltimore, Md., 122, 132–133, 140, 158, 177, 180, 215, 217, 223, 228
Bancroft, George, 196
*Bankrupt Stories,* 236
Baptism, 8, 10
Baptists, 93, 98, 101, 106, 131, 140, 146, 211, 213, 248
Barabbas, 76
Barbados, 86
Barbary pirates, 157
Bar Kochba revolt, 18
Barnabus, 27
Baron, Salo Wittmayer, 78
Barrett, Walter (Joseph Scoville), 236

"Battle Hymn of the Republic, The," 212
Bauer, Bruno, 174
Bayard, Nicholas, 96
Beekman, Gerard C., 110
Belgium, 78
Belmont, August, 180, 181, 185, 186, 187–189, 190, 191, 192, 227
Benjamin, Judah P., 136, 177, 178, 181, 185, 186, 190, 191–192, 200, 227
Bennett, James Gordon, 154–155, 186, 191, 236
Berlin, Germany, 66, 243
Bettelheim, Bruno, 14
Bible, The. *See* New Testament; Old Testament
*Bible History,* 247–248
Bill of Rights (U.S.), 113
Bingham, Caleb, 151–152
Black Death. *See* Black Plague
Black Plague, 60, 67–68, 72, 73, 79
Blair, Francis, 137
Blake, John L., 151
Bloom, Lazarus, 204
Bloom, Leon, 204
Bloom, Moses, 204
B'nai B'rith, 197
Bohemia, 58, 76
*Book of Commerce, The,* 152
Booth, Edwin, 227
Booth, Junius Brutus, 128, 183
Borden, Morton, 168
Boston, Mass., 91, 104, 109, 127, 131, 134, 138, 150, 183, 216, 226, 234, 247
Boston Brahmins, 165, 190, 202, 215, 220, 238
*Boston Daily Evening Traveller,* 101
*Boston Evening Transcript,* 190
Bourges, France, 62
Brackenridge, Henry M., 168–169
Brackenridge, Hugh Henry, 161, 162
Bradford, William, 92
*Bravo, The,* 164, 166
Brazil, 89, 90
*Bridal Eve,* 235
Briggs, Charles F., 165, 236
British Navigation Act of 1660, 95, 98
British West Indies, 85–86
"Broadway," 223
Brooklyn, N.Y., 218, 223, 247

*Brooklyn Tablet*, 247

Brown, Charles Brockden, 128, 134

Brown University, 102, 151

Browne, Ross J., 222

Brownlee, W. C., 213

Brownlow, William Gannaway, 191–192, 217

*Brownlow's Knoxville Whig*, 191, 217

Bryant, William Cullen, 183–184

Buchanan, James, 177–178, 182, 194

Buffalo, N.Y., 204, 205, 206

*Buffalo Courier*, 226

Butler, Benjamin F., 192, 198, 200

Cain, 21, 36, 70, 167, 228, 230

California, 193, 195, 218, 240

Calvinism, 107. *See also* Dutch Reformed Church; Puritans

Cambridge University, 102, 170

Cannibalism, 36, 41, 56, 59. *See also* Eucharist

Canon Law, 10, 31, 32, 46, 61, 64, 70, 79

Capitalism, 2, 3, 4, 6

Carolingians, 46

Carroll, John, 140–141, 142

Cartaphilus, 228

Cass, Lewis, 178, 182

Castration, 10, 11, 37, 39–40, 56. *See also* Psychoanalytic theory

Catalonia, Spain, 48

Cathari. *See* Heresy

*Catholic Dictionary, A*, 248

*Catholic Mirror*, 215

Catholics in America, 91, 93, 96, 101, 112, 121, 132, 133, 135, 138, 140–141, 154, 179, 182, 185, 190, 200, 206, 215–217, 246, 247, 248; discriminated against more than Jews, 93, 98, 101, 106

Chamber serfdom. *See* Jews: as royal serfs

Chamberlain, Houston Stewart, 244, 245

Channing, William Ellery, 148–149, 215

Charles II, king of England, 84

Charleston, S.C., 102, 103, 104, 122, 125, 126, 129, 180, 181, 182, 186, 187, 190, 214

*Charleston Investigator*, 13

*Charlestown Gazette*, 107

Chatham Street, N.Y.C., 170, 186, 187, 219, 221, 222, 223, 227, 231, 239

Chaucer, Geoffrey, 69

Chauncey, Charles, 100

Chesnut, Mary, 192

Chicago, Ill., 181, 182

Child, Lydia Maria, 202, 203, 214

Chilton, William P., 197

"Chimerical anti-Semitism," 23–24, 29

Christian American Patriots, 243, 246–247

Christian beliefs/Christianity, 2, 3, 7, 9, 10, 11, 16, 21, 24; Manichean element in, 3, 36, 47, 58, 87; militance of, 3; universalism of, 3, 32–33; Judaism as tribalistic in, 3, 7, 115, 118; Judaism as enfeebled relic in, 3, 22, 30–31, 57, 69–70, 71, 229; Jew as outsider in, 3–4, 6, 7, 8–9, 10, 16, 44, 58, 118, 173; tolerance and sympathy for Jews in, 6, 11, 22, 23–26, 40, 45, 60, 61, 77, 78, 81, 83, 91–92, 94, 143, 144, 145, 200–201, 213; conversion and preservation of Jews in, 6, 40, 42–45, 47–50, 59, 60, 61–63, 64, 73, 74–75, 79, 80, 84, 91–94, 102, 107–109, 126, 129, 141–147, 148–150, 201, 212, 213, 214, 215, 220; criticism of Judaic law and ritual in, 18, 25–26, 28, 61, 93, 96, 108, 141, 142, 143, 147, 148, 209, 212, 232, 248; anti-Semitism in, 18–24, 25, 26–29, 32–37, 42–44, 87, 93–94, 228–229; redemption and salvation in, 24, 25–26, 28, 29, 32–37, 39–43, 51, 92–94, 108, 144–145, 147–148; displacement of Jews in, 25–27, 30–31, 33–37, 91, 93–94, 107, 109, 141, 142, 143, 145, 148–149; Jews as spurners of Christ in, 25–37, 40–44, 229–230; Augustinian formulation of, 30–31; Jews as depraved, demonic, defilers in, 34–37, 87, 93–94, 140, 142, 144–145, 201, 213, 214, 217, 246–248; Jewish conspiracy against, 59, 67, 68, 69, 73, 92–94, 117, 154–155, 237, 246–247. *See also* Christological anti-Semitism; Crucifixion of Jesus; Desecration of the Host; Israel; Jews/Judaism; Mosaic Law; Psychoanalytic theory; Ritual murder; Well poisoning

Christian Front, 247

*Christian Intelligencer,* 214

Christian Mobilizers, 247

Christian Social Party, 243

Christological anti-Semitism, 10, 16, 17, 18–43, 49, 51, 59, 107, 227–229. *See also* Christian beliefs/Christianity; Crucifixion of Jesus; Oedipal conflict

"Christ's Entrance into Jerusalem," 230

*Chronicles Selected from the Origins of Cartaphilus, the Wandering Jew,* 228

Chrysostum, John, 29–30, 31

Church (Roman Catholic) Councils, 10, 31–32, 46, 60, 64, 70; Second Lateran, 51; Fourth Lateran, 60–61, 70

Church of England, 88, 91, 109

*Churchman,* 214, 217

Cincinnati, Ohio, 125, 205, 226

Circumcision. *See* Castration

Citizens Committee of New York, 209

*City of God,* 30

Civil War (American), 81, 114, 137, 183–184, 188, 190–192, 196–200, 203, 206, 211–213, 215, 220, 223–226, 232, 237, 241

*Clarence Bolton,* 236

Clay, Henry, 125

Cleveland, Henry L., 196–197

Clinton, DeWitt, 125–126, 136, 137, 143

*Clipper Yacht, The,* 233

Coleman, William, 155

Columbia College, 102, 122, 125, 139, 169

*Columbian,* 136

*Columbian Orator,* 151–152

*Commentaries on the Constitution of the United States,* 139

Communism, 174–176, 246, 247; Christianity compared to, 174–176. *See also* Marx, Karl; Socialism

*Condition of the Working Class in England in 1844,* 176

Confederacy (Civil War), 189, 190, 197–198, 200, 206, 211–212, 224–255, 227, 237, 238; Congress of the, 189, 197

*Confidence Man, The,* 231

Congregationalists, 91, 107, 121, 135, 141, 143, 150, 153, 211. *See also* Puritans

Conical hats. *See* Special insignia for Jews

Connecticut, 91, 92, 95, 101, 105, 110, 121, 135, 151, 200

Connecticut Colony Enactment, 92

*Connecticut Courant,* 100

Conspiracy theories, 2–3, 7. *See also* Christian beliefs/Christianity: Jewish conspiracy against; Jews/Judaism: alleged conspiracy for world rule

Constantine the Great, 31

Constitution of the United States, 113, 130–131, 139, 140, 190, 205

*Contrast, The,* 159

*Conversations on Common Things,* 209, 210

Cooke, George Frederic, 128

Cooper, James Fenimore, 164, 166

*Cooperative Commonwealth, The,* 244

Cotton, John, 92–99

Coughlin, Charles E., 246, 247

Counter-Reformation, 44, 76–77, 78–79, 82, 87, 100

*Countess Ida,* 238

Court of Assistants (Connecticut), 95

Cresson, Warder, 180, 217

Cromwell, Oliver, 84

Cromwell, Richard, 88

Cronos, 37, 41

Croswell, William, 227

Crucifixion of Jesus: in Christian theology, 4, 7, 10, 16, 21, 25, 27–31, 34–35, 38–43, 55–59, 75, 87, 93–94, 107–109, 114, 140–141, 142, 147, 148, 149–150, 213, 214, 216, 217, 228–229, 235, 243, 246, 248; in the American popular mind and folklore, 96–97, 110, 111, 151, 163, 191, 192, 194, 201, 209, 218, 227–228, 230, 235, 238, 241

Crusades, 44, 51, 53, 65–66; First, 3, 23, 44, 47, 48–50, 59, 68; Second, 50; Third, 50, 59

*Crusoe's Island,* 222

"Cry Holy," 241

Daly, Augustin, 183

Damascus, 176, 184

Damascus Affair, 176, 184, 212

Dana, Charles W., 196

Davenport, Charles B., 244

Davenport, John, 92–93

Davis, Jefferson, 178–179, 192, 197

"Day of Judgement, The," 149

*Dearborn Independent,* 243, 246

de Gobineau, Joseph Arthur, 173

Deism, 106, 115, 116, 119, 120, 132, 134, 193, 194. *See also* Age of Reason

DeLancey, Oliver, 103

Delaware, 101, 105, 106, 121

Democratic party, 136, 137, 187, 189, 193, 195, 201

Democratic-Republicans, 120, 128, 132, 133, 134, 135, 139, 161

Dennie, Joseph, 134, 159

Department of the Tennessee, 108–109

Desecration of the Host, 47–48, 57–58, 66, 67, 76, 79, 80, 81, 85. *See also* Eucharist

Detroit, Michigan, 193

*Detroit Commercial Advertiser,* 225

Devil. *See* Satan

D'Haert, Balthazar, 95

d'Holbach, Paul Henry Thiery, 114–115

Dickens, Charles, 117, 160, 183

Diderot, Denis, 114–115, 116

Dietrich, Captain Paulson, 179

Disciples of Christ, 246

Dives and Lazarus, 65

Dix, Dorothea, 209–210

Dodge, Nehemiah, 135–136, 140

Dominicans. *See* Inquisition; Mendicant Friars

Dongan, Thomas, 95

Dracula, Count, 57

Dreyfus, Alfred, 242, 243

Drumont, Edouard, 243, 244, 245

Dun and Bradstreet, 204–206

Dutch Reformed Church, 77, 82–83, 84, 107, 143, 146, 147, 214

Dutch West India Company, 89–91

Dutch West Indies, 85–86, 89, 90

Easter, 55, 56, 61, 218

Edwards, Jonathan, 107–108, 143

Egypt, 17–18, 33, 55, 159, 197, 248; pharoahs of, 1, 17, 55; Jewish exodus from, 55, 68, 91–92, 234, 248

"Elements of Religion and Morality in the Form of a Catechism," 149–150

*Elisama,* 147–148

Ely, Ezra Stiles, 140

Emmanuel, David, 122

Encyclopedists, 114–115

Engels, Friedrich, 176

England, 5, 6, 7, 48, 50, 58, 59, 60, 63, 64, 65, 66, 69, 71, 72, 74, 76, 81, 82–84, 86, 89, 97, 98–99, 105, 109, 115, 116, 119, 120, 122, 124, 125, 127, 131, 143, 144, 160, 170–171, 172, 176; Puritan Revolution in, 82–84; Revolution of 1688 in, 89, 100

Enlightenment. *See* Age of Reason

Episcopalians, 122, 125, 146, 150, 180, 188, 211, 214, 215, 227, 233

Epistles of Paul. *See* New Testament

*Epitome of Ecclesiastical History, An,* 141–142, 143

*Epitome of History, An,* 153

Erasmus, Desiderius, 76

Ethnic hostility, 2–4, 11–15. *See also* Xenophobia

Ethnocentrism, 14–16. *See also* Xenophobia

*Etsi Judaeos. See* Papacy: edicts of

Etting, Solomon, 125

Eucharist, 41–42. *See also* Descrecation of the Host

Evangelical Christianity, 139, 143–148, 149, 203, 204, 211, 213, 238, 241, 246

Evangelical Synod of North America, 212

*Evening Star,* 133, 154

Everett, Edward, 189

Evolution, theory of, 7. *See also* Racialism

Fackenheim, Emil L., 115

Fagin, 117, 160, 183. See also *Oliver Twist*

*Faith and Fratricide,* 31

Fascism, 7, 73

Fay, Theodore Sedgwick, 129, 165–166, 238

Federalists, 120, 131, 132, 133, 134, 135, 137, 139, 143, 153, 159, 168

Female Society of Boston and Vicinity for Promoting Equality among the Jews, 127, 144

Fenno, John, 134

Ferdinand, king of Spain, 75

Feurbach, Ludwig, 174

Fichte, Johann Gottlieb, 118

Fillmore, Millard, 182

Finney, Charles Grandison, 143, 204
First Coming, 34
Fischer, David Hackett, 135
Fisher, Miers, 136
Florence, Italy, 78, 79, 159
Florida, 112, 177, 190, 197
Folklore, anti-Semitism in, 69, 96–97, 127, 166–167, 218, 238–241. *See also* Crucifixion of Jesus; Jews/Judaism: demonization of; Ritual murder
Foote, Henry S., 191, 197
Ford, Henry, 243, 246
Forrest, Edwin, 183
Foster, George C., 222–223
Fourier, Charles, 117, 174, 244
Fourth Lateran Council. *See* Church Councils
*Fourth Reader, The,* 127
France, 6, 9, 48, 49, 51, 53, 58, 59, 60, 63, 64, 66, 67, 70, 71, 72, 78, 83, 84, 85, 86, 89, 112, 116–117, 118, 119, 127, 131, 134, 157, 160, 171, 172, 173, 174, 183, 215, 243; Revolution of 1789 in, 6, 85, 113, 116, 117, 120, 128, 133, 134, 135, 216, 243; New World colonies of, 85–86, 112
Franciscans. *See* Inquisition; Mendicant Friars
Frank, Leo, 218
Frank, Michael, 205
Frankfurt, Germany, 81, 179
Franklin, Benjamin, 100, 102, 120, 123
Franks, David, 103
Franks, Phila, 103
Franks, Samuel D., 122
Frederick the Great, king of Prussia, 84
Frederick Town, Maryland, 111
*Freeman,* 217
*Free Presbyterian,* 214
Freneau, Philip, 128
Freud, Sigmund, 11, 28, 39, 40. *See also* Psychoanalytic theory
*Frontier Humor,* 240
Fuller, Margaret, 184
Fundamental Constitutions of Georgia, 87–88

Gadsden, Christopher, 125

Galloway, Benjamin, 132
Garrison, William Lloyd, 138, 201, 202, 203
*Gazette of the United States,* 134
Genoa, Italy, 78
*Geographical Compilation for the Use of Schools,* 152
*Geography for Children, A,* 151
Georgetown, S.C., 122
Georgia, 100, 101, 102, 104, 105, 107, 111–112, 121, 122, 136, 168, 193, 194, 200, 206
Gerber, David, 204, 205
German-American Bund, 243
*German Correspondent,* 169
German Reformed Church, 109
Germany, 2, 7, 49, 50, 60, 65, 66, 67, 68, 70, 75, 76, 77, 81, 83, 84, 97, 102, 115, 116, 118, 120, 127, 144, 171, 172, 173, 174, 176, 183, 208, 215, 229, 237, 242, 243, 245; Nazis in, 1, 15, 18, 22, 57, 62, 68, 75, 157, 160, 165, 187, 188, 240, 243, 244–245. *See also* Hitler, Adolf
Ghettos. *See* Jews/Judaism: Segregation/banishment of
Gilmour, Richard, 247
Girard, Stephen, 193
Glass, Max, 200
Gog, 76, 77
Goodrich, S. G., 127
Grant, Madison, 244
Grant, Ulysses S., 179, 180, 196, 198–199, 206
Gratz, Michael, 110
Great Awakening: First, 107–108; Second, 143
*Great Christian Doctrine of Sin Defended, The,* 108
Great Depression (1929), 8, 244
"Great Sanhedrin, The". *See* Assembly of (Jewish) French Notables
Gregg, Jarvis, 147–148
Gregory I, pope, 46–47
Gregory IX, pope, 62
Grillet, Stephen, 210
Grimm, Jakob, 240
Grimm, Wilhelm, 240
Gronlund, Laurence, 244

*Guardian,* 215–216
Guterman, Norman, 13
"Gypsy of Sardis, The," 164, 230
*Gypsy of the Highlands, The,* 233

Halleck, Henry W., 196, 199
Hammond, James Henry, 194–195
*Harper's New Monthly Magazine,* 224, 239
*Harper's Weekly,* 181, 183, 223–224
Harris, George Washington, 239
Harvard: College, 102, 108, 122, 128, 143, 149, 165, 220; Divinity School, 149, 150, 215
Hawthorne, Julian, 231
Hawthorne, Nathaniel, 164, 230, 231
Hebrew language, 101, 102
Hebrews. *See* Israel
Hegel, G. W. F., 118, 174
Hellenistic Empire, 17–18, 20, 21, 22, 37
Henrici, Ernest, 244
Henry, Jacob, 138
Heresy, 47, 51, 58, 60–62, 64, 67, 70, 76. *See also* Inquisition; Mendicant Friars
Higham, John, 14
Hilton, Robert, 197
*History of the Jews from the Destruction of Jerusalem to the Nineteenth Century, The,* 127, 144–145
Hitler, Adolf, 62, 153, 245. *See also* Germany: Nazis in
Hoffheimer Bros., 206
Hoffman, David, 228
Holland. *See* Netherlands, The
Holocaust, The, 3, 11, 39, 129, 171, 244
Holy Communion, 10, 56, 57, 67. *See also* Desecration of the Host; Eucharist
Holy Roman Empire, 40, 50, 51, 73, 78; Emperor of, 50, 71, 73
*Household Tales:* "The Good Bargain," 240; "The Jew Among the Thorns," 240
Howe, Julia Ward, 212, 227
Hubbard, John, 152
Hugh of Lincoln, 56, 69, 97. *See also* Ritual murder
Hungary, 59, 80, 119, 171, 172, 201. *See also* Austro-Hungarian Empire

Hurlbut, Stephen A., 149
Hutchinson, Anne, 95

I. H. Heinsheimer & Co., 204
Idinopulos, Thomas, 25–26
Illinois, 167, 176, 198
Immaculate Conception, 38, 58–59, 71
Independence Day (American), 8, 123, 124, 140
Indians, American, 87, 106, 168, 169, 218, 231, 232, 238, 240. *See also* Yaqui Indians
*Inequality of Human Races, The,* 173
Ingraham, Joseph H., 233–235
Innestar, Syria, 32
Innocent III, pope, 53–54, 60–61, 63, 64
Innocent IV, pope, 63
Inquisition, 61, 63, 64, 75, 76, 112. *See also* Heresy; Mendicant Friars
International Research Associates Survey of 1954, 14
*Introduction to the American Common-School Reader and Speaker,* 206–207
Irish-Americans, 161, 200, 205, 206, 218
Isaac, 40
Isabella, queen of Spain, 75
Israel, 2, 7, 16, 18, 25, 41, 54, 55, 63, 76, 83, 100, 107–108, 124, 141, 147, 148, 149, 151, 152, 154, 163, 167, 207, 208, 227, 234–235, 248; Jewish wars against the Romans in, 2, 18, 21–22; Christian beliefs about, 22, 25–29, 33–37, 63, 82, 91–93, 100–101, 234–235
Italy, 6, 48, 51, 63, 73, 78–79, 81, 102, 116, 226
*Ivanhoe,* 127–128

Jackson, Andrew, 136, 137, 153, 185
Jacob, 100
Jacob, Morris, 217
Jacques, Moses, 137
Jamaica, 85–86
James II, king of England, 89
Japan, 7
Jefferson, Thomas, 100, 120, 123, 124, 130, 133, 183
Jehovah, 19, 28, 33, 37, 40, 41, 55, 109, 148, 221, 230, 235

Jerome, Saint, 30

Jerusalem, 7, 49–50, 53, 141, 149, 161, 163, 180, 186, 213, 227, 235, 248

Jesus of Nazareth, 3, 11, 16, 19, 20, 23, 24, 25, 26, 27, 28–29, 31, 32–37, 39–43, 51, 54–59, 62, 67, 69, 75, 76, 88, 89, 91–94, 96–97, 107–109, 111, 181, 192, 194, 206, 208, 210, 213, 217, 218, 227–230, 246, 247, 248

Jew badge. *See* Special insignia for Jews

"Jewing and Chewing," 239

Jewish congregations, 125, 126, 225

Jewish funerals and cemeteries, 49, 71, 79, 80, 112, 223

Jewish males and females contrasted, 158–159, 160

Jewish Oath, 64, 83, 99

Jewish population in America, 94, 120, 125–126, 186–187

"Jewish Question, The," 15, 118, 178, 175

Jewish Wars, The. *See* Israel

Jews/Judaism: alleged conspiracy for world rule, 1–2, 3, 7, 30, 59, 117–118, 245–248; demonization of, 1–3, 4, 10, 12, 16, 23, 25, 27–28, 34–35, 42, 46–48, 54–59, 60, 61, 62, 66, 67–70, 71, 72, 73, 75, 76, 77, 79, 80, 83–84, 85–86, 92–94, 96–97, 119, 153, 163, 166, 176–177, 201, 218–219, 227, 229, 232, 236, 237, 240, 244, 245–248; as alleged betrayers of their nation of residence, 3, 4, 6, 7, 8, 117, 118, 135–136, 172–173, 190, 191, 197, 198, 200, 237, 246–247; economic fear of and discrimination against, 3–5, 6, 7, 8, 49, 51–55, 56, 61, 62, 66, 72, 74, 76, 77, 78, 79–80, 83–84, 85, 86, 87, 89–91, 99, 109–110, 115, 116, 117, 118, 119, 134, 135, 136, 137, 144, 152, 156–157, 158, 159, 160, 161, 162, 164, 165, 167–168, 170, 172, 173–175, 186, 188–189, 191, 194, 196–200, 203–206, 207, 216, 217, 220–227, 231–241, 242, 244, 245, 246; feared as radicals, 4, 6, 7, 216, 245–246; as calculating cosmopolitan urbanites, 5, 6, 7, 173; emancipation of, 5–6, 81, 84, 85, 86, 98–106, 113, 114, 115, 116–119, 121–126, 132–133, 170–171, 175,

177; as royal serfs, 5, 53, 71–72, 74; as sexual degenerates, 6, 27, 29, 56–58, 68–69, 71, 84, 98, 110, 115, 154, 158–159, 166, 201, 232, 236; violence against, 7, 18–19, 22, 32, 47–50, 59, 60, 64, 66, 67, 68, 73, 77, 78, 79, 80, 81, 99, 118, 171, 243, 247; as morally corrupt and nihilistic, 7, 8, 15, 118, 129, 150–151, 155, 162, 173–174, 176, 201, 235–236, 237; as flamboyant nouveaux riches, 8, 110, 115, 165, 170, 176, 242; aloofness and clannishness of, 16, 115, 117, 118, 175; rabbinic aspect of, 51, 59, 62, 77, 142, 153; as malevolent sorcerers, 56–59, 60, 66, 67, 70, 76; scatological references to, 57, 58, 68–70, 71, 83, 135, 232; identified with other outcasts, 58, 66, 70, 71, 73, 93, 94, 106, 111, 124, 131, 132, 133–134, 139, 140, 153, 154, 194, 216; segregation/banishment of, 64, 66, 67, 68, 71, 72, 73, 74, 77, 78, 81, 229; portrayed on the stage, 76, 117, 128, 156–160, 183, 226–227, 232, 233, 247; favorable treatment of, 81, 83, 85, 86–87, 91–92, 95–96, 98–99, 100–106, 113, 114, 115–117, 119–129, 150, 155–156, 162, 165–166, 169, 177–184, 213, 220, 243–244, 245, 249; blasphemy charges against, 88, 89, 94, 101, 139–140, 214; intermarriage with Christians, 103, 122; military service of, 103, 122, 137, 179, 192, 196, 198, 224; in textbooks, 127, 150–154, 206–211; as culturally barren, 142, 153, 173, 175, 201, 220, 238. *See also* Christian beliefs/Christianity; Passion plays; Racialism; Ritual murder

*Jews, Turks and Infidels,* 168

John, Saint, 28

John Birch Society, 14

Johnson, Andrew, 190, 191

*Johnson's and Walker's English Dictionaries Combined,* 239

Jones, John Beauchamp, 197–198, 237–238

Jones, John Richter, 184

Jordan, David Starr, 244

Joseph, father of Jesus, 38

Joseph II, emperor of Austria, 85, 208; Edict of Toleration of, 85, 116, 208
*Joseph and His Brethren,* 159–160
Judas Iscariot, 30, 41, 53, 191, 198, 218, 221, 224, 236, 238, 240
Judea. *See* Israel
*Judgement of Solomon, The,* 159–160
*Judith Bensaddi,* 162
*Julian,* 128–129
Jung, Carl, 43
Jupiter, 19, 28, 37–38
Justinian Code, 46

Kant, Immanuel, 115
Kean, Edmund, 128
Kennedy, Thomas, 132
Kenny, James, 110, 111
Kent, James, 139–140, 210
Kiddush ceremony, 41
King, Charles, 168
"King John and the Bishop," 240
*Knickerbocker, The,* 221, 239
Know-Nothing party. *See* American party
Kossuth, Lajos, 171, 201
Kuhn, Fritz, 243
Ku Klux Klan, 14, 219, 242, 244, 246

Langmuir, Gavin I., 2, 23–24, 29, 59
Larkin, Oliver, 193–194
Larrabee, William C., 211
Lassalle, Ferdinand, 174, 175, 176, 244
Last Judgment, 35
Last Supper, 41, 56. *See also* Eucharist
*Leah, The Forsaken,* 183
*Lectures on Revivals of Religions,* 143
Le Mans, France, 47
Lenin, V. I., 153
"Leper, The," 230
Lepers. *See* Jews/Judaism: identified with other outcasts
*Lessons for Schools, Taken from the Holy Scriptures,* 209, 210
*Letters from New-York,* 202
Levin, Louis, 178, 191
Levi-Strauss, Claude, 3
Levy, Asser, 76
Levy, Moses, 122

Levy, Uriah Phillips, 137, 138, 179, 196
Liberal Christianity. *See* Unitarians
*Liberator,* 138, 201, 238
*Libre Parole, La,* 243, 245
*Life and Adventures of a Country Merchant,* 237
Lincoln, Abraham, 179, 199, 212, 234
Lindo, Moses, 104
Lippard, George, 232–233
Livermore, Abiel Abbott, 219
Livingston, John, 145–146
Locke, John, 88, 120
Loeb, Samuel, 205
Logan, James, 106
London, England, 63, 84, 104, 112, 159, 234
London, Jack, 244
Longfellow, Henry Wadsworth, 183
Lopez, Aaron, 102, 105
Lorraine, France, 84, 140
Los Angeles, Calif., 180, 181
*Los Angeles Star,* 195
Louis I, king of France, 46
Louis IX, king of France, 63
Louisiana, 112, 138, 177, 190, 205, 206, 241
Lowe, Albert T., 152, 153
Lowenthal, Leo, 13
Lucena, Jacob, 95
Lucifer. *See* Satan
Lueger, Karl, 243
Luke, Saint, 28
Lumbrozo, Jacob, 88, 101
Luther, Martin, 77
Lutherans, 77, 89, 106, 107, 211, 248
Lyman and Cooledge, 203

Maccoby, Hyam, 41
Madison, James, 123–124, 133
*Magazine of the Dutch Reformed Church,* 162
Magog, 76, 77
Malchus, 228–229
*Mameluke, The,* 238
Mammon, 176
*Manchester Weekly Mirror,* 189
Marchand, Albert G., 190
Marcus, Jacob Rader, 95
Mark, Saint, 28

Marlowe, Christopher, 76

Marr, Wilhelm, 174

Marranos. *See* Christian beliefs/Christianity: conversion and preservation of Jews in

Marseilles, France, 84

Marsh, John D., 141–143

Marty, Martin, 146

Martyrdom in Christian eschatology, 34–37, 42

Marx, Karl, 174–176, 244

Mary, mother of Jesus, 34, 38, 56, 59, 71, 139, 158

Maryland, 87–89, 100, 101, 105, 106, 177, 121, 132–133

Maryland "Jew Bill," 126–127, 132–133, 156

Masonry, 3, 102, 118, 122

Massachusetts/Massachusetts Bay Colony, 91–94, 101, 105, 106, 107, 121, 131, 132, 139, 140, 157, 191, 192, 209

Massachusetts Constitutional Convention of 1820–1821, 131–132, 140

Massachusetts Constitution of 1780, 106–107

Mather, Cotton, 92–93

Mather, Increase, 92–94

Mathews, Cornelius, 222

Matthew, Saint, 28

May, Samuel J., 168

McCarthy, Joseph, 14

McClure, David, 109

McGuffey, William, 153–154, 208–209

*McGuffey's: Eclectic Reader(s),* 153; *Newly Revised Eclectic Fourth Reader,* 208–209; *Rhetorical Guide; or Fifth Reader,* 208, 209; *New Fifth Eclectic Reader,* 209

McKenzie, Andrew, 110

McMaster, James A., 215

Medieval debates between Christian and Jewish theologians, 63

Megapolensis, John, 90, 94

Melville, Herman, 164, 231–232

Memphis, Tenn., 196, 199, 225, 226

Mendicant Friars, 61, 63, 66, 72, 76. *See also* Heresy; Inquisition

Mennonites, 247

*Merchant of Venice, The,* 76, 127, 128, 207, 209, 226

*Methodist Review,* 162

Methodists, 146, 191, 192, 211, 246

Michaelis, Johann David, 115

Michelberger, Maximilian, 206

Michelet, Jules, 173–174

Michigan, 193, 223

Middleton, Henry, 126

Milan, Italy, 30, 78

Miles, William Porcher, 197

Milledoler, Philip, 145

Millennium, 42, 47, 61, 84, 91–92, 94, 130, 143, 145, 212, 213, 227, 229. *See also* Second Coming

Milwaukee, Wis., 178, 181

Minis, Philip, 168

*Miriam, Avenger,* 235

*Miser's Heir, The,* 236–237

Mississippi, 191, 241

*Modell of Christian Charity, A,* 92

*Modern Chivalry,* 161

Mohammed, 153

Molech, 40, 176, 228

Monis, Judah, 102

Monotheism, 10, 20–21

Monroe, James, 138

Moravians, 101

Mormons, 240

Mortara, Edgar, 179, 216

Mortara case, 179, 215–217

*Morton's Hope,* 165

Mosaic Law, 33, 162, 209, 211, 248

Moses, 21, 33, 38, 40, 100, 114, 142, 206, 234, 247, 248

*Moses and Monotheism,* 11. *See also* Freud, Sigmund; Psychoanalytic theory

*Mother Goose,* 240; "Old Mother Goose," 240

Motley, John Lothrop, 165

Muhlenberg, Henry Melchior, 106, 108

Murray, Lindley, 210

*Murray's English Reader,* 209, 210

Muslims, 45, 48, 49, 50, 59, 60, 70, 81, 93, 131, 132, 153, 166

Myers, Peter Hamilton, 236–237

*Mystery of Israel's Salvation Explained and Applied,* 94

Myths, 3, 36–43, 69, 96–97, 127, 166–167, 173, 176–177, 218–219, 227–230. *See also* Jews/Judaism: demonization of;

Nationalism; Oedipal conflict; Ritual
murder

Naples, Italy, 64, 66, 78
Napoleon Bonaparte, 6, 9, 116–117, 118,
171, 172
Nationalism, 2, 3, 4, 6, 7, 9, 62, 75, 81, 83,
100, 114, 115, 117, 118, 172–174, 229;
romantic, 5, 118, 173, 229; republican,
5, 173–174; volkish, 11, 15, 243, 245;
liberal, 172, 173–174; racial, 172–174,
244–245; Christian, 174, 229, 243, 246.
*See also* racialism
*National Pronouncing Speller, The,* 207
*National Reader,* 150–151
National Reform Association, 212
Nativist movement, 178, 200, 219, 237. *See
also* American party
Navigation Act of 1660, 95
Negroes. *See* African-Americans
Netherlands, The, 6, 78, 82–84, 91, 98–99,
116. *See also* Dutch West Indies
New Amsterdam/New Netherland, 6, 89–91,
95, 96, 98, 99, 100, 104. *See also* Dutch
West India Company; Stuyvesant, Peter
New Christians. *See* Spain
New England Election Day sermons, 100,
108–109
*New England Spectator,* 138
New Hampshire, 101, 105, 121, 177, 185
New Jersey, 99, 105, 121, 143, 248
New Mexico, 218
New Orleans, La., 112, 180, 181, 190–191,
192, 198
Newport, R.I., 101, 102, 109, 112, 124, 125
*Newport Mercury,* 101
New Testament, 1, 10, 22, 23–29, 30, 32,
33, 38, 41, 47, 51, 54, 65, 121, 149,
152, 207, 210, 215, 229
*New York American,* 137
*New York by Gas-light,* 222–223
New York City, 96, 103, 104, 109, 112,
125, 126, 128, 133, 135, 136, 137, 159,
168, 179, 180, 181, 183, 186–187, 188,
200, 202, 204, 209–210, 220, 221, 222,
223, 224, 226, 233, 234, 236, 237, 244,
247
*New York Commercial Advertiser,* 126, 137

*New York Evening Post,* 137, 155, 225
*New-York Freeman's Journal and Catholic
Register,* 215
*New York Herald,* 137, 154–155, 186, 189,
201, 217, 219
*New York in Slices,* 222–223
*New York Journal,* 133
New York State, 95–96, 99, 101, 102, 103,
104, 105, 106, 121, 136, 139, 143, 144,
185, 218; assembly of, 105–106; senate
of, 178
*New York Tablet,* 216
*New York Times,* 188
*New York Tribune,* 188
*New-York Weekly Journal,* 110
Nicholas I, emperor of Russia, 171
Niles, Hezekiah, 155–156
*Niles Weekly Register,* 155–156
Nisbet, Charles, 134
Noah, Mordecai Manuel, 136, 137, 138,
154, 157, 169, 185, 186, 187, 193, 201,
203, 219
Nordic race, 7, 173
*North American Review,* 181, 220
North Carolina, 94, 105, 110, 121, 133,
138, 177, 185, 192

Oedipal conflict, 10, 11, 174; in Christian
anti-Semitism, 37–44, 71; between com-
munism and capitalism, 174
Oesterreicher, John M., 24–25, 29
Oglethorpe, James, 111
Old Testament, 17, 21, 24, 33–34, 36, 40,
49, 51, 62, 91–92, 100, 107, 124, 130,
141, 147, 149, 160, 163, 208, 211, 228,
234–235, 241. *See also* Christian
beliefs/Christianity; Israel;
Jews/Judaism
*Oliver Twist,* 17, 60. *See also* Fagin
*On the Jewish Question,* 175
*On the Jews and Their Lies,* 77
Origen, Saint, 31
*Origin and Feast of Purim,* 159–160
Otto, M., 168–169
*Our Mutual Friend,* 183
Oxford University, 102, 170

Pacheco, Rodrigo, 104

Pagans, 17–19, 20, 37, 38, 40, 45, 140, 216
Pale of Settlement in Russia, 119, 171
Palestine, 50, 60, 61, 92, 179, 231. See also
    Israel
Papacy, 45, 47, 48, 51, 52, 59, 60–63, 74,
    76, 79, 179, 215, 216, 248; edicts of, 64,
    70, 74
Paris, France, 62, 66, 84
Parker, Theodore, 200–201, 209, 214
Parliament (British), 105, 106, 170
Passing of the Great Race, The, 244
Passion plays, 69, 240, 247
Passover, 7, 41, 55, 56, 57, 67, 201
Paul IV, pope, 79
"Paul at Rome," 207
Paul of Tarsus, 24–28, 39, 149, 150, 162,
    215
Payne, John Howard, 157, 159
Peasants and Jews, 12, 60, 70, 240, 245
Peasants' War, 76, 77
Peasant War in Germany, The, 176
Peddler of Very Nice, The, 227
Peet, Harvey D., 214
Pelayo: A Story of the Goth, 129
Pelley, William Dudley, 243, 246–247
Pen-and-Ink Panorama of New York City, 222
Penn, William, 94
Pennsylvania, 94, 101, 102, 103, 105, 106,
    121, 122, 134, 161, 177, 178, 190, 195,
    218
Pennsylvania Evening Post, 106
Pentecostals, 248
People, The, 173
"Peste of the Marranos," 75
Peter, Hugh, 95
Peter the Hermit, 49
Philadelphia, Pa., 109, 112, 122, 123, 124,
    134, 157–158, 168, 178, 179, 180, 181,
    182, 187, 232, 234
Philadelphia Gazette, 110
Philip Augustus, king of France, 53
Philip IV, king of France, 60
Pierpont, John, 150–151, 163
Pierre, 231
Pilate, Pontius, 21, 34–35, 41, 107, 141,
    149, 184, 228, 235, 247
Pilgrim, James, 226
Pilgrims. See Plymouth Colony

Pillar of Fire, The, 234
Pilot, The, 216–217
Pittsburgh, Pa., 110, 134
Plantation Act of 1740, 101, 105
Plymouth Colony, 92
Pogroms. See Jews/Judaism: violence against
Poland, 59, 66, 79–80, 81, 106, 118, 119,
    171, 184, 187, 209, 238
Police Gazette, The, 221
Polonies Talmud Torah, 125–126
Polytheism, 20–21
Poore, B. Perley, 238
Populism (American), 245
Portugal, 6, 23, 73, 74–75, 76, 82, 85, 89,
    229
Prague, 81
Presbyter, 218
Presbyterian General Assembly, 213
Presbyterians, 77, 100, 101, 107, 128, 140,
    143, 144, 146, 153, 162, 190, 211, 213,
    214, 218
Prince of the House of David, 234, 235
"Prioress' Tale, The," 69
Progressive Fourth Grade Reader, 207
Prophets of Deceit, 13
Prostitutes. See Jews/Judaism: identified
    with other outcasts
Protocols of the Elders of Zion, 243, 246
Proudhon, Pierre Joseph, 174
Prussia, 84, 116, 118, 119, 122, 171, 208
Psychoanalytic theory: of Christianity, 10; of
    anti-Semitism, 10–12, 37–44, 59. See
    also Castration; Oedipal conflict
Puritans, 77, 82–83, 91–96, 97, 99, 248.
    See also England: Puritan Revolution in

Quaker City, 232–233, 236
Quakers, 89, 91, 93, 98, 121, 136, 156,
    180, 184, 210
Quaker Soldier, The, 184
Quincy, Edmond, 201, 202, 214, 220, 238

Racial anti-Semitism, 6, 7–8, 12, 69, 75,
    118, 231, 232, 242, 244–245, 246; com-
    pared to Christian anti-Semitism, 69, 75,
    246
Racialism, 7–8. See also Xenophobia
Rameau's Nephew, 114–115

*Ramero,* 233

"Rare Ripe Garden Seed," 239

*Redburn,* 231

Reformation, 5, 76–77, 87, 91, 229

Religious revival (1850s–1860s), 211–213

Renaissance Humanism, 76

Republican party, 185, 196

Reuchlin, Johannes, 76

Revolution of 1848, 171, 172, 173, 174

Rhode Island, 91, 95, 99, 102, 104, 105, 106. 110, 112

Richmond, Va., 122, 125, 177, 180, 189, 198, 206, 215, 224, 225, 226

*Richmond Examiner,* 234

Ritual murder, 4, 11, 12, 18, 20, 29, 32, 51, 54–59, 60, 66, 67, 69, 73, 76, 79, 80, 84–85, 96–97, 119, 136, 158, 166, 176, 182, 201, 218–219, 227, 229, 240. *See also* Jews/Judaism: demonization of; Myths

Rivington, James, 106, 133

*Rivington's New-York Gazetteer,* 106

"Robert Slender Argueth with the Parson," 128

Rogers, Robert, 110

Roman Empire, 2, 5, 16, 17, 18–19, 20, 21, 22, 30, 31–33, 38, 44–47, 74–75, 100, 141, 144, 150, 184, 209, 228, 235, 241

Romania, 59, 80, 119, 177

Rome, Italy, 30, 59, 73, 79, 179, 209, 216

Rose, Paul Lawrence, 176

Rosenberg, Alfred, 244, 245

Ross, Edward Alsworth, 244

Rothschild family, 177, 179, 185, 188, 189, 191, 219, 227, 237

Rousseau, Jean Jacques, 115, 120, 209

Rowson, Susanna Haswell, 157, 159, 160, 166

Rubin, Theodore Isaac, 12

Ruether, Rosemary, 25, 35, 44

Ruffner, Henry, 162

Rush, Benjamin, 120, 123, 130

Russia, 9, 112, 118–119, 171, 242, 246–247

Rutledge, Edward, 125

Sabbath: Jewish, 17, 41; Christian, 111, 139–140, 169, 195–196, 203–204

St. Louis, Mo., 179, 203

"St. Paul's Defense Before Agrippa and Festus," 152, 208

Saltonstall, Leverett, 131

San Francisco, Calif., 180, 182, 198, 205, 215, 226

Sanhedrin, 163, 247

Santa Fe, N.M., 180

Satan, 3, 30, 47, 54, 60, 93, 166; identified with Jews, 28, 29, 30, 35, 47, 56, 58, 68, 69, 70, 76, 92–94, 135, 153, 166, 227, 246

Savannah, Ga., 104, 107, 111, 168

Schwartz, Joseph, 205

Scott, Sir Walter, 127–128

*Scripture Lessons for the Young,* 214

Seal of the United States, 100

*Seclusaval,* 162

*Second Class Book,* 152–153

Second Coming, 35, 47, 50, 107, 229. *See also* Millennium

Second Lateran Council. *See* Church councils

Seixas, Gershom Mendes, 122, 125

Seleucid Kingdom, 18

*Self-Raised,* 235

Seligman, J., 180

Seligman, W., 180

*Selumiel; or, A Visit to Jerusalem,* 148

Sermon on the Mount, 51

Shaftesbury, First Lord of (Anthony Ashley Cooper), 87–88

Shakespeare, William, 54, 76

Sherman, William Tecumseh, 198, 199

Shylock, 6, 54, 117, 128, 133, 136, 157, 164, 167, 197, 201, 207, 209, 221, 226–227, 236, 237, 238

*Sidney Clifton; or, Vicissitudes in Both Hemispheres,* 129, 165–166

Silverman, Leon, 185

Silver Shirts. *See* Christian American Patriots

Simms, William Gilmore, 129

"Sinners in the Hands of an Angry God," 108

Sisebut, Visigoth king, 45

*Slaves in Algiers,* 157–158, 159, 160, 166

Smith, Gerald L. K., 246, 247

Smith, Sarah Pogson, 162–163

Smith, William, 106
Social Gospel, 245
Socialism, 5; anti-Semitism in, 117, 174–176, 243–244, 245. *See also* Communism; Marx, Karl
Social Reichsparty, 244
South Carolina, 87–88, 101, 102, 103, 104, 105, 106, 121, 122, 125, 132, 177, 178, 184, 185, 186, 187, 239
*South Carolina State-Gazette,* 126
*Southern Illustrated News,* 224–225, 239
*Southern Literary Messenger,* 162
Southern Mutual Insurance Company, 203
*Southern Punch,* 224
Southworth, E. D. E. N., 235
Spain, 6, 48, 49, 50, 55, 59, 60, 63, 64, 66, 70, 71, 72, 73, 74–75, 76, 82, 83, 85, 112, 129, 229; New Christians in, 75; New World colonies of, 85, 112
Special insignia for Jews, 61, 70, 73, 77, 79, 80
*Spirit of the Times,* 221, 222, 239
Stamp Act, 100
"Star of Calvary," 230
Stephen, Saint, 29
Stiles, Ezra, 100, 101, 105–106, 109
Stoddard, Lothrop, 244–245
Stoecker, Adolf, 243
Story, Joseph, 139, 193, 194, 210, 220
Story, William Wetmore, 220
Stow, William W., 195–196
Stowe, Harriet Beecher, 231
Straus, Lazarus, 200
Strong, George Templeton, 220
Strong, Pascal, 137, 140
Stuyvesant, Peter, 89–91, 95
Sue, Eugene, 176, 183, 227
Switzerland, 65, 66, 77, 78, 116, 171, 178, 182
Synagogues, 28, 29, 32, 47, 49, 58, 63, 76, 80, 93, 95, 101, 109, 112, 119, 123, 124, 125, 126, 202, 208, 218, 220, 221, 225, 230, 247
*System of Modern Geography, A,* 207

Talbotton, Ga., 200
"Tale Told Too Often, A," 240

Talmud; attacks on, 51, 62, 63, 76, 77, 79, 80, 119, 154, 161, 219
Tappan, Lewis, 204
Tennessee, 190, 191, 192, 197, 198
Test oath, 101, 106, 121, 122, 131, 132–133, 138, 139, 169, 177
Texas, 177, 200
Thanksgiving proclamations, 126, 194–195, 211–212
Thatcher, Samuel, 149
Theodosian Code, 46
Third Reich. *See* Germany; Hitler, Adolf
Thomasville, Ga., 200
*Throne of the House of David, The,* 234–235
Timayensis, Telemachus Thomas, 242, 244
"To Jew," 238–239
*Tortesa the Usurer,* 159, 164
*Tree of Liberty,* 134
*Trial without Jury; or, The Magpie and the Maid,* 157, 159
Tuckerman, Joseph, 131
Turkey, 146, 182, 213, 244
Turks, 80, 159, 164; identified with Jews, 77, 93, 94, 106, 124, 131, 168
Tyler, John, 177, 178, 194, 227
Tyler, Robert, 227–228
Tyler, Royall, 159–161, 162

*Uncle Tom's Cabin,* 232, 233, 234
*Union Questions,* 146–147
Unitarians, 128, 131, 132, 139, 140, 148–150, 203, 209, 214–215
U.S. Christian Commission, 212
U.S. House of Representatives, 178, 217
University of Pennsylvania, 102, 115
Uranus, 37, 40
Usury, 2, 51–55, 56, 60, 61, 64, 67, 68, 72, 73, 77, 79, 80, 89, 127–128, 144, 158, 164, 165, 166, 167, 175, 186, 217, 221, 222, 227–229, 233, 237, 238. *See also* Jews/Judaism: economic fear of and discrimination against
Utah, 240

Van Buren, Martin, 136, 154, 182
Van Rensselaer, Stephen, 143
Vienna, Austria, 81, 119, 243

*Vigor,* 236
*Vincennes Weekly Gazette,* 189
Virginia, 94, 101, 102, 111, 121, 123, 124, 125, 162, 177, 225, 227; Act for Establishing Religious Freedom in, 123; House of Burgesses of, 123; Constitutional Convention of 1829 in, 125, 177; House of Delegates of, 177
*Virginia Constitutional Whig,* 126
Visigoths, 45
Voltaire (François-Marie Arouet), 115, 120

Wagner, Richard, 173
Walker, James, 149, 215
Wallace, George, 14
Wallack, James W., 159
*Wandering Jew, The,* 176, 183, 227
Wandering Jew legend, 76, 116, 167, 176, 183, 208, 227–230
Ward, Nathaniel, 92
Ward, Roy Bowen, 25–26
Ware, Henry, 128, 129
Ware, William, 128, 129, 184
Washburne, Elihu, 196
Washington, D.C., 191, 196, 218, 226
Washington, George, 124, 206
*Washington Chronicle,* 225
*Washington Globe,* 137
Waters, Ronald, 203
Webster, Daniel, 193, 194
Well poisoning, Jews accused of, 58, 60, 66, 67–68, 72, 73, 79, 81, 85. *See also* Black Plague; Jews/Judaism: demonization of
*Wensley,* 238
*Western Merchant, The,* 237
Weston, E. P., 207
West Point Military Academy, 122
Whig Party, 137, 189
Whitman, Walt, 223
Whitney, Lorenzo, 203

Whittier, John Greenleaf, 183
William of Trent, 56. *See also* Ritual murder
Williams, Roger, 92–94
Williamsburg, Va., 128
Willis, Nathaniel Parker, 159, 164, 230
Wilson, Henry, 191, 202
*Winkles, The,* 237–238
Winrod, Gerald, 246–247
Winthrop, John, 92
Wirt, William, 209
Wisconsin, 185, 193, 203
Wise, Isaac M., 178
Witches, 58, 60; Jews identified with, 93
Worcester, Joseph E., 153
"Worcester Catechism, The," 149, 215
*World's Own, The,* 226
World War I, 2, 6, 9, 120, 246
World War II, 2, 36, 119, 120, 130, 242
Wright, Richard, 248

Xenophobia, 7–8, 11, 15–16. *See also* Ethnic hostility; Ethnocentrism; Racialism

Yale College, 102, 107, 109, 122, 143, 153, 181
*Yankee Jack,* 226
Yankees, identified with Jews, 167, 239–240
Yaqui Indians, 218
Yiddish dialect; as anti-Semitic stereotype, 134, 208
Yom Kippur, 218
Young Germany, 71, 72
Young Men's Christian Association, 218
Yulee, David, 177, 178, 179, 185, 186, 189–190

*Zenobia,* 128–129, 184
*Zerah, The Believing Jewess,* 162–163
Zeus, 27–28
Zubly, John, 100